Reshaping the International Order

A REPORT TO THE CLUB OF ROME

Jan Tinbergen, coordinator

Antony J. Dolman, editor

Jan van Ettinger, director

E. P. DUTTON & CO., INC. | NEW YORK

Design RIO-vignette: Wim A. Brekelmans

This publication was realised in cooperation with
the Foundation Reshaping the International Order (RIO).

Library of Congress Catalog Card Number: 76-41058
ISBN: 0-525-19250-6 (cloth)
0-525-04340-3 (paper)

Published simultaneously in Canada by
Clarke, Irwin & Company Limited, Toronto and Vancouver

PRINTED ON RECYCLED PAPER

Preface

The project 'Reshaping the International Order' (RIO) originated from the initiative taken by the Executive Committee and in particular the President of the Club of Rome, Dr. Aurelio Peccei. This initiative followed the 'Salzburg Meeting' held in February 1974 at which President Echeverría of Mexico strongly advocated the proposals contained in the 'Charter of Economic Rights and Duties of States' and the resolutions adopted by the Sixth Special Session of the U.N. General Assembly. Realizing the importance of the U.N. resolutions and the Charter, but being equally aware of the vagueness and controversy surrounding the subject area covered by them, Dr. Peccei suggested that I form and coordinate a group of specialists who would be able to address the following question: what new international order should be recommended to the world's statesmen and social groups so as to meet, to the extent practically and realistically possible, the urgent needs of today's population and the probable needs of future generations? An answer, inevitably tentative, to this question is presented in the following pages. The work of the group has been made possible by the generous financial support of the Netherlands Minister for Development Cooperation, Mr. Jan Pronk. Neither the Club of Rome nor the Netherlands Government imposed any kind of restrictions on the group, leaving it completely free to formulate and express its own opinions.

The group consisted of 21 specialists (see box) drawn from a variety of countries, social systems and specializations. I wish to thank all of them for having devoted so much of their time to the RIO project and for the cooperative spirit in which they have worked. A considerable effort was made in forming the RIO group to achieve balanced First, Second and Third World participation. Unfortunately, however, it did not prove possible to secure the required representation of the centrally planned nations, even though we were fortunate to receive advice on several points from Messrs. Jozef Pajestka and Kazimierz Secomski. I regret this deficiency because it is my firm belief that the establishment of a new international order requires the active participation of the Second World as well as First and Third World Nations. My work as coordinator would not have been possible without the strong support of a staff of 6 part-timers (see box). I thank all of them, through mentioning Mrs. Carolien Bos who — by admirably fulfilling the awesome task of organizing the in- and outflow of information — made us all function. Furthermore, it was highly facilitated by the numerous services provided by the Bouwcentrum in Rotterdam, where the group held most of its meetings (December 1974; June and October 1975; February, April and June 1976) and by far the largest part of our work was done.

Given the complexity of the subject, the RIO project could only realistically aim at attempting to make a modest contribution to the growing dialogue on the new international order. Therefore, rather than placing the emphasis on the contribution as such (a product orientation), the project aimed throughout its execution at increasing the dialogue between the various groups involved in attempts to shape a new international order, not only between specialists working on related issues but also between specialists and politicians on the one hand and the general public on the other (a process orientation). Drafts of RIO documents were in fact despatched through a mailing list to more than 350 individuals and institutes all over the world. The Interim Report, drafted in our June 1975 meeting as a contribution to the Seventh Special Session of the U.N. General Assembly, had a circulation of more than 5000 copies. Many of the comments received on these various drafts now form part of the text and I sincerely thank all those who took the trouble to think and work with us. I must also take this opportunity of thanking the organizers of meetings in Algiers, Brussels, Copenhagen, Davos, Geneva, The Hague, Linz, Philadelphia, Rome, Santa Barbara and Stockholm where provisional conclusions were presented by some of us and helpful comments received from panels and audiences.

Every attempt has been made to ensure than the RIO report reflects the results of the many and intensive discussions of the group. This, however, does not mean that every word printed necessarily meets with agreement of all 21 members of the group. Those of the group who felt it necessary, have clarified their position vis-à-vis the report through short statements, which can be found at the end of the report. I intend to finish my task on the occasion of the official presentation of the Report in Algiers in October and Amsterdam in November 1976. These meetings will mark the starting point of the activities of the RIO Foundation, as a follow-up to the project and its report. May these endeavours be successful and thus continue to contribute to an ongoing and growing dialogue on attempts to shape a fairer world.

Jan Tinbergen

Participants

Strategies of Change
Silviu Brucan
Inga Thorsson
Víctor L. Urquidi

The International Monetary Order
Duncan N. Ndegwa
Robert Triffin

Income Redistribution and the International Financing of Development
James P. Grant
Mahbub ul Haq

Food Production and Distribution
Sukhamoy Chakravarty
Maurice Guernier

Industrialization, Trade and International Division of Labour
Ibrahim Helmi Abdel Rahman
Helmut Hesse

Energy, Ores and Minerals
Robert Gibrat
Tetsuo Noguchi

Scientific Research and Technological Development
Alexander King
Aklilu Lemma

Transnational Enterprises
Idriss Jazairy
Pieter Kuin
Juan Somavía

Human Environment
Ignacy Sachs

Arms Reduction
Inga Thorsson

Ocean Management
Elisabeth Mann Borgese
Arvid Pardo

Coordinator
Jan Tinbergen

Staff
Carolien J. Bos, Administrative Officer
Wim A. Brekelmans, Graphic Designer
Antony J. Dolman, English Editor
Jan van Ettinger, Director
Dick A. Leurdijk, Dutch Editor
Jan van den Oudenhoven, Financial Officer

Table of contents

Chapter 1   The Aims and Scope of the Report

1.1   *General Introduction*

This report deals with a subject of vital importance to current and future generations: the removal of manifest injustices endemic in the present system of relationships between nations and peoples with a view to creating a new international order in which a life of dignity and well-being becomes the inalienable right of all. It is prompted by the results which emerged from the Sixth Special Session of the United Nations General Assembly held in April and May 1974, following initiatives taken by Algeria and supported by the Group of Non-Aligned countries. The session culminated in the adoption of two important resolutions: the first expressing the collective desire of member states to work towards the 'Establishment of a New International Economic Order'; the second concerning the 'Programme of Action' required as a basis for attaining the new order. These resolutions suggest general agreement on the need for international reforms; that the present system of relationships between nations fails to serve the common interests of mankind as a whole and that only through the establishment of a new international order can existing injustices be rectified and the basis established for a more just and peaceful world.

The present report is designed to serve as a contribution to the necessary further elaboration of the important ideas contained in the Declaration and the Programme of Action and to stimulate and contribute to the necessary further *exchange of ideas* between the many parties involved in attempts to shape a fairer world.

Whilst proposals and recommendations are, where appropriate, expressed quantitatively, this report does not pretend to contribute directly to scientific quantitative research. Rather, it makes an attempt to translate into politically feasible first steps the courses of action which the existing international community might choose to take in the direction of a more human and equitable international order, *on the basis of the knowledge currently available on the community's operation.*

The authors do not believe that it is possible to advocate proposals for change from a position of value neutrality. Moreover, since proposals for change must also be based upon an analysis of deficiencies in the existing system of international relations, they feel compelled to point clearly at what they believe to be the reasons for such deficiencies. This in itself implies a value position. This value position they have attempted to make explicit choosing to call it an equitable social order. As such, as will become clear in the following pages, they contend that the construction of a 'better' world implies acceptance by society of the responsibility to ensure the satisfaction of the individual and collective needs of people and the creation of international and national systems in which opportunities and the means to use those opportunities are much more equitably distributed than at present.

The authors do not believe that proposals for change should be limited exclusively to economic relations between nations. Indeed, the almost exclusive preoccupation with economic questions in the past has contributed towards exacerbating many of today's problems. The world is too complex to be viewed in purely economic terms. The establishment of a New International Economic Order entails fundamental changes in political, social, cultural and other aspects of society, changes which would bring about a *New International Order*. For this reason, in this report the latter expression is chosen in preference to the former.

1.2 *The Layout of the Report*

The report consists of four main parts. In Part I, 'The Need for a New International Order and the Main Problem Areas', the magnitude and complexity of some of the problems facing mankind are sketched and the processes leading up to the call for a new international order and the progress made to date in negotiating it are described.

Having discussed the magnitude of the tasks before us, Part II, 'The Architecture of the New International Order; Initiating and Steering the Process of Planned Change', discusses the ways in which the required change can and should be organized. As such, it deals with the process of initiating, organizing and guiding change in prefered directions. Since prefered directions imply explicit statements with respect to the goals and objectives of development, it is in Part II that the group presents its view of what should constitute development. In that it 'takes a position' with respect to development, it is deliberately normative.

In Part III, 'Proposals for Action', the main proposals and recommendations which have emerged from the project's working groups are presented. An attempt has been made to list the proposals in order of assumed priority, those deemed important in the medium term and those more relevant in the long term. The different proposals have been selectively grouped into three packages which should preferably be negotiated comprehensively. These packages are intended to contribute towards the further negotiation of the new international order.

Part IV is devoted to the Technical Reports prepared by the project's working groups. Some ten major subject areas relevant to the establishment of a new international order are discussed in some depth and pro-

Some Concepts and their Definition

A number of central concepts are used in this report to analyse the general interdependencies between nations, the interactions between problem areas and to formulate proposals for action. Some of the most important are defined below.

Fundamental aims (or goals) are defined as ideals which can be expressed in abstract terms. They comprise ideals to be pursued, even though rarely susceptible to total fulfilment. They embrace all the elements of mankind's welfare and are of both a material and non-material character. They range from the flow of consumer goods necessary for a healthy life to the principles of justice or equity, participation and freedom.

Fundamental aims are, of course, much too general to serve as a basis for drawing up specific policy recommendations. They need, therefore, to be translated into harder statements of intent. These we will call *derived or intermediate* aims (or objectives). Examples of derived aims include the production of the necessary food, the building of the necessary houses, the construction of the legal system required to exercise justice and to warrant some forms of freedom or of participation in decision-making.

Policies or strategies can be defined as proposals of concerted action to achieve derived aims. Common to both are the *means* which authorities — whether at th national, a lower or a higher level — have at their disposal to attain the objectives. Examples include import duties and other taxes, public works (e.g. the building of roads), public utilities (e.g. the provision of energy and water), the education system; in short, the whole of the government and intergovernmental machine. A distinction can be made between *direct means* (those under direct control) and *indirect means* (e.g. private production stimulated by a price or a price subsidy). A logical chain runs from fundamental aims, through derived aims, to indirect means and finally to direct means. A causality chain links the levels in the opposite direction; means are used in order to attain indirect means through them intermediate aims and, finally, the fundamental aims. In some cases the chain may be long, for example from public subsidies to encourage a private producer of food, through production and trade, wholesale and retail, to the final consumer. In other cases the chain may be so short that the means coincide with the aim, as may be said of a school.

The means are controlled, not by one abstract all-embracing authority, but by a number of more or less separate *institutions*. Institutions are organizations in either the *concrete* or *abstract* sense. Examples of concrete institutions are ministries and their respective parts, trade unions, and political parties.

Examples of abstract institutions include markets and other customary or spontaneous ways of behaviour.

By the *social order* we will understand the group or set of all institutions which together constitute a society and control the means to attain the aims of that society. Included are not only the *formal* institutions of a legal or customary character, but also the *informal* structures, such as action committees formed spontaneously in some situation and existing often only until some aim has been achieved.

Part of the world's social order will be called the *international order*, which brings us to our main subject. *The international order we will define as comprising all relations and institutions, both formal and informal, which link persons living in different nations.* It ranges from the family of United Nations agencies to all forms of bilateral and multilateral contacts, including such organizations as the Andean Group of States, the European Community, CMEA, OECD, large numbers of international non-governmental organizations, transnational enterprises, and international professional organizations – in short, all of the iceberg of world order above the national level.

A final central concept which will be used is that of *power structure*. Among all the individuals living and institutions existing in the world, some have more 'power' than others. Their power is reflected in the fact that the present system allows their aims to be more fully attained than those of others. The forces which give more power to some are of different origin. Power is a multi-dimensional concept and consists of different components. These, we contend, are of five basic types. Firstly, there is *physical violence* such as used by armies, police forces, and informal groups or even individual political extremists and terrorists. The second and third components are of an economic character: power deriving from *coalitions and monopoloid organizations*; and power deriving from the *possession of scarce resources*, whether natural resources or human qualities (e.g. intelligence, leadership, or personal attractiveness). A fourth component is the power of *custom or law*, sometimes recognized as a legal basis for certain types of behaviour. The fifth component we propose to identify is the power of *ideas*, rational or ethnical.

The existing power structure is a product of the forces exerted by these five components as they have developed over time. It advantages some whilst disadvantaging others. At the international level, the components of power combine with differences in size, strength and development among nations. Changes in the international order designed to redress existing inequalities and imbalances call, therefore, for changes in the forces which define the power structure.

posals and recommendations for change are made. Part IV is by far the most extensive and represents the foundation upon which much of the three preceding parts are constructed.

The organization of this report in its four main parts provides different entries into the subject matter treated. The most important division is that between Parts I-III and Part IV. The first three parts represent what might be called the 'main text' with Part IV serving as the main 'supporting evidence'. Those with only a general interest in the subject matter treated may find it sufficient only to read the first three parts. Those familiar with the growing literature on the new international order and the various viewpoints prevailing will, it is hoped, also find the reading of Part IV a rewarding experience.

Finally, it should be noted that this report draws upon the published work of certain RIO participants.

Part 1   The Need for a New International Order and the Main Problem Areas

'Many new nations, having won political independence, find themselves still bound by economic dependency. For a long time it was thought that the solution to this problem was aid and assistance. It is increasingly clear however, that a new international economic order is essential if the relations between rich and poor nations are to be transformed into a mutually beneficial partnership. Otherwise, the existing gap between these groups of nations will increasingly represent a potential threat to international peace and security.

'Moreover, the dependence of the developing world upon the developed is changing – indeed in certain cases has been reversed. Many developed nations are also finding themselves in serious economic difficulties. The international system of economic and trade relations which was devised 30 years ago is now manifestly inadequate for the needs of the world community as a whole. The charge against that order in the past was that it worked well for the affluent and against the poor. It cannot now even be said that it works well for the affluent. This is an additional incentive for evolving a new economic order . . .'

Kurt Waldheim, 1975

Introduction to Part I

Part I is devoted to the 'why' of the new international order. It comprises three chapters. The first of these — Chapter 2 — briefly reviews the problems confronting the First, Second and Third Worlds and the process which led up to the call for a new international order. Chapter 3, the longest of the three chapters, reviews eleven major substantive problem areas and some of their interlinkages with a view to identifying the areas in which action is required if progress towards the creation of a fairer world is to be made. It does not deal with possible solutions; proposals for change are presented in Part III. Chapter 3 also briefly discusses the complex nature of problem interactions and of planetary interdependencies. Finally, Chapter 4 attempts to review the major landmarks in the process of negotiating a new world order and the positions, roles and responsibilities of the principal parties.

'. . . the international economic system is not as free as is often
claimed and our choice is not one between a free system based
on free enterprise and a fully centrally planned economy. The
real choice we have to make is between sticking to our present
system, which is largely guided and manipulated for the benefit
of the rich countries, and opting for a system directed towards
finding solutions to the problems of an equitable division of income and property, of scarcity of natural resources and of des-
poliation of the environment.'

Joop den Uyl, Netherlands Premier, 1975

2.1   *The Industrialized World: From Cornucopia to Pandora's Box*

The call for a new international economic order was made in a period of
economic turmoil without precedent in the post-war world. The industrialized countries were experiencing economic dislocations unknown since the
agonies of the Great Depression of the 1930's. The international system,
which they had largely created and which had appeared to serve them well,
was in serious disequilibrium.

Behind them was a period of unparalleled economic growth. The planetary
product, for which they were responsible for by far the largest part, had
trebled in the twenty years between 1950 and 1970, a period in which
most of the world's industrial capacity was created. This growth had
brought material prosperity for most of their citizens, a more equitable
income distribution within their societies, and achievements in many
fields of science.

The rich countries had created an enormously powerful industrial
machine. Fed by stimulated demand, it was, in the Western world, fired by
abundant and cheap supplies of oil. At just over one dollar a barrel, oil
supplies stimulated growth in energy consumption at between 6 and 11
per cent a year. The very cheapness of the supplies ensured rapid growth.
It also encouraged extravagance and waste.

A colonial history had also helped bestow upon many countries in the
Western world access to cheap supplies of other of the Third World's raw
materials. Of the nine major minerals (excluding oil) required to sustain
an industrial economy, the industrialized market economy countries
consumed nearly 70 per cent of the world's output. The Third World,
economically tied to the industrial machine, was compelled to sell for the
price determined by international market mechanisms which worked to
the advantage of the industrialized importing countries.

The two most powerful nations were able to construct a mighty military
capability and devise weapons of incredible destructiveness in order to

Table 1   *Gross national product and population, 1973 (percentages)*

	GNP	Population
North America	30.0	6.1
Europe (excluding U.S.S.R.)	31.8	13.2
U.S.S.R.	10.7	6.5
Asia (including Middle East and excluding Japan)	10.2	52.7
Japan	8.3	2.8
Central and South America [a]	5.2	7.9
Africa	2.4	10.2
Oceania	1.5	0.6
Total	100.0	100.0
Developed Market Economies [b]	65.7	17.9
Centrally Planned Economies [c]	20.2	32.0
Developing Countries	14.2	50.1
Total	100.0	100.0

[a] includes Mexico.
[b] Australia, Austria, Belgium, Canada, Denmark, Finland, France, Fed.
Rep. of Germany, Iceland, Ireland, Italy, Japan, Luxembourg, Nether-
lands, New Zealand, Norway, Portugal, Puerto Rico, South Africa,
Sweden, Switzerland, United Kingdom, United States.
[c] Albania, Bulgaria, People's Rep. of China, Cuba, Czechoslovakia, Dem.
Rep. of Germany, Hungary, Dem. Rep. of Korea, Poland, Romania,
U.S.S.R., Dem. Rep. of Vietnam.

Note: In 1973, world GNP was $ 4.8 trillion; population was 3.8 billion.

Source: Based on *World Bank Atlas, 1975: Population, per Capita
Product, and Growth Rates* (Washington, D.C.: World Bank Group, 1975).

protect their competing social systems. This military capability not only
required the industrial machine to sustain it, it also made it possible for
the machine to grow still further. It was, moreover, a capability which
threatened the lives of every single man, woman and child.

By the early 1970's it had become clear that the cornucopia of economic
growth was turning into a Pandora's box. The main props upon which the
economic system was resting began to crumble, for the industrialized
countries, in uncomfortably quick succession. The world monetary
system, agreed upon by the Western powers at Bretton Woods towards the
end of the Second World War, had all but collapsed by 1971. Despite the
fact that this laid the basis for gigantic financial disruptions, world wide
inflation, trade dislocations and, for some countries, enormous balance of

payments difficulties, the Western powers found it hard to cooperate on international monetary reforms.

The disruptions contributed to wild movements in the price of most primary products which, because of their unstable markets, were already prone to serious fluctuation. Prices of industrial products had increasingly risen, partly as a consequence of increased demand and partly because of wage claims far surpassing increases in labour productivity. These developments not only jeopardized the growth prospects of the industrialized countries but also resulted in continuous increases in the import bills of most Third World countries.

The Development Strategy for the Second United Nations Development Decade, solemnly adopted by the U.N. General Assembly in 1970, and reviewed in 1973, had hardly been taken seriously by the larger industrialized countries and a general feeling of frustration prevailed among the countries of the Third World. A sudden and historically important change took place, however, when in 1973 the Organization of Petroleum Exporting Countries (OPEC) took the initiative to use their power and raised the price of crude oil — which in real terms had actually declined between 1950 and 1970 — to about four times the previous level. This development, facilitated by a temporary and perhaps unexpected coincidence of interests between Western oil companies and OPEC nations, caused the industrialized countries considerable distress and brought vailed threats of military retaliation. It did, however, result in a temporary two per cent transfer of the GNP of the industrialized countries to the OPEC nations; it also contributed towards accelerating the recession in economic activity which had started in 1972.

The world situation was further aggravated by adverse weather conditions which brought disastrous crop failures in many parts of the world, and by the concerted action of the main producers of basic staple foods which enabled them to increase their prices in 1974 to a level some three to four times higher than in 1970. This placed enormous pressure on world reserve stocks of food grains — which dwindled to virtually nothing in 1972 as well as in 1975 — and on the importers of staple foods, especially the poorest countries.

The full impact of all these developments were felt in the industrialized world in 1974 and 1975 when the recession assumed proportions larger than any experienced since the Second World War. Economists struggled to explain 'stagflation', the unique combination of high inflation and industrial recession; Keynesian economics, which had helped to steer courses away from impending crises in the past, this time seemed perilously inadequate. Industrial production in many industrialized countries fell in 1975 for the first time since the Second World War. In Sep-

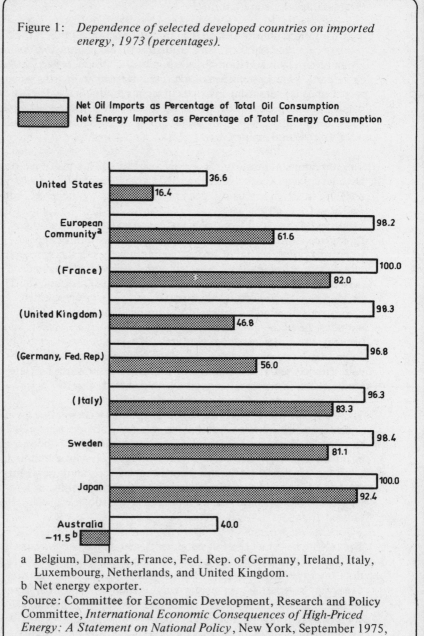

Figure 1: *Dependence of selected developed countries on imported energy, 1973 (percentages).*

☐ Net Oil Imports as Percentage of Total Oil Consumption
▨ Net Energy Imports as Percentage of Total Energy Consumption

United States — 36.6 / 16.4

European Community[a] — 98.2 / 61.6

(France) — 100.0 / 82.0

(United Kingdom) — 98.3 / 46.8

(Germany, Fed. Rep.) — 96.8 / 56.0

(Italy) — 96.3 / 83.3

Sweden — 98.4 / 81.1

Japan — 100.0 / 92.4

Australia — 40.0 / -11.5[b]

a Belgium, Denmark, France, Fed. Rep. of Germany, Ireland, Italy, Luxembourg, Netherlands, and United Kingdom.
b Net energy exporter.
Source: Committee for Economic Development, Research and Policy Committee, *International Economic Consequences of High-Priced Energy: A Statement on National Policy*, New York, September 1975, p. 77.

14

tember of that year, seventeen million people flooded the employment offices of the richest countries. Nor was it the industrial machine that alone was misfiring; some sectors of Western agriculture, which only a few years earlier had appeared strong, were in difficulties.

To many it became increasingly apparent that the economic crisis which plagued the Western world was more than a temporary phenomenon, a pocket of economic turbulence along the route towards even greater riches. They view it as a crisis in the very international structures and mechanisms which the Western world itself has largely created. If the inexorable workings of market forces have helped create the problems, it is clear that they, if left to their own devices, will not be able to solve them. Some economists even warn us that the much heralded 'recovery' might prove little more than a brief respite, a lull before an even greater economic storm, not long off, even more damaging than the last.

Prosperity has brought anxiety to the Western world, a gnawing fear that the good times might well be over, even though aspirations for still greater material benefits remain. If the Western world is to come to grips with this, with its growing list of problems − social as well as economic − it must, in its own long term interests, seek to create new international structures based upon global cooperation.

2.2 *The Third World: From Deference to Defiance*

If the period since the Second World War was an era of growth in the industrialized world, it was an age of political liberation in the Third World. In little more than one decade, some one third of the world's then population was freed from foreign suzerainty. But the poor nations found that with fewer resources, less know-how, and limited opportunities to utilize that which they had, they were in fact less free than the rich countries. They discovered that political liberation does not necessarily bring economic liberation and that the two are inseparable: that without political independence it is impossible to achieve economic independence; and without economic power, a nation's political independence is incomplete and insecure.

This economic dependence is rooted in the main institutions of the international system created largely by the industrialized countries to deal essentially with their own problems at a time in which the voices of the world's poor were unheard in international fora. The poor nations have been forced to question the basic premises of an international system which leads to ever widening disparities between the richest and poorest nations and to a persistent denial of equality of opportunity. They contend that the 'free' market is in fact not 'free' but works to the advantage of the industrialized nations, who have used it to construct a protective wall around their affluence and life-styles. And even if it were 'free', it would still work to the advantage of the industrialized nations because of their enormous political and economic strength. As at the national level, the market mechanism tends to mock poverty, or simply ignores it, since the poor hardly have the purchasing power to influence market decisions. This is even more true at the international level, since there is no world government and none of the established mechanisms which exist within countries which create pressures for the redistribution of income and opportunity.

Inevitably and rightly, the Third World is demanding change in an international system which, it contends, systematically discriminates against its interests and is characterized by institutional distortions which, according to some estimates, cost the poor nations in the order of $ 50 - $100 billion* a year. It is insisting on fundamental structural change; not remedial tinkering at international institutions but a new world order which will redress past patterns of hopeless dependency and provide real opportunities to more equitably share in global growth.

Meeting in Dakar in 1975 the poor nations declared that to achieve their 'full and complete economic emancipation', it was necessary 'to recover and control their natural resources and wealth, and the means of economic development.' They agreed that there was 'an urgent need for the developing countries to change their traditional approach to negotiations with the developed countries, hitherto consisting of the presentation of a list of requests to the developed countries and an appeal to their political goodwill which in reality was seldom forthcoming.'

It must be made clear that the Third World is not demanding massive redistribution of the past income and wealth of the rich nations. It is not seeking charity from the prosperous nor equality of income. It is asking for equality of opportunity and insisting on the right to share in future growth. The basic objectives of the emerging 'trade union' of poor nations is to negotiate a 'new deal' with the rich nations on the basis of reasonable demands through the instrument of collective bargaining and participation. In attempting to secure greater equality of opportunity, they are simply insisting on the right to sit as equals around the bargaining tables of the world.

2.3   *The Centrally Planned Nations: We Do Not Live in a Hothouse*

The economic and financial crises besetting the industrialized world sent

---

* The word billion when used in this report represents one thousand million, being equivalent to 'milliard' used in Continental Europe. Trillion refers to one million million. All dollars are U.S. dollars.

their ripples into Eastern Europe. The effect of OPEC's increase in oil prices, for example, has been felt by all the oil-importing countries of CMEA, particularly Hungary, Czechoslovakia, the German Democratic Republic and Bulgaria. Since most obtain their oil from the Soviet Union, the shock was delayed; it was not until 1973 that CMEA substantially increased the price of oil in line with the world market. Poland and Romania were the least affected: Poland derives over 80 per cent of its energy from its coal resources while Romania is a producer of crude oil. Even Romania, however, failed to escape the economic dislocations. Its refining capacity is greater than its production and the difference had to be made up by imports from the Middle East (1).

Most Eastern European nations ran balance of payment deficits with the West in 1974 and 1975 and were seriously affected by world inflation. An unusual editorial in a Hungarian newspaper, under the eloquent heading: 'We do not live in a hothouse' observed: 'Sometime ago we believe that we are not affected by what is happening on the world capitalist market. Inflation could be stopped, as an unwelcome guest, at our borders and here in our country we could live and work under the same conditions as before. That 'hothouse' atmosphere has cost us 20 billion forints' (2).

The situation is somewhat different with the Soviet Union, a global economic power. The Soviets produce about 8 million barrels of oil daily (nearly the same as Saudi Arabia), but export only one-fifth. The increase in gold prices has also advantaged the Soviet Union as has the general increase in the price of raw materials. Soviet exports to the West amounted, for oil alone, to $ 3 billion in 1974 and were expected to increase to $ 3.5 billion in 1975 (3).

Despite this, Western European nations ran a $ 1.6 billion trading surplus with Eastern Europe in 1973 (a figure slightly higher in 1974) (4). Soviet-American trade in 1975 resulted in a $ 1.5 billion surplus to the advantage of the U.S. mainly as a result of the Soviet Union's substantial grain imports. The Soviet-American grain agreement points to a continued U.S. trading surplus.

The main cause of Eastern Europe's trading deficit lies in the asymmetrical structure of East-West trade. The share of manufactured goods in Eastern European exports is relatively small (less than 20 per cent in the late 'sixties and early 'seventies), whereas the machinery imported from the West accounts for over 40 per cent of total West-East intercourse. The highly unfavourable structure of trade is compounded by the privileged position of Western currencies in financial transactions. As Soviet economist Pichugin has pointed out: '. . . such a situation can become a brake on the further expansion of exports from industrial capitalist countries to socialist nations, in as much as the latter's purchasing capacities with regard to capitalist countries are determined in the ultimate end by the size of their export receipts from those countries' (5).

The centrally planned nations are disadvantaged on international markets with the manufactured goods of their infant industries, barely competitive both in prices and technological performance with the products of the industrially advanced nations. Moreover, the debts incurred by Eastern European countries with Western banks have reached an all-time high and run into billions of dollars. These observations lead inescapably to the conclusion that we are dealing here with a *specific pattern generated by a disparity in development* and that difficulties in East-West economic relations are in some cases more the result of different levels of development than of differences in social and economic systems (6). Indeed, development is not an exclusive North-South or West-South problem affecting the developing continents only. Europe has a *'development gap' of its own*, in a milder version to be sure, but nevertheless one that makes for an important factor in correctly understanding the vital stake of Eastern Europe in the restructuring of international economic relations.

As things stand now, in spite of the tremendous efforts of the Eastern European nations to industrialize and to develop a modern economy, their main economic indicators still lag behind those of their Western counterparts. Whereas per capita GNP in Eastern Europe ranges *grosso modo* from $ 1,000 to $ 3,000 annually, the same indicator in Western Europe goes as high as $ 2,500 to $ 6,000 (7). This is an imbalance with serious economic, political and ideological consequences.

To really understand the peculiarity of this phenomenon, it must be realized that it has a much longer ancestry than that currently accorded to it by authors who deal with the East-West conflict as though it were purely and exclusively an ideological antagonism that started with the Russian Revolution and took shape in the aftermath of the Second World War with the extension of the revolution into Eastern Europe. Such an approach may at best help explain the origins of the Cold War, but not its underlying economic background. This goes back to the very inception of the modern international state-system, when the two major convergent processes, namely the vigorous expansion of capitalism and the formation of nation-States in Europe, gave the Western part of the continent a strong edge over its Eastern part.

It was the Renaissance with its blend of antiquity and feudalism that at once produced the many breakthroughs in science and the historical turning point from which Europe outdistanced all other continents. And since the Renaissance was a Western European phenomenon, *par excellence*, both the early start of the Absolutist state as the maker of modern nations and the capitalist expansionist thrust established *there* the centre of the new international system.

Such were the historical conditions that allowed the Western nations to fully benefit from the industrial revolution. Eastern European peoples (most of them still struggling for nationhood) remained in predominantly agrarian economies with strong feudal structures which survived until the twentieth century. And since the socialist revolution started in backward Russia and subsequently expanded into underdeveloped or less developed countries, they were all faced with the enormous task of industrialization at a pace as rapid as possible, a task so overriding that the whole social, economic and political fabric of those new societies bear its imprint.

It would logically follow that Eastern Europe has a vital interest in the creation of a new international order that would eliminate existing imbalances among nations. Indeed, all centrally planned nations have supported the drive initiated to that end by the Group of 77; Romania even recently joined the Group (8).

2.4 *The Need for a New International Order*

The inequities in the international system are of tremendous significance. They have given rise to essentially two worlds and the disparities between them are growing. One is the world of the rich, the other the world of the poor, united by its heritage of common suffering. A poverty curtain divides the worlds materially and philosophically. One world is literate, the other largely illiterate; one industrial and urban, the other predominantly agrarian and rural; one consumption oriented, the other striving for survival. In the rich world, there is concern about the quality of life, in the poor world about life itself which is threatened by disease, hunger and malnutrition. In the rich world there is concern about the conservation of non-renewable resources and learned books written about how the world should be kept in a stationary state. In the poor world there is anxiety, not about the depletion of resources, but about their exploitation and distribution for the benefit of all mankind rather than a few privileged nations. While the rich world is concerned about the impact of its pollutive activities on life-support systems, the poor world is concerned by the pollution of poverty, because its problems arise not out of an excess of development and technology but out of the lack of development and technology and inadequate control over natural phenomena.

We have today about two-thirds of mankind living – if it can be called living – on less than 30 cents a day. We have today a situation where there are about one billion illiterate people around the world, although the world has both the means and technology to spread education. We have nearly 70 per cent of the children in the Third World suffering from malnutrition, although the world has the resources to feed them. We have

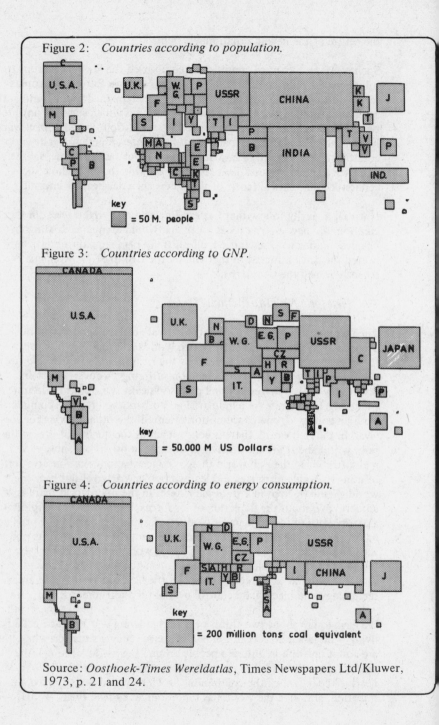

Figure 2: *Countries according to population.*

key
= 50 M. people

Figure 3: *Countries according to GNP.*

key
= 50.000 M US Dollars

Figure 4: *Countries according to energy consumption.*

key
= 200 million tons coal equivalent

Source: *Oosthoek-Times Wereldatlas*, Times Newspapers Ltd/Kluwer, 1973, p. 21 and 24.

Table 2 *Growing income disparities: per capita income ($ U.S.) in selected regions, 1913 and 1957*

Region	1913		1957	
	Population (millions)	Income/capita ($ U.S.)	Population (millions)	Income/capita ($ U.S.)
North America	105	917	188	1,868
N.W. Europe	184	454	211	790
S.E. Asia	323	65	318	67
China	370	50	640	61
World population	1,463		2,373	

Source: L.J. Zimmerman: *Arme en Rijke Landen*, The Hague, 1959, p. 29, 31.

maldistribution of the world's resources on a scale where the industrialized countries are consuming about twenty times more of the resources per capita than the poor countries. We have a situation where, in the Third World, millions of people toil under a broiling sun from morning till dusk for miserable rewards and premature death without ever discovering the reasons why.

Both the rich and poor worlds have pressing, unparalleled problems. They are not separate; they cannot be solved independently. Mankind's predicament is rooted in its past, in the economic and social structures that have emerged within and between nations. The present crisis, in the world economy and in the relations between nations, is a crisis of international structures. What both worlds must come to grips with is basically a sick system which cannot be healed by expeditious economic first aid. Marginal changes will not be sufficient. What is required are fundamental institutional reforms, based upon a recognition of a common interest and mutual concern, in an increasingly interdependent world. What is required is a new international order in which all benefit from change.

Whatever agreements are eventually negotiated, they must balance the interests of the rich and poor nations. All nations have to carefully weigh the costs of disruption against the costs of accommodation and to consider the fact that any conceivable cost of a new deal will be a very small proportion of their future growth in an orderly cooperative framework.

Not only is there an overwhelming need for change, but there are increased opportunities for organizing change also. Mankind's history is the story of a continuous process of change, of evolution in the face of threats and dangers. It is this process which provides the dynamism in the struggle to continually improve living conditions and to increase control over nature. The process, always subject to autonomous human interference, is occasionally subject to 'historical discontinuities', breaks or 'mutations' in trends which provide increased opportunities for taking new initiatives in redirecting the evolutionary process. Four such discontinuities have recently occurred and are of very great importance internationally.

The process of social change is subject to a variety of *quantitative development patterns*. These, familiar in many sciences, have a time dimension and may apply to any system of interaction. *Cycles* ('l'histoire se répète') are a familiar component of such patterns. Well-known examples include cycles in climate and business. Other components may be one-sided rather than cyclical movements. These can be either downward or upward, either accelerated (*'runaway'* or 'escalating') or decelerated, moving towards some *saturation* level ('trees don't grow into heaven'). In some cases saturation might constitute an optimum and therefore comprise a desirable target. In other cases, it may move to a level deemed too low, suggesting, among other possible states, *stagnation*. Of these various prototypes of evolution only a movement towards saturation or harmony is generally considered desirable. In contrast, cycles or stagnation often mean waste or annoyance and runaway movements are prone to result in disaster.

All the movement types described can be suddenly interrupted by great 'mutations' or unexpected interferences. In the field of technological development, such proved to be the case with, for example, the discovery of the steam engine, electricity and nuclear power. Social mutations have sometimes taken the form of *revolutions*, the French, the Russian, the Cuban, the Chinese and the Algerian revolutions being important examples. In terms of the process of change, the events comprised a moment of great 'historical discontinuity' for the countries concerned and were of such momentous importance that they changed the pattern of world relations. Following the revolutions, decades of evolutionary change were required to attain the aims pursued; the communist phase in Marxist terms, or social equity in the Western European democracies, were by no means achieved overnight and have not been fully achieved yet.

Firstly, one of the world's superpowers was obliged against its will to leave a part of the world where it had intervened in support of a non-representative regime. That this immensely powerful nation was unable to use its full military capability is of enormous importance. Secondly, there are the demands of the Third World, strengthened by the OPEC actions, a development which will be increasingly felt in international fora in the coming decade. Thirdly, there is the increasing incapacity of the rich and privileged nations, the industrialized world, to come to grips with the economic imbalances in the present international system and to deal creatively with the collapse of their own invention; this combined with growing alienation and frustration and the threats to basic human values and human environment engendered by pressures to consume. And fourthly, there is a growing recognition of global interdependencies and of the fact that no nation, however powerful it may believe itself to be, can realistically pursue its policies in isolation.

The demands for a new international order must be placed within this historical process. On one level of reasoning, it is a natural evolution of the philosophy already accepted at the national level: that the government must actively intervene on behalf of the poorest segments of their populations ('the bottom 40 per cent') who will otherwise be bypassed by economic development. In a fast shrinking planet, it was inevitable that this 'new' philosophy would not stop at national borders; and, since there is no world government, the poor nations are bringing this concern to its closest substitute, the United Nations. At another level, the demand for structural change is, as we have seen, a natural second state in the evolution of Third World countries; a movement from political to economic equality.

There is of course nothing new in the existence of rich and poor. History has known nothing else and has in part been shaped by the struggles between them. But the rich and poor have in the past mainly existed within individual societies. What *is* relatively new is the enormous differences among societies. It is moreover a visible difference; the rich cannot conceal their wealth in a 'global village'. The glaring differences are perceived by the poor thanks, perhaps paradoxically, to the rich world's technological dexterity. And their perception of these differences will, in a shrinking world, exert growing stress on already frail international institutions.

Mankind's future depends upon it coming to terms with these differences, with developing a new understanding and awareness, based upon interdependence and mutual interest of working and living together. Recent discontinuities in the process of change have placed mankind on the threshold of new choices. In choosing among them, it will have to accept the harsh fact that, perhaps contrary to previous times, it has just one future or no future at all.

Notes and References

(1) While in the past Romania paid $ 21 per ton for such imports, in 1974 the price increased to $ 126, a loss which had to be offset by exports of petroleum products. This, combined with increases in the price of other imported raw materials, left Romania in 1974 with a balance of payments deficit with centrally planned nations of over $ 200 million.

(2) Magyar Nemzet, Budapest, 1974.

(3) *Oil and Gold-Price Increases Russians Windfall Profits*, The New York Times, January 11, 1975.

(4) Economic Bulletin for Europe, no. 1, vol. 26, 1974.

(5) B. Pichugin: *East West Economic Cooperation*, International Affairs, Moscow, no. 8, 1975.

(6) See Gunnar Adler-Karlsson: *Economic and Trade Policies*, International Institute for Peace, Vienna, no. 3, Sept. 1972, pp. 36-37.

(7) These are figures based upon official exchange rates and do not reflect differences in purchasing power.

(8) In an official document submitted to the U.N., the Romanian Government takes a clear-cut position in favour of the new order: 'In a situation of growing economic inter-dependence between states in which no country can isolate itself from the world economic development, it is clearly necessary that all states, regardless of their social system, the extent of their territories or their economic potential, should make an active contribution to the solution of the major economic problems currently facing the world'.

3.1   *Introduction*

This chapter is devoted to a short review of some of the major problem areas relevant to the creation of a new international order. They are reviewed with a view to defining the magnitude of the tasks confronting the international community and to identifying the areas in which action is required if progress towards a fairer world is to be made. In reviewing them, we will not deal with possible solutions: these are presented in Part III. The final section of this chapter is devoted to a brief discussion of the nature of planetary interdependencies.

3.2   *The Armaments Race*

We must begin our review of the world's major problems with the competitive armaments race since this more than any other carries the very real threat of the destruction of virtually all life on our planet. World military expenditures are now approaching $ 300 billion a year – nearly $ 35 million every hour of every day – and they continue to rise. The military alliances in general, and the superpowers in particular, are the great military spenders, accounting for 80 per cent and 50 per cent respectively of world military expenditures (1). More and more Third World countries, however, are devoting an increasing share of their limited resources to the acquisition of weapons. Their share of world armament and military expenditures rose from 6 per cent in 1954 to 17 percent in 1974 and an increasing number of Third World countries now possess their own weapon manufacturing capability.

The armaments race deprives mankind of enormous financial and human resources. The net transfer of financial resources from rich to poor countries amounts to about one thirtieth of world military expenditures and they are 163 times more than the sum spent on peace and development through the United Nations system. Close to half a million scientists and engineers – almost half the world's scientific and technological manpower – devote their skills to military research and development, at a cost of between $ 20 and $ 25 billion. These sums represent about 40 per cent of all – public and private – research and development expenditures.

Increasingly sophisticated nuclear arms represent a very particular threat to the future of mankind. Few who have studied the use of nuclear weapons believe they are in fact useable and even question the value of the weapons as a real deterrent. As an instrument of power, nuclear threats no longer seem particularly effective, if indeed they ever were. And even assuming their usefulness for 'brandishing' purposes, it has been estimated

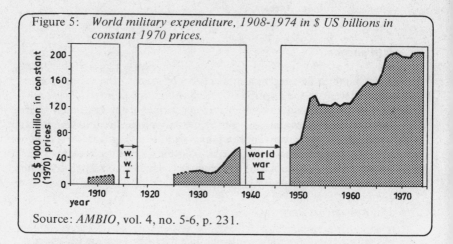

Figure 5: *World military expenditure, 1908-1974 in $ US billions in constant 1970 prices.*

Source: *AMBIO*, vol. 4, no. 5-6, p. 231.

that one fifth to one tenth of the present total of weapons held by the superpowers would be sufficient to act as a deterrent (2).

Any country with a large nuclear reactor and access to facilities for separating uranium and plutonium (the fissionable by-product of reactors) is a potential nuclear power. According to some estimates there could be more than 500 reactors operating in 52 countries by the end of the decade. By the 1980's, the world's reactors will have produced about one million pounds of plutonium — enough to manufacture 50,000 explosive devices. And even if countries should prove wise enough not to manufacture nuclear weapons, there is the growing danger that fissionable material will fall into the hands of political extremists and terrorist groups.

These circumstances place current arms reduction negotiations in a completely new light. They point to the absolute need that such negotiations produce immediate and concrete results. Since the competitive armaments race has deep structural causes, it will take more than a few compromise conventions to change a trend which, if allowed to continue, can only lead to one inevitable result. The problem is not to shift from a war to a peace economy, but from a war to a peace mentality. Whether mankind is able to achieve this will largely determine its chances of surviving the twentieth century (3). It would be perverse indeed if this mentality could only emerge from the rubble of a nuclear holocaust.

3.3   *Population*

The subject of world population growth has been the cause of much controversy. Some in the industrialized countries have viewed it much too simplistically, being quick to attribute many if not most of the world's problems to 'soaring birth rates' in the developing continents. Some poor countries, on the other hand, have been reluctant or have refused to initiate population control programmes even when it has been clearly demonstrated that such programmes could comprise powerful means for achieving some of their development objectives.

Population growth is a complex subject that defies easy generalizations. Some demographers contend that the constantly reiterated references to 'soaring birth rates' in the poor nations have little factual basis and in many instances no basis at all. Some poor, essentially agricultural, societies clearly suffer from 'under' rather than 'overpopulation' pressures. In other countries, the population problem is more one of distribution than of total numbers: the migration rate of people from rural areas to the cities is often twice as rapid as total population growth and slums are growing much faster than cities as a whole. No sensible person could expect a man and woman to deliberately choose to limit the size of their family when they expect five out of six of their children to die before the age of three and when a large family is the only safeguard against the hopelessness and destitution of old age. Given this, it is hardly surprising that some Third World countries view the population control exhortations of the rich countries as a failure to confront the real issues.

It is however clear that, given the many uncertainties and unknowns facing mankind, there is every need to exercise caution in discussing the population that our planet can ultimately support. This applies just as much to the rich as the poor nations because of the vastly disproportionate share of the earth's fruits they consume and of the disturbances to the world's eco-systems they generate. That there must be limits to the earth's support capacity is obvious, even though we do not know what these limits are.

The lowest growth projections indicate that during the first decades of the twenty-first century the earth's population will be almost twice as great as it is now — over 7 billion people compared with the present 4 billion. Although the rate of growth is itself slowing down, the 1970's will witness the greatest population growth so far in history: over 800 million will be born — more than 600,000 per month — of whom nearly 88 per cent, some 700 million, will be in the Third World. This will obviously place tremendous pressures on the social and economic systems of the poor countries. Without major changes, the doubling of the Third World's population will necessitate a doubling of all investments in social and physical infrastructure simply to retain existing standards of living. It should be noted that a doubling of population calls for a trebling of the total number of jobs needed.

Demographers are not agreed on how long and how far this exponential population growth can continue. Probably the rate of growth will slow down in the early part of the next century, and what is now being discussed is the possibility of achieving a *reasonably stationary population*, somewhere in the middle or the latter half of that century, at a level of 12, 15 or 20 billion people.

It is clearly of no little importance where, and at what level, growth may be halted. Even the lowest estimate – in a situation where the then comparatively poor peoples of the world still constitute nearly 90 per cent of the world's population – will present us with a situation with serious international tensions and conflicts, leading to appalling strains in international cooperation especially if the world is still being run along the same lines as at present.

New perceptions of population growth have shown us that there can be no single solution to balancing birth and death rates. High birth rates clearly have a cause and effect relationship with poverty, illiteracy and underdevelopment. To curb high growth rates calls for a concerted attack on poverty, unemployment, illiteracy, hunger, malnutrition and disease; and for the provision of essential social services as well as population limitation measures. This package of measures must be geared to the specific conditions prevailing in the country concerned. That population curtailment cannot be achieved without economic development is obvious. The central question is whether 'the vicious circle' of poverty and high birth rates can be broken.

3.4   *Food*

Estimates of the number of people currently suffering from hunger and undernourishment vary from close to half a billion to one and a half billion. Women and children are hunger's principal victims. Some 40 per cent of the world's underfed are children and in the Third World, half of all children are estimated to be undernourished. As a direct result, more than 300 million children are believed to suffer from grossly retarded physical growth and development. The absolute number of hungry and malnourished in the world in the early 1970's was greater than ever before except in times of famine. Before the Second World War all the developing continents were exporters of cereals; today they are all major importers (Table 3).

The annual rate of growth in food production at the global level was 3.1 per cent during the 'fifties and 2.7 per cent during the 'sixties, compared with population growth rates of 2.0 per cent and 1.9 per cent respectively. Although Third World food production growth rates over the past two decades were the same as those recorded in the industrialized countries, gains were greatly reduced because of higher rates of population growth (averaging 2.4 per cent a year over the same period). The growth in food

Table 3 *International trade in cereals 1934/38 - 1975 import/export in million tons*

		1934/38		1975	
		Import	Export	Import	Export
From surplus	Latin America	9		3	
to deficit	Africa	1		10	
	Asia	2		47	
	USSR	5		25	
Remaining in deficit	Western Europe	24		17	
Becoming major exporters	North America	5			94
	Australia/ N. Zealand	3			9

Source: Lester R. Brown: *The Politics and Responsibility of the North American Breadbasket*, Worldwatch Paper 2, October 1975.

production per capita in the Third World in fact narrowed from 0.7 per year in the 'fifties to 0.2 per cent in the 'sixties. A growth rate of 0.2 per cent represents a yearly gain of only 400 grams per capita. The gain in the industrialized countries over the same period was nearly thirty times greater and averaged 11,250 grams.

It was during the early 1970's that development in world food production, already precarious for hundreds of millions, took a sharp turn for the worse. In 1972, world food production declined for the first time in over 20 years as adverse weather struck the Soviet Union, China, India, Southeast Asia and parts of Africa. At about the same time, agricultural growth rates in many poor countries, in some of them stimulated by the 'green revolution', began to slow. This was followed in some parts of the world by drought and monsoon failures.

As world food demands increased, world grain reserves – already a perilously inadequate buffer against the vagaries of weather and plant disease – dwindled to their lowest in over a decade (4). Production shortfalls led to shortages and this to price increases on world grain markets, a development which put basic foodstuffs beyond the reach of many of the most needy countries.

The situation was further aggravated by the increased rate of inflation generated by the market economy industrialized countries during the 'seventies. This was due in part to the closure of fertilizer plants in the United States from 1970 onwards because of a shortage of natural gas. This gave rise to a substantial increase in the prices of the main categories of fertilizers which doubled between June 1972 and September 1973, 85 per cent of world fertilizer production being controlled by the industrialized countries. In 1974, the United States, Japan and Western Europe took a series of decisions which resulted in a reduction in the exports of fertilizers; the United States reduction alone — 2 million tons — prevented the production of 20 million tons of cereals in the Third World. As inflation raged in the industrialized countries, the price of agricultural equipment began to skyrocket; tractors, for example, doubled in price in two years. Some pesticides and herbicides trebled in price in one year, seed prices also turned sharply upwards. These and other developments not only brought hundreds of millions of hungry people in the Third World closer to the brink of starvation, but also some sectors of agriculture in the market economy industrialized countries — dependent on increased mechanization and copious supplies of fertilizers, pesticides, herbicides and fungicides — into difficulties.

There is no single cause of the world food problem. Part of the explanation is to be found in the operation of many of the world's international systems which deprive Third World countries of the opportunities to develop the resources required to meet their own food needs. Part can be found in the distribution of available food and, in particular, the emergence of meat eating in the industrialized countries as a consequence of affluence, a development which requires an enormous indirect consumption of grain to sustain it (5). It is also true that many Third World countries have themselves contributed, sometimes unwittingly, to the world food problem. In some cases they have not given domestic food production the priority it deserves, choosing instead to invest their scarce resources in their cities or in 'prestige' projects. They have sometimes subordinated their food needs to those of the industrialized world, using some of their most productive areas for cultivating the cash crops required by the industrialized world rather than for producing their own food. In many cases they have also failed to free the small farmer from the poverty, ignorance, exploitation and discrimination which are traditionally his lot and thus prevented him from making the major contribution to development he is able to make. They have sometimes, as a matter of policy, kept prices of farm products very low with the net result that the small farmer overwhelmingly carries the burden of development. Many have been reluctant to initiate the land reforms required to expand food production and have failed to come to terms with post-harvest food losses which, in some countries, account for 50 per cent of total grain production.

No country can allow itself to be permanently and greatly (say 80 per cent) dependent on others for its foodstuffs. Without international and,

where necessary, national reforms, the humble wheatsheaf seems destined
to become a powerful weapon of economic warfare and the hungry
millions of Africa and Asia, pawns in the game of international politics.
A CIA report prepared shortly before the Rome World Food Conference
pointed to the fact that the United States' food surplus provided 'virtual
life and death power over the fate of the multitudes of needy'. This power
has been recognized by, for example, the American Secretary for Agriculture who has observed: 'Food is a weapon. It is one of the principal
tools in our negotiating kit' (6). Without a major change of course, the
present hunger crisis seems destined to become a starvation crisis.

3.5   *Human Settlements*

The twentieth century increasingly witnesses an astonishing change in the
pattern of human settlements. At the beginning of this century, our planet
was almost entirely rural; by its close, it will be largely urbanized. The
world's urban population has doubled in the last 25 years and is expected
to double again in the next generation. Some 3.2 billion people – half the
world's population – are expected to live in the world's cities and towns
by the end of the century, and two out of three urban dwellers will live in
the Third World.

Traditionally, the size of the city has served as an index of 'progress' and
'development'. In 1950, the urban population of the rich countries was
nearly double that of the poor countries (439 million compared with
265 million). Today, half of the 15 largest cities, measured in population,
are in the Third World. By the end of the next decade, almost 60 per cent
of the world's urban population will be living in the cities of the Third
World. By the end of the century, three-quarters of all Latin Americans,
and one third of all Asians and Africans, will – if present urbanization
trends continue – be living in cities. If city size was ever a satisfactory
index of prosperity, it is barely so today, and will certainly not be so in
the near future.

The tremendous increase in the level of urbanization is largely the result
of mass migration from the rural areas. It has been estimated that between
1970 and 1975, about 106 million persons moved from rural to urban
areas. Of these, 70 per cent (73 million) were in the nations of the Third
World. It is generally the largest cities which attract the most newcomers.
The number of cities with one million inhabitants or more in 1950 was
75, accounting for 25 per cent of the world's urban population. Today,
there are almost 200 'million cities'. By 1985, there may well be close to
300, housing nearly 40 per cent of the world's urban population. It will
be in the Third World where large cities will grow the most rapidly.

It is in cities where the glaring disparities between the 'haves' and 'have nots' are most apparent. It is also in cities where poverty and disadvantage are the most concentrated. Migrants to the city are no ordinary people. They have taken the courageous decision to dig-up their rural roots, to seek a 'new life' for themselves and their children. In coming to the city, they bring with them their expectations and aspirations. If cities cannot meet these, if cities can offer no alternative to poverty, it will be in cities that future structural changes in national orders will be wrought. In the past, modernization has tended to mean urbanization. In the future, it cannot do so.

3.6 *Human Environment*

That our life-support systems are under unprecedented attacks from the combined effects of urbanization, industrialization, agriculture and our daily life-styles is undisputed. How much disruption these systems can absorb without breaking down, however, is simply not known. Some scientists fear that, in certain areas, we might be closer to transgressing the 'outer limits' imposed on our activities by the environment than we might care to think. And to exceed the limits set by nature could conceivably result in a planet unable to support human life.

Our emergence from the Dark Ages of almost total environmental ignorance has brought with it the discovery of appalling lacunae in the strategic knowledge required to address a complex array of problems. Certainly, the agenda of unanswered questions is long, and growing. What, for instance, will be the long term effects on our well-being of continued exposure to the half million compounds and poisons which we carelessly dispose of? How much man-made interference can oxygen and nitrogen cycles tolerate before breaking down? What influence do aerosols exert on the ozone layer, and what will be the effect of supersonic jet transports? Will the continued pollution of our air, rivers, lakes and seas constitute an eventual limit to the expansion of human activities? Does increasing thermal pollution represent a bigger threat to human survival than the continued generation of carbon dioxide? How will massive deforestation, caused by the need for firewood, by overgrazing, urbanization and commercial timber exploitation, effect our terrestrial environment and, ultimately, our planet's atmosphere and climate? And how, above all, do the many and varied environmental problems interact; are there 'synergisms' which will accelerate our journey towards the 'outer limits'?

It is in the sphere of human environment that the interdependencies between nations are perhaps most clearly evident. Third World countries acknowledge that, far from being an exclusive problem of the industrialized world, environmental degradation and overtaxing of nature form very much a part of their own predicament. The industrialized countries are increasingly recognizing that patterns of resource use and maldistribution are an important aspect of the 'environmental crisis'. Both sides subscribe to the concept of 'spaceship earth'. The sad fact is that very few practical steps have yet been taken to translate the implied awareness into a genuine blueprint for ecological survival. The current negotiations on the management of ocean space and resources demonstrate the difficulties involved.

Failure to take such steps, given the unprecedented scale of human interference with nature and ecological balances, might prove disastrous to all. Environmental concern must be reflected in the more balanced management of world resources and human environment. Balanced management must aim simultaneously at waging an immediate battle against poverty and at safeguarding the interests of future generations through the legacy of a habitable planet. Both are predominantly political and not technical issues; both belong to attempts to shape a new international order.

3.7 *International Monetary and Trading Systems; Concessional Assistance*

The international system has evolved with in-built and self-propelling mechanisms which have tended to ensure that the industrialized countries are not only able to retain their privileged position but also, in many instances, to enhance it.

In the present *international monetary system* international liquidity is largely created by the national decisions of the richest industrialized nations since their national reserve currencies are in international circulation. Because of the over-reliance on the dollar, the growth of international reserves became increasingly the unintended by-product of the United States' balance of payments deficits. This system served the rich countries reasonably well — as far as *global* liquidity creation was concerned — provided that the United States' payments deficits did not exceed the normal needs for the growth of world reserves in an expanding world economy. The accumulation of dollar balances by foreign central banks between 1950 and 1969 accounted for approximately $ 14.5 billion (or about half) of the total growth of $ 31 billion in world reserves, i.e. about 2.5 per cent a year. Between 1970 and 1972, however, world reserves, expressed in dollar terms, increased as much as they had in all previous years since Adam and Eve. The increase in U.S. liabilities to foreign central banks accounted for nearly 69 per cent of the total, and the increase in other countries' reserve liabilities for another 24 per cent, i.e. 93 per cent in all.

The inflationary implications of such an 'explosion' of world reserves and of gold-convertible U.S. liabilities, exceeding five times the global U.S. gold and other reserve assets, led to the virtual collapse of the international monetary system based on the Bretton Woods agreement. This has not stopped, however, the continued inflation of world reserves, measured in dollars: 15 per cent in 1973 and 20 per cent in 1974.

While Third World countries continue to invest their monetary reserves in the national currencies of the richest industrialized nations, they obtain little benefit from the creation of new international liquidity; of the $ 102 billion of international reserves created in the period 1970-1974, the Third World received $ 3.7 billion, or less than 4 per cent of the total. Deposits in reserve currencies admittedly contributed to the ability of the richer nations to expand their loans and investments in the Third World, but such a lending and investment pattern runs directly contrary to the oft-repeated resolutions of the United Nations calling for an expedited transfer of real resources.

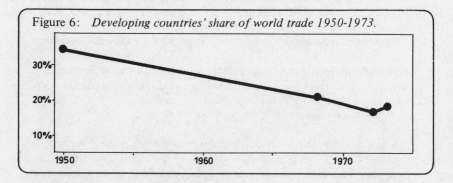

Figure 6: *Developing countries' share of world trade 1950-1973.*

With respect to *international trade*, most Third World nations are still tied to the Western World. However, their share of world trade is decreasing due to deteriorating terms of trade (Figure 6). Fully 75 per cent of their trade is with the countries of the OECD. The Third World produces only 7 per cent of the world's manufactured exports and some of these often face fierce tariffs and quotas in the industrialized countries. Its major exports are commodities and although twelve of these (excluding oil) account for about 80 per cent of its export earnings, Third World commodity trade amounts to only one-fifth of total world trade in commodities. Although the final consumers in the industrialized countries pay over $ 200 billion for Third World commodities and the products derived directly from them, the poor nations receive only $ 30 billion. Moreover, the Third World's export earnings from commodities, being dependent upon the requirements of the rich countries, fluctuate violently according to market conditions. And given the inflationary monetary practices of the rich nations, the purchasing power in terms of the manufactured goods produced by the industrialized countries is constantly declining. The price of industrial products increased by 33 per cent in 1974-1975 and in 1974 the poor nations paid 65 per cent more for their imports although their volume increased by only 20 per cent.

These developments have resulted in an enormous increase in the trading deficits of most of the poor nations: the annual deficits of oil-importing poor nations increased from $ 18 billion in 1973 to $ 40 billion in 1974 and are expected to be even higher in 1975.

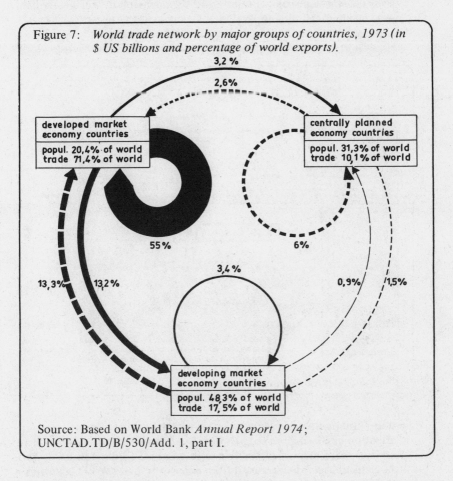

Figure 7: *World trade network by major groups of countries, 1973 (in $ US billions and percentage of world exports).*

Source: Based on World Bank *Annual Report 1974*; UNCTAD.TD/B/530/Add. 1, part I.

The disadvantages facing Third World countries in the international monetary and trading systems have not been compensated by *concessional assistance* from the industrialized nations. As early as 1961, the rich market economy countries agreed in principle to target 1 per cent of their GNP to the poor nations, with 0.7 per cent in the form of 'Official Development Assistance' (concessional transfers from or guaranteed by governments). By 1974, following constant reaffirmations of the transfer targets, only one country — Sweden — had achieved the figure, the example of which is expected to be followed by the Netherlands in 1976. In 1975, the flow of ODA from the rich market economy countries amounted to 0.30 per cent of their combined GNP. At $ 11 billion, it represented $ 6 billion in 1970 prices, the lowest 'real' flow of the 1970's. There are few signs that the concessional transfers of the main donors will rise in the near future. According to World Bank estimates, this assistance is even expected to fall to 0.28 per cent by the end of the decade.

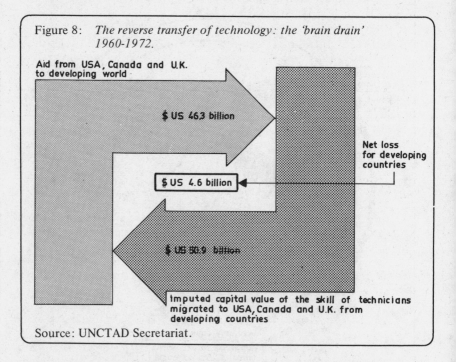

Figure 8: *The reverse transfer of technology: the 'brain drain' 1960-1972.*

Aid from USA, Canada and U.K. to developing world

$ US 46.3 billion

Net loss for developing countries

$ US 4.6 billion

$ US 50.9 billion

Imputed capital value of the skill of technicians migrated to USA, Canada and U.K. from developing countries

Source: UNCTAD Secretariat.

Where international resource transfers have taken place, insufficient attention has been given to their terms and conditions. Interest payments on loans have increased steadily and stood at $ 2.5 billion in 1973. About 11 cents of every dollar earned from exports by Third World countries flow out again to pay off debts and interest. Much larger than interest payments has been the outflow of profits on direct investments. According to reports on 73 countries, the profit outflow stood at $ 12 billion in 1973 (7). The reverse flow of funds — interest and profits — takes away about one half of fresh assistance each year. The amounts differ among countries, but in some it amounts to about a third of their export earnings. The reverse flow would be even higher if it were to include the advantages to the industrialized countries of the 'brain drain'.

3.8   *Natural Resources and Energy*

Fears for the exhaustion of natural resources combined with the actions of OPEC have brought raw materials in general and non-renewable resources in particular to the forefront of international discussions. The OPEC actions and the realization that the industrialized countries are vulnerable to the collective pressures of Third World raw material producing countries have afforded natural resources a strategic importance. It should be noted, however, that Third World countries do not have exclusive possession of raw materials. About one half of total world raw material production in fact takes place in the industrialized countries. Overall measures designed to raise prices of raw materials will not, therefore, have a major impact on world income distribution. It is through selective measures only that this distribution can be changed to the advantage of the Third World.

The present situation is characterized by three reactions on the part of resource rich Third World nations: a growing tendency towards ownership and management of natural resources traditionally controlled by Western 'multinationals'; a new impetus to the longstanding aspiration to process locally the raw materials they produce and so obtain a higher percentage of the final price paid by consumers; and the realization that information on their own known or potential reserves has become a political question and that they do not as yet possess all the relevant data. The changes in attitude have brought many in the industrialized countries to the conclusion that changes are necessary in present mineral resource investment, production, trade, and research and development patterns from the viewpoint of the interests and needs of their own societies. Moreover, it was clear to many, even before the 'energy crisis', that some industrialized countries had commodity problems which called for the creation of new international structures. The commodity problem is thus one of the areas where the negotiation of agreements, in this particular case guaranteeing Third World producing countries a fair and stable price for their products and guaranteeing the consuming industrialized countries uninterrupted supplies, is in the interest of both sides.

Recent analyses have shown that the fears expressed in recent years concerning the exhaustion of natural resources may well be exaggerated, at least in some cases. The oceans, for example, represent a potential source of enormous supplies of some raw materials. There is reason to believe that new technologies can be developed which will help solve problems of exploitation, extraction, substitution and environmental degradation. Several of these new technologies, however, will take many years, possibly decades, to develop. They will also be more costly, in terms of both money and energy, thereby making access to natural resources increasingly difficult to Third World countries and thus increasing inequalities rather than expanding opportunities. The need for such technologies is intimately linked to the evolution of consumption patterns, especially in the industrialized countries.

The two main resource problems are likely to be energy and water supplies. The industrialized countries have a history of lavish energy consumption combined with enormous waste. Nearly 86 per cent of global energy consumption occurs in a band between 30° and 60° north: the Third World, with 71 per cent of the world's population consumes only 16 per cent of the energy produced (Figure 4). The problem now is to develop new sources of clean energy, diversified in kind and in source, adequate to assure dependable long term supplies at acceptable cost, especially to the poorest countries.

The question of water supplies has so far received less attention than energy. One per cent (38,000 cubic kilometres) of the world's water — that in the 'hydrological cycle' — is available for human consumption; the remainder is stored in the oceans, polar ice caps and underground. This one per cent, although sufficient to meet forseeable needs, is unevenly distributed. Africa as a whole, for example, receives only 12 per cent of the water distributed by the hydrological cycle whereas the United States receives over 33 per cent.

Water may be the most important single factor for improving the well-being of the world's poor majority. Some 70 per cent of the world's population is without safe, dependable water and the consequences are enormous. Waterborne diseases are estimated to kill more than twenty-five thousand people daily. Schistosomiasis and filariasis, the world's biggest cause of blindness, afflict 450 million people in more than 70 nations. Many other diseases, such as typhoid, cholera, dysentery and hepatitis, are spread by contaminated water.

Some industrialized countries are on the verge of consuming more water than is produced by their natural cycles. Since the 1950's the water requirements in the industrialized countries for industrial purposes have exceeded those required for agriculture. Modern technology has very high water requirements, as part of its chemical processes for the removal of waste and, above all, for cooling. This is often wasteful of water but can be overcome by multiple recycling. Indeed, the management of water resources at all stages is perhaps the greatest need at present.

Intervening in the hydrological cycle in order to divert water and to redistribute it more equally seems to offer some possibilities. The ecological and climatic consequences of such intervention, however, are difficult to foresee and may produce strong effects at great distances from the place of intervention. All these matters will be reviewed by the U.N. World Water Conference to be held in March 1977 in Buenos Aires.

3.9   *Science and Technology; Transnational Enterprises*

Nowhere is the disparity between the industrialized and Third World countries more marked than in the field of scientific research and technological development. Although 90 per cent of all the technologists and scientists that have ever lived are alive today, over 90 per cent are at work in the industrialized countries. Over 90 per cent of their activities are concentrated on research for the rich world and on converting their findings into protected technical processes. The rich minority thus commands an overwhelming proportion of techno-scientific development.

Science and technology still hold out great promise for the improvement of the human condition. New research is urgently required, for example, on the improvement of agriculture and food production, the understanding of the climatic system, the production of new energy sources and the development of new technologies for the extraction of metals from low grade ores, at present unsuitable ores. It must be remembered, however, that the lead time of research and development is very long; the planning of research must be undertaken many years before its results are needed.

Third World countries have been largely dependent upon transnational enterprises for acquiring and expanding their technological development capability and the rapid growth of the so-called 'multinationals' has been one of the major forces which have shaped the international system. They are a Western phenomenon. Of the 650 largest transnationals, 638 have their headquarters in North America, Western Europe or Japan. The largest 300 U.S. enterprises and their 5,200 foreign subsidiaries alone account for 28 per cent of world exports, including 47 per cent of exports of primary products and 20 per cent of manufactured goods. Without changes in present trends, transnational enterprises could control more than 40 per cent of world production (excluding the centrally planned nations) before the end of the 1980's.

Facts like these, combined with the fact that some transnationals have proved to be politically disturbing elements, have been the subject of much controversy. Surprisingly little is really known about transnationals and this has given rise to the tendency to generalize about them. They undoubtedly excel in two fields: they have accumulated vast technological and marketing knowledge; and they have developed a highly effective process of transnational decision-making. The use of these capacities, unless channelled by the public interest, will increasingly clash with larger human and social dimensions of development emerging throughout the rich and poor world. It is obvious that transnational enterprises are not only a North-South issue, but a global one.

It has become clear that the development fostered by transnationals, especially in the Third World, is not always responsive to social needs and particularly those of the poor. Because of their necessity to continually expand and grow, they must have an increasing number of responsive buyers. Since their capacity to sell largely determines their capacity to increase their profits, they must inevitably produce for those that can afford rather than those in need. Thus, they have become essentially linked to and dependent on the affluent sectors of society because they are the principal consumers. This has not necessarily been the conscious policy of the transnationals; in some cases it is an inevitable consequence of the failure of governments to guide productive capacity of transnationals in desired directions. Although transnationals can be powerful engines of growth, their activities are not per se geared to the goals of development and, in the absence of proper government policies and in some cases social reform, they tend to accentuate rather than reduce income inequalities in poor societies. When allowed to operate on the principle of artificially stimulated demand (and thus waste), it is inevitable that they tend to repeat the patterns of Western market economy societies through a type of technology very often inappropriate to the needs of Third World countries.

Despite this, it is generally acknowledged that these enterprises can contribute to a poor country's development efforts. Although the bargaining power between the enterprises and host governments appears, in recent years, to have shifted in favour of the latter, there are still anachronistic arrangements dating from the colonial era which are in need of adjustment. The main problem is thus one of reconciling the interests of transnationals in security of investment and reasonable returns with the economic independence and development objectives of the host country.

3.10   *The Oceans*

It is only in recent decades that mankind has come to realize the immense potential offered by the oceans — an enormous envelope, largely unexplored, covering two-thirds of the earth's surface and with all the features of emerged land. The vastness of the oceans has constantly defied our imagination. It led us to implicitly assume that their living resources were inexhaustible and that all conceivable uses could be easily accommodated without the need for regulation. It encouraged us to view the oceans as the ultimate 'sink' through which we could dispose of all the things too dangerous or unpleasant to store or discard on land. Moreover, we came to believe that because the oceans were so vast and their uses so limited, serious conflicts of use were impossible.

This belief is now obsolete. The oceans are important and will increasingly become so as we search for new ways of solving some of our land-based problems. They are economically important: they contain 95 per cent of our planet's water, probably more hydrocarbons, and certainly a greater range of hard minerals than are found on land. Exploitation of manganese nodules could, according to some estimates, yield $ 15-20 billion over the next few decades. Moreover, in an energy-hungry world, the oceans are a potential source of vast supplies of power. The oceans have a military importance, for conventional and nuclear naval fleets. The oceans are important nutritionally, containing as they do vast living resources which could, if harvested sensibly, make an enormous contribution to meeting growing world food needs. The oceans are important environmentally, indeed to life on earth. Fully a quarter of the oxygen we breathe is produced by the effect of sunlight on the phytoplankton lying on the oceans' surface, exactly that area most vulnerable to the growing volume of pollutants and toxic wastes produced by our expanding industrial society. And the oceans are of fundamental importance to climate. It remains to be seen how this will be influenced by our apparent desire to turn the oceans into the ultimate cesspool.

The oceans are the last and, in some respects, the greatest resource of our planet. They are also a battlefield of conflicting interests. They are a 'common heritage' and as such 'belong' neither to the countries with the capability to exploit them nor exclusively to coastal States or powerful vested marine interests. As a common heritage, all mankind must benefit from their exploration, exploitation and conservation. That this cannot be guaranteed by the traditional law of the high seas or by unilateral national policies has become patently obvious. It is also clear that no attempt to fashion a new international order can afford to exclude the oceans. This question represents a historic opportunity, not only to ensure that all will benefit from the exploitation of the oceans, but also to develop new forms of international cooperation.

3.11 *Outer Space*

Outer space, often referred to as the 'new frontier', has a vast potential for both good and evil. By the early 1970's, some 900 American and Russian instrumented satallites were circling our globe. Many were known to be serving useful purposes; the purpose of others was a military secret. Space has provided the superpowers with new opportunities for expanding their already enormous sphere of influence: through spying; through the detection of unknown reserves and resources; and through the opportunities which communication satellites offer for influencing the attitudes and perceptions of people everywhere. Space is also the medium used by man's most destructive weapons, and space weaponry has become a field of fact as well as speculation.

The problem posed by outer space is, therefore, like the planet's oceans, much more than the accommodation of a proliferation of users or the allocation of scarce resources — frequencies, orbital areas and the like. Outer space, again like the oceans, must be viewed as an obvious example of a geographical entity forming a 'common heritage of mankind'. As such, the main problem is one of ensuring that all nations, not only the powerful and rich, benefit from its exploration and exploitation. That this is possible is evidenced by the usefulness space has already demonstrated for earth-oriented programmes, such as weather forecasting, geodetic survey and some forms of communication. It would appear to have considerable potential in such fields as education and health care. Even 'sky spies', if operated by a world agency rather than a nation-State, have a clear potential for international peace-keeping.

The effective management of space, ensuring its use for peaceful purposes and common benefit, is becoming increasingly necessary and important. Disturbingly, there is at present, apart from INTELSAT, no international body responsible for such management.

3.12 *International Institutions*

Many of the world's international institutions were established by the rich nations in the period immediately following the Second World War essentially to deal with the considerable problems then confronting them. Most of the world's population at that time lived under foreign suzerainty and the political liberation movement which was to sweep across the world in the following decades was only gathering momentum. The Third World, as we understand it today, simply did not exist and, as a result, its needs and requirements did not figure prominently — if at all — in the grand designs for the international institutions that were then drawn up. The United Nations, for example, had 41 founder members when it was established in 1945. Today it has more than 140 and most of those living today were not yet born when the Charter of the United Nations was adopted.

If the period following the Second World War was largely the world of the rich, today's world is predominantly the world of the poor. Political realities have changed but these changes have not yet been reflected in all international institutions. In pursuing its affairs, the Third World has discovered that policies and practices are still those largely determined by the industrialized nations and that the instruments at its disposal remain essentially those created, in different circumstances, by the industrialized world.

The Third World is clearly no longer prepared to accept its *de facto* marginal status in international affairs and is determined to make full use of all available international machinery in pursuing its goal of a more equitable world order. Many international institutions have become immovable parts of the international status quo and the guardians of powerful vested interests. Whether they are able to adapt to changing realities has become one of the key questions of our time.

That some international institutions are able to adapt has been demonstrated by the U.N. system through the establishment of new agencies and programmes. However, partial adaptation of international institutions will not be sufficient to bring about a new international order; they must be integrated into an all embracing approach aimed at facing the global challenge of the world of today. This approach should be guided by three fundamental objectives, i.e. greater democracy, greater efficiency and greater solidarity.

Until the need for change has been clearly demonstrated and the fact realized that all can benefit from change, an equitable basis for cooperation through international institutions cannot be established. In seeking this basis, we must choose to focus our attention on the U.N. system: it may be weak and imperfect yet it remains the only machinery with the potential for constructing a fairer world.

3.13   *Planetary Interdependencies*

No single major problem in the world today can be attacked in isolation. To attempt to do so will almost inevitably increase the difficulties in other and apparently unrelated problem areas. That we have in the past been guilty of simpleminded approaches to complex problems, the inevitable result of the 'tunnel vision' engendered by scientific specialization, is evident. In the field of technology, for example, the desire of Western man to conquer nature has often meant that the probability of small inconveniences has been reduced at the cost of increasing the possibility of very large disasters. Technological development has itself been distorted by the strategic armaments race.

Not only have the world's problems become more complex substantively, the world has also become more complex politically. The world's nations are more than a collection of giants and dwarfs. There are a great many middle powers of rising importance and strength, both in the industrialized and the Third Worlds. There are also today many levels of intercourse or interactions in addition to the strategic, the political or the economic: energy and technological relationships are obvious examples. A world in which a large number of powers — super, great and middle — attempt to maintain stability by means of bilateral diplomacy at several levels of interaction, some of which are vital to some but not to others, increase the chances of domestic as well as international confusion and tensions. The internal organization of nations is generally not suited to cope effectively at the policy level with interactive problems. Ministries, for example, have traditional sectoral competences and inter-ministerial committees normally reach agreement on the basis of the lowest common denominator.

The interpenetration of domestic as well as international issues has made nations increasingly interdependent. Interdependencies have always existed although the industrialized countries, judged by the actions, have in the past been generally slow to acknowledge them. The joint action by OPEC nations clearly led to a change in the industrialized world's perception of international relations, and interdependence is now generally recognized as being characteristic of North-South relations.

North-South interdependencies are of four basic kinds. Firstly, there are interdependencies caused by the need for food. There are countries, usually rich, with food surpluses, and there are countries, often poor, with deficits. Secondly, there are interdependencies caused by the need for energy and minerals in a world where supply and demand have different geographical patterns. Thirdly, there are interdependencies caused by the possibility of disrupting or destroying 'spaceship earth's' life-support systems, the consequences of which would affect all mankind. Finally, there are basic interdependencies generated by the hopes for reducing the glaring disparities between the world's rich and poor. Different nations afford different priorities to these different kinds of interdependencies. It is thus clear that interdependencies can be, have been, and will be interpreted in a number of ways, the perspective dependent upon whether viewed from the positions of the rich or poor nations. Each kind of interdependence carries its own particular opportunities, threats and political implications, and interacts with others. Given this, it is clear that no nation can choose to live in complete isolation from others. Not even the most powerful nation has the option of excluding itself from contact with other nations, nor can it isolate itself from the effects of the actions of others.

Interdependencies are in fact such that international relations are susceptible to quite small tremors or the inconsiderate actions of a single nation. We have seen, for example, that the stability of the international monetary system has become extremely sensitive to the accumulation of the surpluses and deficits of a single nation, and that one nation's economy is much more quickly and drastically affected by changes in the economy of another than it was only a decade ago. The world knows few if any sanctuaries, be they economic, technological or ecological.

Few of mankind's pressing problems have purely national solutions. They call for cooperative solutions: actions organized multilaterally and globally. That they require united action demonstrates the fact that nations, in addition to being economically, technologically and ecologically interdependent, are also politically interdependent. It would be unrealistic, however, given present international inequalities and resurgent nationalism, to expect nations to engage in cooperation simply because it is in their interests to do so and that they will suffer if they do not. It is, at present, easier to point to areas where effective international cooperation is virtually non-existent rather than to areas where it is clearly working well.

However, the discovery of new interrelationships and a growing recognition that, in some cases, interests can best be furthered by united action are beginning to have a major impact on political thinking. Without concern for a common interest, the agenda of 'high politics' is in danger of becoming hopelessly overloaded, wires will undoubtedly become crossed and conflicts will almost certainly occur. True interdependence cannot be dissociated from sovereign independence, but excessive insistence on national sovereignty that exists in theory but barely in practice carries the seeds of confrontation, antagonism and, ultimately, war.

Notes and References

(1) The two superpowers are also together responsible for 83 per cent of world armaments trade; the United States accounts for 53 per cent, the U.S.S.R. for 30 per cent.

(2) View expressed by Georgi A. Arbatov during discussion *Today in the Context of Tomorrow*, as part of the International Conference *Japan and the World of Tomorrow*, Tokyo, October 30, 1974.

(3) Atomic and political scientists from Harvard University and Massachusetts Institute of Technology meeting in November 1975 concluded that an atomic war will certainly occur before the year 2000. This, they believed, could only be prevented by the decision of all nation-States to surrender their sovereignty to an authoritarian world government, a possibility they viewed as unlikely.

(4) In 1961, reserve stocks of grain stood at 163 million metric tons or 105 days of annual grain consumption. Preliminary estimates for 1976 place reserve stocks at 100 million metric tons, or 31 days reserve supply. The 1976 figures are the lowest in the 16 year period 1961-1976.

(5) Between 1951 and 1971, a period in which world grain production doubled, at least one-third of the increased demand for food reflected increases, not in population, but in the diet of affluent countries. In North America alone per capita consumption of cereals rose from 1,000 lbs. a year to nearly 1,900 lbs. Only 150 lbs. of this is eaten directly, the remainder is consumed indirectly in the form of meat, milk and eggs. Per capita beef consumption in the United States doubled in the period 1940-1972. Between 1960 and 1972 meat consumption increased by one-third in West Germany, in Italy it almost doubled, and in Japan it increased by over three and a half times. It has been estimated that the livestock population of the United States alone (excluding household pets) consume enough food to feed 1.3 billion people.

(6) Both quoted in the 1975 Dag Hammarskjöld Report *What Now*, p. 32.

(7) It should not be forgotten, however, that profit payments are accompanied by a higher level of production in the country concerned than would have existed without the investments made in the past, from which the profits are transferred. In this sense, the figures for a single year are an incomplete picture.

'. . . it is nothing short of wishful thinking to suppose that solutions to global poverty could be found in case-by-case adjustments of an essentially marginal character. In coming to terms with the tasks with which it is confronted in this field, the international community has to demonstrate a new resolve for urgent and imaginative action.'

Commonwealth Group of Experts, 1975

4.1   *Some Recent Developments*

The process of negotiating new international relationships in a number of interrelated fields has already started. Although the past few years have been characterized by sharp and sometimes bitter confrontation between the market economy industrialized countries and the Third World, there are a number of encouraging signs that politicians on both sides of the 'poverty curtain' are beginning to demonstrate a new awareness of common interests generated by global interdependencies and to adopt a new flexibility in the search for solutions. In this chapter we will briefly review the progress made in negotiating a new world order and the positions adopted by and the responsibilities of the major parties.

It is certainly true that the majority of Western politicians are being driven to the world's negotiating tables, not by the plight of the poor nations, but by the plight of their own economies and by the serious dislocations in the international system which has helped make the wealthy nations wealthy. Hence their inevitable preoccupation with safeguarding the flow of supplies of raw materials and oil. The Third World has refused to discuss these problems independently of more fundamental institutional reform. It has repeatedly stressed that any attempt to construct a new world order will have to be comprehensive and not piecemeal. Such reform, it contends, must be based upon the right of nations to control and expropriate foreign owned property and enterprises in accordance with national rather than international law. It must also involve the transfer of real resources to the Third World and include a code of conduct for the transfer of technology from rich to poor nations. The Third World demands the restructuring of the world monetary system and of international trade. It seeks not only the stabilization of commodity prices at equitable levels but also a linking, or 'indexing', of these prices to those of the manufactured goods produced by the industrialized countries.

All these and more elements are incorporated in the 'Plan of Action' adopted without a vote by the U.N. General Assembly at its Sixth Special Session on 1 May 1974. They were reaffirmed in the 'Charter of Economic Rights and Duties of States' adopted by the Assembly on 12 December

47

Significant Recommendations of the U.N. Sixth and Seventh Special Sessions

I. International Trade
(a) Appropriate international stocking and other forms of market arrangements for securing stable, remunerative and equitable prices for commodities of export interest to developing countries.

(b) Adequate international financing facilities for such stocking and market arrangements.

(c) Improved compensatory financing of export revenue fluctuations through the widening and enlarging of the existing facilities.

(d) Promotion of processing of raw materials in developing countries.

(e) An increase in the share of developing countries in transport, marketing and distribution of their primary commodities.

(f) Reduction or removal of non-tariff barriers affecting the products of export interest to developing countries. The Generalized Scheme of Preferences should be improved through wider coverage, deeper cuts and other measures.

II. Transfer of Real Resources
(a) Financial aid needs to be increased substantially, its terms and conditions softened and its flow made 'predictable, continuous and increasingly assured'.

(b) Developed countries should reconfirm their commitment to reach annual transfers of concessional resources amounting to 0.7 per cent of gross national product no later than 1980.

(c) The International Monetary Fund should consider establishing a link between special drawing rights (SDRs) and development assistance when it creates new SDRs. A Trust Fund should be set up, to be financed through IMF gold sales and voluntary contributions. Other transfer means which are predictable, assured and continuous should also be considered.

(d) International organizations should enhance the real value of assistance. The capital of the World Bank Group, and in particular the resources of the International Development Association, should be increased substantially in the near future.

(e) The resources of the United Nations' development institutions, UNDP in particular, and the funds of the regional development banks should be augmented. Such increases in multilateral and regional aid should be without prejudice to bilateral flows.

(f) All donors should ensure that the developing countries obtain the largest possible share in the procurement of equipment and consultancy services. Bilateral assistance should, as a general rule, be untied.

(g) UNCTAD was invited to consider convening a conference of major donor, creditor and debtor countries to devise ways and means to mitigate the debt burden of developing countries, taking into account their development needs and paying special attention to the plight of the countries which were most seriously affected by the economic upheavals of 1973-74.

(h) Developing countries should be granted better access, on favourable terms, to the capital markets of developed countries. U.N. bodies and other intergovernmental agencies should examine means of increasing the flow of public and private resources to developing countries, such as an international investment trust, and expansion of the capital of the International Finance Corporation.

(i) Developed and developing countries in a position to do so, were urged to contribute as soon as possible to the United Nations Special Fund.

(j) The least developed, land-locked and island developing countries should be given aid mainly in grant form. All traditional and new donors should undertake specific measures to aid the most seriously affected countries.

(k) The role of national reserve currencies should be reduced and special drawing rights (SDRs) should become the central international reserve asset. There should be greater international control over the creation of liquidity. The role of gold should be diminished; new international liquidity should be distributed in an equitable fashion, emphasizing the needs of developing countries.

(l) Decision-making in international institutions should be fair, responsive to change, and reflect the new economic influence of developing countries.

III. Science and Technology

(a) Developed and developing countries should cooperate in the establishment, strengthening and development of the scientific and technological infrastructure of developing countries.

(b) Developed countries should expand assistance to developing countries for direct support to their science and technology programmes, and increase the proportion of their research and development devoted to problems of interest to developing countries.

(c) An international code of conduct for the transfer of technology corresponding, in particular, to the special needs of the developing countries should be adopted.

(d) Since the outflow of qualified personnel from developing to developed countries seriously hampers development, national and international policies should be adopted to counter the 'brain drain'.

IV. Industrialization

(a) Developed countries should develop new policies to encourage the redeployment of their industries which are less competitive internationally to developing countries.

(b) Developed countries should encourage their enterprises to participate in investment projects within the framework of the development plans and programmes of the developing countries in accordance with the laws and regulations of the developing countries concerned.

V. Food and Agriculture

(a) Urgent and necessary changes in the pattern of world food production should be introduced and trade policy measures should be implemented, in order to increase agricultural production and the export earnings of developing countries.

(b) Developed countries and developing countries in a position to do so should substantially increase the volume of assistance to developing countries for agriculture and food production.

(c) Developing countries should accord high priority to agricultural and fisheries development, increase investment accordingly and adopt policies which give adequate incentives to agricultural producers.

(d) All countries should accept both the principles of minimum food aid targets and the concept of forward planning of food aid.

(e) Developed countries should increase the grant component of food aid and should accept multilateral channelling of these resources at an expanding rate.

(f) All countries should subscribe to the International Undertaking on World Food Security. They should build up and maintain world food-grain reserves, which should be held nationally or regionally, and strategically located in developed and developing, importing and exporting countries, and should be large enough to cover foreseeable major production shortfalls.

1974. The Charter seeks to establish 'generally accepted norms to govern international economic relations systematically', and to promote the creation of a New International Economic Order. Initiated by President Echeverría of Mexico and prepared over a seventeen month period by a working group of representatives from forty nations under the auspices of UNCTAD, the Charter elaborates standards that would 'protect the rights of all countries and in particular the developing states' and presents fifteen fundamentals which should govern international economic relations.

The Charter of Economic Rights and Duties of States

The Charter is based upon fifteen 'fundamentals of international economic relations'. These are:
— Sovereign territorial integrity and political independence of States;
— Sovereign equality of all States;
— Non-aggression;
— Non-intervention;
— Mutual and equitable benefit;
— Peaceful coexistence;
— Equal rights and self-determination of peoples;
— Peaceful settlement of disputes;
— Remedying the injustices which have been brought about by force and which deprive a nation of the natural means necessary for its normal development;
— Fulfilment in good faith of international obligations;
— Respect for human rights and fundamental freedoms;
— No attempt to seek hegemony and spheres of influence;
— Promotion of international social justice;
— International cooperation for development;
— Free access to and from the sea by land-locked countries within the framework of the above principles.

The demands of the Third World, as contained in the Plan of Action and Charter, caught many industrialized countries unprepared and they were generally dismissed by most as being too far reaching. Of the Western industrialized market economy countries, only Sweden adopted the Charter; the United States, the Federal Republic of Germany, the United Kingdom, Belgium, Denmark and Luxemburg voted against it, as did Japan; most other Western industrialized countries abstained. Caught in internal crises of their own, most industrialized countries were unable to respond to demands for international equity.

Less than one year after the adoption of the Charter, the General Assembly again convened a Special Session to debate the new international economic order. The atmosphere on this occasion was clearly more business-like and constructive. The rich market economy countries, having more carefully analyzed the results of OPEC actions and the potential costs of disruption, seemed to possess a better understanding of the issues and the demands of the Third World and were clearly more prepared. Some, notably the United States, were able to present modest proposals for change. The talk among some delegates was about a movement away from confrontation towards conciliation and constructive dialogue. Henry Kissinger, in a speech read by the United States' Ambassador to the U.N., went so far as to tell the Third World: 'We have heard your voices. We embrace your hopes. We will join your efforts' (1).

Since then we have witnessed a stream of enlightened statements emanating from the leaders of the rich and privileged nations. An extraordinary number of publications, conferences and seminars have increasingly focused attention on the dangers of failing to come to grips with growing global disparities and on what needs to be done. These have contributed towards creating a new sense of urgency among certain groups. We also witness a 'negotiation explosion' in which serious attempts to hammer out agreements on a range of issues are being made.

What is yet to emerge, however, is concrete evidence to suggest that most rich nations are convinced of the need for structural change. The apparent readiness of the industrialized nations to debate international issues cannot yet be interpreted as a recognition of the need for a *new* international order. Certainly most privileged nations realize that the demands of the Third World are legitimate and can no longer be taken lightly and that change in international structures is required to come to terms with some of their own pressing problems. But this understanding has in most cases as yet been reflected in little more than a recognition of the need for the selective streamlining of the international system.

This reluctance to accept the need for structural change can be traced, not only to inevitable attempts to preserve existing positions of privilege and power, but also to two mistakenly held beliefs: firstly, that the international system still basically serves the world well and that the rules of the international game are fair and only require streamlining; and secondly, that, for the most powerful nations, independence is, despite repeated references to interdependence, still a viable option. Neither of these beliefs can withstand serious scrutiny.

4.2   *The Position of Western Nations*

A significant shift appears to have occurred in the tactics of most of the larger Western industrialized nations concerning their response to the demands made by the Third World for a new international order. They no longer appear to subscribe to the call made by the United States following the Sixth Special Session that they should together join forces and confront the nations of the Third World — especially the raw material producers — with a powerful and united bloc. This bloc would be able to use its collective strength to postpone change through a policy of *protracted negotiations* and use the various means at its disposal (e.g. preferential tariffs, aid promises, concessional loans, postponement of debt repayments and arms sales) either to influence the actions of Third World nations or to weaken their solidarity.

The political experience of the last century, reinforced by recent trends, has taught the Western nations that the laws of the world market systematically work to their advantage and that, therefore, the best approach is to continue to allow them to operate 'freely'. Opinions differ within the Western bloc on the role of the market. The United States and the Federal Republic of Germany have particularly stressed the importance of 'free market forces'. But international markets are not free. A free market implies the free movement of labour and capital as well as goods and services. Yet immigration laws in almost all rich nations make impossible any large scale movement of unskilled labour in a world-wide search for economic opportunities (except for a limited 'brain drain' of skilled labour); not much capital has crossed international boundaries, both because of poor nations' sensitivities and the rich nations' own needs; and additional barriers have gone up against the free movement of goods and services — e.g. over $ 20 billion in farm subsidies alone in the rich nations to protect their agriculture and progressively higher tariffs and quotas against the simple consumer goods exports of the developing countries, like textiles and leather goods. The rich nations have in fact used the 'free' market to construct a protective wall, which even enhances their privileged position. A large part of the losses in petrodollars incurred in 1974 by the industrialized nations, for example, has already been recuperated by the inflated prices of their manufactured goods and by the other mechanisms which sustain the 'poverty curtain'. Many Western nations which suffered balance of payments deficits in 1974 achieved substantial surpluses in 1975 and will do so in 1976.

Paradoxically, even the newly gained market power of the oil-exporting countries, once absorbed by the international system, increases rather than decreases the leverage in international affairs controlled by the industrialized nations. By purchasing large quantities of modern technology and arms from the West, and by depositing their liquid assets in Western banks or by investing in Western countries, some oil-exporting countries are discovering that they are becoming more dependent for their supplies and, thus, feel committed to maintaining the prosperity and well-being of the rich countries.

In general, as the difference between prices for commodity exports and manufactured goods increases, so does the trading deficit of the Third World, compounded by borrowing from Western banks with soaring interest rates and heavier debt servicing. In Nairobi, UNCTAD was faced with the situation that whereas in the 1960's the collective annual debt of Third World nations was in the order of $ 12 billion annually, by 1972 it had leapt to $ 30 billion, and is expected to increase to $ 45 billion in 1976. These figures are in no way compensated for by grants provided in the assistance programmes of the industrialized countries (cf. section 3.7). Given this, it is legitimate to pose the question: in which direction does the *net* flow of funds actually go and, therefore, *who is in fact assisting whom?*

While the discussion in the United States and Canada on the use of food as a political weapon has revealed that the political cost seems to outweigh almost any conceivable gain, more subtle applications of the food weapon (price incentives, gratuity, limiting supply, delaying tactics, etc.) have already become standard practice.

It is becoming increasingly evident that all these tactics are dangerously short-sighted. While the results achieved at UNCTAD IV cannot be regarded as satisfactory, some important political signals emerged from the Conference. The solidarity of the Third World withstood all pressures, from both within and outside the Conference. The Third World also refused to consider proposals made at a late stage by the United States, France and Japan; it viewed these proposals as diversionary moves rather than as a serious contribution to constructive negotiation. It also demonstrated its determination to go it alone on the financing of the Common Fund for primary commodities. These are important political signals which simply cannot be ignored by the industrialized countries.

The size and power of the *United States* impose special responsibilities both in continuing the operations of the international organizations of which it is a member and in efforts to secure agreements on means of making cooperation more effective. It especially must take the initiative in stimulating constructive North-South dialogue. The exercise of real responsibility implies more than a willingness to take the viewpoint of others into account; it implies the readiness to question the validity of one's own position.

Henry Kissinger recently remarked that: 'Where the world is going depends importantly on the United States' (2). And this is true. It is thus to be regretted that the United States, like most other countries, has yet to develop the internal mechanisms which make it possible to discern desirable directions. The boundaries between domestic and foreign policies have become blurred by a world in which virtually every international issue has domestic policy consequences and every domestic issue is partly international. It is possible for the representatives of the same nation to adopt different positions at various international discussions, even at the same one as occurred in the case of the United States at the World Food Conference. Moreover, failure to develop appropriate institutional mechanisms within nations not only jeopardizes serious discussion about options, it also contributes to preventing a government from going to its people on a range of issues which must affect their own and their children's lives.

It became apparent at the Seventh Special Session that, with few exceptions, the *Western European* market economy countries and *Japan* although they have potentially more to lose than the U.S. from a failure to forge new international structures, were not only reluctant to take the initiative in redirecting the process of change, but were quite prepared to take refuge behind the United States' position when discussions became serious. That they are unwilling or unable to take serious initiatives is witnessed by the results of the first meeting of EEC Ministers for Development Cooperation held after the Seventh Special Session (3). It ended in complete failure; no agreement was reached on any important agenda point. Despite a considerable effort, the 'nine' also failed to formulate a common position for UNCTAD IV.

4.3   *The Position of the Centrally Planned Nations*

There is a real danger that the negotiation of a new international order will become restricted to a debate between the developing continents and the industrialized market economy countries. The real reform of the international system should not be conceived and cannot be realized, however, without the participation of the Second World, the centrally planned nations. The assumption that the negotiation of a new world order is an exclusive West-South affair is erroneous both theoretically and practically. For one thing, given the nature of global interdependencies, the West-South system does not and cannot exist in isolation; it is part of the international system and, as such, it is intersected by and is interacting with other international sub-systems, whether East-West or East-South. Interdependence between various systems or sub-systems does not eliminate the autonomy of each one, and vice-versa. Secondly, serious inequalities and economic disparities *do exist* between centrally planned nations (cf. section 2.3). This is why such countries as China, Yugoslavia, Cuba and Romania declare themselves developing countries and why some of them have officially aligned themselves with the Third World.

In drawing up strategies of change, the three worlds cannot be viewed as blocs or monolithic entities in a state of opposition. The world is too complex and the issues too important for such simpleminded viewpoints. The centrally planned nations must be organically included in the negotiation of a new world order. At the practical level, how can substantial changes in the international trade and monetary systems and in the power structure and the U.N. system be seriously suggested without integrating a world sub-system which comprises over one and a half billion people and is responsible for over 35 per cent of the world's industrial output?

Whether the centrally planned countries actively participate in negotiating the new order will depend to a large extent upon the positions adopted by the two centrally planned superpowers — the U.S.S.R. and China. Although, for obvious political reasons, both have supported the Group of 77's call for a new international economic order, they have so far chosen to exclude themselves from the various activities initiated to that end. The Soviet Union would appear to have two main reservations concerning attempts now underway to reshape international structures. The first concerns the nature of existing organizational institutions: all major international economic and financial organizations (GATT, IMF, World Bank, etc.) are perceived by the Soviets as institutions created by the rich capitalist nations in order to serve their own interests. The second stems from the well-known Marxist thesis that a change of systems-transforming dimensions in international economic relations must necessarily affect *political* international relations, namely the existing world power structure, which is not exclusively set on ideological lines. In international fora, Soviet spokesmen have continually argued that the new world order should in fact represent indemnification for former colonial exploitation and that since the centrally planned countries have not participated in this exploitation, it cannot be expected that they should share in the compensation.

Chinese spokesmen have reiterated the indemnification argument. An additional reason, however, would seem to motivate Peking's lack of enthusiasm for current attempts to shape a new world order. It originates in the all too familiar thesis of China: 'The current international situation is excellent, there is great disorder under heaven' (4).

The argument of *indemnification* for past sins has been particularly stressed when the question of rich nations making 1 per cent of their GNP available to the poor nations has been debated in the U.N. General Assembly. The creation of a new international order, however, concerns something much more important in terms of both time and space: it concerns tomorrow's world and all nations. An undertaking of such magnitude and far-reaching implications can neither be indifferent to nor carried out without such a major power as the Soviet Union. After all, tomorrow's world, in terms of the new order, means not only an all-out effort to eliminate the glaring inequalities among nations, which ever since the publication of the Communist Manifesto has been one of the major goals of socialism, but also such momentous practical actions as the reform of the international monetary and trade systems, the solution of the food problem, the industrialization of Third World nations and the transformation of the present division of labour, the rational management of world resources, the transfer of technology etc. — all areas in which the Soviet Union and the other centrally planned nations have a vital stake and, therefore, a significant role to play.

As for the Chinese argument, one should never forget that we live in the nuclear era, and too much 'disorder under heaven' may well become a propitious ground for desperate actions and military ventures. Italian Communist leader Berlinguer, in a major report, warned that an exacerbation of all the contradictions of imperialism may push things to a catastrophe of unprecedented proportions and, consequently, a showdown in world politics must be avoided by all means (5). The famous dictum that the name of peace is today development should have a particular ring in South East Asia. Indeed, the centrally planned nations have shown a high sense of responsibility in safeguarding peace in the post-war period, and both the Soviet Union and China have persuasively maintained that peaceful coexistence is a *must* in the nuclear era. It is now time to realize that, given present conditions, this vital principle requires first and foremost international order based on a more equitable distribution of world incomes, resources and knowledge.

4.4 *The Responsibilities of Third World Nations*

The actions required to obtain a more equitable distribution of income and opportunities are not only the responsibility of the industrialized nations. Whether it is achieved will also depend upon the national actions of the governments of the poor countries. As the Third World itself has pointed out: '. . . reforms in the international order will be meaningless, and often impossible to attain, without corresponding reforms in the national orders' (6).

Although the governing elites in virtually all Third World countries have in general proclaimed themselves in favour of greater income equality and, in particular, of raising the living standards of the poor masses, the actual trend in many of these countries is towards greater inequality although this is often the result of structural problems rather than deliberate policy (7).

There is, however, an intimate link between the reform of national and international orders. If national economic orders in the poor nations remain unresponsive to the needs of their own poor and if their development strategies continue to benefit only a privileged few, legitimate demands for the reform of international structures will be weakened, since much of the benefit of such reforms would flow to the privileged elites.

Given the inequities in the international system, the implementation of international reforms cannot be made dependent on internal social transformations. Third World countries may well discover, however, that changes, where necessary, in their own national orders are of decisive importance – the critical 'bargaining chip' – in pressing for structural reforms at the international level.

4.5 *The Way Ahead*

Any nation that chooses to stand for a rigid adherence to the international status quo must expect to be on the defensive in virtually every international forum since the demands for a new international order pervade all relationships between nations. The new international order is not an empty slogan; it is a phenomenon and the debate on the ways and means of attaining it has only recently begun.

The crisis in international structures and the first tenuous steps to come to terms with a rapidly changing world may yet prove a moment in history in which all nations come to acknowledge the deficiencies of an obsolete international system and seek to further their interests within the framework of a new world order; that all can gain from a creative partnership and that all must eventually suffer from a reckless and short-sighted struggle that pits nation against nation – the rich against the poor.

The new international order is not a panacea for all that is wrong in the world of today. It cannot lead to complete and real equality among nations. But it can result in a reduction in inequalities and in the equitable distribution of global opportunities and, in doing so, lay the foundations for real cooperation. Our strategies of change must be based upon this recognition.

Notes and References

(1) Mr. Kissinger told the Assembly: 'We believe that an effective development strategy should concentrate on five fundamental areas:
– First, we must apply international cooperation to the problem of ensuring basic

economic security. The United States proposes steps to safeguard against the economic shocks to which developing countries are particularly vulnerable: sharp declines in their export earnings from the cycle of world supply and demand, food shortages and natural disasters.

— Second, we must lay the foundations for accelerated growth. The United States proposes steps to improve developing countries' access to capital markets, to focus and adapt new technology to specific development needs, and to reach consensus on the conditions for foreign investment.

— Third, we must improve the basic opportunities of the developing countries in the world trading system so they can make their way by earnings instead of aid.

— Fourth, we must improve the conditions of trade and investment in key commodities on which the economies of many developing countries are dependent and we must set an example in improving the production and availability of food.

— Fifth, let us address the special needs of the poorest countries, who are the most devastated by current economic conditions, sharing the responsibility amongst old and newly wealthy donors'.

Some Third World countries, after carefully reviewing the proposals, pondered the question whether they reflected a desire to negotiate a new order or whether, in fact, they represented an attempt to save the old. They found it difficult, for example, to reconcile the spirit of the proposals with that of the U.S. Trade Act introduced earlier in 1975 which threatens punitive measures against those countries which attempt to increase their control over their natural resources by nationalization, and outlines restrictions on countries attempting to improve their bargaining position with industrialized countries by acting collectively as members of raw material cartels.

(2) Henry Kissinger, interviewed in Time Magazine, October 27, 1975.

(3) Meeting held in Luxemburg on October 14, 1975. The meeting was widely described as 'a fiasco'. The Netherlands Minister for Development Cooperation expressed his deep disappointment at the failure to produce any results and referred to the 'hard' positions adopted by some EEC countries.

(4) Renmin Ribao, Honggi and Jiefangjun Bao: *Nothing is Hard if you Dare to Scale the Heights*, 1976 New Year's Day editorial, Peking.

(5) L'Unità, Rome, December, 1974.

(6) Special Task Force of Third World Forum: *Proposals for a New International Economic Order*, Mexico, August 21-24, 1975.

(7) In many Third World countries it is simply not true that when there are more material goods and services in the system that they can necessarily be redistributed in such a way as to create more social satisfaction. It is not true for at least three reasons. Firstly, poor societies often have very poor means of redistributing incomes. The coverage of the fiscal system is generally very limited. Even when income distribution is extremely skewed, it is difficult to reach through direct taxation. To illustrate, even if 60 per cent of income accrues to 20 per cent of the population in India, this still implies an average per capita income level of $ 300 for the rich which is below the income tax exemption limit of $ 400. In other words, income transfers from one sector to the other can be arranged only to a very limited extent in poor societies through the taxation machinery.

Secondly, income flows are not always financial: they are often in the form of physical goods and services. They are influenced by the initial distribution of income. If the society has increased its income in the form of luxury housing and motor cars, how do you really convert it into low-cost housing and public transport, short of their physical take-over by the poor?

Thirdly, the institutions which create growth are not neutral as to its distribution. Thus, if the growth institutions are characterized by wide disparities in land holdings and concentrations of industrial wealth, the process of growth will strengthen them further and they will resist and frustrate all attempts to take away their powers and privileges through orderly reforms.

Part II   The Architecture of the New International Order; Initiating and Steering the Process of Planned Change

'Peace is progress, peace is growth and development. Peace is welfare and dignity for all people. The nations — developed and developing — must work together; each side has its responsibility to this end. They must do so not merely by transferring resources from those who have to those who have not, in conditions which make progress possible. There must be international, economic, and financial policies which recognize the interdependence of all nations and will help the poorer ones to grow. If after the political, economic, and financial experiences of recent years we still think that states, however proud and independent that may feel, can go it alone in these matters, ignoring each other's interests and above all the interests of the impoverished and backward states, then we are beyond redemption. Before long, in our affluent, industrial, computerized jet society, we shall feel the wrath of the wretched people of the world. There will be no peace.'

Lester B. Pearson, 1968

Introduction to Part II

Part II focuses on the 'what' of the new international order. It comprises three chapters. The first — Chapter 5 — is deliberately normative. It is devoted to defining the aims and scope of development at both the international and national levels. It argues that the attainment of a peaceful and just world is dependent upon the creation of an equitable social and economic order and defines the main elements which should guide efforts to achieve it. It points to the need for new development strategies in the rich and poor nations, identifies the most important components of such strategies, and briefly reviews progress made towards their application in different parts of the world.

Chapter 6 focuses on the growing income disparities between the world's rich and poor. Through a quantitative illustration of world development covering population, food production, and income (per capita and from manufacturing industry), it outlines the magnitude of the challenge confronting the international community if it is to come to terms with a development which, if allowed to continue, must ultimately threaten world peace.

Chapter 7 is devoted to strategies of change. It briefly deals with the process of initiating and steering change and discusses some of the major issues which must be addressed and some of the options open in formulating and implementing such strategies.

The Aims and Scope of Development: Towards an Equitable Social
Order

> 'The idea of brotherhood is not new, but what is special to our
> times is that brotherhood has become the precondition for
> survival.'
>
> Leon Eisenberg, 1974

5.1 *The Fundamental Aims of a New World*

The fundamental aim of the world community should be formulated as:
to achieve a life of dignity and well-being for all world citizens.

This aim must embrace all ethnic groups, including those suppressed as
minorities even though they possess their own cultural identity. It must
also include groups with different human capabilities: those presently endowed with few as well as many talents and with the opportunities to
deploy them; the old as well as the young; the weak as well as the strong.
The fundamental aim must also include both sexes, for discrimination
against women in many parts of the world is an institutionalized practice
and implies injustices comparable to some of the worst of the general
social order.

5.2 *Guiding Elements for the Attainment of the Fundamental Aim*

The fundamental aim formulated above has its root in the conviction that
all human beings have an equal right to a life of dignity and to satisfaction
in their threefold capacities as citizens, producers and consumers.
Acceptance of this as the foundation upon which attempts to construct a
new world should be based, implies the need for guiding elements which
serve to shape our development efforts. Six such elements are likely to
prove of decisive importance. Although not mutually exclusive, they can
be summarized as follows.

Equity: As an expression of the equal value of all human beings and of the
need to fight the many forms of prejudice and discrimination directed at
social groups throughout the world. Equity, or justice, can be viewed as a
widespread and growing desire to reduce inequality in the distribution of
consumption and effort to a minimum compatible with adequate levels
of well-being and production. Given this starting point, we witness a
demand for less inequality between individuals, within as well as among
nations. Furthermore, the distribution of future resources should take
account of the needs of future as well as today's generations.

Freedom: History has shown that an increase in the freedom of one
individual or of a nation can result in the reduction of another's freedom

in the same or a different realm. Freedom must thus be viewed as the maximum compatible with that of others. Many forms of freedom, conceivable and existing, can be identified. It is defined here as the recognition and the acceptance of the basic rights provided for in the *Declaration of Human Rights*.

Democracy and Participation: An open society is an absolute prerequisite for achieving the fundamental aim. It cannot be achieved in a closed society where individuals and groups are deprived of the basic right to exercise power and influence. Democracy must exist in every sense of that term: *political democracy*, through forms of participation congruent with cultural preferences; *social democracy* providing absolutely equal access to all forms of social security; and *economic democracy* providing the right of all those engaged in the process of production to influence that process, keeping in mind the need for an adequate level of production. Democracy and participation have to be attained at different levels. In complicated structures, forms of participation by representation will be necessary. In a world with several billion inhabitants, some form of indirect participation in world affairs is the only one that is feasible. There is no reason, however, why it should not be democratic.

Solidarity: There will be no redirection in the process of societal change unless the majority of the world's population recognizes the strategic importance of forming a united front in the fight for freedom and equity. Solidarity must also permeate society as a whole and engender the feeling of common interest and brotherhood. Solidarity is a precondition for establishing social rights, security and participation. Without it, it will be impossible to mobilize the capacity for imagination and to achieve the real will required to share society's resources.

Cultural Diversity: Development must be based upon a recognition of cultural diversity and acceptance of the basic right of groups — national and international — to pursue their goals within their own cultural context. In a shrinking world, the impacts between cultures are more intensive than ever before. Regrettably they are far from mutual; the Western world has tended to dominate exchanges and this has resulted in the increasing homogenization of cultures. Recognition of cultural diversity as a *positive* and not a dangerous feature of a future world and selective policies to maintain cultural integrity will contribute greatly towards the reduction of social tensions both within and among countries.

Environmental Integrity: A life of dignity and well-being implies concern for human environment. The pursuit of the goal is conditioned by the requirement that the ecosphere, upon which the life of all ultimately depends, be respected and that development efforts do not result in trespassing the 'outer limits' placed by nature on the conduct of mankind's activities.

Acceptance of the above should guarantee the rights of all individuals with respect to their threefold capacities. As a *citizen* the individual is represented at evey level of planning and decision-making; not only by intelligently exercising the right to vote, but by becoming an active member of society. At every level he has a voice of equal importance. As a *producer*, the individual, in offering his capabilities as a worker, is provided with the opportunities to exercise influence and power. And as a *consumer*, he has a voice in the production process regarding, not only how goods should be produced, but also what should be produced so as to satisfy society's basic needs. As a counterpart to these rights, a number of duties must be accepted, especially the duty to use one's capacities in the interests of an adequate level of production and to respect other people's rights.

5.3 *Towards an Equitable Social Order: The Need for New Development Strategies*

The above elements must serve as guidelines which shape our attempts to construct a new international order and to pursue the fundamental aim of a life of dignity and well-being for all people. It is increasingly evident that, in many instances, over-reliance on market forces may jeopardize attainment of the aim and that neither societies that emphasize human rights while neglecting social injustices, nor societies that seek to redress social injustices while neglecting human rights can effectively attain it.

The moral and political obligations suggested by the guiding elements and the overriding need to construct a peaceful and just world point clearly to the need for new development strategies — national and international — defined and designed, not merely to meet the criterion of private or state profitability, but rather to give priority to the expression and satisfaction of fundamental human values. Society as a whole must accept the responsibility for guraranteeing a minimum level of welfare for all its citizens and aim at equality in human relations. The creation of an *equitable social order* — internationally and nationally — can thus be viewed as a precondition for the real pursuit of the fundamental aim.

Many in the RIO group believe that this equitable social order could best be described as *humanistic socialism* since it would aim at equalizing opportunities within and among nations and be founded on universal human values.

The progressive construction of an equitable social order will not be facilitated by doctrinaire responses to national and international problems. Every doctrinaire ideology pretends to be the whole truth and thus tends to be constricting. Orthodoxy and doctrinaire approaches are the enemies of an open society and, by their very nature, are systems maintaining rather than systems transforming. They function as intellectual and operational straight-jackets which inhibit the open-mindedness required to come to grips with the growing catalogue of self-reinforcing problems with which mankind is presently confronted.

5.4 Main Components of New Development Strategies

One of the main deficiencies in traditional approaches to development has concerned its definition. Confusion has been compounded by the identification of 'growth' with 'development'. They are compatible but they are not synonyms. Such an arbitrary simplification ignores one of the most important aspects of development: welfare improvement for all groups of the population. Here, welfare is a synonym for increased well-being.

New development strategies must be shaped by five main components; these are the 'pillars' upon which attempts to construct an equitable social and economic order must rest. These pillars are in principle relevant to the industrialized countries and the Third World and in subsequent sections we will attempt to relate them to both.

5.4.1 *The Satisfaction of Needs* The key to development resides in the satisfaction of individual and collective material and non-material needs within the framework of policies geared to specific sets of circumstances and relevant institutions. In general, material needs tend to be largely individual, whereas most important non-material needs are predominantly collective, although the lines that divide them do not completely coincide.

Most of the basic material needs of individuals are concerned with *survival*. In such cases, the equation is simple: failure to satisfy them means inability to sustain life. This applies to food and water, health care and, to varying extents, to shelter and clothing. That hundreds of millions of people in today's world are unable to satisfy their basic needs or have limited or no access to many essential services — safe drinking water, sanitation, transport, health services and the like — fails utterly to convey the wretchedness of their existence. Here we must concern ourselves with identifying the minima required to guarantee meaningful existence and, having defined them, ensure that they become the right of the hundreds of millions who at present exist below them.

When bare survival has been guaranteed, the satisfaction *derived from labour* assumes a more important role. The satisfaction of needs implies that each person available for and willing to work should have an adequately remunerated job. This further enables him to satisfy material needs and to expand the range of services within his reach. It further implies the satisfaction of needs of a more qualitative nature: a healthy, humane and satisfying environment, participation in the making of decisions that affect the lives and livelihood of people and their individual freedom.

Education is the most important non-material component for fulfilling individual ambitions. At the lowest level, practical education can be viewed, among other things, as a means to achieve higher levels of hygiene and improved standards of, for example, self-built housing. As such, it forms a weapon in the attack on problems of health and shelter. At a higher level, education not only contributes directly to individual satis-faction by developing the individual's spiritual endowment, but also indirectly by preparing the individual, mentally as well as morally, for a future role in a changing world

Educational aims should be expressed in both quantitative and qualitative terms. Quantitatively, it should form the right of the majority rather than the privilege of the minority; it should embrace all those who wish to make use of it. Qualitatively, education — formal as well as informal — should be adapted to each country's or region's culture as well as to the future socio-economic aims of that society. The resources available to a country partially determine the quantity and quality of education it is able to offer.

Only after basic needs have been met can goals in the field of *recreation*, *leisure* and general *socio-cultural activities* be realistically pursued. At present, such goals are largely the prerogative of the industrialized world.

The concept of basic needs is of universal applicability. The specific objectives set will naturally vary according to levels of development, climatic conditions, relevant institutions and cultural context. The con-cept is thus to a large extent a relative one. But there are also certain minimum levels which should be universally regarded as essential to a decent life and should, therefore, be viewed as minimum targets for raising the living standards and well-being of the poorest by the entire international community. Moreover, the satisfaction of an absolute level of basic needs should be placed within a broader framework, namely the fulfilment of basic human rights, which are not only ends in themselves but also contribute to the attainment of other goals.

5.4.2 *The Eradication of Poverty* The satisfaction of basic needs must be combined with measures aimed at the eradication of poverty. Poverty, it should be noted, is not the exclusive concern of the Third World; it also exists in isolated pockets within affluent societies, inflicting those who, for various reasons, are less able to participate in the process of produc-tion. It is, however, in the poor nations where it has assumed desperate dimensions.

According to the World Bank, nearly half of the world's people live in relative or absolute poverty in conditions which are an insult to human dignity. Some 900 million people are estimated to subsist on incomes of less than $ 75 a year in an environment of squalor, hunger and hopelessness. Of these, 650 million live in absolute poverty on incomes of $ 50 or less in conditions so wretched and deprived as to defy any rational definition of human decency. Given present dislocations in international economic structures and the failure of some traditional approaches to development, it seems unlikely that the real income of the desperately poor will increase by as much as 1 per cent a year during the remainder of this decade.

In the poor nations, development efforts should shift to the poorest 40-50 per cent in society. In planning national production targets, the basic minimum needs of the poorest should be taken into account. Simultaneously, a concerted effort should be made to reshape income distribution so that the poorest can acquire the means to purchase the products and make use of the services required to satisfy their basic needs.

It follows that the problem of development must be redefined as a selective attack on the worst forms of poverty. Development goals should be expressed in terms of the progressive reduction and eventual elimination of malnutrition, disease, illiteracy, squalor, unemployment and inequalities. Social indicators must be developed so that the progress of plans can be measured in terms of specific and quantitative objectives in these fields.

5.4.3   *Self-Reliant and Participatory Development*   If development is the development of the individual as a societal being, it must of necessity stem from the inner core of each society. A nation's development must make full use of its peoples' strengths, creativity and wisdom, and of its own resources, its cultural and natural heritage. This does not exclude, however, that society must protect individuals against themselves by setting norms with regard to minimum education, respect for other peoples' rights and community property.

Self-reliant or endogenous development carries many advantages. It enables nations to assume fuller responsibility for their own development within a framework of enlarged political and economic independence. It builds development around individuals and groups rather than people around development and it attempts to achieve this through the deployment of local resources and indigenous efforts. The mobilization of the creative energies of the people themselves — a resource neglected in many previous efforts at development — contributes directly to the formation of new value systems, to the direct attack on poverty, alienation and frustration, and to the more creative utilization of productive factors. Self-reliant development, with its reliance on local rather than imported

Table 4

Regional Distribution of World Population by Per Capita Income Groups, 1973

	Per Capita GNP under $200	Per Capita GNP $200-$449	Per Capita GNP $500-$999	Per Capita GNP $1,000-$2,999	Per Capita GNP $3,000 and over	Total
			(millions)			
Latin America and Caribbean	6	46	204	38	–	294
Africa	223	123	*	2	–	348
Asia, Middle East, and Pacific	1,818	153	69	10	108	2,158
Europe, North America, and Oceania	–	44	32	102	477	655
U.S.S.R. and Eastern Europe	–	–	30	326	–	356
Total	2,047	366	335	478	585	3,811
			(percentage of world population)			
	54%	10%	9%	12%	15%	100%

* Under one million.

Note: Population figures are based on *national* per capita GNP and thus do not reflect higher or lower individual incomes within nations.

Sources: Based on GNP data from Report by the Chairman of the Development Assistance Committee, *Development Co-operation, 1975 Review OECD*, Paris 1975, Table 48, pp. 260-61, and on population data from Population Bureau, Inc., *1973 World Population Data Sheet*, Washington D.C.

institutions and technologies, is a means whereby a nation can reduce its vulnerability to decisions and events which fall outside its control; a self-reliant community will be more resilient in times of crisis. And since it is a style of development predicated upon a recognition of cultural diversity, it is an instrument against the excessive homogenization of cultures.

Self-reliance applies at different levels: *local, national and international.* At the national level it implies that each nation is responsible for its own essential well-being and its own development. It further implies that each nation has the right to organize itself politically, economically and socially as it chooses and that no nation shall interfere in the affairs of others. As such, it provides social and economic content to enlarged political independence. At the international level, self-reliance can be extended through cooperation on equal terms with other nations on the basis of common interest, mutual benefit, and the exchange of goods and services needed to make up for each others deficiencies; it becomes *collective self-reliance.*

It is at the local level, however, where self-reliant development acquires its full meaning for it makes greatest sense when local communities are fully able to practice it. Participation at the local level is a precondition for active and informed citizens which, in itself, is a precondition for active world citizens; concern for and interest in international affairs begins with opportunities to exercise power and influence at the local level. Self-reliance at the local level implies decentralization – political, economic and administrative – and, ultimately, the development of small, self-determining, self-regulating communities.

Self-reliance cannot mean 'self-seclusion', isolationism or autarky. No nation, given the nature of global interdependencies, can exclude itself from the international system. The world has become too complex for that (cf. section 3.13 and 5.8). It does however imply an attempt to attain a high degree of self-sufficiency in the satisfaction of basic needs.

In that each country must determine its own way of practicing self-reliance in the light of its own specific endogenous strengths and resources, there can be no universal approaches or solutions: a diversity of starting points implies a diversity of responses. Endogenous and self-reliant styles of development can only be understood in the plural. As such, they do not require a single, universally valid, normative approach, but rather the systematic exchange of relevant experience.

5.4.4   *The Exercise of Public Power*   The satisfaction of basic needs, the eradication of poverty and the promotion of a self-reliant style of development based upon endogenous resources, calls for the exercise of public power. This is one of the principal instruments for pursuing the goal of an equitable social order and without it there can be little concern with anything other than the short term and with remedial tinkering at social systems. The priorities afforded by governments to the different areas of public expenditure have the greatest possible bearing on the well-being and welfare of the different groups comprising that society. Implicitly, the choices made with respect to taxes, subsidies, and the provision of services, including education, also influence the distribution of income.

The objective of applying public power must be to ensure that the eventual distribution of welfare is as equitable as the social order makes possible. Complete equity, defined as absolute equality of welfare ($=$ satisfaction), may be impossible to attain on the basis of the socio-economic policy instruments now known.

Public power does not necessarily exclude private ownership in some sectors of the economy. It is not necessary for the public sector to control all means of production in order to maximize welfare. In Sweden, for example, a country in which public power is extensively used to safeguard and enhance the welfare of its citizens, some 90 per cent of all productive capacity is in private ownership. In many countries, the private ownership of small establishments of production and distribution will probably be found more conducive to welfare maximization than public ownership. Where private ownership of large enterprises is preferred to socialization, countervailing power in the form of some public control will be required to ensure that the economic power vested in large enterprises is not misused, that their activities further the public good, and that labour is afforded an equal voice in the organization of the production process. However, in many Third World countries, the exercise of national sovereignty over their resources has often required that the State takes over the management of these resources through public enterprises. Land, as an important social commodity, is another area in which public power should be used to ensure its use in the public interest. In many Third World countries, land reform implying public or cooperative ownership and State distribution of land is an essential element for adapting social structures to development oriented objectives (1).

Public power should be used to ensure that education is geared to meet the needs of individuals and the needs of society, that is, all individuals. The supply of qualified types of labour should be so planned as to equal, to the greatest possible extent, the demand for them by society (i.e. by the 'organizers of production'). This should contribute to the reduction of income inequalities, to the enhancement of job satisfaction and to meeting the manpower needs of a developing society.

Society must also deliberately aim at creating *employment* for all those seeking it and at ensuring that the distribution over different types of jobs achieves a balance between the satisfaction derived from the job and the satisfaction of the needs of society. The latter necessitates that certain unpleasant (heavy, dirty, dangerous) activities be performed. If these activities can be learnt relatively easily, they could be performed by all citizens. Their efforts could be organized in the form of 'land' or 'neighbourhood armies' for work in rural areas, in the field of environmental care, in social and health services, such as in hospitals, or by providing assistance to the elderly, infirm or disadvantaged. If the unpleasant activities require high skills, they must be performed by those especially trained for the work. In such cases, it should be the objective of public power to ensure that a lack of satisfaction is compensated for by differences in income, or in working hours, or both.

Effective application of public power implies the need for *middle and long range planning* at different levels. The preparation of national and international indicative plans, or systems of consistent data, is a necessary part of attempts to shape equitable social orders. Much planning of this kind is at present being undertaken but coordination is required in order to achieve a unified approach in a broader sense. The United Nations Economic and Social Council might be best suited for undertaking such a task, perhaps assisted by the United Nations Development Planning Committee.

5.4.5   *Balanced Eco-development*   Development that is in harmony with the environment can contribute, especially at the local level, to the satisfaction of a range of basic needs and to the promotion of self-reliance. There is, for example, an obvious relationship between sound environmental practices and local food production. Unsound grazing patterns and deforestation can result in accelerated soil loss through erosion and denudation; poorly conceived irrigation schemes in soil salinity and the propagation of environmentally induced illnesses; the indiscriminate use of fertilizers in the eutrophication of rivers and lakes and, through the destruction of fish life, in a loss of valuable protein and in unemployment; and the haphazard use of herbicides, pesticides and fungicides constitutes a danger to human health and to animal life.

New development strategies must be based upon a sensitive appraisal of the behaviour of local eco-systems and include an assessment of the impact that developments may have upon them. They must also encourage recycling, especially at the local level; animal and human excrement, together with the cultivation of water hyacinth, for example, can be used to produce bio-gas, fertilizers and protein, a possibility that would enhance the opportunities for local self-reliance.

Nationally and internationally, it is our duty to foster styles of development more capable of meeting the 'inner limits' of basic human needs of all the world's people without violating the 'outer limits' of the planet's resources and environment.

5.5 *New Development Strategies and the Third World*

Faced with the massive scale of their basic needs and poverty problem, the poor nations have no choice but to turn inwards, to the extent made possible by global interdependencies. Whilst vigorously pressing for new international structures and a more equitable world distribution of opportunities, they must pursue genuinely self-reliant styles of development aimed at attacking poverty directly and developing the means to satisfy their own basic needs.

In many countries, two decades of development have produced meagre results indeed. For about two-thirds of humanity the increase in per capita income has been less than one dollar a year for the last twenty years. Even this increase, miserable as it may seem, has been unevenly distributed, with the poorest 40 per cent of the population hopelessly squeezed in the struggle for existence and sometimes getting even less than it received almost a quarter of a century ago.

To conceive the objectives of development in terms of Western living standards may only compound confusion. The poor countries should reject the aim of imitating Western patterns of life. Development is not a linear process, and the *aim of development is not to 'catch up'*, economically, socially, politically or culturally. Many aspects of Western life have become wasteful and senseless and do not contribute to peoples' real happiness. For the poor nations to attempt to imitate the rich may only mean that they trade one set of problems for another and in doing so discard or destroy much that is valuable in terms of their human resources and values.

Nor can mass poverty necessarily be attacked through high growth rates, the advantages of which will eventually 'trickle down' to the masses. It is not always true that because high growth rates enlarge society's options they are invariably preferable to low growth rates. It all depends on the structure of these growth rates. If a high growth rate is achieved through rising military expenditures, or through the production of luxury goods for the rich and the privileged, it is not necessarily better than a lower growth rate which is more evenly distributed. In other words, judgements about different levels of growth rates cannot be made independently of the income distribution implicit in them. It is not merely a question of how much is produced, but of what is produced and how it is distributed. GNP measurements, unfortunately, do not register social satisfaction.

The poor nations must attempt to satisfy their own basic food needs, thereby overcoming the vagaries and uncertainties of international food markets. Small nations will need to organize this effort within the framework of collective self-reliance. If this is to be achieved, *land reform* is one of the most important prerequisites, with land viewed as an essential social good and not a profit object. Land reform must benefit the small and poor farmer, liberating him from exploitation, discrimination and servitude and must be viewed as a means to promote social justice and human dignity. In many cases, this may call for the introduction of cooperative or collective systems of land tenure. Farmers must be offered sufficient inducements and be given the opportunity to charge enough for their products to provide the material rewards required for increased outputs. Agricultural development must also encourage the formation of incomes so as to provide a market for the goods produced by the nation's developing industries.

The creation of employment must be treated as a primary, not a secondary, objective of development since it is the most powerful means of redistributing income in a poor society. This calls for an emphasis on labour-intensive rather than capital-intensive processes, wherever alternative choices of technology of comparable efficiency are available and when the factor endowment, and in particular the natural resources of the country concerned, make this possible. Capital should not necessarily be concentrated in a small, modern sector, enjoying high productivity and savings. In some cases, advantages will be greater by spreading it more thinly over a wide segment of the economy — through public works programmes if necessary — even at the risk of lowering the average productivity of labour and lowering the future rate of growth (2). In general, poor nations should aim at 'walking on two legs': the creation of a modern sector required to increase their productivity and to enhance their competitive position on international markets combined with 'appropriate' technologies which make use of the inventive capacities of local populations and which generate labour-intensive production processes.

Some consumer prices might be kept below their market level by means of *subsidies* and, where appropriate, *tax exemptions*. Such measures are particularly appropriate for first necessities and for 'merit goods', i.e. those afforded high significance in development efforts by policy makers. By the same token, the prices of goods and services deemed marginal or even counterproductive to the main thrust of the development strategy could be raised through the application of special taxes.

Tax collection should, where necessary, be improved. This is required so as to guarantee the full utilization of national financial resources for development purposes and to compel the wealthier classes to participate more fairly in national development efforts. It should also be designed to put an end to the practice of fiscal desertion through tax evasion and the flight of capital to foreign havens. In the poorest countries sales taxes will probably be found to be the most manageable. These can be made progressive by exempting first necessities. The best places for collection are at the country's frontier (import duties) and at the production (factory) level for manufactured goods.

Special attention will in many cases need to be given to the provision of *shelter*. The building programme will to a large extent have to be carried out by people themselves. Faced with this task, they will require the support of an organized community upon which they can call for material and technical assistance and which will take the initiative in mobilizing creative problem-solving capacities. This support should be provided in the development strategy. Sites and services schemes should also be more extensively employed. Special attention may also need to be given to improving *public transport* and subsidizing it so as to make it available to the poorest groups.

The attainment of an equitable income distribution will in the long term be determined by decisions concerning education, public health, the structure of employment and technological development and by policies for population control. The technological innovation process can be expected to increase the demand for skilled labour and educational policies should be geared to meet this demand. Population control policies carry the important indirect consequence of restricting the supply of unskilled labour, thereby raising its price (3).

The satisfaction of basic needs and the eradication of poverty imply that some countries will need to afford high priority to population control policies forming an integral part of their development effort. Large families are encouraged, for example, by the vicious circle of malnutrition leading to high death rates. In rural families in some poor countries, the nutrition of infants is strongly influenced by family size. Almost 70 per cent of the most severe forms of protein-calorie malnutrution seen in some clinics are among the fourth or subsequent children. The incidence of other nutritional deficiencies also tends to be higher in later born children. This suggests that a major improvement in a nation's malnutrition problem could be achieved through family planning practices. These, however, would only be really effective when combined with a range of related measures.

5.6   *New Development Strategies and the Industrialized Countries*

Although the poor world is suffering from the deprivation caused by too little, the rich world is increasingly suffering from the problems caused by too much. The material prosperity of the industrialized countries has brought with it stimulated demand — temporary and artifically generated 'needs' – and a powerful and persuasive industry to ensure that these needs are met.

Mass consumerism has brought enormous waste in a world of want and of finite supplies of most raw materials. Industrial waste, virtually indestructible in the case of some radioactive sludge that remains lethal for hundreds of years, and household waste, often 'non-biodegradable' (i.e. not subject to natural decomposition), are accumulating at a frightening rate, on land, in the oceans, and even as the debris of space colonialism orbiting the earth.

Nowhere is overconsumption more evident than the eating habits of the rich. Affluence has emerged as one of the great claimants on world food supplies. The rich nations in fact feed more cereals to their livestock than are consumed as food by the vast population of the poor world and, inevitably, the international market for animal feedstuffs generates more financial interest than the market in food for hundreds of millions of hungry men, women and children. The indirect consumption of cereals in the form of meat and dairy produce in the rich nations has reached such proportions that it has even become counterproductive to a healthy life. That there is food wastage in the rich countries is evidenced by recent estimates that as much as 65 per cent of food served in U.S. restaurants finds its way into garbage cans; 25 per cent of all food purchased by middle income families is also estimated to be thrown away.

No sane person could seriously envisage a world in which the world's poor live like today's affluent minority, adopt the rich countries' standards of automobile use (at present 96 per cent of all private cars are in the countries of the OECD), use in the form of consumer goods and useless gadgets 11 tons of natural resources, and pollute fifty times more than at present. Nor can we seriously envisage a system of agriculture which permits everyone to develop the affluent minority's appetite for cereals. Such a world would be neither possible, nor desirable. To believe it is possible is an illusion; to attempt to construct it would be madness. To acknowledge it is to recognize the need for changes in the consumption and development patterns of the rich.

Mankind's attempt to construct a new world cannot be based upon the exclusive philosophy of economic growth and material riches. The experiences of the affluent countries show that even unparalleled economic growth does not necessarily lead to increased social equality and increased power sharing. Life in the industrialized world has often been marked by the short-sighted misuse of science and technology and with disregard of the social costs that have accompanied technological advance. The growth ideology that is characteristic of the rich world – both the market and centrally planned economies – has shown itself to be a constant stimulus to overconsumption of goods; the pursuit of quantity and the extravagant and wasteful use of resources has taken place at the expense of the fair distribution of wealth and of the quality of life. And we are increasingly seeing that preoccupation with growth may be morally and ethically corrupting; that fundamental human values may be endangered by the philosophy underlying the mania to consume.

Figure 9: *Relative shares of selected resources and expenditures of developed and developing countries, 1960 and 1972 (percentages).*

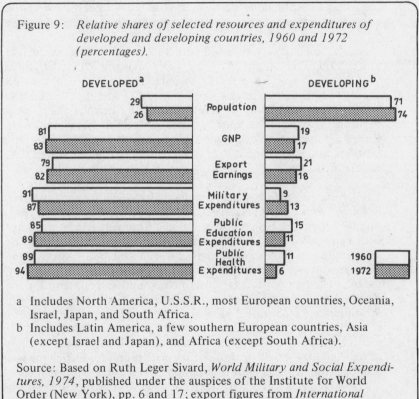

a Includes North America, U.S.S.R., most European countries, Oceania, Israel, Japan, and South Africa.
b Includes Latin America, a few southern European countries, Asia (except Israel and Japan), and Africa (except South Africa).

Source: Based on Ruth Leger Sivard, *World Military and Social Expenditures, 1974*, published under the auspices of the Institute for World Order (New York), pp. 6 and 17; export figures from *International Trade, 1973-74* (Geneva: General Agreement on Tariffs and Trade, 1974), Publication Sales No. GATT/1974-4, Table E.

These characteristics of the consumer society generate dissatisfaction, uncertainty and anxiety, the symptoms of the alienated society and these will be felt with mounting distress. The cases of mass motorization and the problem of waste provide two good examples of the self-defeating nature of the material growth philosophy.

The rich world must be primarily responsible for seeing that new directions are followed. These are required not only as part of attempts to shape an equitable international social and economic order but also to come to terms with its own mounting problems.

In the first instance, the rich nations must demonstrate that they are prepared to move from a growth philosophy to an *overall welfare concept*, replacing the present narrow concept of 'economic profit' by the broader one of 'social profitability'. They must move away from the ostentatious waste of the affluent society towards a sensible husbandry of resources.

Secondly, technology must be submitted to the values of a new society. The *control of technological development* is in many ways more important than economic planning, since the uncontrolled use of technology — allowing the feasible to become the permissible and ranking 'can' higher than 'ought' — preempts future economic options. In particular, the social costs of technological advances must be carefully monitored; it should be clearly recognized that technological development affects directly and deeply the relationships between individuals and groups of individuals as well as societal structures.

Thirdly, the rich nations must promote the economical use of available resources, with a greater emphasis on quality rather than quantity, in order that they should be more fairly distributed nationally and internationally, with a greatly increased flow from the affluent world to the poor world. They could seek, for example, to place a ceiling on meat consumption, encourage greater durability of consumer goods and actively promote the use of public transport. As far as meat consumption is concerned, they could take the initiative in educating consumers to the value of some substitutes and replacement products, for example, vegetable oils for animal fat and vegetable protein for animal protein — a development which would have ecological, health and economic advantages for themselves. And they should institutionalize mechanisms for linking the savings resulting from reduced meat consumption to formal development co-operation projects. Ultimately, they must aim to construct their policies on a series of 'maxima' which define an appropriate style of civilized living in a world of deprivation and declare that all consumption beyond that fixed by the maxima is not only waste but a conscious action against the welfare of large numbers of poor and disprivileged, their own children, and the prospects for a peaceful world.

Fourthly, the rich world must urgently come to grips with its most pressing problem, the sky-rocketing costs of armaments, exposing all mankind to continuous risks of extinction and constituting the most appalling waste of limited planetary resources as well as contributing substantially to environmental pollution.

These changes call for massive innovations in and the redirection of systems of formal and informal education (cf. section 7.6). A new world can only be built through solidarity of the world's people and the participation of large masses of people — hundred of millions, not hundreds of thousands. The development of global awareness is a prerequisite to the peaceful creation of a new world order. It can even be said that the cultural and educational upgrading which global awareness implies, entails — or is equal to — the new order.

5.7 *Progress to Date: The Experiences of the Centrally Planned Nations*

Some countries are already implementing policies which contain many of the elements advocated above. In the Western world, for example, Sweden, and to a lesser extent, the Netherlands, are demonstrating the advantages derived from guiding development through the selective application of public power and are showing that the mixed economies of the industrialized nations are able to meet the challenge of an equitable social order. In this brief review, however, we will focus attention on the development experiences of selected centrally planned nations.

Eastern European countries have made rapid strides in industrialization and demonstrated that benefits can be quickly derived from well focused technological education and research policies. Although economic and technological cooperation within CMEA has been an extremely important factor, the emphasis in development strategies has always been on the all-out mobilization of national material and human potential with a regular allocation of a high percentage of their national income for development (Table 5).

Table 5   *CMEA: Development Fund's Share of National Income (percentages)**

Country	1960	1970	1974
Bulgaria	27.4	29.2	28.5
Czechoslovakia	17.6	27.0	27.7
G.D.R.	18.1	24.0	22.8
Poland	24.2	27.9	37.3
Romania	20.1	29.2	33.7
Hungary	23.1	27.2	29.9
U.S.S.R.	26.8	29.5	28.0

* Calculated on the basis of the CMEA annual bulletins.

According to the prevailing theory in the East, the high rate and efficiency of investment is the decisive internal factor of development, which explains why this rate has been maintained at a high level over recent decades and even slightly raised in recent years. As to efficiency in practice, the recurrent criticism in official documents reveals overcentralization, poor management and lack of incentive against which various remedies are prescribed.

Although as a result of this strategy the share of national income earmarked for consumption has remained comparatively low, the funds allocated to education have always been considerable. The accelerated pace at all levels of education — from the eradication of illiteracy and the training of manpower to the establishment of new colleges and universities — has resulted in a cultural thrust which is probably the most remarkable achievement of the centrally planned economies. The number of scientists and engineers has rapidly grown; in Romania, for example, the percentage of employed with a medium education (high schools and vocational schools — 12 years) has increased from 2 per cent in 1960 to 3.7 per cent in 1974, while those with a higher education (universities and technological institutes) from 0.1 per cent in 1960 to 1.6 per cent in 1974. In that same year, 80 per cent of the managerial cadres who ran economic ministries and enterprises with a republican status were graduates of higher institutes or universities, while 70 per cent of those who ran local industrial units and state farms graduated on a part-time basis. All this clearly demonstrates that a sustained *attack on the educational front* is an essential prerequisite of a rapid rate of development.

In investment policy, whilst the bulk of investments has always gone to the industrial sector (machine tools, means of production) — viewed doctrinally as the key sector of industrialization — there have been, however, situations when a reassessment of the minor role accorded to the consumer sector and agriculture led to a temporary shift in investment distribution, particularly in the mid 'fifties (Malenkov), and more recently in setting the targets of the 1971-1975 plan (when Premier Kosighin argued that while the industrial sector remains primordial strategically, it is not a *must* for every five year plan). Soviet economists took up the official statement and demonstrated rather persuasively that lagging agricultural output may negatively affect even the rate of industrial growth, a theory that is conspicuously confirmed in the targets of the current Soviet five year plan (1976-1980), that were set after the poor grain harvest of 1975.

The investment policy of Bulgaria should be mentioned in this respect (Table 6). In the 'fifties it deviated from the general pattern and increased substantially the funds allocated to agriculture, irrigating practically all arable land. Although other factors are probably involved, the more rational investment policy should certainly be counted among the reasons why Bulgaria, the poorest of CMEA countries, has made the most spectacular advance in Eastern Europe, jumping from under 4 per cent share of industrial goods in her exports in 1950 to over 55 per cent in 1973 (4), and from a pre-war $ 250 per capita GNP to something like $ 1,500-1,600 in 1973 and coming close to $ 1,800 in 1975 (5).

Table 6   *Bulgaria: Total Investment (percentages)**

Sector	1955 1950	1960 1955	1965 1960	1970 1965	1973 1970
Industry	193	204	190	182	110
Agriculture	322	342	97	145	118

* Extracted from CMEA Annual Bulletin 1974, Moscow.

The evening out of the levels of economic development of centrally planned nations, which was considered in the basic 1971 CMEA document as 'an objective historical process in the development of the world Socialist system', has proved a much longer process than was originally envisaged. Czechoslovakia and the German Democratic Republic, which started 30 years ago from an advanced stage, still maintain a substantial lead with respect to all major economic indicators. Whereas their GNP per capita in 1973 reached something like $ 3,000, the estimated figure for the U.S.S.R. and Poland was $ 2,030, Hungary $ 1,850, Bulgaria $ 1,590, Romania $ 900 and Albania $ 460 (6). In recent years, a more concerted effort towards equalization within CMEA countries has followed three courses of action: (a) accelerated rate of development in the lagging national economies, as reflected in a relatively higher rate of investment; (b) specialization and reorganization of industrial production according to the most favourable conditions existing in individual CMEA countries; and (c) optimization of the interaction among national economies through trade, transfer of technology and joint financing and building of industrial projects. Table 7 shows the effects of a higher rate of investment in the two less developed CMEA members vis-à-vis the most developed ones.

The projections anticipate that if present rates of development funds are maintained and an optimization of interaction within CMEA is achieved, the levels of development will be largely equalized by 1990. Yet, such an optimization is still a desideratum if one looks more carefully into the matter, for specialization of industrial production still plays to the advantage of the most developed nations which enjoy a more diversified range of industrial branches (in 1970, Czechoslovakia and East Germany's range was twice as diverse as Romania's). This imbalance is conspicuously reflected in the weight of machine tools in the total exports to CMEA countries: in 1971, Czechoslovakia and the G.D.R. 59.8 per cent, Poland

Table 7   *Comparative Economic Indicators of Development Between Romania, Bulgaria, Czechoslovakia and G.D.R.* (average annual rates in percentage)*

Economic Development Indicators	Romania	Bulgaria	Czecho-slovakia	GDR
1. *Rate of development funds*				
1966 - 1970	30.5	31.7	22.0	21.4
1971 - 1973	33.0	25.2	25.7	22.5
2. *Growth of National Income*				
1966 - 1970	7.7	8.7	6.9	5.2
1971 - 1973	11.1	7.8	5.0	5.2
3. *Growth of Industrial Production*				
1966 - 1973	16.0	12.2	7.6	7.1
4. *Share of Industrial Equip-ment in Total Export*				
1960	16.7	12.9	45.57	49.0
1973	24.4	38.9	48.7	51.4

* Calculated on the basis of CMEA annual bulletins.

57.4 per cent, Hungary 52.2 per cent, whereas Romania only 29.6 per cent, having to direct the bulk of its industrial exports to other markets under adverse conditions. Here one should ponder two things: (a) in a planned economy, the production of industrial goods is also affected, though not completely regulated, by its external market; and (b) exports of machine tools provide a much higher rate of return than those of other commodities.

As for joint industrial ventures, recent data show that the contracts signed with Western enterprises greatly outnumber the arrangements between the Eastern European partners themselves. According to a Soviet publication, thirty projects involving multilateral agreements have been concluded since 1971 among CMEA countries (7), whereas in 1974 and 1975 the Soviet Union alone signed an almost equal number of contracts of cooperation with large enterprises from West Germany, France, Italy, Austria, Finland, Japan and the United States, some of them running into billions of dollars (8). This is quite natural from both an economic and technological viewpoint, since the fundamental strategic task of Eastern European nations requires the acquisition of the most modern technology. Over-all trade compulsions and competition in world markets in the present international system have grown to the point of making interdependence *the law of the world*. It is a factor so strong that it overpowers even ideological differences: joint ventures between centrally planned nations and large capitalist enterprises are emerging every day.

The *Yugoslav* concept of social ownership, on which its entire self-management system is based, is in fact a concept of non-ownership of resources or means of production. Such resources or means of production have three attributes. Firstly, they cannot be owned: not by the State, by companies or enterprises, nor by individuals, and they cannot be appropriated. Secondly, they require a system of management in which all users participate, and it is thus that social ownership forms the basis of self-management, and one cannot exist without the other. Self-management, in turn, requires a participatory political system, where representatives of all self-managing enterprises participate in the decision-making processes of the political system. Thirdly, social ownership in Yugoslavia implies benefit sharing in the widest sense, that is, a sharing not only of financial benefits but a sharing of management prerogatives and the acquisition of know-how.

Relationships based on social ownership and self-management are never determined once and for all, but are redefined in a constant on-going process of amending and complementing the Constitution. Lately, there has been intense work on the improvement of self-management, particularly in its economic aspect. Draft legislation on associated labour has been prepared and is to regulate interrelations among all economic subjects, combining integration at the policy level with a maximum of flexibility and decentralization at the operational level, with the basic organization of associated labour at the centre of the entire system of self-management. Based on the interests of this economic unit — the foundation of the enterprise — all other relations are coordinated, including planning at the level of the Republics, Provinces, and the Federation. It is the expectation of Yugoslav theorists that these processes will constitute a major contribution both to the increase of production and productivity and to the stabilization of economic trends.

Yugoslav theory and practice show a deep awareness of the *interaction between internal and external policies.* The external aspect of Yugoslav policy is non-alignment and the establishment of the New International Economic Order. It is evident that the principles and practices elaborated internally by this multinational community, with its developed and developing Republics, can make a major contribution to the elaboration of the new international order. The concept of social ownership and its attributes are clearly applicable to the 'common heritage' concept.

China especially has given the greatest meaning to self-reliance development. Despite modest economic growth rates and an estimated per capita nominal income of $ 250 a year, the country has apparently been successful in providing adequate levels of nutrition and health care to its vast population, and in attaining near universal literacy. It has shown that, even in a densely populated country, it is possible to attain a very large measure of food self-sufficiency and the advantages of affording very high priority to agricultural and rural development. Within industry it has shown that it is feasible to create a large array of rural and geographically dispersed industries using technology well-suited to local conditions. In doing so, it has pursued a policy of technological independence and proven that — despite the overwhelming experience in other parts of the world — industrialization need not result in large scale urbanization. And economically, it has demonstrated that narrow income differentials combined with modest inducements can, in a socialist society, furnish sufficient incentive to organize a complex economy efficiently with satisfactory output growth.

Above all, China has shown that development can be built around people and geared to meeting their needs; that participatory development is not only possible but necessary if poverty is to be attacked directly and human needs are to be satisfied.

5.8 *The Need for a Reinterpretation of National Sovereignty*

An equitable social and economic order implies that a large number of decisions must be taken at the lowest possible level, so as to enhance participation and the satisfaction derived from it. Decisions with external effects, that is, decisions which have consequences for other than those taking the decisions, must be taken at a level implying these others, that is, at a higher level. Generally, then, the optimum level of decision-making is the one where external effects are negligible. This implies that some types of decisions — those with global consequences — must be taken by international fora representing the world's population. The international order must be organized accordingly.

This implies a voluntary surrender of national sovereignty as conceived today. Each nation must, within the foreseeable future, be responsible for its own well-being and development based upon sovereignty over, and the creative utilization of, its own human and natural resources — the concept of self-reliant development. To make this possible, a nation must have guarantees that its development efforts are not jeopardized by the consequences of other nations' decisions. These guarantees can only be provided by international agreements and thus the international fora in which they are negotiated. A precondition for the effective exercise of territorial sovereignty is thus strong international institutions and international agreements, drawn up between equals, and preferably containing compulsory arbitration mechanisms. Without these, the belief that all aspects of sovereignty can be effectively exercised is at best an illusion, and at worst, a precondition for international conflicts and tensions with the prospects of escalation and all its possible dire consequences.

Nations whose citizens are affected by the external effects of decisions made in another country in whose decision-making process they have no part have in fact, for all practical purposes, lost their sovereignty. The protest made by the Australian and New Zealand governments following the testing of French nuclear weapons serves as a case in point. The Australian government contended that the deposit of radioactive fallout on the territory of Australia and its dispersion in its airspace without the country's consent was a violation of Australia's sovereignty over its territory. It also follows that failure to develop the cooperative machinery required to come to grips with the complex array of pressing global problems is to default on the responsibilities afforded by national sovereignty. This is recognized, for example, in a recent convention on environmental protection between Nordic countries. It enables a citizen in any Nordic country to make formal complaints against a government concerning damage caused to his environment by an activity in any of the member countries.

Moreover, as has been repeatedly stressed throughout this report, the world has become too complicated for any nation to even attempt to pursue all its goals in isolation. Attainment of objectives in many inter-related field is closely dependent upon links with other nations; there is a functional necessity for the joint exercise of sovereignty with like-minded or similarly situated nations — the notion that lies behind the concept of collective self-reliance. The failure to attempt to harmonize the exercise of sovereignties so as to deal with problems which defy national solutions — even when these solutions call for limitations on sovereignty — can be viewed as an implicit decision which erodes rather than strengthens national prerogatives. Failure to make such attempts will harm the interests of all nations and, given the present international power structure, those of the smallest and weakest nations the most.

Many of the guiding elements outlined in section 5.2 apply not only to the national level but to the international level also. Acceptance of these elements calls for a reinterpretation of the concept of national sovereignty. Participation and social control suggest a *functional* rather than a territorial interpretation of sovereignty, or jurisdiction over determined uses rather than geographical space. Conceptually, this interpretation will make possible the progressive internationalization and socialization of all world resources — material and non-material — based upon the 'common heritage of mankind' principle. It also permits the secure accommodation of inclusive and exclusive uses of these resources, or, in other words, the interweaving of national and international jurisdiction within the same territorial space.

Such an approach is suggested for the world's oceans (cf. Chapter 18). It is based upon five attributes of the 'common heritage' concept. The first three have already been mentioned in discussing the Yugoslav concept of social ownership, that is, the common heritage of mankind cannot be appropriated, it requires a system of management, and it requires benefit sharing in the widest sense, including the transfer of technologies and participation in decision-making. These can be extended by the addition of two other attributes: resources and means of production which are the common heritage of mankind can be used for peaceful purposes only — that is, they have a disarmament implication; and they must be preserved for future generations — that is, they have a strong environmental implication. These principles and attributes should eventually be applied to, for example, the earth's air envelope, the world's mineral resources and means of production, and the scientific and technological heritage.

Acceptance of the concept of functional sovereignty will require the creation of new kinds of international institutions comprising a balanced system of functional interests. The aim here should be functional confederations of international organizations, decentralized at the operational level and centralized at the policy-making level. Ultimately, we must aim for *decentralized planetary sovereignty* with the network of strong international institutions which will make it possible.

Notes and References

(1) Land taxes, where land is privately owned, can be administered without excessive difficulty. They carry the additional advantage that they can be used as a powerful incentive to make the best use of available land. Various methods of land tax assessment can be employed. Ranging as they do from the simple to the highly sophisticated, the possibility can be retained of starting with the former whilst preparing for the latter. In designing land taxes it should be borne in mind that land valuation officers have in the past shown that they are not always immune to attempts at bribery. Corrupt practices can be reduced by requesting land owners to make their own evaluation of their property on the condition that public authorities are able to purchase it from them for the assessed value plus some fixed percentage.

(2) The nature of the development process must of necessity vary from country to country; that which constitutes the right course of action for one may well be inappropriate for the other. Under some social systems, for example, it may be that labour-intensive processes can be organized in sufficient volumes in the tertiary sector, thereby increasing the scope for more sophisticated processes in the primary and secondary sectors. This, however, can only be established on the basis of concrete computations covering the economy as a whole.

(3) The positive long term effects that population control policies can have in income distribution have been illustrated by estimates made for India. It can be shown that had population growth from 1941 onwards been restricted to 1 per cent per annum, then the per capita income of the families of unskilled worlers and poor peasants would, by 1971, have been 75 per cent higher than it actually was. The same could be achieved three decades hence if the average size of low-income families could be stabilized at 3.95 persons, the current size of high-income families.

(4) I. Dudinski: *Creative Power of Socialist Internationalism*, International Affairs, Moscow, no. 9, 1975.

(5) World Bank Atlas and CMEA annual bulletins. (Although figures differ slightly, ranking of nations remains the same.).

(6) Calculated on the basis of World Bank Atlas and CMEA annual bulletins; though the methodology differs and the conversion rate of currencies raises difficult problems, the ranking of nations in both is similar and the differences very small.

(7) I. Dudinski, op. cit., p. 4.

(8) B. Pichugin: *East-West: Economic Cooperation*, International Affairs, Moscow, no. 8, 1975, pp. 63-64.

Chapter 6   Reducing the Differential Between the World's Rich and Poor

> 'If a free society cannot save the many who are poor, it cannot
> save the few who are rich'.
>
> John F. Kennedy

6.1   *Introduction*

In this chapter an attempt will be made to define the scale of the income
disparities between the world's rich and poor and to review the prospects
for reducing them. In doing so, we must shift from a qualitative to a
quantitative analysis of world problems and of the means for overcoming
them. Quantitative analysis carries a number of important advantages. It
enables us to determine the extent and character of unfavourable trends
in world development and, as such, to gauge the magnitude of the tasks
before us. By updating the results we have a basis for monitoring performance, identifying the extent to which our efforts are proving successful in moving in desired directions.

We will discuss the prospects for reducing the income differential between
the world's rich and poor through a *quantitative illustration* based upon
four considerations: population growth, world food production, and
income (per capita and that derived from manufacturing industry). Income
differentials will be expressed on a per capita basis, despite the imperfections of the indicator. It should be stressed that the analysis undertaken
is illustrative only and is designed to serve as a partial basis for identifying
qualitative objectives and relevant targets. The alternatives introduced are
not projections based upon extensive statistical analysis nor are they the
result of the application of complex simulation models. Their purpose
is to explore the magnitude of global problems, the feasibility of alternative development scenarios, and to give substance to qualitative analyses.
Above all, the results of the analysis are designed to indicate the magnitude of the challenge facing mankind if it is to succeed in building an
equitable social and economic order.

Before investigating the alternatives before us, we will look briefly at
the situation today.

6.2   *Income Disparities: The Situation Now*

To review the situation today we must of necessity take 1970 as a starting
point for the simple reason that, as a general census year, it is the most
recent year for which sets of relevant data are available.

Certain key data on population and real income levels are shown in Table
8. Total purchasing power and real per capita incomes for Third World

and industrialized countries are presented in columns 2 and 4 respectively, and for the poorest and richest ten per cent of the world population (the upper and lower deciles) in columns 3 and 5. The table shows that even when corrections are applied (table footnote), an individual living in the richest part of the world has an average per capita income of US $ 1,100 (upper decile) compared with a per capita income of only US $ 85 of an individual living in the poorest part of the world (lower decile). The decile ratio is thus 13:1. Purchasing power of the U.S. dollar in the poorest countries is taken as the yardstick.

Table 8   *Population, income per capita and total income 1970 in U.S. $ with purchasing power (p.p.) in poorest countries, world and four groups of countries.*

	World	Third World countries[a]		Industrialized countries[b]	
		Total world	Poorest tenth world	Total world	Richest tenth world
	(1)	(2)	(3)	(4)	(5)
Population (mlns)	3,667	2,588	368	1,089	368
Total income billion $	1,526	490	31	925	405
Income/capita 1970 U.S. $ per person	415	190	85	1,010	1,100

[a] Countries included in lower decile: Afghanistan, Burma, Chad, Dahomey, Ethiopia, Indonesia, Malawi, Mali, Nepal, Niger, Pakistan + Bangladesh (part), Rwanda, Somalia, Upper Volta, Yemen Arab Republic, Zaire.
[b] Countries included in upper decile: Belgium (part), Canada, Denmark, France, Norway, Sweden, Switzerland, United States, West Germany.

Note: Incomes in 1970 U.S. $. Incomes of richest countries divided by 2.25 as a correction for higher price level and for duplication (Tobin-Nordhans) and corrected for price level difference (David 4/9 rule).

Source: *Trends in Developing Countries*, World Bank, Washington, 1973.

This decile ratio of 13:1 and its trend must be deemed unacceptable *for reasons of human decency and for the danger of political instability which they imply.* The existence of such disparities is incompatible with an equitable social and economic order and the redress of them must be afforded the highest priority by the international community. Coming to terms with these differences is not only a precondition for attaining a fairer world; it also has a considerable bearing on mankind's success in surviving the twentieth century.

6.3 *Prospects for the Future: An Illustration of the Challenge*

6.3.1 *Uncertainties: The Need for Alternative Starting Points* Because of lacunae in our knowledge there does not exist, nor is there likely to exist for some time to come, a generally agreed upon stock of knowledge on which a framework can be built for the quantitative analysis of world development. Indeed, the differences of opinion among scientists on quantitative starting points are spectacular. Perhaps the greatest contrast in intuitive outlook can at present be found between, for example, most economists, technologists, geologists and some agronomists on the one hand, and most ecologists (largely biologists) on the other. The differences of opinion compel us to think in terms of alternative quantitative starting points. Two main alternatives will be presented here: the first we will call a 'high' starting point (representing the general viewpoint of the former group); the second we will refer to as a 'low' starting point (the viewpoint of the ecologists). By changing the relative weights of the viewpoints held, the opportunities of introducing sub-versions into the analysis are retained.

6.3.2 *The Assumptions* The analysis has been limited to selected indicators of the world socio-economic situation combined with a limited number of alternatives so as to retain clarity without loss of substance. A number of figures have had to be estimated and we are keenly aware of the highly approximate character of many of our estimates (1).

The analysis is based upon four considerations: population growth, income growth (per capita and that derived from manufacturing activities), and the total demand for food. In the following tables, Alternative B — the 'high' alternative — represents a viewpoint essentially optimistic with respect to future food production as well as to the energy which can be produced without damaging the planet's climate. Alternatives A (i) and A (ii) — the 'low' alternatives — are more cautious in both respects and may be called pessimistic with respect to both issues. A second cautious viewpoint has been introduced in order that the interrelationship between population, income and food production can be more fully examined. All three alternatives, however, have one thing in common: they all assume accelerated rates of development in the Third World.

It should be stressed that the alternatives investigated are based upon several important assumptions and these should be made explicit. They obviously assume the absence of cataclysms, disintegration in the industrialized countries and violent social and economic change. They assume that the industrialized world will, within the next few years, recover from the problems of the present depression even though, given the structural nature of the problem, it will never attain its pre-depression growth rates. The figures mentioned are 42 year averages and are meant to suggest gradual changes in the direction indicated. They further assume that the link between the industrialized countries and the Third World will gradually be reduced, for example through the emergence of regional groupings within the Third World. This implies that during the earlier part of the 42 year period the growth of Third World countries will be largely dependent upon the growth rates of the industrialized countries, which will approximate those attained during the 'sixties. This link will enhance the growth prospects of Third World countries. Gradually, however, the production of the goods now imported by Third World countries will shift to the latter and their growth will become less dependent on their imports from, and their exports to, the industrialized countries.

Before discussing the alternatives, reference should be made to the prospects for world food production. Since food forms the most serious scarcity facing mankind today, it must be afforded a prominent position in our quantitative analysis of world development.

6.3.3   *Prospects for World Food Production*   There are essentially two ways of expanding world food supply from conventional forms of agriculture. The first is to expand the area under cultivation; the second to increase the yields of the land already under cultivation. As far as the first option is concerned, it is wrong to assume that our planet has vast areas of virgin land waiting to be put under plough. One-third of our globe's surface is already utilized for food production, either as tilled land or pastures. Although the Third World has in recent years expanded the area of land under cultivation by 0.7 per cent a year, it is generally agreed that virtually all the most suitable land has already been brought into production. Many of the remaining areas are greatly inferior and could only be made productive at enormous costs. Moreover, it has been estimated that by 1985 all land surfaces, except those so cold or at such high altitudes as to be incompatible with human habitation or exploration, will have been occupied and utilized by man.

The best hope of raising world food production would appear to lie in increasing the yields of land already under cultivation. The high yields obtained in the industrialized countries are not necessarily appropriate indicators of the yields that can be obtained in Third World countries. These high yields are frequently obtained at very high cost and often require enormous fertilizer and energy inputs. Moreover, many poor countries are confronted with special difficulties which inhibit their opportunity to substantially increase yields in the immediate future (2).

There are other constraints to world food production. Water supplies, for example, may well prove to be the most imminent 'outer limit' to world food production (3). Coupled to water is the potential new constraint imposed by natural climatic cycles. Although not yet proven, climatologists are being forced to conclude that our planet has in recent times passed through a period which may well have been optimal as far as food production is concerned. They believe that future decades may well be characterized by extremes — hot and cold, wet and dry — without necessarily a change in average temperatures (4).

Despite the apparent constraints on our ability to increase world food production, some scope for modest growth has been assumed in the quantitative analysis of world development alternatives. The FAO's proposed target of 4 per cent, contained in its World Indicative Plan, appears too optimistic and it has not been used. Instead, a general figure, of 3 per cent a year has been adopted. If this growth rate could be attained and maintained over the next forty or fifty years, the volume of agricultural production would be 3.0 to 4.5 times the 1970 level. More recent estimates, based upon very extensive analyses, made by H. Linnemann and his colleagues, suggest that even the figure of 3 per cent might prove too optimistic in the short and medium term (5). Their own estimates of the probable volume of world food production around the years 2010-2020 are lower and amount to 3 times the 1970 level (6).

6.3.4 *The Results*   The examples of Eastern Europe, Japan and some oil-producing countries have demonstrated the feasibility of annual growth rates in income per capita of 5 per cent or more. This we take as a quantitative target for a first reconnaissance of the alternatives before us and as a first attempt to give concrete content to the Plan of Action adopted by the U.N. General Assembly. Achievement of this target would result in a doubling of per capita income in fourteen years, or an eightfold increase over a period of 42 years. For the poorest 10 per cent of the world's population this represents an increase from $ 85 per annum to $ 680 per annum by 2012. This figure is well below the average of all industrialized countries in 1970. If it is further assumed that the industrialized countries retain the same rate of growth achieved in the period 1960-1970 (approximately 3.3 per cent) for the coming decades — alternative B in Table 9 — then per capita income would increase fourfold by 2010. The average for all industrialized countries would then be in the order of $ 3,670 and for the world's richest ten per cent approximately $ 4,400.

Thus we can see that even when the Third World is able to achieve an ambitious rate of growth and maintain it over a period of 40-50 years, an individual living in the richest part of the world (upper decile) will still have 6 times the real income of an individual living in the poorest part (lower decile). In other words, a 5 per cent target for the Third World, when combined with a rough extrapolation of growth in the industrialized world, still fails substantially to reduce the income differential. There must

Table 9   *Figures in U.S. $ of buying power in 1970 ('real dollars') for Africa, Asia, Latin America and the industrialized countries for alternatives A (i), A (ii) and B.**

Alternative			A (i)		A (ii)		B	
Year		1970	2012		2012		2012	
		a	a	b	a	b	a	b
Population	Africa	349	750	1.8	720	1.7	750	1.8
(Millions)	Asia	1,958	3,700	1.5	3,560	1.4	3,700	1.5
	Latin America	281	550	1.6	530	1.5	550	1.6
	Industr. '70	1,089	1,600	0.9	1,540	0.8	1,600	0.9
	World	3,677	6,600	1.4	6,350	1.3	6,600	1.4
Income per Capita	Africa	200	1,500	5.0	1,550	5.0	1,550	5.0
(Real 1970 $ in	Asia	150	1,170	5.0	1,170	5.0	1,170	5.0
poorest group of	Latin America	483	1,500	2.8	1,830	3.3	3,670	5.0
countries)	Industr. '70	925	1,500	1.2	1,830	1.7	3,670	3.3
	World	407	1,320	2.9	1,430	3.4	2,030	3.9
Total income	Africa	73	1,130	6.7	1,120	6.7	1,170	6.7
(Real $ billions in	Asia	280	4,330	6.6	4,170	6.5	4,330	6.6
poorest group of	Latin America	140	830	4.5	980	5.0	2,020	6.7
countries)	Industr. '70	1,010	2,400	2.1	2,850	2.5	5,870	4.3
	World	1,500	8,700	4.3	9,120	4.7	13,380	5.3
Total Food demand	Africa	30	200	4.6	193	4.5	203	4.6
(Real $ billions in	Asia	140	870	4.5	830	4.4	877	4.5
poorest group of	Latin America	45	147	2.8	163	3.1	243	4.1
countries)	Industr. '70	240	427	1.4	457	1.5	707	2.6
	World	450	1,640	3.1	1,640	3.1	2,030	3.6
Income from Manuf.	Africa	10	430	9.4	410	9.3	430	9.4
(Real $ billions in	Asia	30	1,730	10.1	1,670	10.0	1,630	10.0
poorest group of	Latin America	30	310	5.7	390	6.3	750	8.0
countries)	Industr. '70	420	950	2.0	1,080	2.3	2,200	4.0
	World	490	3,420	4.7	3,550	4.8	5,020	5.7

a: absolute figures
b: growth rate in per cent per annum, average of 42 year period.

* Some more information about methods used is given in Appendix 1 to this chapter.

Note: Countries included in *upper decile 1970*: Belgium (part), Canada, Denmark, France, Norway, Sweden, Switzerland, United States, Western Germany. *Added 2012:* Australia, Belgium (remainder), Eastern Germany, Netherlands, New Zealand, United Kingdom.
Countries included in *lower decile 1970*: Afghanistan, Burma, Chad, Dahomey, Ethiopia, Indonesia, Malawi, Mali, Nepal, Niger, Pakistan + Bangladesh (part), Rwanda, Somalia, Upper Volta, Yemen Arab Republic, Zaire. *Added 2012*: Pakistan + Bangladesh (additional part).

also be doubts as to whether all Third World countries will be able to attain and maintain a 5 per cent annual growth in per capita incomes.

Moreover, the world's total food demand in the same period would increase by 3.6 per cent a year and thus would need to have attained a level almost 4.5 times that of 1970. Given the constraints to world food production, this is probably well beyond the sustainable level discussed in section 6.3.3.

In Alternatives A (i) and B, the low population forecasts of the United Nations have been taken as the demographic basis, since caution with respect to demographic growth is in the interest of all continents. In Alternative A (i) it has been assumed that the growth of incomes in the more prosperous countries will not exceed a level compatible with a growth in world food production of 3.1 per cent a year over the 42-year period. This assumption represents an average per capita income growth rate of only 1.2 per cent or an increase from $ 925 in 1970 to $ 1,500 in 2012. This growth rate is of course considerably less than that achieved by the industrialized world in past decades. The same 3.1 per cent upper limit of food production is also applied to Latin America resulting in an average per capita income growth rate of 2.8 per cent. Given these assumptions it can be seen that even the growth of Africa would be more modest.

In Alternative A (ii) the 3.1 per cent upper limit for food production has been retained but combined with slightly more modest population growth. As such, it represents an alternative approach to the adaptation of food demand. In this case, population growth is reduced by 0.1 per cent in all parts of the world.

Table 9 also contains crude estimates of the income which could be derived from manufacturing industry (excluding mining) in the various continents (7). It illustrates the scale of industrialization needed for the attainment of development targets.

Table 10 shows each continent's share in total world industrial production expressed in both nominal and real dollars for the sets of assumptions made in the three alternatives (8). The figures show that in 1970 Africa had, in nominal amounts, only 0.5 per cent, Asia 2.6 per cent and Latin America 4.0 per cent of the world's total industrial production. Under the three alternatives, the respective shares are raised very substantially. The share of the industrialized world, by the same token, shows a very substantial fall, from 92.9 per cent in 1970 to 35.7 per cent under Alternative A (i).

6.4   *Summary: Challenges Emerging from the Quantitative Illustration*

To determine the magnitude of the development tasks confronting us,

Table 10 *Income from manufacturing for Africa, Asia, Latin American and countries industrialized in 1970, as percentage of total world income from manufacturing: 1970 and 2012; nominal and real estimates; three alternatives.*

	1970		2012 A (i)		2012 A (ii)		2012 B	
	Nom.	Real	Nom.	Real	Nom.	Real	Nom.	Real
Africa	0.5	1.8	16.1	12.6	14.9	11.6	9.8	8.5
Asia	2.6	5.9	36.4	50.6	32.5	46.9	21.4	32.5
Latin America	4.0	6.0	11.8	9.0	13.1	11.1	17.2	15.0
Industrialized in 1970	92.9	86.3	35.7	27.8	39.5	30.4	51.6	44.0
World	100.0	100.0	100.0	100.0	100.0	100.0	100.0	100.0

three alternative world futures — covering population growth, food production and income — have been investigated. The investigations suggest that if (alternative B):
— the limit to world food production is less stringent than assumed in section 6.3.3;
— Third World countries are able to achieve a per capita income growth rate of 5 per cent a year;
— the growth in per capita incomes in the industrialized countries maintains its present rate (approximately 3.3 per cent a year); and
— the 'low' population forecast of the UN are assumed;
then the decile ratio between the world's richest and poorest could be reduced from 13:1 to 13:2 over a 42 year period.

This ratio could be reduced to 13:4, and food production could be adapted to the limits assumed in section 6.3.3, on the basis of the following assumptions (alternative A (ii)):
— 5 per cent growth rate in per capita incomes in Third World countries;
— a growth rate of only 1.7 per cent in the industrialized countries (approximately half the existing growth rate so as to attain zero growth in about 40 years);
— a maximum growth in world food production of 3.1 per cent a year (compared with 2.7 per cent at present); and
— a population growth of 0.1 per cent less than the 'low' U.N. forecasts.

The same ratio of 13:4 could also be obtained over the 42 year period on the basis of the 'low' population forecasts, although in this case, assuming a 3.1 per cent growth in food supply and attainment of the 5 per cent growth target for the Third World, the growth of per capita incomes in the industrialized countries would need to be limited to the order of 1.2 per cent a year (alternative A (i)).

The ratio of 13:4, or about 3:1, is equivalent to the present ratio, considered barely acceptable, between the rich and poor *regions* within the EEC. It is also higher than the one between the richest and poorest *countries* within the industrialized world, where it is less than 2:1. A few industrialized countries have even reached a ratio of 1½:1. And this ratio of 3:1, assumed to be necessary for world political stability, could only be achieved between the regions and the countries of the world, at least on the basis of the assumptions made, over a period of 42 years. The question is of course whether the poor are prepared to wait half a century to attain what is now barely acceptable within the industrialized world.

Table 11   *World Bank forecasts of population and per capita GNP levels and GNP growth rates for developing and developed countries[a], 1970-1980*

	Population[b]	Per capita GNP		Per capita GNP growth rate, 1970-1980
		1970	1980	
	(millions)	(1970 $)		(percentages)
Low income developing countries (under $ 200 per capita GNP)	1,000	105	108	0.2
Middle income developing countries (over $ 200 per capita GNP)	725	410	540	2.8
Developed countries	675	3,100	4,000	2.6

[a] Excludes centrally planned economies and OPEC countries.
[b] Estimates for the latter half of the 1970s.

Note: These figures assume that capital flows to developing countries will increase in nominal terms but not in real terms between 1975 and 1980; that industrialized countries will make a rather rapid recovery from the current recession; and that per capita growth rates for the remainder of the decade will be 1.2 per cent for the low income countries and 2.8 per cent for the middle-income countries.

Source: Robert S. McNamara, *Address to the Board of Governors*, Washington, D.C., September 1, 1975 (Washington, D.C.: World Bank, 1975), p. 7.

In the alternatives, a target of 5 per cent annual growth in per capita incomes among the countries of the Third World has been used. Only 15 countries succeeded in attaining this average during the period 1965-1972. Some 12 countries actually had negative per capita income growth rates over the same period. The strategy for the Second Development Decade called for a 3.5 per cent growth rate in per capita income for all poor countries. Only OPEC and the exporters of manufactured goods are achieving this target. In most poor countries, the growth in per capita incomes has averaged only 2.3 per cent, a growth rate jeopardized by the present recession (Table 11 and Figure 10). And even here the average disguises the fact that, in many cases, much of the new wealth has simply not reached the poorest and most in need. The target of 5 per cent might thus be considered ambitious

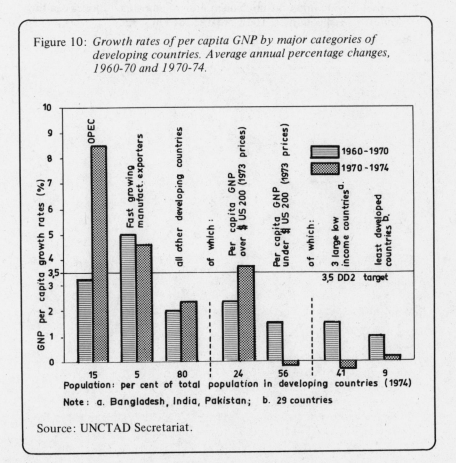

Figure 10: *Growth rates of per capita GNP by major categories of developing countries. Average annual percentage changes, 1960-70 and 1970-74.*

Source: UNCTAD Secretariat.

A third alternative was thus investigated in which the growth in Third World per capita incomes was restricted to 4 per cent a year. This assumption, when combined with an extrapolation of the 3.3 per cent growth rate in the industrialized countries over the period 1970-2012, results in a decile ratio of 13:1.3. In other words, only a marginal improvement in the currently unacceptable situation. The growth rate might thus be considered more reasonable; its consequences, however, are not.

The attainment of the 5 per cent growth rate is thus to a large extent dependent upon Third World countries expanding their share of world manufacturing industry. The target in this field has been set by the UNIDO Lima Conference (1975): it passed a recommendation that the Third World's share in world industrial production should increase from its current level of 7 per cent to 25 per cent by the year 2000. This is a target and not a projection. It is, however, a necessary target. Its attainment will in part depend upon the implementation of adjustment policies in the industrialized countries. These are discussed in section 7.7.

Notes and References

(1) Details and explanations concerning main assumptions are given in Appendix 1 at the end of this chapter.

(2) Some of these difficulties include: soils are sometimes much more fragile, prone to erosion and have inferior nutrient and mineral qualities; the menace of rodent, insect, fungi and weed invasion is frequently greater; indiscriminate use of fertilizers, herbicides, and pesticides is more likely to have detrimental effects on local eco-systems; rainfall and climate generally are less dependable; irrigation projects and the like are much more likely to result in endemic, debilitating environmentally induced diseases in man and animals and in increased soil salinity; the vulnerability of new strains is often higher; and small farmers frequently equate agriculture with poverty, are discriminated against and exploited, and seek desperately to find ways of leaving the land. All these factors, and their many and complex interactions, motivate against high crop yields in parts of the Third World.

(3) Some estimates suggest that 50 per cent more agricultural land must be irrigated if food needs are to be met. Agriculture as practiced in the industrialized countries is very water-intensive. In the United States, for example, some 3,500 gallons of water are required daily in order to produce food for the average diet, and at least 250 more gallons in order to store it and make it nutritionally available. Although vegetarian diets require considerably less water, it should be remembered that the closer a plant comes to the limits of available water, the more water a plant requires (Australian wheat strains for example require more than twice the water of American ones – 850 as against 350 pounds per pound of organic matter). Poor soils with low fertility, those typical of many poor countries, also raise the water consumption: more water is wasted in poor soils in order to produce a certain amount of food than in fertile soils.

(4) There is certainly sufficient evidence for this concern: the Asian monsoons were unsatisfactory for three successive years between 1972-1974; severe droughts in the Sahel and other parts of Africa and the Great Plains area of the United States and Canada in 1974; an unexpected late frost in Brazil in 1975 which may have destroyed as much as 60 per cent of its 1976 coffee crop. The growing season of the best grain producing areas in the Soviet Union is now believed to about a week shorter than it was in the 1950's; an even more pronounced shift appears to have taken place in the United Kingdom.

(5) H. Linnenmann et al. *Moira: Model of International Relations in Agriculture* to be published in 1976 by North Holland Publishing Company, Amsterdam/New York.

(6) These projections do not include the potential of the utilization of non-conventional living resources (both plants and animals) of the oceans, based on new technologies of harvesting and processing. In view of the problems enumerated in footnotes 2, 3 and 4 above, the development of these marine resources may become of increasing importance and urgency for all nations, especially for the poorer ones.

(7) The basis for the estimates is also given in Appendix 1.

(8) Nominal dollar figures are included because they are frequently used in the calculations of U.N. agencies.

Studies Supporting the Quantitative Illustration
Jan Tinbergen

Some observers or students of world affairs believe that income ratios are not a very relevant aspect of political stability and that, for instance, disarmament is much more important. There is a considerable element of common sense in this judgement; but unfortunately the prospects of progress in the field of disarmament are very doubtful. If, then, the direct cause of instability cannot be easily influenced, the question arises whether there are indirect causes co-determining the threat of conflicts and hence the use of arms. These indirect causes are, on the one hand, the arguments used by those in possession of military power, and, on the other, the popular emotions they can use in order to manoeuver their power policies. Among these emotions some of the most formidable are nationalism and religious or cultural differences. These again cannot be easily changed, as is shown by centuries of human history. Next in the list of emotions are those of envy and of feelings of injustice; and these forces are to a considerable extent dependent on differences in well-being. This is clearly related to perceptions of income disparities.

It is usually assumed that the poor countries will quietly take for granted the growing income disparities which our extrapolations of past trends show. But here we have our doubts. The initiatives taken by OPEC, UNCTAD, UNIDO and other institutions show that a new era has started; the age of acquiescence has passed.

The only guideline we were able to find for dealing with growing disparities is based on the observations that: (a) step by step, larger political units have been organized; and (b) within these larger units regional income differences have been reduced. Let us give examples of both.

In a period of two centuries, the most powerful country in the West, the United States, has emerged from a group of isolated colonies. In a period of one century, Germany and Italy have been unified. In a period of half a century, Eastern Europe has been made what it is now. In a period of a quarter of a century the world's most populous nation, China, the 'sleeping giant', has woken up.

Income ratios between the most and the least prosperous regions (each so defined as to have 10 per cent of a country's population) were above 3 in the United States between 1880 and 1930 and for 1960/70 were below 2. In smaller countries, such as France and Germany, they are somewhat smaller than in the United States. In France, the figure fell from 2.6 in 1860 to 1.7 in 1960/70. In the European Community of the 'Six' the figure was 3.2; but this Community is not yet well integrated and experiences an uneasy tension between the Italian South and the North of the Continent. In India the ratio is close to 3. We attempted to summarize this evidence by the conclusion that the ratio of 3:1 goes with an uneasy tension, not too far from political equilibrium.

Our proposition for the world forty years from now is that we should aim at a ratio of 3:1 for the world at large. As an alternative we also consider a situation of 6:1. These two alternatives we use as a basis for a serious attempt to meet minds with those whose responsibility it is to defend the interests of the world's poor masses.

There are other reasons why we chose our ambitious figures. As set out in Annex 2, a drastic income redistribution in poor countries will be needed. We could hardly imagine how this can be organized. One precondition seems to us that the average per capita income of the developing countries has to rise substantially and we opted for a figure of 5 per cent per annum. Together with the limitations expected in world food production this figure of 5 per cent annual growth in income per capita does not leave untouched growth possibilities for income per capita in the prosperous countries. Our two main alternatives were thus continued growth equal to past growth (Alternative B) or about half that growth (Alternative A).

The latter alternative has been considered incompatible, by a number of economists, with our proposed accelerated growth of developing countries. The argument is that the exports to developed countries will grow less than in the past if Alternative A is assumed. In considering this argument it should not be forgotten that our growth figures are averages over the coming forty years, meant to be reached through gradual changes. In the earlier part of the period, figures of the past would still more or less apply. But as time proceeds we take into account the possibilities for developing countries of 'collective self-reliance', that is, of increased trade among themselves. Thus, they would become less dependent, step by step, on the growth rate of developed countries. There is not, therefore, a contradiction between our assumptions of less growth of the developed and more growth of the developing countries.

The estimates of food demand have been based on the U.N. National Accounts Statistics for 1965, from which the share of gross domestic product devoted to food was derived for 40 countries in all stages of development. The figures were compared with those for 1970 and the relationship appeared not to have changed appreciably. The most difficult problem is to estimate the portion for incomes considerably higher than the 1970 per capita income for the United States. Household budgets for higher than average family incomes are not available for the United States. Finally, a few indications were found for the Federal Republic of Germany (1) and for Sweden (2). These were integrated into a formula: Consumption per capita = 210 + 0.13 Income per capita, which was applied to the higher income range in real 1970 dollars (U.S. purchasing power) or 70 + 0.13 income per capita, purchasing power of poorest countries.

The estimates for income from manufacturing industries were based on statistical material supplied by the United Nations Research Institute for Social Development in its Compilation of Development Indicators (for 1960), Geneva 1969, Index 56 (GDP derived from manufacturing as percentage of GNP). An upper limit of 40 per cent was assumed to exist for countries with relatively few natural resources; one of 37 per cent for countries with ample natural resources, implying that they would draw 3 per cent more from agriculture and mining.

No reduction at higher per capita incomes than the ones now prevailing in the most prosperous countries was applied in the way suggested by Jean Fourastié. This probably implies an overestimation of the volume of manufacturing in rich countries and hence an underestimation of the percentage of world industrial activity to be expected, around the year 2000, for the now developing countries.

From the above, the very crude nature of the quantitative illustration will be clear. Programmes of refinement will thus be needed.

Personal income distribution within countries remains at least as important as distribution between countries. For brevity's sake, the reader may be referred to the studies on this subject by Mrs. Irma Adelman and Mrs. Cynthia Morris Taft, summarized by them in *Policies for Equitable Growth*, a paper presented to the Conference on Economic Development and Income Distribution, held at the Institute of Behavioral Science, University of Colorado, April, 1976.

(1) *Statistisches Jahrbuch 1971*, p. 477-480.
(2) *Svensk ekonomi fram till 1977*, Statens Offentliga Utredningar, vol. 21, 1973, p. 124.

Chapter 7   Strategies of Change

> '. . . Laws and insitutions must go hand in hand with the progress of the human mind. With the change of circumstances institutions must advance also to keep pace with the time.'
>
> Thomas Jefferson

7.1   *The Means of Change*

To attain an equitable international social and economic order efforts will need to be made by everyone; not only politicians and decision-makers, but, in principle, every single member of the world's population. Change in desired directions implies action based upon high levels of cooperation; not only the more formalized forms of cooperation within and between established institutions, but also the many other forms of informal and voluntary cooperation which can and must be organized among individuals, between individuals and institutions, and between institutions.

At the highest level, the level of world affairs, international institutions must form the prime movers of planned change. The efforts to be made by institutions at higher levels can be viewed as 'means' which can be mobilized to achieve desired ends. This implies that institutions control a number of 'handles' which can be used to guide change through the efforts of individuals and smaller institutions. The control which institutions can exercise, however, is not unlimited but rather determined by the *power structure* in which they operate. In the case of powerful institutions, the means at their disposal are often organized into *policies*. As such, policies may refer either to the current operation of the socio-economic order or to action designed to execute planned change to the existing order. They can, therefore, be directed towards either reinforcing or transforming the international status quo.

In the present international order huge power is concentrated in industrialized nation-States. Seen from a world viewpoint, this must be deemed undesirable. Some of the means which could be employed to attain those objectives of vital importance to the international community can more effectively be handled by higher levels of decision-making. This in contrast to Third World nations where a reinforcement of the state forms a precondition to the achievement of certain aims, for instance less inequality among citizens. Even so, for smaller Third World countries, the achievement of some aims, such as the creation of larger markets through regional and sub-regional cooperation (collective self-reliance), would be facilitated by decision-making on a level higher than the nation-State.

7.2 *The Institutions of Change*

The most important options for organizing institutions lie in three main areas. The first relates to the way in which the means of operating society are grouped into *bunches* which can appropriately be handled by one institution. From the viewpoint of efficiency, the most suitable approach would be to group together those means requiring similar techniques of control. The second option concerns the various *levels of decision-making* and the hierarchy corresponding to it. This important structural consideration applies to single institutions as well as to the relationships between persons and between institutions. To achieve certain aims, for example, it may be necessary to think in terms of confederations of international organizations as has been proposed for the oceans (cf. Chapter 18). The third option concerns choices which will need to be made with respect to the *membership* of institutions. Membership should not be limited to national governments; it should also embrace non-governmental organizations of many kinds operating at different levels. The objectives of institutions will of course differ, as will the roles they can effectively play.

These options will need to be judged in the light of some *criteria* derived from the community's general aims. Although no criterion will be fully attained, three should be afforded special importance:

(a) *Participation*. If the chosen structure is not genuinely participatory, it cannot hope to succeed. Among other things, it must define the degree of participation appropriate to all interest groups represented.

(b) *Political feasibility*. Crucially important especially during the early phases of the transformation of the existing order, it is by its nature closely linked to the criterion of participation since participation is likely to reflect positions of power. Proposals, however, while taking account of the existing power structure, must attempt at the same time to change it in directions compatible with the attainment of an equitable international social and economic order (1) (cf. section 7.4).

(c) *Efficiency*. The option chosen must possess a favourable ratio between results and efforts. This criterion will express itself in each of the main structural features: in the number of levels in the decision-making hierarchy, the highest level being chosen for a given set of means; in the membership of institutions, their duties and their rights; and in the importance afforded to specialist opinion.

Institutions must function as catalizers of change. Experience has taught us, however, that international institutions are prone to a cataleptic condition brought about by their inability to advance and keep pace with changing circumstances. Established to initiate and guide a process of

The United Nations System

The future of the new international order should not be confused with the future of the U.N. system. Mankind is confronted with a complex array of problems which defy national solutions. They require international cooperation organized through international institutions. Despite its very many achievements in a range of fields — achievements that are frequently forgotten or denigrated — the United Nations remains the only real machinery with the potential for constructing a fairer world.

Its future role will largely depend upon its ability to adapt to changing power realities, to the needs of an expanding world community and on decisions of governments, especially the most powerful, to use it as a major instrument in formulating and implementing those policies which affect others.

That U.N. machinery is in need of restructuring is not disputed. Ways in which its economic efficiency can be improved have already been recommended by the 'Group of 25' *. These recommendations provide an essential, though partial, basis for future adaptation and although several have proved controversial every effort must be made to improve efficiency along the general lines suggested. Some of the Group's most important recommendations are summarized below:

(a) A Director-General for Development and International Economic Cooperation should be appointed, who would be second in rank only to the Secretary-General. The Director-General would provide leadership for the entire international economic system and be responsible for coordination of important economic initiatives at the global level.

(b) All funds for preinvestment activities (except UNICEF) should merge in a 'fund of funds' to be called the U.N. Development Authority, managed by an Administrator who would be a Deputy Director-General. The identity of the present funds would be maintained to allow earmarking of contributions for such purposes as the environment or population programmes. The Development Authority would be governed by an Operations Board which would report to ECOSOC.

(c) The Department of Economic and Social Affairs of the U.N. Secretariat should be reorganized and placed under a Deputy Director-General for Research and Policy. The Department would undertake research, policy planning, and economic analysis for ECOSOC and other elements of the United Nations. A joint research, planning and programming staff would assist in this task.

(d) The Director-General would chair an Advisory Committee on Economic Cooperation and Development composed of the heads of the major specialized agencies and the regional economic commissions.

(e) The Economic and Social Council should be strengthened to provide central policy guidance on economic and social affairs. Most of the commissions and subordinate bodies should be abolished.

(f) A small body of independent experts should be created to evaluate the implementation of the U.N.'s economic activities.

* *A new U.N. Structure for Global Economic Cooperation*, United Nations, New York, May 1975, E/AC 62/9.

change, they can become a vested interest and consequently status quo rather than change oriented; they outlive their purpose. Such institutions may ultimately devote the greatest part of their energies and resources to preserving their own power position and guaranteeing their survival.

This would suggest that some new institutions should be operated for limited periods only rather than established as a permanent feature of the international order, for example, to undertake a specific task or set of tasks. Such institutions, at their inception, must be furnished with an in-built 'self-destruct' mechanism; periodic evaluation of the future need for the institution in the light of changing circumstances should be mandatory and result in decisions to either terminate operations or to adapt its role and function.

7.3   *Steering the Process of Change: Alternatives; Second-Best Solutions; Compromises*

Given the growing list of problems confronting mankind, every effort must be made to stimulate processes which point in directions which can be deemed desirable. This would certainly apply, for example, to the tendency towards the increasing centralization of decision-making involving issues with considerable external effects. The promotion of decision-making beyond national frontiers should be viewed as a logical continuation of the process of change and a precondition for the effective assertion of national sovereignty. By the same token, the continuation of trends towards decentralized decision-making based upon the need for genuine participation is also in line with historical developments , such as decolonialization. There is nothing paradoxical or incompatible with these trends towards increasing centralization and decentralization. They are different sides of the same coin. Together they represent a movement in the direction of what, in section 5.8, was termed 'decentralized planetary sovereignty'.

In addition to stimulating and steering desirable processes, we must also be wise enough to judge in which areas 'mutations' are required. The aim here must be to cause breakthroughs in processes which, if allowed to continue, will only worsen prospects for real change. Such processes might be either of the runaway or stagnatory type. Examples of the former include the armaments race, the proliferation of nuclear capability, the growing disparities between the world's rich and poor, overconsumption in the rich industrialized countries, and the growing inability of Third World countries to secure the means to satisfy the basic needs of their poor. Stagnatory processes calling for intervention include quiescence in the field of development cooperation and inertia in the renewal of obsolete social systems.

Given the present power structure and perceptions of 'political feasibility', deterministic blueprints of long range change must be avoided: pre-occupation with these may actually jeopardize rather than enhance the prospects for redirecting the process of social evolution. We must of necessity restrict ourselves to a number of guiding principles which can serve as a basis for steering change in desired directions (see box). In applying these principles we must strive for optimality even though it would seem intrinsic in the human condition that it never be achieved. In pursuing it, however, we must honestly scrutinize the alternatives before us, be prepared to make compromises if failure to do so would result in no progress, and to be wise enough to accept a second-best solution when the alternative is no solution at all.

Guiding Principles for Generating Decision-Making Alternatives

(a) Forms of international decision-making can range from *very loose* to *highly organized*. The loosest form is one in which, for example, a country continues a particular policy but informs those countries likely to be affected by its actions of its intentions. The second form comprises a process of *consultation* without binding decisions. Third in degree of organization are attempts to arrive at *unanimous decisions*, and, fourthly, through a system of majority voting. A still more organized form is given by the introduction of some form of *dispute settlement*. A desirable form of international decision-making, however, is one in which a genuinely supranational *authority* takes decisions based on a qualified majority principle. A qualified majority may comprise a system of weighted votes, be based on a simple majority, or be based on a system in which not only the total number of representatives but also the representatives of some well defined groups must together form a majority. Combinations of these alternatives are also conceivable.

(b) A decision-making body can be initiated by several *pioneering countries* on a *voluntary* basis and then be gradually extended. Some of the means used could first be applied at low levels, for example, a *tax* on consumer durables, and be gradually *raised* and extended to include more categories and eventually more countries.

(c) Membership of an international decision-making body should be open to both public authorities and private organizations, whether non-profit or profit-making, or a combination of these categories.

(d) Because an effective international order requires institutions at the regional as well as the world level, decision-making bodies at the regional level can be established prior to institutionalizing a decision-making capability at the world level. In certain cases it might be appropriate to make a start at the sub-regional level on the basis of the principles outlined under (c).

(e) Proposals should preferably contain a *time-table* outlining the future action in those areas in which agreement has been reached. This would enable a political check to be built into the proposals although this would of course also depend on the experiences and results of successive phases.

The creation of an equitable international social and economic order entails changes in the existing distribution of power. The development of global awareness has not yet reached the stage where the rich and privileged nations are prepared — in their own long term interest — to voluntarily surrender some of their power to international institutions. The required awareness can be expected to develop only slowly. The Third World, however, is impatient for change and it must draw upon its own strengths and resources to enhance its power position vis-à-vis the industrialized countries. The redress of power imbalance is not only required to establish a more equitable basis for forthcoming negotiations between the main parties on a new world order; it should also contribute towards promoting the necessary changes in the attitudes of the industrialized nations.

In the short term, changes can be effected in the power structure through violent action and, indeed, many violent reactions to existing inequalities, both within and between nations, can be expected in the coming decades. Resorting to violence at the international level, however, would inevitably bring mankind even closer to the nuclear brink. The resolution of conflicts through force opens the way to escalation and this is one of the preconditions for nuclear war, a possibility unknown to the fathers of revolutionary thinking. In redressing power imbalances, Third World nations must seek to use instruments other than violence.

The Third World can enhance its power position by exercising *control over its scarce natural resources*. The effectiveness of this strategy has in part been demonstrated by the OPEC group. The prosperity of the industrialized countries is dependent upon regular supplies of raw materials from the Third World (Table 12). Of the 13 basic raw materials required by a modern industrial economy, the United States was, for example, in 1950 dependent on imports for more than half its supplies for only four. By 1970 the list had grown to six, and by 1985 the list is expected to grow to nine.

Third World countries can, in the absence of internationally agreed rules, increase their power by exercising *control over foreign investment*. Many industrialized countries have large and growing stakes in the economies of many poor nations. To take but one case, in the United States foreign earnings on direct investment as a proportion of total domestic profits rose from 9 per cent in 1950 to 28 per cent in 1969. Control over the investments of the industrialized countries, provided for in the Charter of Economic Rights and Duties of States, is a powerful weapon and would need to be used with discretion.

Table 12   *United States, European Community, and Japanese dependence on selected imported industrial raw materials, 1973 (percentages)*

	United States	European Community	Japan
	(imports as percentage of consumption)		
Bauxite[a]	86	60	100
Chromium	91	100	100
Cobalt	96	100	100
Copper	6	96	83
Iron ore	20	59	99
Lead	26	70	70
Manganese	98	99	86
Natural rubber	100	100	100
Nickel	72	100	100
Phosphates	b	100	100
Tin	87	99	93
Tungsten	68	100	100
Zinc	63	60	68

[a] Raw material for the production of aluminium.
[b] Net exporter.

SOURCE: *International Economic Report of the President*, transmitted to Congress March 1975, U.S. Government Printing Office, Washington, D.C., 1975, p. 61.

Some Third World countries will also be able to raise their negotiating power as a result of their natural products regaining a *comparative advantage* over synthetics. In some instances this possibility might be increased as industrialized countries approach the limits of their water supplies (2).

New structures can be built up through the creation of '*new coalitions*'. These might be formed at the national and international level and be of a political character, aiming at establishing new combinations of influence and power. It should be understood that such coalitions must be formed on the basis of completely equal partnership, as must any practical implications of the concept of 'interdependencies' between nations. The proposal of the Group of 25 on the restructuring of the U.N. system that some type of 'negotiating' or 'consultative' groups should be established within the framework of ECOSOC might open up possibilities to explore such 'new coalitions'.

Many other types of new coalitions can be envisaged. They might be forged, for example, between Consumer Unions in industrialized countries and UNCTAD, between producers of capital goods and UNIDO, and between food and raw materials producers and FAO. Consumer interests in the rich countries run parallel with a reduction in import impediments; the interests of producers of capital goods run parallel with increased development financing; the interests of producers of food and raw materials run parallel with an adequate world supply of food.

Coalitions might also be forged between small and middle-sized industrialized countries, with common interests, against the great powers. Especially important is the need for a vastly expanded effort for exploring the borderlines of cooperation among the countries of the Third World within the framework of policies designed to promote self-reliance. Such cooperation could be organized at many levels and around different problems: among neighbouring Third World countries; among countries with similarities in levels of development; among countries with common commodities to sell; among countries having complementary products to exchange; and among countries with common problems e.g. incidence of debt servicing. OPEC countries in the Middle East, a water deficit area, and countries in South Asia with a water surplus could possibly benefit from mutual cooperation. There are many new and exciting opportunities for arranging collaborative alliances between OPEC and the Third World. These and other types of new coalitions could and should eventually result in the institutionalization of a new power structure.

The greatest power which the Third World possesses is its *solidarity*. It is of absolute importance that the Third World retain its collective 'poor power'. Without it, it will prove infinitely more difficult to obtain major concessions from the rich nations and to arrange for a genuine transfer of resources.

7.5 *The Search for Relevant Ideas: The Responsibilities of Specialists*

In the final analysis, our world is ruled by ideas — rational and ethical — and not by vested interests. The 'power of the idea', the particular weapon of scientists, moralists and concerned citizens, must prove of decisive importance in constructing a fairer and more peaceful world and the search for relevant new ideas must be organized and intensified so as to support it.

One of our main weapons in this search is the vast arsenal of scientists we are potentially able to deploy. To fully utilize this resource, we must deliberately choose to focus investigation in directions we believe to be really *relevant*. Given the present state of the world, relevance must be determined by the extent to which thought supports action designed to alleviate the crushing poverty suffered by the majority of mankind and reducing the enormous differences in opportunity and income between the world's rich and poor.

One area of relevant research is *recycling in the wider sense*, that is, deliberately trespassing the frontiers between industrial sectors and areas of knowledge. Recent research has demonstrated the feasibility of using the wastes of one industrial process as inputs into another. Many technologists and industrialists have grown up in the narrow environment of single industries and, as such, many new recycling possibilities, with their promise of savings in non-renewable resources, may have escaped their attention. Just as interdisciplinary research has proven to be particularly productive, we can expect that the systematic search for interindustrial links will prove to be especially fruitful. The justification for such a search is supported by the emerging realization that failure to use part of the output of one productive process as an input into another constitutes an unnecessary *waste* of both human and physical resources to society as a whole.

In political processes too, the search for '*new combinations*' can be expected to produce valuable results. Such a search is likely to demonstrate the responsibilities which scientists and other specialists have, not only to their nations, but also to the constituency of mankind. In the past, specialists have often been reluctant to engage in political debate or to share their knowlegde and fears with the general public. Given social dilemmas, they have often preferred to adopt neutral rather than value positions, to tacitly advise rather than openly advocate. This generalization no longer holds true. In many branches of science there are radical movements. Increasingly, both in the rich and poor worlds, scientists are involved in active advocacy which they see as an intellectual and ethical duty.

The idea that scientists should be advisors and politicians decision-makers must, in the light of the awful complexities of contemporary problems, be viewed as questionable. In order to take responsible decisions, a decision-maker must be aware and take account of the consequences of his actions. Today's complexities are such that he can no longer depend upon purely intuitive responses nor gear his actions to predominantly short term expedients. Increasingly, he must make use of specialist opinion (3).

These observations suggest that specialists be provided with greater opportunities to participate in the making of decisions in areas of vital importance to the future of mankind. This is not to suggest the creation of a technocracy nor that political will can ever be substituted by scientific expertise; only that it may prove short-sighted not to more effectively use the insights and understandings which are at present available and required to build paths to a more just world. Specialists must serve as 'advocates for the unborn' and the expansion of their role can be viewed as an example of *functional representation* in international decision-making.

Not only must specialists advocate courses of action in international fora, they must also more fully commit themselves to development efforts at the local level. Their commitment must be total, their allegiance to a problem or community unstinting. Experts operating through bilateral and multilateral channels have not always met these requirements. The 'new expert', in actively promoting local self-reliant development, may need to subordinate his own values, even his knowledge, to those of the community he is attempting to serve. We have seen the rise of 'barefoot doctors'; we must encourage the rise of 'barefoot experts'.

If the Third World is to carry out its development within a framework of enlarged independence and collective self-reliance, it must strive for its own intellectual liberation. There is a great need today for the Third World to debate its choices frankly and honestly in the fora of the Third World itself. The organization of the Third World Forum thus represents a most timely initiative. It has been created with the task of fashioning relevant development strategies within national value systems and to provide the analytical underpinnings for negotiations on the establishment of a new international order. Its intellectual presence is already being felt in international debates.

7.6   *Public Opinion in the Industrialized Countries: The Task Ahead and the Need for Information Reforms*

The possibility of implementing ideas of a new power structure would, in democratic societies, necessitate the acceptance of such ideas by wide sectors of public opinion. It is of paramount importance, therefore, that new ways and means be found to establish, within industrialized countries, contacts between formal and informal groups of concerned citizens, scientists and politicians, and to maintain a continuous dialogue and debate within and between these groups on the need to find and accept new approaches to increasingly common problems.

In stimulating and organizing such a debate, it is essential that discussions be taken out of the realms of 'Christian charity', 'assisting the poor'. 'humanitarianism' — expressions suggestive of 'crumbs for the starving'. The issues are no longer, indeed never were, those which can be addressed by international do-gooding. The questions which need to be asked must be placed in a much broader perspective. To what kind of life do the prosperous of the industrialized countries aspire, for themselves and — perhaps even more importantly — for their children? Cannot the rich nations, at present struggling to retain the 'good life' on their islands of prosperity and relative calm, read the first signs of failure to take the demands of the Third World more seriously: the uncertainties surrounding their foreign investments and the future activities of their transnational enterprises, the rising number of immigrant workers, the increasing activity of political extremists, and the continuous threat of internal disputes escalating into international conflicts?

It must be doubted that public opinion is in general as resistant to change as some Western politicians would apparently have us believe. On the contrary, many citizens of the industrialized countries seem to possess a clearer recognition of the need to devise new ways and means of dealing with some of today's pressing and increasingly common problems — and the possible consequences for themselves and their families of doing nothing — than do many of their elected representatives and appointed officials (4).

Governments repeatedly and inherently underestimate their people. History has frequently shown that people, in times of crisis and once convinced of the necessity for change, are prepared to accept policies which demand changes in their behaviour so as to help secure better lives for themselves and their children. The creation of an equitable social and economic order does make such demands upon them: for instance, the need to gradually modify their life-styles and consumption patterns. The governments of the industrialized countries must go to their people on some of the choices ahead. They must take the initiative in structuring a national debate, not simply on internal issues or selective aspects of foreign policy, but on a range of policy choices which will directly affect the lives of their citizens in the years ahead.

That public recognition of many of today's problems has so far found little expression in national policies is not only a reflection of inertia and innate conservatism but also of a refusal by the governments of most industrialized countries to admit that post-colonial technological and economic domination is almost as strangulating as that exerted by direct colonial rule.

The governments of the industrialized nations simply cannot use public opinion to justify their reluctance to accept structural change at the world's negotiating tables. Public opinion is no phenomenon *sui generis*. It is in part the result of government policies and by definition politicians cannot hide behind their own creation. If some sectors of public opinion in the industrialized countries are immersed in the rhetoric and slogans associated with misunderstanding, then much of this may be inherited from their political leaders. And if these leaders are in part responsible for a situation which impedes acceptance of the need for change, then they themselves must be held responsible for changing this situation.

Whereas national public opinion may exist in the singular, internationally it exists in the plural. Analogous groups with similar roles and functions in different societies are much more quickly aware of each others' positions, tactics and actions than they were only twenty years ago. Groups of many different kinds, both in and outside the production processes — students, trade unions, scientists — from both the Third World and the industrialized countries should join forces in their attempts to shape public and political opinion. The aim here must be the internationalization of attempts at 'conscience-raising'. There would appear to be tremendous scope for a range of non-governmental organizations in this field and for cooperation among them.

Much effort has been made in the past ten years, in some industrialized countries, to bring the disadvantages facing many Third World countries to the attention of large numbers of people. If it has met with only limited success, it is probably because it has failed to bring out the concept of interdependence of countries and issues. More attention must in future be focused on information and education on how our planet functions and on the 'survival fact' that the claim of the whole is wider and deeper than the claim of any of its parts. There is also a fundamental need to develop a broadly educated political class which is capable of understanding science and the broad implications, possibilities and dangers of technological advance, and which can harness technological advance for constructive social purposes.

It must also be recognized that international information dissemination has long formed the subject of discriminatory practices. Flows of information from the Third World to the industrialized countries are controlled by a handful of Western news agencies; information is bought and sold in a highly oligopolistic market. As such, information is subject to manipulation and can be and is used as a means of perpetuating preconceived ideas, ignorance and apathy. It serves to maintain systems rather than to transform them.

Public opinion in the industrialized countries will not have real access to full information on the Third World, its demands, aspirations and needs, until such time as information and communication patterns are liberated from the market-oriented sensationalism and news presentation which characterize them at present and until they are consciously stripped of ethnocentric prejudices. The *widening of the capacity to inform* must be viewed as an essential component of attempts to create a new international order and, as such, the monopolistic and discriminatory practices inherent in current international information dissemination must be deemed as one of the worst, though subtle, characteristics of the present system.

That there is a need for reform is obvious. Such reform should include the creation of a Third World information centre to specifically serve Third World needs and to facilitate the dissemination of information on the Third World, both in industrialized and Third World countries. There is also considerable scope for increased cooperation between the national news agencies of the Third World countries. Existing bilateral arrangements and multilateral exchanges should be more fully utilized and, where necessary, new ones created.

7.7 *Adjustment Policies*

One of the most urgent requirements of strategies of change is that they result in raising the productivity of the poor nations — individually as nation-States and collectively in regional groupings. The most powerful means of raising productivity is the expansion of the volume of employment, which is itself one of the principal means for improving the distribution of income. This implies that, if a new international order is to be created, the rich nations must be prepared to give up part of their future productive capacity. To be able to do this smoothly they will need to resort to adjustment policies and such policies must form part of their development strategies. Most rich countries already employ adjustment policies for addressing their own regional imbalances; the EEC recently established a regional development fund for promoting development of the poorer regions of some of its member states. The creations of an optimal international division of labour, and as such the selective development of economic activities in Third World countries, calls for the substantial extension of such adjustment policies, to take account, not only of the inequality of opportunity within the rich world, but also of the much greater inequalities between the rich and poor nations.

The productivity of Third World countries must be increased for two main reasons. Firstly, to increase the country's capacity to meet the basic needs of its poor and thus to attain a higher level of self-reliance. By implication, this must be organized on a country-by-country basis. Secondly, to improve the competitive position of the Third World's manufactured products on international markets. This can best be organized at the regional and sub-regional levels within the framework of collective self-reliance.

It is no longer desirable that the industrialized countries adopt policies of protecting their labour-intensive industries in the manufacturing sector. Rather, they should seek, as must the Third World, to develop those industries in which they have a comparative advantage. This does not mean that they must 'abandon' whole industries. This would be neither politically feasible nor necessary. Just as there is a division of labour between industries, there is also one within industries. Those sectors within industries with a comparative advantage would be retained; no effort would be made to protect the sectors which are not competitive. The industrialized countries, for example, have a comparative advantage in the manufacture of textile machinery but not necessarily in the manufacture of all textile goods. Several of these could best be produced in the countries of the Third World. Other examples in which the industrialized countries have a comparative advantage include most metal-working industries, the electronics industry, and research-intensive industries.

The process described, albeit with distortions, is already taking place: some sectors of Western manufacturing industry are moving to Third World countries. The movement of Western European garment industries to North Africa is a case in point. As such, private initiative will no doubt prove responsible for a large part of the adjustment required. That adjustments are at present insufficient is witnessed by the millions of workers who migrate from the Third World to seek employment in the Western industrialized nations. To the extent that the adjustments brought about by private initiative on the strength of international market forces will be inadequate, and in view of the fact that private enterprises may not be sufficiently creative nor responsive to the needs of countries, adjustment must be stimulated and guided by selective taxes and subsidies. Subsidies should be offered to those industries with a clear potential for contributing to a country's or a region's development efforts. Such subsidies could aim at supporting changes, where necessary, in the production mix of enterprises.

Governments of Third World countries, whilst they should do all in their power to expand the volume of employment, must exercise their judgement in accommodating industries from the industrialized countries. They should know what they want. Experience has taught us that industries do not decide to move to poor countries for altruistic reasons: the decision might be motivated by 'abundant supplies of cheap labour', the desire to escape pollution regulations, the search for excessively generous tax concessions and similar motives. At their worst, unscrupulous industries represent a direct extension of neocolonialism. There can be no objection to foreign industries receiving a reasonable return from their activities in a Third World country, however, provided those activities contribute directly to the development efforts of the host country. And for a poor country to be certain a contribution is being made, it must have a declared development strategy, including an industrialization policy, which clearly specifies its industrial, technological and employment requirements.

Implicit in the process of adjustment is the spectre of unemployment in the industrialized countries. This spectre can be exorcised by manpower training and retraining programmes combined with industrial development and financial incentive policies. These will be required not only in the event of conscious policies for encouraging the industrialization of the Third World, but also in anticipation of international market forces. Few countries are as yet employing such policies on anything like the scale or with the precision required.

To ensure the effectiveness of adjustment policies, there is a clear need for coordination of policies both between the industrialized countries and between public authorities and the private sector. Unless the industrialization of the Third World comprises the common effort of all industrialized countries − should it take place in a haphazard and piecemeal way − some industrialized countries will stand to lose more than others. There should, for example, be a mechanism for adjusting imbalances which might arise between the industrialized countries. These could best be redressed by an OECD adjustment fund for the creation of new employment or for the support of retraining programmes or, preferably, both. Possible imbalances within the EEC countries could also be addressed by a special adjustment fund. The possibilities offered by the introduction of shorter working hours should also be reviewed.

The implementation of adjustment policies on the scale required is no doubt hampered by the present recession. For the planning of longer term policies we may assume that the recession will be overcome, even though a return to the very high growth rates averaged in the period 1945-1970 seems very unlikely. Part of both a remedy for the recession and the adjustment needed in the long term is undoubtedly to be found in an increased flow of funds from the rich to the poor nations.

7.8 *Legal Aspects of the New International Order: The Need for a Framework Treaty*

The aims, means and institutions of the new international order should eventually be laid down in legal rules and standards governing the behaviour of States, international organizations, transnational enterprises and other subjects of law. The law should also provide legal remedies and effective sanctions in case of transgressions of these rules and standards.

A strategy of planned change may use the power of rational and ethical ideas inherent in certain principles of law that have been developed in national economic law, such as the principle of non-discrimination in its more equitable form, which not only prohibits unequal treatment of equal cases, but also equitable treatment of unequal situations. Such principles should be adapted to the international context and find wider acceptance in international society than at present.

The legal challenge posed by the new international order can be viewed as the transformation of a system of law based upon Western European culture into the law of a world community (see box). In answering this challenge, attention will need to be devoted to the contributions which,

Sources of International Law

Traditional international law originated in a Christian and essentially European World. It has passed through a number of qualitative phases: the period of 'Christian Nations', terminating in the middle of the nineteenth century; the period of 'Civilized Nations', in which attention was primarily directed at regulating the freedom of a small number of powerful nations and, following decolonialization and the creation of the United Nations, the period of 'Peace Loving Nations', a condition for membership of the U.N. (article 4). Given its origins and evolution, the traditional law of nations has the inclination to serve primarily the interests of the powerful.

The period of 'Peace Loving Nations' has not only brought an enormous increase in the number of nations covered by the system of law, but also the need for qualitative changes in the law. The majority of subjects are no longer powerful but rather weak and disprivileged states. They have different legal needs. They require more of the law than merely the regulation of freedom. They require, firstly, provisions for the *sharing of freedom* (e.g. participation in the law-making process, membership of the U.N.) and secondly, the *abolition of all negative discrimination*, coinciding more or less with the proper realization of freedom, but also the acceptance of 'positive discrimination', such as *protection*, by the law, against the more powerful members of the international community. This suggests the need for certain *rights of the weak*, established in international law, such as: the right to determine their own socio-economic system; the right to form producer associations (as a means to become stronger); the right, at least as long as inequity in international affairs prevails, to nationalize (e.g. natural resources); and the right to formulate conditions concerning foreign investment. It also suggests certain *duties of the powerful*, such as: non-intervention nor the creation of sanctions as a result of the weak exercising their rights; and respect for the sovereignty of others.

Present sources of international law provide possibilities for establishing a legal basis for a new world order. While the traditional instrument is a treaty between sovereign states, lawyers also recognize the source consisting of decisions taken by *permanent international organizations*. According to Article 38 of the Statute of the International Court of Justice, other sources of international law are formulated as: '(c) the general principles of law recognized by civilized nations', and, as an important subsidiary means for the determination of rules of law '(d) . . . judicial decisions and teachings of the most highly qualified publicists of various nations . . . .'

Moreover, the law of existing regional organizations and of many Specialized Agencies offer a wide variety of institutions, procedures and instruments designed to promote the quality and effectiveness of policy-making and supervision that may be adopted and adapted by other organizations charged with the implementation of a strategy of planned change. Interesting examples concerning such techniques include the quasi-legislative procedure of the International Labour Organization, the use of conditional financial incentives by the World Bank, the International Monetary Fund and the European Communities, the refined system of sanctions of the International Monetary Fund, the persuasive force of the Annual Review procedures and escape-clause supervision in the Organization for Economic Cooperation and Development, and the concept of 'enforceable community rights' enabling individuals to request the national courts in the European Communities to apply community law so as to force the national administration to abide by their international obligations under that law.

for example, the Hindu, Buddhist and Moslem States can make to its progressive development on the grounds of their spiritual background.

It must be recognized, however, that it is in the nature of positive law to legalize change after it has taken place and following its general acceptance; positive law thus seldom serves as a instrument for catalizing change. It should also be recognized that developments in international law in the past two decades have resulted in an increase in the number of reservations made by States to treaties adhered to by them. Participants to multilateral treaties have become more numerous but the legal content of treaties has become 'shallower'. New uncertainties concerning the legal content of treaties may in fact have added obstacles to the attainment of a new international order.

These problems would be most effectively overcome through the negotiation and adoption by both the rich and poor nations of a *framework treaty* which clearly lays down the ground rules for international cooperation and the guiding principles to be adopted by nation-States in building the new order. It would comprise an umbrella treaty based upon cooperation rather than competition and would clearly demonstrate that all can benefit from organized change.

The treaty would not represent an attempt to negotiate a new world order in 'one go'. That would not be its purpose. Neither should negotiations currently underway be postponed until such a framework treaty is negotiated. Negotiation would be facilitated, however, by distinguishing between procedural and substantive issues. The treaty would define the procedures and principles on the basis of which substantive issues could be progressively negotiated.

In that it would lay down the 'rules of the international game', the framework treaty might resemble an international Treaty of Rome, although inevitably much less detailed. Once ratified by a nation it would, in accordance with the legal principle *pacta sunt servanda*, be legally binding. To be effective, it would need to contain some specific *dispute settlement* procedures, perhaps on the lines of Part IV of the Single Negotiating Text of the Law of the Sea Conference (cf. Chapter 18 and Annex 10).

In addition to laying the legal basis for the creation of a new world order, the framework treaty, which could be negotiated within the U.N. system, would carry several advantages. It would, for example, make it easier for, and might actually encourage, the governments of the industrialized democracies to go to their people on a whole range of policy choices which could be discussed in a broad perspective. It would clearly demonstrate the readiness of the industrialized countries to accept international structural change and the willingness of Third World countries to undertake, where necessary, internal reforms. Moreover, since the treaty would provide the foundations upon which the new order would be constructed, it would be difficult for the centrally planned economies to exclude themselves from its negotiation.

The Charter of Economic Rights and Duties of States (cf. section 4.1) already lays down the fundamental principles which should govern international economic relations. The transformation, over time, of the Charter into the proposed framework treaty would greatly facilitate the establishment of a new international order. If this is to be done, some more specific provisions, omitted from the Charter, should be considered for inclusion in the framework treaty. Such provisions could include:

(a) All States shall facilitate access to technology and scientific information;
(b) All States have the obligation to expand and liberalize international trade;
(c) Ocean space and the atmosphere beyond precise limits of national jurisdiction are the common heritage of all mankind: as such they shall be administered exclusively for peaceful purposes through international mechanisms with the participation of all States and their resources shall be exploited with particular regard to the interests of poor countries;
(d) Developed countries have the duty to ensure that net flows of real resources to poor countries shall not be less than the targets established by the United Nations General Assembly;
(e) No State shall allow itself to be permanently and greatly dependent on others for its basic food stuffs;
(f) All States shall encourage the rational utilization of energy, with particular attention being given to non-renewable resources, and develop new sources of non-conventional energy which would particularly contribute to reinforcing the self-sustained growth of the poorest countries;
(g) All States shall accept an internationl currency to be created by an international authority;
(h) All States shall accept the evolution of a world organization with the necessary power to plan, to make decisions and to enforce them.

The transformation of the Charter into a treaty with dispute settlement procedures would help ensure that attempts to establish a new international order are supported by the force of international law.

Notes and References

(1) In this respect it should be noted that functional problems lend themselves more easily to coordinated decision-making than broader or more general political and economic ones. During the early phases, a clear distinction should preferably be made between those relationships which can be institutionalized and those which, at least in the immediate future, must inevitably remain politicized. Even here, however, as the experience of the European Community has demonstrated, functional cooperation does not necessarily eliminate political frictions.

(2) It takes for example 1,250 gallons of water to manufacture the synthetic fibres required for one man's suit. Some 400-500 times more water are required to produce one pound of nylon than one pound of cotton.

(3) The usefulness of scientific opinion is illustrated by the experiences of the Pugwash Committee. On some of the issues of armaments control, the scientists involved reached agreement before politicians, simply because they had a sounder understanding of the subject matter, including, for instance, the discovery possibilities and limitations of nuclear testing. And in the case of current attempts to construct an ocean regime, specialist opinion has played a crucial role in shaping political opinion.

(4) The contention, for example, that citizens of the United States are indifferent to international cooperation and unaware of their dependence on others for part of their prosperity is not supported by a Harris poll taken in late 1974 for the Chicago Council on Foreign Relations. 88 per cent of the public sampled believed that the United States had 'a real responsibility to take a very active role in the world'; 88 per cent believed that international cooperation is essential if their goverment is to cope with the problems of inflation, food and energy; 87 per cent that foreign policy had a direct impact on the availability of raw materials, 59 per cent an impact on employment and 56 per cent an impact on domestic interest rates. Sixty per cent felt that the United States government should conduct its foreign policy through international organizations.

Part III: Proposals for Action

'Enough has been said about
the theory of wealth-getting;
we will now proceed to the
practical part'

Aristotle

Introduction to Part III

Part III is devoted to the main recommendations and proposals for action which have emerged from the work of the RIO group.

It comprises twelve short chapters. Chapter 8 serves as a general introduction to the proposals and deals briefly with the time frame for their implementation. Chapters 9 to 18 are devoted to proposals and recommendations for each of the ten main subject areas addressed by the RIO project. Each chapter forms a summary of the main proposals contained in the Technical Reports which together make up Part IV of this document. Readers seeking an elaboration of the proposals together with their respective underpinnings should thus consult the appropriate section of Part IV. In Chapter 19, three packages of proposals which should preferably form the subject of comprehensive negotiation are presented. These packages, formed by selectively combining proposals made in chapters 9 to 18, focus on: the need to reduce gross inequalities; the need to ensure harmonious global economic growth; and the creation of a global planning system.

8.1   *An Agenda for International Action*

The proposals and recommendations made in subsequent chapters are
presented as an agenda for phased international action. If adopted and
implemented by the international community they will help to ensure the
establishment of an equitable international social and economic order and
that a life of dignity and well-being be attained by all by the end of the
century.

Proposals are grouped according to their assumed relevance for the
medium and long range. The medium range is defined here as the first
ten years, i.e. the period 1976-1985. Long range is understood as the
period from the middle 1980's to the end of the century. Since this
report focuses on the structural changes necessary to reshape the international system, proposals of a purely short range and remedial nature
have been excluded.

In each of the ten subject areas addressed, the proposals made draw
heavily upon the discussions taking place and analyses made within the
United Nations system. The proposals are intended to selectively identify
the most urgent steps which need to be taken by the international community in the main fields relevant to the creation of a new international
order.

The order in which the subject areas are discussed is in no way meant to
suggest the importance attached to them. Essentially, this order is based
upon the historical process which led to the formation of the present international system. An attempt has been made, however, to comply with
some economic logic. For this reason, proposals for changes in financial
and monetary institutions are first presented; means of payment comprise an instrument pervading almost all activities of international
intercourse, although sometimes in an auxiliary rather than a substantive
manner.

8.2   *Long Range Proposals: Monitoring Performance and Organizing Research
Effort Required*

Although a distinction has been made between medium and long range
action, this does not mean that proposals for the latter can for the time
being be disregarded. It is true that most medium range proposals constitute the first phases of planned longer range action; that they serve
to clear the way so as to achieve the structural changes required as part
of the new international order. It is also true, however, that excessive

121

General Perspective for Proposals

The proposals listed in the following chapters should be viewed in the following general perspective.

(a) *Convincing Public and Political Opinion*   Coordinated and intensified effort should be made, particularly in industrialized countries, to publicize the need to create an international social and economic order which is perceived as more equitable by all peoples. There can be little question that unless public opinion is aware of the need for change and of the benefits that all mankind can obtain from establishing a more equitable world, progress towards a new international social and economic order will be very slow and present tensions and conflicts could result in an acute world crisis. The primary task of many non-governmental organizations must be to undertake the effort suggested.

(b) *Reform of the United Nations System*   The political and economic efficiency of the U.N. system must be improved within the context of the Charter of the U.N. which remains an invaluable guide to the world community. For the political side, the reform should aim particularly at the democratization of the operations of the Security Council. For the economic side, it should take place along most of the lines suggested by the Group of 25. An improvement in efficiency is required in order that the U.N. is able to become an effective major instrument of international political and economic cooperation for the benefit of all. Such an improvement is in fact essential to the implementation of many of the proposals listed in this report.

(c) *Ensuring World Security*   One of the vital concerns of mankind today is to make the world safe from the risk of nuclear destruction. Since there is a far greater chance of conflicts in an unjust world, it must be recognized that the implementation of the proposals made to improve equality of opportunity and to make the world increasingly more just will also simultaneously reduce chances of such conflicts. The planned and phased reduction in world defence spending, the reinforcement of the U.N. Peace Force together with the democratization of the Security Council, and the establishment of a World Disarmament Agency should contribute towards ensuring greater world security. It should also be stressed that a major effort to develop new energy sources, such as solar, geothermal and nuclear fusion, would make all countries more self-reliant and would slow greatly the proliferation of nuclear fission plants with all the associated risks to the environment and the danger of the spread of nuclear weapons.

(d) *Negotiating a Framework Treaty*   When major steps have been taken for the creation of a new world order, it could be advisable to consider the negotiation of a framework treaty based on the Charter of Economic Rights and Duties of States adopted by the United Nations in 1974. The purpose of such a treaty would be on the one hand to lay the legally binding foundation for a new structure of economic relations between all States and, on the other, to provide the legal basis for the negotiation of such international agreements as may be required for the implementation of a new world order. It is stressed in this connection that negotiation of a framework treaty should not delay implementation of the main proposals contained in this report and indeed should not be envisaged until major elements of the new order have been adopted by international agreement.

(e) *Sovereignty and the Common Heritage of Mankind*   If all are to live in a better and more stable world in which all members of the international community deal among themselves as equal partners, the first objective to be achieved is the attainment by Third World countries of full sovereignty over their resources in compliance with the U.N. Charter of Economic Rights and Duties of States. Only after this objective has been achieved can the concept of the common heritage of mankind, traditionally limited to resources considered as *res nullius* such as the oceans and outer space, be expanded to new domains such as mineral resources, science and technology, means of production and other sources of wealth. After the exercise of national sovereignty has contributed towards the creation of a more equitable international order, the aim should be to pool all world resources — material and non-material — with a view to ensuring effective planning and management of the world economy and of global resource use in a way which would meet the dual objectives of equity and efficiency. In this perspective, resources would need to be managed on the basis of decentralized planetary sovereignty (cf. section 5.8). Proposals contained in the following chapters for the application of the common heritage concept to particular fields should thus be viewed in this broader context.

concern for the immediate future can distract attention from problems as well as opportunities which could emerge many years hence.

A concern for the medium term – even more so for the short term – in no way guarantees the attainment of long range objectives. Approaches based purely on 'problem solving' will not and cannot be sufficient. Preoccupation with today's 'energy crisis', for example, might conceivably result in the expansion of nuclear energy programmes and the development of fission reactors. This may result in the satisfaction of energy needs; but at a cost that may need to be paid by future generations. It may open the door to a range of new problems – nuclear wastes, proliferation, thermal pollution and so on – about which at present we can only speculate. Concern for the long term necessitates an intensification of efforts to develop new sources of energy which, unlike nuclear fission, would appear not to carry potential threats to mankind or its environment.

Similarly, it is of utmost importance that an equilibrium eventually be established between the world's total population and the capacity of 'spaceship earth' to satisfy the needs generated in conditions of dignity and well-being. Here too we can only speculate on when and how this equilibrium can be achieved. It is clear, however, that its attainment cannot be achieved through population planning alone but rather through the creation of conditions conducive to lower birth rates on the one hand and through recognition of the need by the prosperous for modified styles and consumption patterns on the other. This, in turn, requires the implementation of a series of interrelated measures, some of which are matters of the greatest urgency. Long range attainment of global equilibrium is thus dependent on decisions taken today and tomorrow.

Two main conclusions can be drawn from the above. Firstly, it is important that an effort be made to monitor performance towards the attainment of an equitable international social and economic order; to systematically evaluate the effectiveness of the strategies adopted by the international community. The eradication of poverty, for example, a precondition for the attainment of global economic justice, requires the formulation of indicators of poverty which can serve as a basis for guiding action towards this end (cf. Chapter 10). The creation of a fairer world does not only depend upon the formulation of the right goals and objectives; it is also dependent upon the establishment of a monitoring system for measuring progress towards their attainment and which takes account of the needs, not only of today's generation, but also of the unborn.

Secondly, it follows that development centres and research institutes all over the world must devote a good deal of their time and energy to a thorough analysis of all the concrete proposals contained in this report and carry out the necessary research for this purpose. It also follows that some groups must today devote their efforts to the preparation of long range proposals in order to ensure that they will be operative on time. This applies especially to investigations into the feasibility of the more ambitious long range proposals, such as the creation of a World Treasury. It also applies to the development of new technologies since many of these have long lead times.

Chapter 9   The International Monetary Order

9.1   *Main Proposals and Recommendations*

Proposals for international monetary reform should be inspired by the consensus — or near-consensus — that had previously emerged, after more than ten years of intensive debates and negotiations, about the major shortcomings of the system and the reforms most essential to their correction.

These were clearly outlined in various official documents, and particularly in those published by the Committee of Twenty. They were unfortunately set aside in the proposed amendments to the Fund's Articles of Agreement that emerged from the January 1976 meeting of the IMF Interim Committee in Jamaica. These amendments, now in the process of ratification, glaringly ignore the problems and proposals on global liquidity, adjustment and convertibility long regarded as crucial by the negotiators themselves as well as by outside experts. They can be regarded only as a major — but, let us hope, temporary — setback in the negotiations for a viable world monetary order.

Proposals for constructive action must therefore, first and foremost, aim at the reaffirmation and implementation of the consensus that had been reached prior to the Jamaica meeting concerning the essential requirements of a new international monetary order capable of serving the obvious goals of the international community. These essential requirements are:

(a) that reserve creation should aim at adjusting the expansion of world reserves to the requirements of feasible, non-inflationary, real growth in world trade and production. It should take primarily the form of international reserve deposits with the IMF — broadly similar to, but more flexible and attractive than, the present SDRs — the amounts of which would be collectively concerted and decided upon by the international community. The interim redefinition of SDRs and the increase in interest earnings on SDR claims are a useful first step in this direction; and

(b) that the lending power derived from the acceptance of such IMF reserve deposits in settlement by the surplus countries should be used for collectively concerted and agreed objectives, with emphasis on the financing of development of the Third World. This should entail a democratic redistribution of voting power among all IMF members.

These two basic reforms obviously imply — to use the official jargon — the 'phasing out' of gold and, particularly, of national 'reserve currencies' from the international settlement and reserve system, and would help restore essential pressures for balance of payments adjustments. They should also reduce to a more manageable size, and facilitate, the official 'recycling' of the disruptive movements of private capital prompted by exchange-rate speculation and which are largely responsible for the wild, reversible, and excessive fluctuations of exchange rates in recent years and months. It is evident that other measures necessary to the reconstruction of a viable world monetary order can hardly be seriously negotiated in the absence of agreement on these basic reforms.

It should also be noted that the earlier adoption and implementation of these reforms would have prevented the wild world inflation which contributed to the explosion of oil prices, and would have provided in any case the most appropriate mechanism for the investment and 'recycling' of the temporary surpluses of the oil-exporting countries, as well as of those of all other countries. This makes all the more bizarre and regrettable – no matter how understandable in the present context – the decision to postpone, rather than accelerate, the basic monetary reforms which have repeatedly and rightly been proclaimed to be both urgent and imperative, in view of the utter collapse of the Bretton Woods system.

It is generally accepted, however, that political obstacles are likely to block, for months and even years to come, the *world-wide* negotiation of these reforms, indispensable to the creation of a new international monetary order serving all its members in a fair and constructive way, and repeatedly – even though not unanimously – endorsed in principle by the IMF, the Committee of XX, the Group of XXIV, etc. Obviously, every effort must be made to encourage the political will necessary to change this gloomy forecast.

In the meantime, feasible progress should not be sacrificed to the unanimity rule.

The most urgent recommendation must therefore be to spur the efforts and determination of all countries prepared to do so, to adopt and implement whichever of the above reforms they can put into operation unilaterally or by regional agreements. Existing and emerging regional groups – such as the European Community, the Comecon, the Central American countries, the Andean countries, the ESCAP countries, the West African countries – should do everything possible to palliate the present monetary chaos through faster progress towards their affirmed goal of closer economic and monetary cooperation and integration.

These regional arrangements should be viewed as complementary and indispensable, rather than alternative, to the long term objective of continued progress towards a world-wide monetary system. They can help serve the double, convergent need for centralization and decentralization of the world order and should facilitate the membership of centrally planned countries in the new IMF.

9.2 *Medium Range Proposals*

(a) Phasing out of national reserve currencies as well as gold from reserve creation, confining increasingly the latter to SDR type assets created by joint decisions and used for jointly agreed objectives, with emphasis on the financing of development in the Third World.

(b) Developing and enforcing guidelines for official interventions in exchange markets and better adjustment policies. Assign responsibility for market interventions, within periodically reviewed guidelines and maximum amounts — and/or provisional maximum range of fluctuations — to a permanent executive committee.

(c) Both of the above objectives to be pursued by all countries ready to accept them, especially through regional organizations, whenever not yet negotiable on a world-wide scale.

9.3 *Long Range Proposals*

World-wide agreement on an international reserve unit as common denominator for exchange rates and many international contracts and as medium of intervention, settlement and reserve accumulation for national monetary authorities. Formulation of concerted policies on truly international reserve creation aimed at promoting and sustaining feasible noninflationary growth rates of world trade and production, and use of the resulting lending potential for internationally agreed objectives, with due weight to the financing of development in the Third World (the 'link' proposal).

World-wide agreement on desirable methods for exchange-rate and/or other adjustments, especially between regional groups.

Regional currency mergers (full monetary integration) among countries which have been able: (a) to preserve stability of their mutual exchange rates through a sufficient integration of their domestic policies and adequate commitments to mutual monetary support; and (b) to consolidate and institutionalize such economic integration and financial commitments through the necessary transfers of authority from *national* to *regional* advisory and decision-making bodies, administrative and political.

10.1 *Main Proposals and Recommendations*

In an increasingly interdependent world of rising expectations and of possibly slower overall growth of output, economic policy will need to give much more attention to issues of distribution within and among nations. The implicit social compacts shaped within and among societies during the past generation were based upon the expectation that a sharing of the benefits of high world growth rates between the rich and the poor would occur. This sharing has fallen much below expectations but, with a slowing of global growth rates, there will be increased pressures to devote greater attention to the distribution of the benefits of growth and to addressing mass poverty. Such pressures can be expected to grow within societies; more predictably, they will grow between societies.

The achievement of a more equitable income distribution would be facilitated by the reduction and eventual elimination of inflation of incomes. One side of such anti-inflationary policies consists of reducing demand by limiting monetary circulation. Proposals designed to combat inflation, however, if they are to achieve the desired results, must be complemented by effective incomes policies in the industrialized countries. Without these, monetary reform could conceivably result in more unemployment which would be both socially unacceptable and economically undesirable.

Very much more is required, however, if the poorest third of the world's population — with an annual income of $ 200 per capita or less — is to have access to the bare essentials of life by the end of this century. An equitable social order requires that the worst manifestations of mass poverty be eliminated by the year 2000 and this through the application of three broad sets of measures:

(a) substantially increased transfer of resources from the rich to the poor nations — with particular attention to the use of increased concessional resources for directly addressing the problem of mass poverty in the poorest countries;

(b) increased transfer of resources from the richer and privileged minority within most Third World countries to the poor majority; and

(c) revision of the development strategies of most Third World as well as some industrialized countries with a view to paying far more attention to ensuring employment and minimum levels of nutrition, shelter and clothing, health and education, for their poorest groups.

In view of the scale of the transfers required, the often repeated claim of Third World countries, first made in 1961 and reaffirmed at the Seventh Special Session of the U.N., to fix a public aid target of 0.7 of the GNP of the industrialized countries to be achieved before 1980 seems a very modest goal.

There is encouraging recent evidence from a number of Third World countries, operating under a wide range of economic systems, that the minimum needs of human well-being can be met for the great majority of the population even under very modest per capita income levels when specific attention is given in development strategies to addressing the needs of the poor majority rather than to the indiscriminate pursuit of GNP growth objectives.

It should also be noted that unless international mechanisms are developed in poor nations which permit external resource transfers to be channelled in such a way that they contribute directly towards alleviating the worst manifestations of poverty, the case for any expansion of external resource transfers will loose much of its legitimacy. This inevitably suggests the need, in some cases, for internal structural reforms. The major burden of a nation's development effort must be borne by the nation itself; external resource transfers may contribute towards enhancing prospects for increased self-reliance but can play only a supporting role.

The three sets of measures outlined above together suggest the need for a *new framework* for international resource transfers as an essential component of strategies to establish a new world order. This framework must be based upon some internationally accepted *indicators* of poverty and need rather than upon the uncertain generosity of the rich. Indicators are required as a means of determining priorities and for ensuring the optimal distribution of transfers among deserving countries. In formulating the strategy for the Second Development Decade (DD2) indicators were drawn up on the basis of assumptions concerning the *needs, performance* and *prospects* of developing nations. Indicators should not only embrace per capita income but also include a strong social component. It is suggested that the indicators be such that they make it possible to measure progress towards attainment of the following national objectives for all countries by the end of this century: life expectancy 65 years +; literacy 75 per cent +; infant mortality 50 per 000 or below; birth rate 25 per 000 or below.

In shifting the focus of international assistance to the poorest countries and to the poorest groups within them, there is need for greater automaticity of resource generation and for a greatly increased grant component so as to avoid mounting debt service liability at extreme levels of poverty. (Higher income Third World countries require greater access to international capital markets and expanding trade opportunities rather than greater concessional assistance.) Linking international assistance to national programmes aimed at satisfying minimum human needs — however difficult it may be to define the concept precisely — would give both a focus and direction to international assistance efforts and make it a limited period affair until some of the worst evils of poverty are overcome and the ability of national governments to launch concerted and sustained attacks on poverty is expanded.

If the framework of international resource transfers is to be restructured along the lines indicated above, it follows that multilateral channels should be used for directing this assistance in preference to bilateral channels. This would be consistent with greater automaticity of resource generation, allocations based on poverty and need rather than on special relationships, and a more orderly system of burden sharing. It is also essential that the structure of international institutions be revised to enable them to work more effectively and to reflect new realities. Thus, the United Nations structure needs to be revised (the efforts now underway initiated by the report of the Expert Group of 25 may result in more effective and realistic arrangements), and the World Bank and other multilateral financial institutions need to provide for greater participation of new net donors (e.g. OPEC nations) and of recipient countries. A new resource transfer framework also requires that a major effort be made to design mechanisms whereby the richer centrally planned countries are able to play a much more substantial role than their present limited contribution.

Not only will future resource transfers have to be much higher than they are at present, but also a much higher percentage of these should take the form of *current budget expenditures*. Development financing through a current budget carries the advantage that it is not only administratively much simpler but also avoids the *debt problem*, one of today's principal financing bottlenecks. In this respect, it should be noted that the implementation of national development and social policies has been made more effective by allowing Treasuries to play a much more active role in development processes. In large well-organized nations these frequently occupy a stronger position than Central Banks and Investment Banks. Technically and organizationally, there is no reason why this trend towards expanding the role played by Treasuries should not be extended beyond national boundaries, provided, of course, that the criteria of participation, political feasibility and efficiency can be adequately met (cf. section 7.2).

These observations would suggest that, in the long run, a *World Treasury* could form an effective instrument for attaining some of the aims of an international community. In that it would operate from a current budget of expenditures, it would require a current budget of income. This could be derived from two obvious sources: revenue from *international taxes* and from the world community's *ownership of productive resources*. Taxes and incomes, profits, the use of scarce resources and the royalties received from concessions could figure among the most important types of revenue. Financial lending power could be derived from loans on the capital market, voluntary contributions from industrialized and other affluent countries and from parts of new issues of SDRs (the so-called 'link'). In particular, Third World countries with important external liquid assets should determine with other countries in this group, within the context of collective self-reliance, the ways and means of channelling a larger part of their funds for investment in one another rather than investing and depositing in the industrialized economies.

The structure of institutions sketched strongly implies national, regional and world levels of decision-making. National institutions could engage in bilateral cooperation, regional institutions in regional cooperation. The gaps existing in lower level operations would need to be filled by the results of decisions taken and operations organized at the world level. The alternatives here would also need to be judged against the criteria of participation, political feasibility and efficiency.

10.2   *Medium Range Proposals*

(a) A vigorous effort should be made to reach a concessional resource transfer target of 0.7 per cent of GNP by 1980 and to increase it to 1 per cent thereafter through various forms of international taxation and voluntary transfers.

(b) All rich nations should be required to submit a concrete time-table for the implementation of the 0.7 per cent target which should be monitored by the United Nations on behalf of the international community. Those nations unable to implement the target by 1980, because of the time already lost, should accept to compensate by much higher levels in subsequent years.

(c) An increased element of automaticity should be built into international resource generation by linking it to the creation of international liquidity and to the introduction of international taxes on undesirable forms of consumption in the rich nations and on armament spending. Efforts should be made to place at least one-half of the total resource transfers on an automatic basis over the next decade.

(d) The allocation of concessional assistance must be shifted to the poorest nations with per capita incomes below $ 200. Since these nations presently receive only one-half of total concessional assistance, there is considerable scope for reallocation from middle income Third World countries to the poorest nations and for compensating the former through larger trade concessions.

(e) These concessional resources must be directed to national programmes aimed at satisfying minimum human needs in the poorest nations. The international community should agree to provide about $ 10-12 billion a year (in 1974 prices) over the next decade for investment in basic anti-poverty programmes in collaboration with a vigorous internal effort in the poorest nations themselves who will have to ensure that these programmes are maintained.

(f) Arrangements must be made to provide a negotiating forum for an orderly settlement of the past debts of the poorest nations. The most appropriate form of debt relief would be to consolidate their past debts and to refinance them on highly concessional, IDA-type, terms.

(g) In future, assistance to the poorest nations should be provided on the most concessional terms possible. As a target, it should be accepted that at least 90 per cent of international public assistance would be provided to them in the form of either outright grants or loans on IDA term.

(h) Middle income Third World countries (above $ 200) should be provided greater access to the international capital market and expanding markets for manufactured exports. Institutional arrangements must also be made to provide them an orderly roll-over of their short term debts through the capital market and additional 'safety nets' and international liquidity to cushion them against short term fluctuations in their increasingly vulnerable balance of payments.

(i) Resource transfers should preferably be channelled through multi-lateral institutions. Besides a substantial real increase in IBRD and IDA lending and a major augmentation of the resources of the regional development banks, arrangements should also be considered to supply greater funds on intermediate terms through 'Third Window' type arrangements.

(j) The role of Third World countries, including OPEC, and of the centrally planned economies in the management of international financial institutions should be greatly increased.

(k) A mechanism should be devised to permit an orderly renegotiation of the past concessions, leases and contracts given by Third World countries to transnational enterprises. This should be done within a specified period of time under some international supervision (cf. Chapter 15).

10.3 *Long Range Proposals*

Ultimately, there is a need for the equivalent of a World Treasury, the resources of which are derived from international taxation and ownership of international productive resources (such as the resources of the oceans).

The basic objective of the World Treasury would be to promote equitable world development and the eradication of world poverty.

A target should be established to considerably reduce the existing relative income disparity between the industrialized and Third World countries by the year 2000 (cf. Chapter 6), with special attention given to the eradication of absolute poverty well before the end of this century.

11.1   *Main Proposals and Recommendations*

Without the urgent and positive intervention of the world community in potentially the most serious of all production problems, major food shortages are likely to become a permanent feature of the coming decades. Such shortages seem destined to threaten certain parts of the world — parts of Asia, Africa and certain Arab regions being particularly vulnerable — and these threats might well be exacerbated by increasing population pressures and deteriorating climatological conditions.

Plans of action to deal with the food problem must not be exclusively based upon the transfer of food from surplus to deficit nations and regions. Even if total world food production were able to keep pace with an expanding world population (100 million new mouths to feed every year), the difficulties surrounding the distribution and transportation of food, as well as the availability of means to pay for it, would be insurmountable. International food transfers — predominantly cereals — presently amount to 100 million tons annually and it would be unrealistic to assume that these could be expanded much beyond 200 million tons. Moreover, virtually all of the cereals currently involved in food transfers are produced in the industrialized countries at high cost and are energy intensive.

Although international food transfers will form a necessary component, plans of action must seek a more permanent solution to world food problems. This is to be found in the application of the principle of self-reliant development. Each nation or group of nations must strive towards *self-sufficiency in food production*, aiming at the maximization of its natural resources for meeting its basic food needs. This objective must not only be viewed as an economic imperative but also as a human and political imperative: the principles of self-reliance — underlying all development efforts — requires that nations assume full responsibility for producing their own food and minimize their dependence on others for the satisfaction of their basic needs. Since some countries will not be able to achieve the self-sufficiency objective, even in the long term, they must organize their food production efforts within the framework of regional cooperation and of collective self-reliance.

The expansion of a nation's or group of nations' food production is not exclusively a question of increasing investment, fertilizers and seeds. In many instances, it calls for *structural reforms* covering the political, social and economic aspects of agricultural development. It may require real land reform and action designed to ensure that the small farmer and landless peasant are freed from the exploitation and discrimination which are traditionally their lot and thus able to play their proper role in development processes. To be able to do this they may require the support of rural organizations active within the framework of rural development strategies.

Since self-sufficiency cannot, in many cases, be achieved in the short term, a range of transitional and supporting measures — some of a more permanent nature — will be required.

As a first priority, food production in the Third World must be increased very substantially, not only because it is here that major shortages are most likely to develop, but also because, in many cases, current yields can be increased easily at low cost. Fertilizers, new crop varieties and new tools, for example, can contribute more to overall food production when used appropriately in the Third World than when used in the industrialized countries.

While plans to transfer food from industrialized countries having surpluses to Third World countries suffering from severe shortages can serve as useful instruments in certain situations, they must be so arranged that these transfers do not interfere with programmes for increases in food production, especially in countries having significant growth potential. Transfers should be organized so as not to affect the prices received by farmers.

Since water is very often the key factor to increasing agricultural production, international capital transfers to facilitate construction of small and large scale *irrigation projects*, the largest sometimes covering several countries, can serve as a very powerful stimulus for the growth of food production.

A *price guarantee* and *production scheme* for basic foodstuffs of interest to Third World countries should be organized. The price level should be sufficiently high to act as an incentive to small farmers in the Third World in order to facilitate their adoption of improved technological practices.

Fertilizer production in the Third World should be expanded, for example, through cooperation programmes with oil-exporting countries. The proposal made by the Heads of States of OPEC in Algiers (March 1975) to supply fertilizers at cost price to countries of the Third World deserves particular consideration in this respect.

The present food situation calls for a more permanent structure to meet emergencies. World grain reserves must be built up to a higher level than those currently prevailing and made subject to increased international control. The present level of world food stocks, including working stocks, should be expanded from 100 million tons by 60-70 million tons. In financing the build-up and maintenance of adequate reserves, concessional finance might be made available to Third World countries if the resources are to be held on a decentralized basis.

Of special importance in the short term are attempts by Third World countries to reduce food wastage arising out of untreated plant diseases, pests, deficient storage and inadequate transportation arrangements. Rates of return on investments in these areas may in many cases be very considerable. Efforts to reduce post-harvest food losses should be organized with a view to reaching at least a 50 per cent reduction by 1985, as proposed and adopted by the U.N. Seventh Special Session.

More attention must be given to technical factors involved in food production, especially in the Third World. The problem here is essentially two-fold: ensuring the effective transfer of appropriate technologies from the industrialized world; and, more importantly, the development of completely new techniques and technologies specifically geared to the requirements of agricultural production processes in the countries of the Third World, especially in the tropics. These new technologies must be labour-intensive, ecologically sound, and low or medium energy intensive. New technologies are especially required for increasing yields and for purposes of irrigation and drainage and the generation of artificial rain.

Research into ways and means of expanding food production would be facilitated by the creation of *regional research institutes*, for example in Latin America, Northern, Sahalian and Central Africa, the Middle East, South East Asia and the Indian subcontinent. Such institutes would focus and coordinate research efforts on all aspects of food production in their respective regions. They would also be responsible for determining present and possible future regional food balances and monitoring performance towards the achievement of regional food self-sufficiency.

The creation of conditions conducive to a reduction of *population growth*, especially in countries or regions where progress towards high levels of self-sufficiency will be slow, and *changes in the consumption patterns* of the prosperous, are the two most powerful instruments on the demand side for bringing about an appropriate balance between food production and food requirements in the long term. With respect to the latter case, the per capita consumption of grain-intensive meats in many industrialized countries often exceeds that required for a healthy diet and absorbs part of the grains required by the poor for a minimum diet. In such countries, government should be encouraged, in the interests of their own people as well as the hungry, to reduce meat consumption, for example through the introduction of meat substitutes and replacement products and of taxes on meat consumption or on grains fed to cattle. Countries introducing such measures must devise the appropriate mechanisms for making indirect food savings available to those in need.

If the world is to be liberated from the continual nightmare of hunger and malnutrition, these and the various measures proposed by the FAO World Food Conference should be implemented to the full and call for the creation of a *World Food Authority*, with extensive and real powers; or, as a second best, the World Food Council proposed by the World Food Conference.

11.2   *Medium Range Proposals*

(a) Implementation of measures designed to enhance the self-sufficiency of Third World countries in food production within the framework of (collective) self-reliance, including, where necessary, land reform programmes.

(b) Implementation of decisions of World Food Conference: adequate stockpiling, to be furthered by pressure of agricultural organizations on governments of industrialized countries.

(c) Further contributions to the Fund for Long Term Development of Agriculture in the Third World, for which pressure can be exerted on governments of the industrialized countries by, for example, producers of fertilizer plant. Promotion of international capital transfers to facilitate the construction of small and large scale irrigation schemes, especially in tropical and sub-tropical regions.

(d) Agreements on price and production schemes for basic foodstuffs of interest to Third World countries so as to stimulate food production in the Third World. The price level should be such as to act as an incentive to small farmers in Third World countries in order to facilitate their adoption of improved technological practices.

(e) Furthering transfers of fertilizer gifts or supplies on concessionary terms to the Third World, for which pressure on governments by fertilizer producers is to be applied.

(f) Measures designed to reduce food wastage in industrialized countries, including propaganda for reduction in per capita consumption of grain-intensive meats supported by tax and price policies for meat and coarse grains. Creation of mechanisms for making savings in coarse grains available to food deficit countries.

(g) Efforts to be increased in Third World countries to reduce food wastage arising out of untreated plant diseases, pests, deficient storage and inadequate transportation arrangements. Such efforts should aim at achieving a 50 per cent reduction in post-harvest losses by 1985.

(h) Major emphasis to be given in national development strategies to rural community development with the aim of enhancing the quality of life through improved education, health care and institutional support so as to reduce the rate of urban-rural migration. Development strategies should also aim at preserving the productive capacity of women in the agricultural modernization process and at raising the incomes of the poorest city inhabitants through employment creation and income redistribution so that they can purchase their basic food requirements.

(i) Major expansion of research efforts into ways of increasing food production and related subjects. Studies to start on long term nutritional targets, at both macro- and micro-levels, as guidelines for the direction of production expansion. Efforts to be continuously made to develop newer varieties not only of cereals but also of pulses, oilseeds and vegetables and of non-traditional and new sources of food, especially food from the sea, so as to provide a nutritionally more adequate diet and to partially alleviate pressure on cereal crops. Agricultural research should be broadened to include research on the development of new agricultural technologies geared to the needs of Third World countries, on better water management, the desalinization of water and the production of artificial rain. Increased experimentation with village communities and rural development organizations, especially on the sociological and psychological levels. Research efforts would be facilitated by the establishment of rural research institutes in the main regions of the Third World.

(j) Urgent attention to be given to the creation of a monitoring system in cooperation with the World Meteorological Organization. The monitoring system should take into account not only crop forecasts but also provide a continuous assessment of changing land use patterns, including changes in the ecosphere.

11.3   *Long Range Proposals*

Following the implementation of the medium term proposals, most countries should have attained a large measure of self-sufficiency in food production, with smaller countries organizing their production within the framework of collective self-reliance policies. At such time, food production should be mainly regulated by manoeuvring with the surface areas of agriculturally productive land in the richest countries. Large scale projects designed to improve irrigation and flood prevention in the large Asian deltas, to develop production in arid and semi-arid lands, and to improve and expand (local) transportation networks should be implemented. These projects will require heavy investments and will to a large extent need to be financed by international means.

Emergency stocks of food grains of several hundred million tons will need to be held in the world's main regions. These will especially by required to offer safeguards against possibly deteriorating climatic conditions.

Population pressure on food supplies should, following the implementation of the various measures contained in this report, gradually be alleviated.

12.1   *Main Proposals and Recommendations*

Future developments in these areas should aim at the eradication of mass poverty and unemployment and at guaranteeing the ability to satisfy basic human needs — especially food and shelter — through the optimum utilization of human and physical resources in the world as a whole. This entails the most efficient production and equitable distribution of goods and services and their accessibility to users within the limits imposed by the natural environment and within the framework of the global objectives of a new international order. It also entails the rational use of non-renewable resources and the development of alternative patterns of production and consumption and of programmes of exploitation and substitution.

The current pattern, practices and institutions in the fields of international trade and industrialization have evolved essentially from the requirements and according to the various interests of the industrialized countries. The present international division of labour is in reality neither universal in coverage nor does it conform to a set of rational and global objectives. One of the objectives of the new international order must thus be to aim at the establishment of a truly optimal and dynamic international division of labour — optimal in terms of growth and of distribution.

It should be noted that the expression 'international division of labour' refers to the geographical location of economic activities in the world, or to 'what is produced where'. This is frequently misunderstood to mean a static redistributive device which implies a shift of existing manufacturing infrastructure from one country to another. The expression 'international division of labour' is used here in a much more dynamic sense: the progressive shift in the pattern of production between regions and countries over time, so that all will benefit from changing comparative advantages and specializations.

The main objectives in the field of industrialization are contained in the Declaration and Plan of Action resulting from the Second General Conference of UNIDO held in Lima in March 1975. The Declaration and Plan, endorsed by the Seventh Special Session of the U.N. General Assembly, call for the expansion of the share of Third World countries in world industrial production from 7 per cent as at present to 25 per cent by the year 2000. To attain this and related objectives there is a need for a new framework of rules and institutions to regulate and encourage industrialization, trade and development. This is required to eliminate patterns and practices which have evolved essentially on the basis of bilateral and group interests, many of which are incompatible with the attainment of an equitable international economic and social order.

The Declaration and Plan stress the need for establishing an international system of consultations and agreements between industrialized and Third World countries as regards policies and investments in the industrial field. These should also increase the multilaterality of trade relations and include systems of commitments, surveillance and obligatory arbitration related to specific aspects of production and trade, not only for industry but also for agriculture.

This may effectively lead to the establishment through agreements of an *international industrialization strategy* comprising a set of world programmes aimed especially and whenever possible at the regional level. Such programmes would assist nations in formulating consistent industialization policies and could serve as a basis for negotiations with other parties, especially transnational enterprises. They should also include measures designed to attain a more rational management of raw materials, minerals and basic industrial commodities, especially in situations of scarcity or in cases of fears for depletion. Codes of conduct could also be drafted as part of the strategy and agreed upon internationally. They could cover such areas as specific trade procedures, the transfer of technology, normalization, the transfer of capital and of managerial and technological skills. Nations participating in such codes must naturally assume certain internal responsibilities with respect to their enforcement. The implementation of such a strategy would require supporting procedures and facilities for the identification and financing of viable projects, preferably on a competitive basis, so as to create a 'market' for industrialization projects.

Third World countries in formulating their industrialization policies will, with due consideration to differences in factor endowment and stages of deveopment, need to give priority to the creation of employment and to the production of the goods required to satisfy basic human needs, the processing of local materials and the expansion of exports of manufactured goods. Such policies should include measures which provide the poorest population groups with the necessary purchasing power – through employment creation and income redistribution – to acquire the basic goods and services produced and should form part of national development plans which cover industrial interlinkages. Opportunities for the expansion of exports of manufactured goods to the markets of the industrialized countries should be accorded, whenever feasible, a high priority so as to pay, in part, for the acquisition of capital goods and knowledge-intensive goods. Utilization of these opportunities would contribute towards the eventual development of intra-industry trade with the industrialized countries in manufactured goods.

Appropriate measures will need to be taken in the field of development, adaption and transfer of technology (cf. Chapter 14). New technologies specifically geared to the needs of Third World countries will need to be developed, especially since a *dual system of technology* – the use of different levels of technology for different sectors – will most likely have to be maintained in most Third World countries so as to cater simultaneously for employment generation on the one hand and for industrial growth and the expansion of exports of manufactured goods on the other. If the growth rates required to attain the Lima industrial production objectives are achieved, this duality may disappear within the next decade or two. A plan to establish an *International Industrialization Institute* has been under examination by some industrialized countries and was recently recommended to the U.N. General Assembly by the United States' delegation.

The industrialized countries, on their part, will have to introduce *policies of adjustment*, develop specialization in knowledge-intensive products and gradually introduce and enforce environmental protection standards. This implies a further reduction or even abolition of the tariffs imposed by the industrialized countries on the semi-manufactured and manufactured products of the Third World, a trend that would contribute towards combating inflation in the industrialized countries. Likely to be of even greater importance is a *reduction of non-tariff barriers* since these form a major hindrance to intra-industry trade. If this is not possible without the inclusion of some escape clauses, it should be ensured that temporary protection mechanisms are *degressive*, i.e. are in accordance with a specific time-table and strictly connected with adjustment measures.

Endeavours to improve the international division of labour should not be concentrated exclusively on industry but also embrace the agricultural sector. Here, the first step should be to identify the products which different countries are presently producing or could potentially produce *with comparative advantage* in a dynamic and development oriented context. Agricultural policies should then be organized so as to encourage the production of these products and induce the reallocation of resources respectively. At the same time, trade policies must gradually bring about free access to the markets of all agricultural products. In addition, they should aim at multilaterally negotiated insurances, such as contracts guaranteeing to every country a minimum supply of essential foodstuffs. The objectives of these contracts could even be enlarged, aiming at for example lowering price fluctuations and raising floor prices for the products of Third World countries. It is clearly of importance that the centrally planned economies be included in attempts to shape a new international division of labour in the fields of both industry and agriculture.

The integrated commodity programme launched by UNCTAD forms an example of what might be done. In any event, the principal objective to be achieved is to regulate the prices of the main exports of Third World countries in such a way as to continually improve the derived purchasing power in terms of the prices of imports from the industrialized countries. Means to achieve this include indexation, compensatory financing, greater control of and participation in down stream activities — local processing, storage and banking, transport and marketing processes. The achievement of the objective and the application of the various means could form the responsibility of a *World Trade and Development Organization* formed by expanding the activities and competence of UNCTAD — as suggested by the Manilla Conference of the Group of 77.

In order to achieve *full multilateralism* in trade relations, an extensive exchange of information and consultation and cooperation on the inter-governmental level are required. The existing institutional framework, namely the United Nations Economic Commission for Europe, UNCTAD, UNIDO and their Secretariats should broaden appropriately the scope of their activities.

12.2 *Medium Range Proposals*

(a) Intensification and, where possible, conclusion of international consult-ations to arrive at more multilaterality in trade relations.

(b) Reduction of import impediments vis-à-vis semi-manufactured and manufactured products from the Third World, with the aid of pressures of Consumer Unions on their governments for this purpose.

(c) Implementation of the UNCTAD integrated programme on commod-ities, in particular unstable markets to be regulated with a common fund to finance the necessary buffer stocks or through compensatory financing so as to regulate export incomes as appropriate.

(d) Transform UNCTAD into a comprehensive World Trade and Devel-opment Organization with the task of regulating the prices of the main exports of Third World countries with a view to continually improving the derived power in terms of the prices of imports from the industrialized countries. This to be achieved through the application of a range of means designed to increase Third World particpation in and control of down stream activities — local processing, storage and banking, transport and marketing processes.

(e) Increase in the negotiating power of Third World countries through control over their natural resources and the intensification of their efforts towards collective self-reliance.

(f) Establishment of a world strategy and policies and programmes of industrial development so as to achieve the Lima industrial production objectives including adjustment policies in the industrialized countries; regional cooperation in industrialization programmes. Industrial redeployment should be considered a principal instrument of such programmes.

(g) Review the feasibility of the International Industrialization Institute recently recommended to the U.N. General Assembly.

(h) Integrate employment and income distribution objectives in national and international industrialization strategies.

12.3   Long Range Proposals

A full employment policy should be adopted by all governments as part of their development plan. Trade policies cannot be decided upon at national or even regional levels: they are a matter subject to obligatory arbitration, as already envisaged in the Havana Charter for the International Trade Organization. Protection is reduced *pari passu* with a country's level of development.

By the horizon year of 2000, the Lima Conference objective concerning the 25 per cent share of world industrial production by Third World countries should have been attained. At such time, the qualitative aspects of a genuine industrialization policy must come to the fore as a result of the introduction of a more equitable international intra-sectoral division of labour.

Chapter 13   Energy, Ores and Minerals

13.1   *Main Proposals and Recommendations*

Although fears expressed in recent years for the rapid exhaustion of
natural resources appear, on the basis of available data, to be in some cases
exaggerated, this must not be interpreted as freedom to continue to
squander our natural heritage. The continued availability of natural
resources will depend upon, firstly, their rate of exploitation which is
intimately linked to the evolution of consumption patterns in the industrialized countries and, secondly, the results of technological research and
development into new production processes, substitutes and reserve
location methods. There is cause for concern in both cases. With respect to
the latter, it is important not to fall into the easy optimism that technological solutions to natural resource problems will necessarily appear in
time. The lead time for new technologies to become operative in this field
is long, (in the order of 10-20 years) and since changes are occurring at
such a rapid rate there is a danger that appropriate technological responses
might not be able to keep pace with natural resource problems.

In recent years, Third World countries have increasingly tended towards
assuming full territorial sovereignty and control over their natural
resources, especially those in the hands of transnational enterprises. In that
this development reduces imbalances in the present international power
structure, it must be deemed, in the short term, compatible with attempts
to shape an equitable international economic and social order. Third World
countries have also more vigorously pursued long standing aspirations to
process locally the materials they produce, to expand their share in down
stream operations, and thus to obtain a higher share of the final price paid
by consumers in the industrialized countries. These developments
have brought many in the industrialized countries, some of which are
strongly dependent on raw materials imports from the Third World, to
the conclusion that changes are necessary in present patterns of investment, production, trade and research and development of mineral resources from the viewpoint of the needs of their own societies.

The question of natural resources in general and energy in particular is a
North-South issue in that the position taken by the oil-exporting countries
has set off a round of global negotiations between industrialized and Third
World countries. Natural resources, however, are not exclusively a North-
South issue. Mineral resources are not distributed evenly over the face of
the earth: many industrialized countries are major producers of some
minerals and many Third World countries are deficient in mineral endowment. Essentially, then, the issues are two-fold; the increase in the

revenues received by Third World countries from exports of raw materials so as to arrive at a more equitable international income distribution; and the creation of the necessary safeguards for uninterrupted supply for consumer countries.

Plans of action in the field of raw materials must take account of the following:

(a) Producer countries should receive for their products a fair proportion of the prices paid by consumers. Market organization and price formation should be studied in order to determine the benefits which could be derived by producers through local processing, by the elimination of market imperfections and excessive trade margins, by better credit facilities and distribution systems.

(b) Large fluctuations should be avoided. Price stabilization or indexation should not form a pretext for avoiding higher prices where these are reasonable. Unstable markets, such as those of mineral resources, should be subject to regulation through international agreement.

(c) Consumer countries must be provided with the safeguards which guarantee uninterrupted supply.

(d) Producer associations for primary commodities should be accepted as legitimate instruments of collective bargaining. These should prepare for negotiations prior to meeting with consumer countries. In a situation of unequal power on both sides of the market, this procedure may enhance the power of the weaker party.

The creation, as part of the proposed World Trade and Development Organization (cf. Chapter 12), of a *World Agency for Mineral Resources*, is recommended. This agency would be responsible for supervising agreements entered into by governments. More specifically, it would be responsible for:

(a) Coordinating and continuing the activities of agencies specialized in individual products and arranging for agreements on products not yet covered.

(b) Compiling and circulating information on known reserves, reserves likely to be exploitable in the future, ten-year trends in operating costs and in demand. This information will be useful to public and private concerns in formulating their prospecting and exploration programmes.

(c) Periodically putting forward comments and suggestions to countries on the conduct of their mining policies, with individual countries retaining full sovereignty and complete freedom to reject such suggestions.

(d) Compiling and circulating information on commercial transactions.

In the long term, and assuming progress towards the creation of an equitable international economic and social order leading to a pooling of material and non-material world resources, mineral resources will need to be viewed as a common heritage of mankind. This concept implies both a real world market for all mineral resources and a system of world taxation to replace national mining taxation. The revenues collected should be redistributed among Third World countries — possibly through such an agency as IDA —according to certain criteria (taking account of, for example, the size of population, the need to eradicate mass poverty and to satisfy basic human needs, income redistribution projects, etc.) and which would not necessarily exclude the producing countries themselves.

This tax could, for instance, be introduced as one of a moderate rate and gradually be raised to something in the order of 70 per cent of profits on fossil fuels and 50 per cent of the value of production of ores (including uranium).

Such a tax would, like the present taxes on oil products, in fact be paid by the consumers. It would have three advantages as compared with higher prices:

(a) it would help all Third World countries, whilst a price increase only improves the situation of producer countries (which includes some of the most industrialized);

(b) it would not disequilibrate the market, since it would not raise the price received by producers and hence not raise production beyond demand;

(c) it would not affect the relative competitive situation of one mineral in comparison to others.

Such a tax, at the rates proposed, would probably induce consumers to restrict their consumption of mineral raw materials (economizing on their use, recycling and substitution by non-mineral materials, etc.). A slight slowing down of the sales of mineral resources by Third World countries could result, but the revenue of the tax, which they would share, would enable them to create other industries, or to embark upon further exploration of their resources.

With regard to *energy* resources, future needs are subject to opposing forces: on the one hand, savings in the excessive use of energy may emerge in the industrialized countries as a result of slower rates of economic growth and the implementation of energy conservation programmes; and on the other, the industrialization and development of the Third World will result in a greatly increased demand for energy. New technologies required for processing low-grade ores and for securing future supplies of fresh water may also result in increased energy demands.

A considerable effort will need to be made to develop new energy sources capable of replacing finite supplies, such as oil, gas and even coal. This effort is in the interest of all countries, of the Third as well as of the industrialized world. Given the considerable lead time required for the practical development of new resources, the efforts currently being made need to be intensified. The forms of nuclear energy used at present carry some heavy risks, such as the dangers of proliferation and the threats they may pose to the world's climate. Interdisciplinary research and policies related to economic and, for example, environmental matters should be concentrated on such alternative energy sources as geothermal, solar, tidal, and nuclear fusion as well as small scale non-conventional sources, such as biogas. Failure to pursue these alternatives could result in the expansion of breeder programmes with consequent high risk of plutonium theft and diversion as well as grave environmental hazards. These consequences appear to be of such a magnitude that they must weigh heavily against the spread of such programmes.

The creation of a *World Energy Research Authority*, within the framework of the United Nations, might prove the most effective means for intensifying research activities and for functionally integrating the various existing organizations, national and international, active in the energy field. Its activities might in part be financed by revenues derived from a tax on the kilowatt hours of nuclear fission energy produced, so as to establish the necessary link between the expansion of nuclear fission energy programmes and the volume of energy research.

13.2 *Medium Range Proposals*

(a) Urge the negotiation of commodity agreements with a view to stabilizing production, markets and the prices in real terms of the most important mineral raw materials.

(b) Encourage and accept the formation of producers' associations in primary commodities which, as legitimate instruments of collective bargaining, can help offset the considerable concentration of economic power presently vested in the buying end.

(c) Urgent examination of the present marketing and price structure of primary commodities to determine the advantages which can be derived by

Third World producer countries from, for example, the further processing of primary commodities and participation in down stream activities.

(d) Creation, as part of the proposed World Trade and Development Organization, of a World Agency for Mineral Resources with the following tasks: preparation and supervision of future commodity agreements; compilation and circulation of information on commercial transactions, ore reserves and trends in their exploitation; and putting forward comments and suggestions to countries on their mining policies.

(e) Expand information on endowment with ores; internationalization of information derived from earth satellites.

(f) Intensification of research into recycling possibilities, especially of non-renewable resources, and the expansion of recycling activities shown to be feasible and environmentally sound.

(g) Strongly stimulate research on geothermal, solar, tidal, biogas and nuclear fusion energy, possibly coordinated by a World Energy Research Authority (within U.N. framework) and partly financed by revenues derived from a tax on the kilowatt hours of nuclear fission energy produced.

(h) Implementation of measures to save energy in energy-intensive countries and to better use waste low grade heat, including the recuperation of part of heat losses, particularly from thermal power plants.

(i) Expansion of research into the thermal pollution consequences associated with energy development programmes, concentrating on their effects on climate and including the role which can be played by deep ocean waters.

13.3   *Long Range Proposals*

After the exercise of national sovereignty by Third World countries over their natural resources has helped to establish more equality between mineral producing and consuming countries, a switch to the concept of the 'common heritage of mankind' is recommended and a gradual transformation of the principle of territorial sovereignty into functional sovereignty. This must be viewed as the most desirable approach to the world management of natural and other resources, material and non-material.

Future policies must focus upon the maintenance of a remunerative price to producers, a non-disrupted foreseeable supply of the resources covered, and the avoidance of heavy price fluctuations. The proposed

World Agency for Mineral Resources, to be established in the next ten years as part of the World Trade and Development Organization, will have a more operational role to play in the long term in managing resources and, more precisely, in managing a real world market for all mineral resources and a system of world taxation so as to partly replace national mining taxation. The revenues so collected should be redistributed to Third World countries in recognition of the fact that mineral resources are a common heritage and all must benefit from their exploitation.

Recycling of a much larger proportion of non-renewable resources will need to become customary; technological development must continually aim at adding new forms of recycling.

As for energy, it is hoped that it will prove possible to avoid nuclear fission and to switch to solar radiation and nuclear fusion as the main sources; this hope can be reinforced by the adoption of the much larger research effort advocated. The use of hydrogen as an ecologically attractive and easy to transport energy bearer is another long range energy alternative which should be seriously investigated.

Chapter 14   Scientific Research and Technological Development

14.1   *Main Proposals and Recommendations*

Scientific research and its application in technology are fundamental to the development process. The new international order, in attempting to overcome the enormous disparities in research and development capability existing between the industrialized and Third World countries, must fulfill four main requirements:

(a) the access of Third World countries to technological know-how must be greatly improved;

(b) the research capacity of the Third World must be greatly increased through the establishment and expansion of high quality research institutes organized on a national, sub-regional and regional basis;

(c) the industrialized countries should devote a greater proportion of their research and development to the problems of the Third World; and

(d) priority under (a) and (b) must be directed towards meeting the needs of the world's poor majority.

Since applied research is more important for development than fundamental research, the type of research to which improved access is desirable can often be supplied by private enterprises in the industrialized countries. The knowledge concerned, however, is generally carefully guarded and subject to international patent law. The governments of the industrialized countries are in no position to force their industries to part with their technological property which, in many cases, has involved exceedingly high research and development costs and which determines their competitive position in both domestic and international markets. As a result, Third World countries must generally purchase technological knowledge in national and international markets; private firms must charge a price for the knowledge which covers their costs and which allows them a reasonable profit required for investment in their own future research activities.

There is considerable scope for improvement in this situation. Negotiations between the market economy industrialized countries could be aimed, for example, at the establishment of agreed, preferential terms for the sale of various categories of patents and know-how to Third World countries or of policies whereby the governments of such countries subsidize the sale of technological property to Third World countries as part of their official development assistance policy. Such *subventioned research* should concentrate on production processes which, in general, are neither too sophisticated nor capital intensive, which call for the maximum utilization of local raw materials, and which enhance a country's prospects for satisfying human needs and self-reliant development. Transnational enterprises could serve as the means for making the results of research available to recipient countries.

An increase in research and development activity does not automatically result in an increase in economic performance. This is largely determined by the kind of research undertaken and the conditions for assimilating research results in the development process. Attention must of necessity focus on the process of technological innovation in which R&D, whether indigenous or imported, is viewed as an initial though essential input. *National policies for science and technology* should therefore be elaborated in articulation with economic, social, educational and other policies. It is extremely important that Third World countries, in the evolution of their technoligical capacities, should not regard policies in this field as autonomous but rather link them with economic and social policies and plans in an organic fashion.

Deliberate policies for technological development related to long term social and economic objectives imply the existence of detailed knowledge on the process of technological innovations and a capacity to select the appropriate processes. Experience has shown, however, that, when lacking sufficient knowledge of world scientific and technological trends, it is easy for a country to innovate at high cost to obsolescence. Ability to select the appropriate processes would be greatly enhanced by the creation of *technological knowledge registers* covering technology which might be imported together with its social and economic values, its training needs and the behaviour and efficiency of the various firms selling the technology. Such international organizations as UNCTAD and UNIDO should engage further in the compilation of such registers.

The second important requirement is to establish an *indigenous capacity for research and development.* This is essential for long term purposes, since otherwise countries depending on imported technology will always be running several decades behind the technologically active countries. Unless a country is able, through its own research activities, to achieve an awareness of the significant developments of world science it is unlikely to reach a threshold of technical awareness which enables it to select, negotiate the purchase and ensure the effective assimilation of the technology which its economic and social objectives require. It is thus of considerable importance that *high quality research institutes*, with high level manpower training programmes, be established and expanded in the Third World. These should be organized on a national, sub-regional and regional basis and should give special attention to research in such fields as nitrogen fixation for grains, pest resistant crop varieties, schistosomiasis and river blindness in arid and semi-arid lands. The creation of an indigenous research and development capacity, mentioned in the Development Strategy for the Second Development Decade, also provides a powerful means to counteract the 'brain-drain', one of the major problems of Third World countries. Financing of this capacity should be one of the main objectives of international financial transfers (cf. Chapter 10).

The third requirement is that new and existing research institutes must focus their efforts on the *needs of the poor* and seek innovative responses to raising the opportunities for self-reliant development, especially at the *local level.* Research should also focus less on the improvement and adaptation of technologies developed in the industrialized world and more on the development of completely new technologies specifically geared to the requirements of each country and its factor endowment, and, where appropriate, related to the traditional technologies used by local populations.

Two major reforms are proposed which would not only make international cooperation in research and development more efficient, but also help ensure that Third World countries are able to participate in major decisions taken in this field and have improved access to the results of research and development work.

The first proposal aims at making the research and advisory functions of the United Nations, its Specialized Agencies and Programmes, more relevant, effective and coherent than the somewhat fractional and ineffective performance of today. To achieve this, it is suggested that the strategic and planning functions in this field of the United Nations itself should be strengthened to make possible a clear formulation of major objectives and priorities for research, considered within a socio-economic framework and with due recognition of the conflicts and reinforcements likely to result in meeting those objectives sector by sector. This would be followed by a planning and programming exercise which the United Nations' Agencies and Programmes would undertake together to determine the broad lines of a coherent U.N. *research and development programme.* They would delegate responsibility for the carrying out of the various elements to the various organizations themselves, making use, not only of the in-house capacities of the various cooperating units, but also by using the most appropriate facilities, whether national or international.

Secondly, it is suggested that many of today's problems and deficiencies could be resolved through the creation of a *World Technological Development Authority*, backed up by an *International Bank for Technological Development.* The authority, which could be formed by expanding the powers and competence of an existing international institution, would not be an operational agency, undertaking work itself, but rather a planning and programming body which would carry out feasibility studies, devise the detailed programmes, arrange their implementation, by contract with the most appropriate organizations in each specific case — research institutions, corporations, state enterprises and/or universities — supervise the progress of the work and act as custodian of the resulting technological projects on behalf of all nations. The advantages to Third World countries would be their association in the planning stages, their joint ownership of the property and long term benefits of training and of intimate knowledge of new techniques and know-how through the association of their nationals in the specific projects.

These two suggestions might serve as subjects for discussion at the U.N. Conference on Science and Technology, to be held in 1979.

14.2 *Medium Range Proposals*

(a) Promotion of a system of subsidizing prices at which technological know-how can be made available to Third World countries. Such subsidized research should focus on increasing the ability of Third World countries to expand employment opportunities, to satisfy basic needs and to promote self-reliant styles of development.

(b) Organization of a pool of technological information (a register of such knowledge) which can be used by governments of the Third World in their negotiations on technology transfer and in their efforts at formulating deliberate policies for technological development organically linked to the attainment of social and economic objectives; this should result from cooperation between the U.N. agencies involved.

(c) The elaboration of an international code of conduct for the transfer of technology under different forms and the revision of the Paris Convention on the protection of industrial property in the light of the development needs of Third World countries.

(d) Appropriate reexamination and reinforcement of the U.N. system. Urgent attempts to be made to formulate coherent programmes of scientific research and technological development; such programmes to give due attention to developments within the U.N. system and to be drawn up as a cooperative endeavour by the specialized agencies. Such programmes should contribute towards the improvement of the efficiency of such agencies; the planned U.N. Conference on Science and Technology should be directed, among other ends, to this improvement of efficiency.

(e) High quality research institutes with high level manpower training programmes must be established and expanded in the Third World, especially in arid and semi-arid regions, on a national, sub-regional and regional basis in order to focus research on the problems of poor countries and to reduce the 'brain-drain'. Special priority should be given to research of particular benefit to the poorest groups within countries and regions. Examples of such research include nitrogen fixation for grains, pest resistant crop varieties, schistosomiasis and river blindness in arid and semi-arid lands. Emphasis should also be placed on the development of 'appropriate' technologies.

14.3   *Long Range Proposals*

Forty years hence, it is assumed that there will be a more equitable distribution of research and development effort between different parts of the world, with the emergence of high quality research centres organized on both a national and international basis in countries now constituting the Third World. A large proportion of the total scientific and technological effort in both industrialized and Third World countries should be concerned with problems of human welfare rather than with military matters, national prestige, and in support of a consumption economy as at present. Furthermore, a considerable body of research should be devoted to problems of an inherently global character, through programmes agreed internationally, although not necessarily carried out in international laboratories.

World technological development is likely to increase considerably in cost and the global needs for new technology will call for cost-sharing; the proposed World Technological Development Authority with its Bank will provide an institutional framework for this. By this time also, considerable progress should have been made in evolving efficient, labour-intensive technologies which should reinforce cultural diversity. Much of the new research will inevitably need to be of a multidisciplinary and systems character and this will require much modification in educational and research structures and attitudes.

Ultimately, science and technology must be viewed as the common heritage of mankind.

15.1 *Main Proposals and Recommendations*

Because of their growing size, expanding areas of activities, globalization process, increasing concentration and productive factors they control, transnational enterprises have considerable power in forging the structure of national and international development. This power implies that, in pursuing their normal business activities, their decisions are able to influence the societies in which they operate in a number of non-business ways. By the very act of investing in a foreign country they are able to create conditions for international disputes. This has led to cases of subversive political interventions, acute confrontations over the exercise of the right to nationalize, use of businessmen as cover for intelligence activities, political and economic retaliation by home governments, situations where affiliates of transnational enterprises have been subjected to unilateral measures by host governments, conflicts of jurisdiction and a number of politically related problems.

Under these conditions, and from the viewpoint of a new international order, the basic problem to be resolved is what functions transnational enterprises are to perform in the future and according to which criteria these functions will be defined at national and international levels. As noted in section 3.9, transnational enterprises have accumulated vast technological and marketing knowledge and have developed a highly effective process of transnational decision-making. These capacities can play a positive role in improving the living conditions of the poor masses in the Third World insofar as they comply with rules, formulated nationally and internationally, directed towards this end.

The possibility of setting limits to corporate size and to the process of concentration should be investigated. Criteria which could serve as guidelines for this should be developed. Linked to this is the question of social control and accountability of transnational enterprises. The concept of efficiency or optimum size can vary considerably when judged by public (i.e. social costs) as distinct from private criteria. It is not a question of eliminating private property but of controlling private by public rationale in shaping research and production priorities.

Governments of 'host countries' should base their negotiations with transnational enterprises on a socio-economic policy in which the interests of the poor are strongly represented. Their principal aim should be to pursue a less unequal distribution of purchasing power thereby enabling low-income groups to buy the goods required to satisfy their basic needs. Such a policy should be expressed in a *development plan*, the objectives of which the transnational enterprises should comply with.

In order that the activities of transnational enterprises result in the effective and appropriate increase in the GNP of the host country, in the strengthening of its industrial basis, and in the maximization of local value added, adequate management in the economic, financial, commercial and technological fields should be exercised by the enterprises in compliance with the policies of the host country and under its control. To ensure that the activities of transnational enterprises result in the creation of as much employment as possible, *appropriate technologies* should be chosen and thus form the subject of negotiation. In order that governments can effectively conduct such negotiations, their access to technological knowledge must be improved. Governments of the industrialized countries should be encouraged to subsidize the prices at which transnational enterprises are able to make available the most relevant technologies (cf. Chapter 14).

The power position of Third World countries in their negotiations with transnational enterprises must be increased. It would be enhanced through the formation of regional groupings, such as the Andean and similar groups, and of producers' associations. Such groupings and associations can establish joint investment codes for the purpose of organizing negotiations with transnational enterprises. Codes should address themselves to such questions as ownership and control, financial flows and balance of payments, research and development, commercialization of technology, employment and labour, consumer protection, competition and market structure, transfer pricing, taxation, accounting standards and disclosure. In formulating the codes, particular attention should be given to exploring the following policy alternatives: limits to direct or indirect profit remittances; orientation of research and development towards labour-intensive activities; use of transnational enterprises as consultative rather than productive entities, as direct investors or suppliers under contract to state or other local partners of plant equipment, production technology, and/or market outlets; elimination of discriminatory tax exemptions; restriction of the use of the local capital market to local enterprises; strict control of intra-company transactions; and minimum disclosure standards.

The only suitable agreements between governments and transnational enterprises are equilibrated agreements. This requires greater transparency and larger disclosure of the activities of transnational enterprises. A systematic renegotiation after a certain period and immediate renegotiation of palpably unequal contracts should be considered.

The international community could apply several instruments to influence the relative power positions. One instrument is to have labour and consumer representatives serve on the board of the enterprise together with representatives of − public or private − capital owners. A start could be made along these lines in, for example, the transports or the pharmaceutical industry. Another instrument is the creation of public international enterprises, for example, to exploit ocean resources. A third would be a *code*, with legally enforceable elements, of internationally agreed upon *minimum standards of behaviour* and criteria for the assessment of *maximum size* concerning transnational enterprises. Although all transnational enterprises respond to similar motivation patterns, too strict generalizations can be misleading. When dealing individually with them differences in behaviour emerge reflecting such factors as: the size and power of their country of origin; their policies of research and development; location; the nature of their internal decision-making process; the extent to which political pressure or illegitimate practices are resorted to; and their ability to adapt to local circumstances. This suggests that an international register of individual enterprises should be set up in order to be able to pin-point specifically, with respect to each individual company, the positive and negative aspects of their activities in a disaggregated manner. An international body of voluntary technical advisors could assist in the compilation of such a register as well as advise on a number of other issues related to transnational enterprises.

The effective handling of some of the conceivable instruments at the disposal of the international community would be facilitated by the establishment of an *International Authority on Transnational Enterprises*. This might most appropriately be formed by expanding the powers and competence of an existing agency. In any event, as a 'countervailing power', trade unions should be afforded a role in the conduct of the authority.

A follow-up of the work of the U.N. Group of Eminent Persons might consider these various suggestions.

15.2 *Medium Range Proposals*

(a) Agreement to be negotiated on minimum information to be supplied by transnational enterprises on their activities, employment created, total and local capital attracted, investment per capita and some technology characteristics (productivity, capital intensity, as compared with countries of origin).

(b) Building up a pool of technological knowledge (cf. Chapter 14) to service governments of the Third World in negotiations with transnational enterprises, and a register of performance of transnational enterprises in different countries.

(c) Compliance by transnational enterprises with the host nation's development plan, which specifies the aims of highest urgency such as the creation of employment, the increase in food production and the redistribution of incomes.

(d) Research on alternative ways of performing the function of trans-national enterprises including public international enterprises.

(e) Increased cooperation between governments to establish counter-vailing power and to make tax structures more uniform.

(f) Increased cooperation of transnational enterprises with the U.N. Research and Information Centre. Creation of an international body of voluntary technical advisors.

(g) Formulation of a Code of Conduct, with legally enforceable elements, on transnational enterprises so as to meet the most urgent needs of the host countries. This code should address such questions as ownership and control, financial flows, local value-added and balance of payments, research and development, commercialization of technology, employment and labour, consumer protection, competition and market structure, transfer pricing taxation, accounting standards and disclosure, and refrain-ing from intervening in a host country's political affairs.

15.3   *Long Range Proposals*

In the long term, transnational enterprises will still form part of the world structure, in either their present form of private enterprises or in a renovated form comprising genuine international ventures. Multinational ventures of different varieties are natural whenever different nations can be suppliers of complementary production factors.

The statutes of transnational enterprises should be under the supervision of, and their profits taxed by, an inter- or supranational authority. Trans-national enterprises should form a part of an international framework of concrete economic activities and their labour conditions should be negotiated with representative national and international trade unions.

16.1   *Main Proposals and Recommendations*

The Stockholm Conference of June 1972 proclaimed environment — the global habitat of man — a matter of continuous concern for the nations of the world and set up in the form of the United Nations Environment Programme embryonic machinery to deal with this newly recognized dimension both of development and international affairs. In the long series of U.N. conferences, Stockholm stands thus high for its success in identifying a new global problematique and in reaching North-South consensus on ways of approaching it. Confrontation was avoided. Both sides grasped that they were living on *only one earth* and that the existence of international commons — oceans, sea-bed, weather and climate — as well as the finiteness of spaceship earth, were binding them into a pattern of real interdependence.

Failure to take this into account, given the unprecedented scale of human interference with nature and ecological balances, might prove disastrous to all. Egoistic policies of resource appropriation by the rich minority, the dumping of waste into seas progressively transformed into cesspools and the release of ever increasing quantities of heat, must give way to the more balanced management of world resources and environment. Balanced management must aim simultaneously at waging an immediate battle against poverty and at safeguarding the interests of future generations through the legacy of a habitable planet. Both are predominantly political and not technical issues; both belong to attempts to shape a new international order.

The combined effects of industrialization, population growth and urbanization witnessed in the twentieth century, and more particularly so since the end of the Second World War, lifted the Gross World Product to a level undreamt of by the generation of our grandfathers. At the same time, however, they magnified the income differentials between rich and poor. They also brought us nearer to the brink of irreversible ecological disasters and the depletion of some essential resources. Can we afford to continue undisturbed along this path, piling up wealth, maldistribution and ecological hazards?

These questions were raised in a dramatic (and possibly overdramatized) way by the 'Limits to Growth' report and several other more or less apocalyptic writings. All of them stem from the trivial and indisputable observation that exponential growth in a finite environment cannot last for ever.

The question, however, is not whether outer limits, the transgression of which would be fatal, do exist at all. Unless one indulges in wild and totally unwarranted technological optimism, their existence can be taken for granted. Instead, we should try to ascertain how close we have moved to them and, still more important, what can be done to push them further away.

Viewed in this perspective, rates of economic growth are less important than rates of exploitation of nature, supposing, that is, that we know how to measure them. Situations can be imagined where a low or even a negative rate of growth is accompanied by rapid depletion of the stock of non-renewable resources (capital of nature) and considerable environmental degradation. Conversely, a fairly high rate of economic growth may prove ecologically sound and sparing of potentially scarce resources by resorting to the flow of renewable ones. This is easier said than done; it has the merit, however, of showing that there may be a way out of the (false) dilemma; growth versus environment.

The more so if, instead of pursuing present patterns of growth inequality, we look at the possibility of changing the uses of growth by giving priority to the satisfaction of the fundamental needs of the whole population, starting with the eradication of poverty. Growth in equality would make it less difficult for people to accept the principle of self-restraint in the satisfaction of material needs, the ideological cornerstone of the future 'steady state'. It would equally create the necessary social conditions for self-control of family size and the consequent reduction of population pressure; birth-control campaigns are likely to remain largely ineffective (unless enforced by coercion, which is clearly unacceptable) up to the time that peasants are freed from material insecurity, that infant mortality rates go down, and that the use of unpaid child labour is no longer necessary to make ends meet.

In the light of the previous argument, the environment appears as an additional and important dimension of development, rather than as a subject per se, a sector, or an alternative to development. It affects development in two ways: as a challenging resource potential that ought to be used for the benefit of mankind in an ecologically sound manner; and as a direct component of the quality of life through the physical and aesthetic values of its natural, man-transformed or man-made components. From another viewpoint, environmental awareness means in reality the introduction of the long term, of the diachronic solidarity with future generations. To the extent to which the protection of the environment may entail costs, these should be looked at as an investment in the future, offset as always by a sacrifice in current consumption and in most cases justified on economic grounds by the reduced cost of preventive actions as compared to the costs of remedial ones.

In this report it is argued that development should be self-reliant and endogenous — i.e. based on an autonomous decision-making and future designing capacity — need oriented and environmentally sound. In order to make the latter condition operational we require:

(a) a set of expanded social rationality criteria for resource management and use, based on development ethics;
(b) an institutional machinery for global resource management; and
(c) a specific strategy to harmonize social and ecological objectives.

The need is, therefore, to explore alternative development styles. This calls simultaneously for the reassessment of lifestyles and consumption patterns, the search for appropriate technologies and the skilfull location of human activities.

The concept of ecodevelopment, actively sponsored by UNEP, is an application of the approach outlined above. It stresses the need to look for concrete development strategies capable of making a good and ecologically sound use of the specific resources of a given ecosystem in order to satisfy the basic needs of the local population. Ecodevelopment insists on the variety of ecological and cultural situations and, therefore, on the diversity of proposed solutions as well as on the importance of citizen participation in the identification of needs and resources, the research of appropriate techniques, the design and implementation of development schemes and structural changes when needed. It is not a mere set of ecotechniques, although redefinition of technological options is likely to play a major role.

Ecodevelopment was first thought of as a guideline for defining micro-regional or regional development strategies in predominantly rural tropical areas. Hence its interest in evaluating, through ethnobotanical and botanical surveys, the potential of local forest, field and water plants, domesticating local animal species, designing and testing mixed crops, fish and cattle breeding systems well adapted to the forest, ecological farms producing their energy from waste, wind, small waterfalls etc. and emphasizing to the maximum all the complementarities. Of course, there is always room left for the introduction of 'exotic species', but preference is given in such a case to plants and animals from similar ecosystems.

Applied to housing — both rural and urban — the ecodevelopment approach stresses the need for ecologically sound designs for both human settlements and for individual dwellings. Software in this area is decisive and, furthermore, it should be possible to supplement it with some low-cost, soft technologies for water cooling and heating, climatization, etc. Local building materials are of course to be used and trees and plants must play an important functional as well as an aesthetic role.

The argument in favour of development of industries based on bio-conversion of solar energy may be interpreted as the addition of an 'industrial floor' to ecodevelopment strategies and in this way extending enormously their applicability, both in Third World and industrialized countries.

16.2   *Medium Range Proposals*

Some research priorities relevant in the medium term can be summarized as follows:

(a) We require a better understanding of the working of outer limits and, in this connection, of the interactions between natural and social processes. 'Nature accounting' must be developed to enable us to follow the changes in the stock of nature capital. It must be then brought in line with social indicators of quality of life and economic accounting of costs of development strategies. Ways must be equally found to quantify the wastefulness of present patterns of resource use. A major reassessment of technological effort is called for in order to foster new uses of solar energy and renewable resources, with special emphasis on technologies for decentralized use of non-conventional sources of energy. We must learn to design techno-industrial structures as true systems and to explore the interfaces between lifestyles, urban design and production systems. Ecodevelopment requires mass mobilization of participatory research on specific solutions to local problems. The range of subjects explored in an ecodevelopment perspective should cover all basic needs in the realm of food, habitat, health and sanitation, as well as education. As ecodevelopment also calls for bold institutional and organizational innovations, life-size experiments should be promoted with active support from UNEP, UNDP and international lending organizations without forgetting, however, that the primary responsibility for endogenous development is by definition vested with concerned populations and their political bodies.

(b) National agencies should be created with responsibilities for global resource management. They should be entrusted with the supervision and coordination of the activities of sectoral and regional bodies.

(c) The viability of the proposal to change development styles depends upon our ability to outline transitional strategies. Such strategies should give special attention to alternative uses of existing productive capacities, redeployment of industrial activities, substitution of non-renewable by renewable resources, and the creation of new job opportunities in resource management and social services activities. Work on these should start as soon as possible.

(d) Life-size ecodevelopment experiments should be promoted in different ecosystems and cultural settings and the experience thus gained compared, analyzed and disseminated.

(e) At the international level, it is necessary to define the regime of the 'international commons' and to set up an agency to exploit their resources in the interest of the poorest section of the world's population. The introduction of ocean-tolls and air-tolls should be considered. Another agency should be established to control the use of 'international commons'. UNIDO could be entrusted with setting up a technical assistance unit specialized in the evaluation of environmental impacts of new industrial projects.

16.3   *Long Term Proposals*

Global management of resources and environment will have to be increasingly tackled at a regional, inter-regional even at the world level, as well as at the national level. The issues involved are very complex and politically sensitive. We do not have as yet effective machinery for dealing with conflicts arising out of the management of rivers, lakes and sea basins belonging to several countries nor for the transnational effects of pollution. Attention must be given to this matter by the United Nations and, above all, by UNEP.

Useful as it may be, an institution for conflict resolution cannot replace positive machinery for dealing with global resources and environmental management; this latter way, it is to be hoped, would prevent the emergence of conflicts. A supranational agency does not seem feasible even in the long run given the sensibility of governments to the question of sovereign control over resources. Efforts must, therefore, be directed towards some form of continuous formulation and voluntary coordination of national resource, environmental and locational policies. Ultimately, such a procedure will involve a considerable degree of harmonization between economic plans that will have internalized environments as one dimension of development. This is a major and very difficult challenge to the new international order, even as a long term objective. It is to be hoped that the Mediterranean Project initiated under UNEP sponsorship will provide some relevant inputs and lessons. At any rate, thinking on possible institutional designs should start without further delay and UNEP should afford it high priority. Proposals made in Chapter 18 and Annex 10 on ocean management for the establishment of functional confederations of international organizations and the creation of integrative machinery would appear particularly relevant in this respect.

Chapter 17   Arms Reduction

17.1   *Main Proposals and Recommendations*

The present level of armament expenditures represents a very particular threat to the future of mankind and a tremendous waste of human and physical resources which could otherwise be used for purposes of development.

Apart from the continuous threat of new wars, which could easily enough escalate into nuclear war, the armaments race and its manifold implications has a direct bearing on the possibilities to rectify past and on-going human errors which have resulted in severe inequalities, suffering and devastation. The arms race is incompatible with the quest for a new international order.

The results of arms limitation talks have up till now been far from impressive. The reasons for this are many but some of the most important include the following:

(a) Technical development in the armaments field, particularly by the two superpowers, seems to have a life of its own and to follow its own laws as if directed by 'anonymous forces'. This gives rise to new military doctrines and strategies, resulting all too often in new obstacles to real and genuine disarmament.

(b) The military-industrial complex in the powerful countries seems to exercise considerable pressure on political authorities and forms an obstacle to concessions which might lead the way towards disarmament.

(c) Excessive secrecy concerning present levels of armament expenditure as well as type, quality and capacity of various types of arms seems to create an atmosphere of mutual fear and distrust, leading to probably unnecessary countermeasures and a spiralling arms race.

(d) New weapons and/or weapon systems seem to be introduced as 'bargaining chips' into disarmament talks; if these momentarily fail to achieve results, they are further developed and, in some cases, ultimately deployed, leading to new and higher levels of the arms race.

(e) The concept of national security still seems – in year 31 of the nuclear era – to be equated with military security, a concept which gradually assumes less credibility with every phase of continuing horizontal and vertical nuclear proliferation.

(f) Military strength and capability, and in particular the possession of a nuclear capacity, still seem to confer prestige and esteem on nations.

These factors — of a material and a non-material character — will need to be carefully examined and assessed as part of continued disarmament efforts. Given the enormous threats and the waste involved in the competitive armaments race, it is clearly essential that on-going multilateral and bilateral arms limitation negotiations be requested to yield more decisive results than has hitherto been the case. While the applied step-by-step approach still seems to be necessary, it should be noted that this has led to the domination in multilateral negotiations of so-called collateral and even sub-collateral measures, leaving most of the major issued untouched.

The case for uniting the support of the overwhelming majority of human beings behind disarmament efforts has never been stronger than at present. It must be hoped that informed and united public opinion can prove to be of decisive importance in giving new impetus and shape to disarmament negotiations. Many disarmament experts seem to be increasingly of the opinion that the partial disarmament measures aimed at so far only seem to have assisted in pushing the arms competition into new and more virulent directions and that the only way out may be through a comprehensive approach. If, as seems to be their view, it has been futile to engage military technicians in arguments over technical details, perhaps more success could be achieved by adding to this method of work matters of principle, questions of economics, morality and, quite simply, survival.

Matters of principle are indeed involved in disarmament efforts. Since mankind's future is inextricably linked with drastic changes in world management, disarmament must be included as an integral and important part of the global issue of survival, that is, of the new international order.

The present efforts being made within the United Nations to examine the possibility of a reduction in the military budgets of states with a major economic and military potential must be pursued with urgency. Support should be given to all efforts to establish a negotiated time-table for consecutive reductions in military budgets with the simultaneous and effective transfer of resources thus released to constructive civilian use, including development purposes. It is likewise recommended that all countries with upward trends — measured in real terms — in their military budgets give serious attention to the possibilities of and the advantages which could be gained from reversing this phenomenon.

Measures aimed at the balanced reduction of military budgets would be facilitated by increased openness between countries with respect to their real armament expenditures. There is also a clear need to establish means for regulating the expanding trade in arms, through national legislation or otherwise.

Special attention must continue to be given to efforts to halt the horizontal and vertical proliferation of nuclear arms and nuclear explosion capability, as well as to a very considerable strengthening and extension of safeguards of all kinds concerning nuclear facilities and material, in use, transport and shortage.

A ban must be sought on the use of indiscriminate and unnecessarily cruel conventional weapons.

So far very few countries have pledged their support of and contribution to a standing U.N. Peace Force. Every effort should be made to promote progress in establishing such a force as a means for peace-keeping and this should be organized within the context of the democratization of the U.N. Security Council.

A welcome development is the establishing by the XXX Session of the United Nations General Assembly of an Ad Hoc Committee to review the role of the U.N. in the field of disarmament. The committee will formulate proposals on ways and means whereby this role can be strengthened and submit them to the XXXI Session of the Assembly. It is contended, however, that in order to make multilateral disarmament efforts truly effective, as well as to supervise the gradual implementation of existing and future disarmament agreements, there appears to be a need to establish, within the framework of the United Nations, a *World Disarmament Agency*.

17.2 *Medium Range Proposals*

(a) Exert strong political and moral pressure on the superpowers through national and international actions to redirect military expenditures towards development because of the enormous threats posed by such expenditures to all mankind and in view of the waste they constitute of financial, material and human resources.

(b) Achieve a Treaty on a Comprehensive Nuclear Test Ban and start genuine nuclear disarmament.

(c) Achieve a Convention banning chemical weapons.

(d) Ban indiscriminate and unnecessarily cruel conventional weapons.

(e) Gradually transfer scientific and technological resources now used for military purposes to development purposes.

(f) Establish means for regulating the arms trade, through national legislation or otherwise.

(g) Reinforcement of the United Nations Peace Force within the context of the democratization of the U.N. Security Council.

(h) Review the need for and feasibility of a World Disarmament Agency within the framework of the United Nations.

17.3   *Long Range Proposals*

The reduction of social tensions both within and among countries and regions is one of the most important fundamental forces mankind has at its disposal to reduce the need for armament. The main precondition for the operation of this fundamental force is the recognition, on all sides, of cultural diversity as a desirable and not a dangerous feature of the future world community. A degree of tolerance is required from all types of social systems in order that each country's and each region's social change is left to the country or the region concerned. Arms reduction will be a consequence of the development of this tolerance. As such, there is considerable need and scope for confidence building between nations. A first step would comprise increased openness between countries with respect to armament expenditures.

Chapter 18   Ocean Management

18.1   *Main Proposals and Recommendations*

One of the most challenging questions facing the international community
is that of *ocean management*, and of how to adapt the traditional law of
the sea to conditions of intensifying and diversifying use and exploitation
of the marine environment resulting from the contemporary technological
revolution. The *Third United Nations Conference on the Law of the Sea*,
which was to deal with these questions, offered a historic opportunity to
develop new forms of international cooperation and organization which
could have had a profound and immediate effect on the concrete implementation of a new international order. The discussions which have so
far taken place, however, demonstrate the great difficulties involved in
dealing with interdependent issues and conflicting uses of ocean space and
in trying to accommodate divergent interests of States.

The Conference was convened in 1973. Since the end of its third session
in Geneva, 1975, discussions have been based on a document called the
Informal Single Negotiating Text. While this text is still subject to
amendment and change, the basic trends are clear: the main effect of a
Treaty based on this document would be a radical shift in the balance
of the traditional law of the sea from the principle of freedom of the high
seas towards that of coastal State sovereignty; national jurisdiction would
be recognized to extend over at least 35 per cent of ocean space and
further extension would be possible on the basis of the imprecise provisions regarding the drawing of straight baselines and the limits of the
legal continental shelf as redefined in terms of the continental margin.
While it is true that the Single Negotiating Text introduces some substantial changes in the traditional law of the sea, it is unfortunate that the
concepts, on the one hand, of the freedom of the high seas and, on the
other, of expanded and virtually unrestricted national sovereignty are
maintained.

Freedom of the high seas was based on the assumption that the seas were
so immense, their uses so limited and their living resources so vast in
relation to needs and exploitation capability that international regulation
was not required. These assumptions are patently obsolete. On the other
hand, the principle of sovereignty is rooted not only in the security needs
of States but also on the assumption that individual coastal States are best
suited to regulate effectively all uses of offshore ocean space. This could
be true with regard to uses of the sea connected with the extraction of
mineral resources. It is less applicable to the exploitation of living
resources — even those which spawn and live within the maritime jurisdiction of the coastal State. In most other matters, the nature of the
oceans and of their present and foreseeable uses emphasizes interdepen-

dence: fragmentation of ocean space between a hundred or more different sovereignties would seriously hamper vital common uses of the oceans, such as navigation, overflight, and scientific research, and would make effective control of marine pollution virtually impossible. Very important commercial fisheries overlap jurisdictional boundaries and cannot be managed in a regime of exclusive sovereignty.

The shift of the Conference focus from the building of a new international order based on the 'Common Heritage of Mankind' concept, to the allocation of ocean space and resources to coastal States has accentuated divisions and hardened the lines, not only between industrialized and developing States but also between the developing States themselves. Fundamental questions, such as the powers and structure of the new International Seabed Authority, the rights of land-locked States in the marine areas under coastal State jurisdiction, or the nature of the dispute settlement system, are still unresolved. What is even worse, issues of vital importance for ocean management are either totally neglected or treated on the basis of obsolete criteria, such as unilateral definition of the maximum sustainable yield of one species. Perceived national interests are accommodated on the basis of ambiguities inviting future conflict and further expansion of national claims. It is indeed to be feared that any Treaty resulting from the present negotiations may create more problems than it solves.

The moment has come for a fundamental reassessment of strategies and policies, if the immense wealth of the oceans is to be utilized for the benefit of all peoples — especially those of the poorer countries — within the wider framework of a new international economic order.

The basic structure that must emerge is simple and rooted in developments which are going on, and must go on, regardless of the outcome of the next phase of the Law of the Sea Conference.

The concept of territorial sovereignty in the seas must be replaced by the concept of jurisdiction defined as the legal power to control and regulate defined uses of ocean space in defined areas subject to treaty limitations designed to protect the interests of the whole of which the area under national jurisdiction is only a part. In other words, the traditional concept of territorial sovereignty should be replaced by the concept of *functional sovereignty*, which distinguishes jurisdiction over specific uses from sovereignty over geographic space. This would permit the interweaving of national jurisdiction and international competences within the same territorial space and open the possibility of applying the concept of the common heritage of mankind both beyond and within the limits of national jurisdiction.

The most promising way of articulating the complex relationships between national and international jurisdictions and management systems would be a *functional confederation of international organizations*, based on existing but restructured agencies of the United Nations system and adding to these the proposed *International Seabed Authority* (ISA). The whole system would be linked through an *integrative machinery*, integrating the now disparate policies of these bodies at a level that cannot be that of inter-secretariat cooperation but must be based on their policy-making or Assembly structure. The advantages of such an approach are that it can utilize and further evolve the work accomplished by the Conference: that it combines integration at the policy level with a maximum of decentralization at the operational level; and that it could serve as a model for other sectors of the new international order (cf. section 19.5.3).

The principal elements of the U.N. machinery dealing exclusively with ocean uses are: the Inter-Governmental Maritime Consultative Organization (IMCO), for navigation; the Commission on Fisheries (COFI) of FAO, for living resources; and the Intergovernmental Oceanographic Commission (IOC) of UNESCO, for oceanographic sciences. The structure and functions of these organizations should be reshaped in order to enable them to assume the required regulatory and managerial competences, analogous to those of the new International Seabed Authority.

This is not enough, however. An *integrative machinery* is required to:

(a) integrate the work of these organizations at the policy level;
(b) deal with ocean activities not falling within the specific competence of any of these organizations;
(c) establish guidelines for multiple ocean space use, taking into account the need for cooperation between national and international management systems;
(d) ensure cooperation with technologically less advanced countries in the development of national ocean space;
(e) ensure equitable sharing of the benefits derived from the exploitation of international ocean space;
(f) promote the progressive development of the law of the sea; and
(g) assume some functions with regard to dispute settlement.

Medium and long range proposals are formulated in terms of three assumptions.

The first group of proposals could be implemented regardless of whether or not there is a Treaty. They would bring some incremental improvements and enhance the participation of Third World countries in ocean management.

The second group of proposals assumes the adoption of some Treaty, together with the establishment, by the Law of the Sea Conference, of some *continuing mechanism* to supervise the implementation of the Treaty and coordinate the restructuring of the U.N. agencies dealing with ocean uses. Such a continuing mechanism could conceivably consist of a periodic meeting of signatory States supported by a small Secretariat and complemented by an intergovernmental committee or, better, Commission of Eminent Persons to advise on appropriate measures to accelerate and coordinate the process of restructuring of COFI, IOC and IMCO and undertake other studies as requested by States.

The third group of proposals (long range) presupposes the conclusion of a Treaty and the establishment, not only of some continuing mechanism, but of an integrative machinery linking an effective system of ocean management institutions.

18.2 *Medium Range Proposals*

A *Independent of Treaty*

(a) Strengthening of *regional cooperation and organization* in fishing and the management of living resources, scientific research, the transfer of technology, and the furnishing of science-based services, the protection of the marine environment and the interaction of all uses of marine space and resources: such arrangements to be viewed as complementary and indispensable, rather than alternative, to the long term objective of continued progress towards a world-wide system. Action could be initiated through regional economic commissions and fisheries commissions and through ad hoc agreements among States bordering enclosed or semi-enclosed seas.

(b) Establishment of *regional institutes* for marine sciences and technology and their coordination through global organizations such as IOC. Action could be initiated by any group of nations, especially in less developed regions, through regional banks or UNDP.

(c) Enhancement of participation of developing land-locked States and developing islands in the marine economy, through bilateral or multilateral agreements, in the wider context of UNCTAD recommendations.

(d) Increase of participation by developing nations in world shipping tonnage and sea-borne international trade.

(e) Enforcement of the UNCTAD Code of Conduct for Liner Conferences.

(f) Extension of the concept of zones of peace and security to other ocean areas, such as the Mediterranean. The U.N. General Assembly has approved the establishment of a zone of peace in the Indian Ocean.

(g) Restructuring of COFI, IOC, and IMCO, to respond to changing political, economic, ecological and technological needs; strengthening of cooperation with organizations outside the U.N. system, such as the International Hydrographic Bureau. Action must be initiated within the agencies themselves, but could be encouraged by resolutions or recommendations adopted by the General Assembly and/or by the Law of the Sea Conference.

B *On the Basis of a Treaty and the Establishment of a Continuing Mechanism*

(a) Clarification of major ambiguities contained in the Treaty and consideration, as appropriate, of such matters of an urgent and important nature for which there are no provisions in the Treaty.

(b) Clarification as appropriate of the Law of the Sea with regard to military uses of ocean space, a subject disregarded, for all practical purposes, in the Treaty.

(c) Establishment of criteria for the harmonization of ocean space uses both within and beyond the limits of national jurisdiction; another subject ignored by the Treaty.

(d) Establishment of links, at the national, regional and international levels, between development of marine resource management and land-based development in such areas as food, mineral production, energy production, international trade, collective self-reliance, relations with transnational enterprises, etc.

(e) Inclusion of the goal of a new international economic order in the oceans on the agenda of other international continuous or ad hoc fora such as UNCTAD, U.N. Regional Economic Commissions, Non-Aligned Summit, etc.

18.3 **Long Range Proposals On the Basis of a Treaty, the Restructuring of the Agencies, and the Establishment of Integrative Machinery**

(a) Effective preservation of the marine environment, including its fauna and flora.

(b) Rational management and development of the living and non-living resources of ocean space, both within national jurisdictional areas and beyond clearly defined limits of national jurisdiction, through cooperative action between international institutions and national authorities.

(c) Harmonization of ocean space uses through the coordination of measures at the national and international levels.

(d) Active sharing of benefits, with particular regard to the needs of less developed countries, through a variety of devices including *international public enterprises* (cf. Chapter 15), especially *for fishing* and *offshore oil production*; *international tax on ocean uses*, etc.

(e) Effective cooperation in the transfer of technology relating to ocean space activities.

(f) Effective regulation of the activities of transnational enterprises in ocean space, in cooperation with coastal States.

(g) Cooperative undertaking through international mechanisms of services to the international community such as ice patrol, monitoring of the marine environment, etc., now undertaken on a national basis.

(h) Effective compulsory and binding dispute settlement system.

Chapter 19   Packages for Comprehensive Negotiation

19.1   *Introduction*

A major theme of this report has been that the existing international system requires fundamental structural changes, not marginal reforms. A number of proposals have been made with this objective in mind. These proposals, although fairly selective, cover almost all sectors of human activity. It may be felt that too many proposals have been made and that they are too loosely integrated. (All medium range proposals are listed in Appendix 2 at the end of Part III). It may also be felt that there is insufficient discussion of the time frame within which the proposals can be implemented and the actual process of negotiation that it will take to implement them. This chapter is, therefore, devoted to a discussion of some of these issues.

It should be recognized at the outset, however, that international economic activity has not so far proceeded through an orderly and planned process of change and is unlikely to do so for at least some time to come. The changes proposed in the world system are essentially long term ones, the negotiation and implementation of which is likely to stretch over several decades. All that can be done at this stage is to indicate some order of priorities and to draw up certain packages of proposals which should preferably form the subject of comprehensive negotiation. At the same time it must be recognized that these packages are merely to stimulate international thinking and concern around certain issues of the highest urgency rather than to suggest a concrete blueprint for action.

19.2   *Selection of Priorities*

While there are a number of relevant criteria for establishing priorities among the proposals for change listed, one is paramount: the *urgent need to remove gross inequities* from the world order. Whether or not the world political system is ready for it, and whether or not it serves the interests of all nations, there is no more urgent task today than to ensure that the instances of gross inequalities of income and economic opportunities in international life are eliminated as rapidly as possible. Without this, the concept of equality of opportunity among people and nations will remain an empty phrase. Both developing and developed nations must afford this objective absolute priority if the powerful forces of justice and equity are to be effectively mobilized in support of constructive change.

Subject to this overriding consideration, there are three distinct criteria that can be used to assess the relevant priority of the proposals made in this report. These are:

176

(a) *Political Feasibility*   Those proposals which have the maximum chance of being acceptable to the international community in the near future should be taken up first. Generally, this would imply that proposals which balance the enlightened interests of various groups of countries should be afforded first priority since they are likely to find a much wider degree of international political acceptance. This does not mean, however, that the present international political framework should be taken as given. On the contrary, a conscious attempt must be made to organize intellectual and political lobbies to re-educate international public and political opinion (cf. section 7.6). However, there will be a clear advantage in focusing negotiations on those proposals regarded as politically feasible; the consensus achieved in the first stage would help establish a viable basis from which to move on to more thorough proposals involving the effective redistribution of power. This would reflect the growing awareness by the developing world of its role in the world bargaining process and the parallel recognition thereof by its partners from the industrialized countries.

(b) *Net Benefits Expected*   High priority should be given to those proposals where the net benefit to the international community is the largest compatible with an optimalization of the well-being of the poor countries. This also means that the net costs and benefits of each proposal must be worked out very carefully at a technical level so that it becomes possible for the decision-makers to evaluate the relevant merits and priority of each proposal. This is a stage which will be reached during serious negotiations when concrete decisions will need to be taken by evaluating the costs and benefits of various proposals and by carefully studying the potential benefits for Third World countries with special regard to the poorest.

(c) *Early Results*   Since the negotiation of a more equitable international social and economic order is an on-going process, it is essential that those proposals should be taken up first which yield early and discernible results. Such a strategy will also have the advantage of keeping the hope of the developing world alive for an orderly change through the process of negotiation and would ensure that interminable discussions do not become a delaying tactic for postponing fundamental reforms.

19.3   *Need for Comprehensive Packages*

There are a number of reasons for attempting to bring together the various proposals made in this report into some viable packages for real negotiation.

Firstly, such packages are needed to demonstrate the interlinkages between proposals. Action taken in one field is likely to set off a chain-reaction and have ripple-effects in a number of other fields. It is important to recognize this and to present various proposals in a more integrated fashion.

Secondly, packages are also needed in order to balance the divergent interests of the rich and the poor nations. While these interests may be entirely compatible over the long term, as has been argued in this report, the perception of these interests may differ and the shorter term costs of longer term reforms may at times encourage the rich nations to resist change. It becomes important, therefore, even a tactical necessity, to devise packages which balance the long term interests of all sides whilst developing greater awareness in the industrialized countries of the real costs and benefits of each package. The poor nations, for instance, have an interest in stable export earnings in terms of their imports after having obtained more equitable prices for their exports. The rich nations have an interest in assured and uninterrupted longer term supplies. Both should be equally concerned by the necessity of fighting against the wasteful use of scarce and non-renewable resources. Similarly, just as Third World nations have an interest in the greater sharing of the benefits resulting from the investments of transnational enterprises and more effective control over their activities, the enterprises themselves have a corresponding interest in ensuring the long term security and growth of their investment. Industrialized countries also have a special stake in the promotion of exports not only of manufactured goods but also, to an increasing extent, of means of production through forms other than direct investment, such as joint ventures or production contracts involving in time marketing arrangements or the like. This may also be the best means for Third World countries to develop rapidly, provided the choice of industry optimizes the value added for the host country and that conditions of finance, conditions of transfer of technology and of training and the development of local research are appropriate. Furthermore, if the poor nations have a special need to be largely self-reliant in their food supply, their potential for lower cost agricultural production can contribute towards slowing the inflationary rise in the costs of food production in the industrialized countries. There are many other instances of this kind and it should be possible to package various proposals in such a fashion as to take maximum advantages of this complementarity of interests.

Thirdly, a certain degree of packaging of proposals is necessary in order to see more clearly how ultimate objectives can be achieved through the process of actual negotiations. In the diverse fora of the world, where negotiations on the new international order are proceeding, it will be a distinct advantage to consider various packages rather than individual proposals. This is likely to increase their degree of acceptability to all parties concerned. They are also needed in order to achieve some comprehensive results rather than getting bogged down in the detailed technical analysis of each individual proposal.

19.4 *Packages and the International Power Structure*

The negotiation of packages reflecting the legitimate interests of both the poor and rich nations in achieving a more equitable distribution of economic opportunity and wealth implies a process of give and take, an element of collective bargaining. Given the present state of international affairs, this 'bargaining' approach must be deemed sensible. It must be recognized, however, that bargains make most sense when negotiated between equals. As we have seen, unequal power relationships between nations lie at the heart of the existing inequality of global opportunity and, consequently, the negotiating position of most Third World countries is undeniably weaker than that of the industrialized countries. The negotiation of packages based upon 'bargaining' thus carries the danger that it results in a perpetuation of the existing international system, streamlining it to meet the pressing needs of the rich and privileged nations. The creation of a new international order must ultimately be shaped by the forces of equity and this calls for a substantial strengthening of the negotiating position of the most disadvantaged countries. Such a strengthening must be viewed as a precondition for the successful negotiation of comprehensive packages.

In fact, the power position of the Third World has already increased considerably, both politically and, more recently, economically. The structure and operations of the international economic and financial system, however, still lag behind this evolution and must first be made to adapt to it and then to accelarate it.

Various proposals have been made in this report which are designed to redress imbalances in the international power structure and to democratize world economic decision-making processes. Some of these are summarized below:

(a) The dependency relationships of Third World countries must be reduced through new-style self-reliant development, greater self-sufficiency in basic foodstuffs, a new framework for resource transfers from the rich to the poor nations which is automatic and less dependent on the fluctuating generosity of the rich nations, and through a more equitable functioning of international markets and financial mechanisms;

(b) Third World countries should exercise full sovereignty over the exploitation of their own natural and other resources, play a larger part in the processing thereof, and all their contracts with foreign investors and transnational enterprises should be reviewed in that light;

(c) Since Third World countries are often weak when they stand alone in international negotiations, it is legitimate for them to develop the umbrella of collective bargaining through United Nations fora and through the organizations of regional associations and the establishment of mechanisms of collective economic security;

(d) Third World countries can pursue the goal of collective self-reliance, encouraging more trade and transfer of technology between themselves so as to be increasingly independent of the economic and political fluctuations in the industrialized countries;

(e) It is legitimate for Third World countries to organize producers' associations in selected commodities in order to develop a countervailing power to the considerable concentration of power already existing at the buying end and thus exercise greater control over the prices of their products and obtain a greater share of the value added derived from their processing;

(f) It would be desirable to develop public international enterprises to enable Third World countries to develop their own resources, thus providing an alternative to private transnational enterprises. Furthermore, codes of conduct, with legally enforceable elements, for the regulation of the activities of transnational enterprises and for the transfer of technology should be developed so that there is international policing in those areas where the poor countries are presently vulnerable or where they have very weak bargaining power individually;

(g) 'New coalitions' should be developed with interested groups in the industrialized nations to achieve the objectives of Third World countries, e.g. a lobby of consumers in the industrialized countries to agitate for the dismantling of trade barriers; a coalition with equipment producers in the industrialized nations to support programmes of foreign assistance, etc.;

(h) A new type of international institution should be established with resource management capacities and responsibilities for the exploitation of the common heritage of mankind, such as the resources of the oceans. Without such an institution, these resources will be unilaterally exploited by the rich nations for their own benefit since most Third World countries have neither the technology nor the capital at present to engage in such activities;

(i) There should be a democratization of international financial institutions, particularly the Bretton Woods institutions, to give adequate voting strength to Third World nations.

All these proposals will take time to implement, but their basic purpose is to bring about a new structure of international economic power which will enhance the negotiating position of the weakest nations. Unless the present imbalances in the world power structure are reduced considerably, if not removed entirely, it will not be possible to extend equality and opportunity between nations in any meaningful fashion. The same principle also applies within nations.

19.5   *Priority Packages*

In line with the approach outlined above and assuming continuing efforts to redress power imbalances, at least three distinct packages of proposals for comprehensive negotiation can be identified:

(a) proposals aimed at removing gross inequities in the distribution of world income and economic opportunities;

(b) proposals to ensure more harmonious growth of the global economic system; and

(c) proposals to provide the beginnings of a global planning system.

9.5.1   *Redressing Gross Inequalities*   One of the major ways to remove gross inequalities in income distribution and economic opportunities is to pay special attention to the problems of the poorest nations (those in the lower decile, cf. Chapter 6). These countries are being left far behind in the process of development. Between 1960 and 1975, the income disparities between the poorest nations and the industrialized nations have increased in terms of real buying power from 10:1 to 14:1 and the disparity between them and the least disadvantaged other Third World countries has also gone up from 2:1 to 3:1. In many of these Third World countries a majority of the population is at present unable to satisfy the basic needs of nutrition, health care, shelter and other social services required for any minimal level of human decency and for creating the conditions under which families have the motivation and opportunity to substantially reduce their birth rates. To bring these nations at least to the threshold of economic survival and respectability, so that they can begin to participate in the mainstream of international economic life, should be regarded as one of the most urgent items on the agenda of mankind.

A global compact on poverty designed to attack the worst forms of poverty all over the globe over the course of the next decade should be afforded the highest priority. The essential objective of such a compact should be to provide for at least minimum basic human needs for the vast majority in the poorest nations through their own action as well as through adequate help by the international community. A number of proposals made in this report fall under such a compact on poverty.

The poorest nations should help their own cause by undertaking programmes aimed at accelerating food production, at a greater domestic resource mobilization, particularly of their human capital, at a basic restructuring of their investment priorities and social institutions in favour of their poorest segments of society and at population control, an objective which becomes feasible when these other measures have yielded concrete results. The rich nations can give their support to this global effort by speedily reaching the target of 0.7 per cent of their GNP in net ODA, by redirecting their assistance in favour of those programmes which benefit directly the poorest people and by rescheduling the external debt of Third World countries so as to permit an increased net flow of resources.

Tentatively, it is estimated that the target of alleviating the worst forms of poverty by the mid 1980's will require an annual investment of $ 15-20 billion over the next decade. Since the poorest nations are already spending about $ 3-4 billion annually on such programmes, and can increase this effort considerably, what it requires from the international community is something in the order of $ 10-12 billion a year for the next 10 years. If such a joint, coordinated effort is made, it may well be possible to take care of the overwhelming inequalities in economic opportunity which face the poorest nations today over a manageable period of time. Such an effort, effectively administered, would serve not only the cause of equity and justice but should improve political stability and advance the dates when population stability would be achieved and concessional aid would no longer be required.

This is an urgent task. It does not require detailed technical studies. It requires a commitment of political will. In order to mobilize such political will, the world community should elaborate, as a matter of greatest urgency, a global strategy to combat poverty. Once the direction is clear, a number of detailed technical studies can be undertaken around many of the proposals in this report which link up with the idea of such a compact.

19.5.2   *Harmonious Global Growth*   A number of proposals have been made in this report, the basic objective of which is to ensure more harmonious growth of the world economic system. Such proposals, if implemented, would avoid a return to the ruinous rates of inflation experienced worldwide in the first half of this decade and to the impoverishment of the already disprivileged masses of the Third World. The costs of interruptions in global economic growth are very high and increasing and the prevention of such interruptions is one area in which there is a large degree of compatibility between the interests of the poor and the rich nations.

The international economic system needs urgently to be reformed so as to work more efficiently and smoothly for all nations. As noted earlier, a precondition for the participation of Third World countries in these essential reforms is that they are afforded a greater share in the international system's decision-making processes and in the benefits of growth emerging from a reformed system.

The following proposals are designed to ensure harmonious global growth:

(a) Fundamental reforms in the international monetary system so that international liquidity is not created in such an unplanned fashion that it generates alternate cycles of inflation, stagflation and depression. If national reserve currencies are replaced by an international reserve currency, to be created and managed by the international community in line with the genuine needs for the growth of the international economic system and with special regard to the pressing needs of the Third World, it can considerably help in avoiding some of the present unplanned fluctuations in economic activity. Other proposals would also contribute towards reducing global inflation. For example, a substantial increase in food production in Third World countries — especially those with large areas with underutilized capacity — is required so as to avoid a 250 per cent increase in the price of grain following a 3 per cent shortfall in world production;

(b) The internationalization of information in a number of fields like transnational enterprises and technology, the transfer of technology as such and the development of appropriate markets and financial mechanisms which safeguard the interests of Third World countries should contribute towards the smoother running of the world economy;

(c) As discussed in section 19.5.3 below, many proposals will introduce conscious elements of global planning so as to safeguard the international economic systems from unilateral and uncoordinated national decisions;

(d) For the longer run, it is essential that some fundamental changes in growth patterns and development strategies be made so as to ensure more harmonious global growth. This requires a basic change in the consumption styles, both in the poor and the rich nations. The poor nations must devote their limited resources in the first instance to the satisfaction of basic human needs, to the provision of low-cost social services, and to the development of consumption styles more consistent with their stage of development and with their own cultural and social values. The rich nations, on the other hand, must develop new consumption styles which are less wasteful, less resource-intensive and geared to the consumption of social services rather than of superfluous consumer durables. Another important element is that new development strategies be constructed on the foundation of balanced ecodevelopment as outlined in Chapter 16;

(e) One of the important aspects of a more harmonious world economic system is the necessity to achieve a balance between population growth and food production, particularly in the poorest nations. Since many poor countries are extremely vulnerable in regard to their basic food requirements, an international food supply system must be evolved which protects the poor countries against major fluctuations in world supplies through the mechanism of adequate world grain reserves and the possibility of emergency food relief.

19.5.3   *System for Global Planning and the Management of Resources*   One of the major themes in this report has been the unforeseen consequences of uncoordinated national action. Within nations, there has been an evolution over time of institutions and mechanisms which ensure greater planning and coordination of diverse economic activities within the framework of overall national objectives. The growth of progressive taxation systems, central banks and planning commissions represent various elements in this evolution. A similar evolution at the international level is only a question of time. Often, the evolution of international institutions has followed the same route taken by national institutions, though with a time lag of several decades. One of the basic questions which today faces the international community is whether it should accelerate the process of this evolution and consciously put in place the various elements of a system for global planning and the management of resources. Many proposals relate to this objective:

(a) The gradual introduction of a system of international taxation which should be handled by a World Treasury, both to meet the current as well as the development needs of the poorer nations;

(b) The creation of an international reserve currency by an international authority, such as an International Central Bank, which should be under international management without being dominated by the interests of one particular group of nations;

(c) A number of measures have been proposed which should bring greater planning and coordination in the field of domestic food production and international supplies of food, including the establishment of world grain reserves, the strengthening of the role of the proposed International Fund for Agricultural Development, and the institutionalization of emergency food relief. In the last analysis, it may require the setting up of a World Food Authority to supervise this vital area of human activity and survival;

(d) In the trade field, an International Trade and Development Organization, formed by expanding the responsibilities of UNCTAD, should be set up with a very broad mandate for overall coordination of policy issues relating to international trade in primary commodities and manufactured goods. Likewise, UNIDO's responsibilities should be increased to enable it to participate in the planning of a more equitable world industrial order;

(e) In addition, the establishment of a number of other international mechanisms and agencies has been proposed, such as an International Industrial Development Bank, a World Energy Research Authority, an international system of ocean management institutions, a World Disarmament Agency, etc. While we must be conscious of the multiplicity of organizations that this involves, such institutions can only operate efficiently in the more effective planning and coordination of the global economic system;

(f) Effective planning and management calls for the fundamental restructuring of the United Nations so as to give it broad economic powers and a more decisive mandate for international economic decision-making. It is hoped that this will be the basic thrust of the report that the United Nations Committee of the Whole is presently being asked to produce on this subject. It is also hoped that major changes in the United Nations structure will be made over the next decade so that it is not only able to play a more forceful role in world political affairs but it is also able to become more of a World Development Authority in managing the socio-economic affairs of the international community.

To be able to plan, make decisions and to enforce them, a world organization working on a *truly democratic basis* must be empowered by its members to do so. The most effective way of articulating the planning and management functions of this organization would be through a functional confederation of international organizations, based upon existing, restructured and, in some instances, new United Nations agencies — to be linked through an integrative machinery. This system and its machinery, if it is really to reflect interdependencies between nations and solidarity between peoples, should ultimately aim at the pooling and sharing of *all* resources, material and non-material, including means of production, with a view to ensuring effective planning and management of the world economy and of global resource use in a way which would meet the essential objectives of equity and efficiency.

The achievement of this global planning and management system calls for the conscious *transfer of power* — a gradual transfer to be sure — from the nation State to the world organization. Only when this transfer takes place can the organization become effective and purposeful.

Whether this historical challenge will be adequately met by nations is one of the key questions of the new international order.

19.6 *Time Frame*

The time frame for the implementation of these packages of proposals will vary according to the international community's understanding and acceptance of their feasibility. However, it is urgent to pursue the compact on poverty since its objective is to remove some of the worst forms of human deprivation. In terms of timing, the proposals aimed at ensuring more harmonious global growth will probably be found the most acceptable since they are in the interests of all nations, even in the short term.

Not all proposals can be accorded the same urgency or implemented at the same time. For instance, the main elements of a more conscious global planning system will take considerable time to develop, as was the case within national systems. It is important, therefore, that, in terms of tactics and timing of negotiations, the proposals mentioned in the above paragraph should be taken up first.

19.7 *Process of Negotiation*

The purpose in presenting various packages for comprehensive negotiation was to show the interlinkages of these proposals and how they relate to the ultimate goals that the international community must pursue. This does not imply that one particular package must be negotiated in one particular forum, nor that the packages presented above are the only ones which should be developed and negotiated. It is obvious that the actual process of negotiation will proceed in a number of different fora. There are three elements, however, which need to be stressed. Firstly, as suggested above, there is an urgent need for the world community to elaborate a global strategy to combat poverty, preferably during 1977. Secondly, it may be necessary to use the on-going North-South dialogue in Paris, or similar fora, for serious and detailed negotiation of the various proposals. They may be presented to the international community for final approval after they have been sufficiently detailed. Thirdly, a restructured United Nations system is the best hope for constructive and continuing negotiations between the rich and the poor nations on a basis of greater equality and participation.

19.8 *Concluding Note*

The past few decades have brought prosperity to some nations and a complex array of problems to all. They have brought the need to question many of the values, ideas and concepts upon which the relationships between and within nations have been forged. They have linked nations in a complex network of interdependence from which no nation, however powerful, can realistically exclude itself. They have placed mankind on the threshold of new choices and opportunities and exposed it to unprecedented dangers.

This report has attempted to review some of the choices and to suggest
ways in which new opportunities for forging new international structures
from which all can benefit from change can and must be used. It has
argued that mankind's future lies in the development of a new global ethic
based upon cooperation, better mutual understanding, the necessary
reduction in suspicions and short-sighted self-interest, and on the setting of
norms for survival rather than on seeing survival as a norm. It has cata-
logued the enormous efforts which must be made if the abysses surrounding the narrow path to an equitable world order are to be avoided.

There will certainly be those that question the realism of the proposals for
change contained in this report. There will be others who will not find
them radical enough for the needs of our time. The purpose of this report
is to join neither the pessimists nor the radicals, but rather to sketch the
kind of evolution in human institutions which could best ensure greater
equality of opportunity between people and nations. This is a challenge
for the entire human race. We can only hope that we, as individuals and as
nations, have the wisdom, the courage and the foresight to meet this
supreme challenge.

General Perspective for Proposals

(a) *Convincing Public and Political Opinion.* A coordinated and intensified effort, particularly in industrialized countries, should be made to publicize the need to create an international social and economic order which is perceived as more equitable by all peoples. There can be little question that unless public opinion is aware of the need for change and of the benefits that all mankind can obtain from establishing a more equitable world, progress towards a new international social and economic order will be very slow and present tensions and conflicts could result in an acute world crisis. The primary task of many non-governmental organizations must be to undertake the effort suggested.

(b) *Reform of the United Nations System.* The political and economic efficiency of the U.N. system must be improved within the context of the Charter of the U.N. which remains an invaluable guide to the world community. For the political side, the reform should aim particularly at the democratization of the operations of the Security Council. For the economic side, it should take place along most of the lines suggested by the Group of 25. An improvement in efficiency is required in order that the U.N. is able to become an effective major instrument of international political and economic cooperation for the benefit of all. Such an improvement is in fact essential to the implementation of many of the proposals listed below.

(c) *Ensuring World Security.* One of the vital concerns of mankind today is to make the world safe from the risk of nuclear destruction. Since there is a far greater chance of conflicts in an unjust world, it must be recognized that the implementation of the proposals made to improve equality of opportunity and to make the world increasingly more just will also simultaneously reduce chances of such conflicts. The planned and phased reduction in world defence spending, the reinforcement of the U.N. Peace Force together with the democratization of the Security Council, and the establishment of a World Disarmament Agency should contribute towards ensuring greater world security. It should also be stressed that a major effort to develop new energy sources, such as solar, geothermal and nuclear fusion, would make all countries more self-reliant and would slow greatly the proliferation of nuclear fission plants with all the associated risks to the environment and the danger of the spread of nuclear weapons.

(d) *Negotiating a Framework Treaty.* When major steps have been taken for the creation of a new world order, it could be advisable to consider the negotiation of a framework treaty based on the Charter of Economic Rights and Duties of States adopted by the United Nations in 1974. The purpose of such a treaty would be on the one hand to lay the legally binding foundation for a new structure of economic relations between all States and, on the other, to provide the legal basis for the negotiation of such international agreements as may be required for the implementation of a new world order. It is stressed in this connection that negotiation of a framework treaty should not delay implementation of the main proposals contained in this report and indeed should not be envisaged until major elements of the new order have been adopted by international agreement.

(e) *Sovereignty and the Common Heritage of Mankind.* If all are to live in a better and more stable world in which all members of the international community deal among themselves as equal partners, the first objective to be achieved is the attainment by Third World countries of full sovereignty over their resources in compliance with the U.N. Charter of Economic Rights and Duties of States. Only after this objective has been achieved can the concept of the common heritage of mankind, traditionally limited to resources considered as *res nullius* such as the oceans and outer space, be expanded to new domains such as mineral resources, science and technology, means of production and other sources of wealth. After the exercise of national sovereignty has contributed towards the creation of a more equitable international order, the aim should be to pool all world resources — material and non-material — with a view to ensuring effective planning and management of the world economy and of global resource use in a way which would meet the dual objectives of equity and efficiency. In this perspective, resources would need to be managed on the basis of decentralized planetary sovereignty (cf. section 5.8). Proposals for the application of the common heritage concept to particular fields should thus be viewed in this broader context.

The International Monetary Order

(a) Phasing out of national reserve currencies as well as gold from reserve creation, confining increasingly the latter to SDR type assets created by joint decisions and used for jointly agreed objectives, with emphasis on the financing of development in the Third World.

(b) Developing and enforcing guidelines for official interventions in exchange markets and better adjustment policies. Assign responsibility for market interventions, within periodically reviewed guidelines and maximum amounts — and/or provisional maximum range of fluctuations — to a permanent executive committee.

(c) Both of the above objectives to be pursued by all countries ready to accept them, especially through regional organizations, whenever not yet negotiable on a world-wide scale.

Income Redistribution and the Financing of Development

(a) A vigorous effort should be made to reach a concessional resource transfer target of 0.7 per cent of GNP by 1980 and to increase it to 1 per cent thereafter through various forms of international taxation and voluntary transfers.

(b) All rich nations should be required to submit a concrete time-table for the implementation of the 0.7 per cent target which should be monitored by the United Nations on behalf of the international community. Those nations unable to implement the target by 1980, because of the time already lost, should accept to compensate by much higher levels in subsequent years.

(c) An increased element of automaticity should be built into international resource generation by linking it to the creation of international liquidity and to the introduction of international taxes on undesirable forms of consumption in the rich nations and on armament spending. Efforts should be made to place at least one-half of the total resource transfers on an automatic basis over the next decade.

(d) The allocation of concessional assistance must be shifted to the poorest nations with per capita incomes below $ 200. Since these nations presently receive only one-half of total concessional assistance, there is considerable scope for reallocation from middle income Third World countries to the poorest nations and for compensating the former through larger trade concessions.

(e) These concessional resources must be directed to national programmes aimed at satisfying minimum human needs in the poorest nations. The international community should agree to provide about $ 10-12 billion a year (in 1974 prices) over the next decade for investment in basic anti-poverty programmes in collaboration with a vigorous internal effort in the poorest nations themselves who will have to ensure that these programmes are maintained.

(f) Arrangements must be made to provide a negotiating forum for an orderly settlement of the past debts of the poorest nations. The most appropriate form of debt relief would be to consolidate their past debts and to refinance them on highly concessional, IDA-type, terms.

(g) In future, assistance to the poorest nations should be provided on the most concessional terms possible. As a target, it should be accepted that at least 90 per cent of international public assistance would be provided to them in the form of either outright grants or loans on IDA terms.

(h) Middle income countries (above $ 200) should be provided greater access to the international capital market and to expanding markets for manufactured exports. Institutional arrangements must also be made to provide them an orderly roll-over of their short term debts through the capital market and additional 'safety nets' and international liquidity to cushion them against short term fluctuations in their increasingly vulnerable balance of payments.

(i) Resource transfers should preferably be channelled through multilateral institutions. Besides a substantial real increase in IBRD and IDA lending and a major augmentation of the resources of the regional development banks, arrangements should also be considered to supply greater funds on intermediate terms through 'Third Window' type arrangements.

(j) The role of Third World countries, including OPEC, and of the centrally planned economies in the management of international institutions should be greatly increased.

(k) A mechanism should be devised to permit an orderly renegotiation of the past concessions, leases and contracts given by Third World countries to transnational enterprises. This should be done within a specified period of time under some international supervision.

Food production

(a) Implementation of measures designed to enhance the self-sufficiency of Third World countries in food production within the framework of (collective) self-reliance, including, where necessary, land reform programmes.

(b) Implementation of decisions of World Food Conference: adequate stockpiling, to be furthered by pressure of agricultural organizations on governments of industrialized countries.

(c) Further contributions to the Fund for Long Term Development of Agriculture in the Third World, for which pressure can be exerted on governments of the industrialized countries by, for example, producers of fertilizer plant. Promotion of international capital transfers to facilitate the construction of small and large scale irrigation schemes, especially in tropical and sub-tropical regions.

(d) Agreements on price and production schemes for basic foodstuffs of interest to Third World countries so as to stimulate food production in the Third World. The price level should be such as to act as an incentive to small farmers in Third World countries in order to facilitate their adoption of improved technological practices.

(e) Furthering transfers of fertilizer gifts or supplies on concessionary terms to the Third World, for which pressure on governments by fertilizer producers is to be applied.

(f) Measures designed to reduce food wastage in industrialized countries, including propaganda for reduction in per capita consumption of grain-intensive meats supported by tax and price policies for meat and coarse grains. Creation of mechanisms for making savings in coarse grains available to food deficit countries.

(g) Efforts to be increased in Third World countries to reduce food wastage arising out of untreated plant diseases, pests, deficient storage and inadequate transportation arrangements. Such efforts should aim at achieving a 50 per cent reduction in post-harvest losses by 1985.

(h) Major emphasis to be given in national development strategies to rural community development with the aim of enhancing the quality of life through improved education, health care and institutional support so as to reduce the rate of urban-rural migration. Development strategies should also aim at preserving the productive capacity of women in the agricultural modernization process and at raising the incomes of the poorest city inhabitants through employment creation and income redistribution so that they can purchase their basic food requirements.

(i)   Major expansion of research efforts into ways of increasing food production and related subjects. Studies to start on long term nutritional targets, at both macro- and micro-levels, as guidelines for the direction of production expansion. Efforts to be continuously made to develop newer varieties not only of cereals but also of pulses, oilseeds and vegetables and of non-traditional and new sources of food, especially food from the sea, so as to provide a nutritionally more adequate diet and to partially alleviate pressure on cereal crops. Agricultural research should be broadened to include research on the development of new agricultural technologies geared to the needs of Third World countries, on better water management, the desalinization of water and the production of artificial rain. Increased experimentation with village communities and rural development organizations, especially on the sociological and psychological levels. Research efforts would be facilitated by the establishment of research institutes in the main regions of the Third World.

(j)   Urgent attention to be given to the creation of a monitoring system in cooperation with the World Meteorological Organization. The monitoring system should take into account not only crop forecasts but also provide a continuous assessment of changing land use patterns, including changes in the ecosphere.

Industrialization, Trade and the International Division of Labour

(a)   Intensification and, where possible, conclusion of international consultations to arrive at more multilaterality in trade relations.

(b)   Reduction of import impediments vis-à-vis semi-manufactured and manufactured products from the Third World, with the aid of pressures of Consumer Unions on their governments for this purpose.

(c)   Implementation of the UNCTAD integrated programme on commodities, in particular unstable markets to be regulated with a common fund to finance the necessary buffer stocks or through compensatory financing so as to regulate export incomes as appropriate.

(d)   Transform UNCTAD into a comprehensive World Trade and Development Organization with the task of regulating the prices of the main exports of Third World countries with a view to continually improving the derived purchasing power in terms of the prices of imports from the industrialized countries. This to be achieved through the application of a range of means designed to increase Third World participation in and control of downstream activities – local processing, storage and banking, transport and marketing processes.

(e)   Increase in the negotiating power of Third World countries through control over their natural resources and the intensification of their efforts towards collective self-reliance.

(f)   Establishment of a world strategy and policies and programmes of industrial development so as to achieve the Lima industrial production objectives including adjustment policies in the industrialized countries; regional cooperation in industrialization programmes. Industrial redeployment should be considered a principal instrument of such programmes.

(g)   Review the feasibility of the International Industrialization Institute recently recommended to the U.N. General Assembly.

(h)   Integrate employment and income distribution objectives in national and international industrialization strategies.

Energy, Ores and Minerals

(a)   Urge the negotiation of commodity agreements with a view to stabilizing production, markets and the prices in real terms of the most important mineral raw materials.

(b)   Encourage and accept the formation of producers' associations in primary commodities which, as legitimate instruments of collective bargaining, can help offset the considerable concentration of economic power presently vested in the buying end.

(c)   Urgent examination of the present marketing and price structure of primary commodities to determine the advantages which can be derived by Third World producer countries from, for example, the further processing of primary commodities and participation in down stream activities.

(d)   Creation, as part of the proposed World Trade and Development Organization, of a World Agency for Mineral Resources with the following tasks: preparation and supervision of future commodity agreements; compilation and circulation of information on commercial transactions, ore reserves and trends in their exploitation; and putting forward comments and suggestions to countries on their mining policies.

(e)   Expand information on endowment with ores; internationalization of information derived from earth satellites.

(f)   Intensification of research into recycling possibilities, especially of non-renewable resources, and the expansion of recycling activities shown to be feasible and environmentally sound.

(g)   Strongly stimulate research on geothermal, solar, tidal, biogas and nuclear fusion energy, possibly coordinated by a World Energy Research Authority (within the U.N. framework) and partly financed by revenues derived from a tax on the kilowatt hours of nuclear fission energy produced.

(h)   Implementation of measures to save energy in energy-intensive countries and to better use waste low grade heat, including the recuperation of part of heat losses, particularly from thermal power plants.

(i)   Expansion of research into the thermal pollution consequences associated with energy development programmes, concentrating on their effects on climate and including the role which can be played by deep ocean waters.

Scientific Research and Technological Development

(a)   Promotion of a system of subsidizing prices at which technological know-how can be made available to Third World countries. Such subsidized research should focus on increasing the ability of Third World countries to expand employment opportunities, to satisfy basic needs and to promote self-reliant styles of development.

(b)   Organization of a pool of technological information (a register of such knowledge) which can be used by governments of the Third World in their negotiations on technology transfer and in their efforts at formulating deliberate policies for technological development organically linked to the attainment of social and economic objectives; this should result from cooperation between the U.N. agencies involved.

(c)   The elaboration of an international code of conduct for the transfer of technology under different forms and the revision of the Paris Convention on the protection of industrial property in the light of the development needs of Third World countries.

(d)   Appropriate reexamination and reinforcement of the U.N. system. Urgent attempts to be made to formulate coherent programmes of scientific research and technological development; such programmes to give due attention to developments within the U.N. system and to be drawn up as a cooperative endeavour by the specialized agencies. Such programmes should contribute towards the improvement of the efficiency of such agencies; the planned U.N. Conference on Science and Technology should be directed, among other ends, to this improvement of efficiency.

(e)   High quality research institutes with high level manpower training programmes must be established and expanded in the Third World, especially in arid and semi-arid regions, on a national, sub-regional and regional basis in order to focus research on the problems of poor countries and to reduce the 'brain drain'. Special priority should be given to research of particular benefit to the poorest groups within countries and regions. Examples of such research include nitrogen fixation for grains, pest resistant crop varieties, schistosomiasis and river blindness in arid and semi-arid lands. Emphasis should also be placed on the development of 'appropriate' technologies.

Transnational Enterprises

(a) Agreement to be negotiated on minimum information to be supplied by transnational enterprises on their activities, employment created, total and local capital attracted, investment per capita and some technology characteristics (productivity, capital intensity, as compared with countries of origin).

(b) Building up a pool of technological knowledge to service governments of the Third World in negotiations with transnational enterprises, and a register of performance of transnational enterprises in different countries.

(c) Compliance by transnational enterprises with the host nation's development plan, which specifies the aims of highest urgency such as the creation of employment, the increase in food production and the redistribution of incomes.

(d) Research on alternative ways of performing the function of transnational enterprises including public international enterprises.

(e) Increased cooperation between governments to establish countervailing power and to make tax structures more uniform.

(f) Increased cooperation of transnational enterprises with the U.N. Research and Information Centre. Creation of an international body of voluntary technical advisors.

(g) Formulation of a Code of Conduct on transnational enterprises with legally enforceable elements so as to meet the most urgent needs of the host countries. This code should address itself to such questions as ownership and control, financial flows, local value-added and balance of payments, research and development, commercialization of technology, employment and labour, consumer protection, competition and market structure, transfer pricing, taxation, accounting standards and disclosure, and refraining from intervening in a host country's political affairs.

Human Environment

(a) We require a better understanding of the working of outer limits and, in this connection, of the interactions between natural and social processes. 'Nature accounting' must be developed to enable us to follow the changes in the stock of nature capital. It must be then brought in line with social indicators of quality of life and economic accounting of costs of development strategies. Ways must be equally found to quantify the wastefulness of present patterns of resource use. A major reassessment of technological effort is called for in order to foster new uses of solar energy and renewable resources, with special emphasis on technologies for decentralized use of non-conventional sources of energy. We must learn to design techno-industrial structures as true systems and to explore the interfaces between lifestyles, urban design and production systems. Ecodevelopment requires mass mobilization of participatory research on specific solutions to local problems. The range of subjects explored in an ecodevelopment perspective should cover all basic needs in the realm of food, habitat, health and sanitation, as well as education. As ecodevelopment also calls for bold institutional and organizational innovations, life-size experiments should be promoted with active support from UNEP, UNDP and international lending organizations without forgetting, however, that the primary responsibility for endogenous development is by definition vested with concerned populations and their political bodies.

(b) National agencies should be created with responsibilities for global resource management. They should be entrusted with the coordination and supervision of the activities of sectoral and regional bodies.

(c) The viability of the proposal to change development styles depends upon our ability to outline transitional strategies. Such strategies should give special attention to alternative uses of existing productive capacities, redeployment of industrial activities, substitution of non-renewable by renewable resources, and the creation of new job opportunities in resource management and social services activities. Work on these should start as soon as possible.

(d) Life-size ecodevelopment experiments should be promoted in different ecosystems and cultural settings and the experience thus gained compared, analyzed and disseminated.

(e) At the international level, it is necessary to define the regime of the 'international commons' and to set up an agency to exploit their resources in the interest of the poorest section of the world's population. The introduction of ocean-tolls and air-tolls should be considered. Another agency should be established to control the use of 'international commons'. UNIDO could be entrusted with setting up a technical assistance unit specialized in the evaluation of environmental impacts of new industrial projects.

Arms Reduction

(a) Exert strong political and moral pressure on the superpowers through national and international actions to redirect military expenditures towards development because of the enormous threats posed by such expenditures to all mankind and in view of the waste they constitute of financial, material and human resources.

(b) Achieve a Treaty on a Comprehensive Nuclear Test Ban and start genuine nuclear disarmament.

(c) Achieve a Convention banning chemical weapons.

(d) Ban indiscriminate and unnecessarily cruel conventional weapons.

(e) Gradually transfer scientific and technological resources now used for military purposes to development purposes.

(f) Establish means for regulating the arms trade, through national legislation or otherwise.

(g) Reinforcement of the United Nations Peace Force within the context of the democratization of the U.N. Security Council.

(h) Review the need for and feasibility of a World Disarmament Agency within the framework of the United Nations.

Ocean Management

A *Independent of Treaty*

(a) Strengthening of *regional cooperation and organization* in fishing and the management of living resources, scientific research, the transfer of technology, and the furnishing of science-based services, the protection of the marine environment and the interaction of all uses of marine space and resources: such arrangements to be viewed as complementary and indispensable, rather than alternative, to the long term objective of continued progress towards a world-wide system. Action could be initiated through regional economic commissions and fisheries commissions and through ad hoc agreements among States bordering enclosed or semi-enclosed seas.

(b) Establishment of *regional institutes* for marine sciences and technology and their coordination through global organizations such as IOC. Action could be initiated by any group of nations, especially in less developed regions, through regional banks or UNDP.

(c) Enhancement of participation of developing land-locked States and developing islands in the marine economy, through bilateral or multilateral agreements, in the wider context of UNCTAD recommendations.

(d) Increase of participation by developing nations in world shipping tonnage and sea-borne international trade.

(e) Enforcement of the UNCTAD Code of Conduct for Liner Conferences.

(f) Extension of the concept of zones of peace and security to other ocean areas, such as the Mediterranean. The U.N. General Assembly has approved the establishment of a zone of peace in the Indian Ocean.

(g) Restructuring of COFI, IOC, and IMCO, to respond to changing political, economic, ecological and technological needs; strengthening of cooperation with organizations outside the U.N. system, such as the International Hydrographic Bureau. Action must be initiated within the agencies themselves, but could be encouraged by resolutions or recommendations adopted by the General Assembly and/or by the Law of the Sea Conference.

B   *On the Basis of a Treaty and the Establishment of a Continuing Mechanism*

(a) Clarification of major ambiguities contained in the Treaty and consideration, as appropriate, of such matters of an urgent and important nature for which there are no provisions in the Treaty.

(b) Clarification as appropriate of the Law of the Sea with regard to military uses of ocean space, a subject disregarded, for all practical purposes, in the Treaty.

(c) Establishment of criteria for the harmonization of ocean space uses both within and beyond the limits of national jurisdiction; another subject ignored by the Treaty.

(d) Establishment of links, at the national, regional and international levels, between development of marine resource management and land-based development in such areas as food, mineral production, energy production, international trade, collective self-reliance, relations with transnational enterprises, etc.

(e) Inclusion of the goal of a new international economic order in the oceans on the agenda of other international continuous or ad hoc fora such as UNCTAD, Regional Economic Commissions, Non-Aligned Summit, etc.

Introduction to Part IV

Part IV is devoted to the reports prepared by the ten RIO working groups. These reports form the main 'supporting evidence' of the RIO project and comprise the foundation upon which much of the three previous parts of this report have been built.

In general, each report begins with an analysis of the main problem area addressed and then deals with prospects for the future. The reports end with proposals and recommendations for action in the medium and long term.

Annex 1 The International Monetary Order
Duncan Ndegwa* and Robert Triffin

1.1 *Money and Monetary Institutions*

Money serves as lubricating oil for the socio-economic order. Means of payment are indispensable for trade and other transactions within or across national frontiers. Commodity currencies evolved from shells and cattle to precious metals; then gold and silver gave way to token coins and paper instruments. Credit money has totally replaced precious metals in domestic trade; and the use of gold bullion for international settlements had been largely superseded by paper currency — convertible or not into gold — even before August 1971. The residual use of gold as a reserve stock for central banks should and will be phased out gradually.

Confidence in monetary management and in monetary authorities is an important consideration. Such confidence has been severely shaken by price inflation throughout the western world, associated with an uncontrolled expansion of the supply of money both owned within issuing states, and owned by banks and monetary authorities of other states.

Central banks are largely responsible for management of national currencies and for maintenance of orderly markets wherein their national currencies may be exchanged for other currencies for current international payments. Although many national currencies are usable in international trade it has been convenient for each central bank to use one or two widely held currencies as 'reserve currencies', for control of the market for its own currency, and to use only market forces (arbitrage) to maintain orderly cross rates for others.

Exchange transactions do not equilibrate from day to day, nor even over fairly long periods of time and, in the absence of official intervention, disequilibria could result in substantial price (i.e. *exchange rate*) variations. Official intervention to counteract a tendency for national currencies to appreciate causes accumulation of reserve currencies in the ownership of the intervening authorities.

Excess and uncontrolled accumulation of reserve currencies in the hands of official and unofficial institutions, and in relatively liquid form, has facilitated the *continual increase in world prices*. Speculative movements of such liquid funds may tend towards equilibrium, but may also be severely disruptive.

1.2 *The Movement of Monetary Reform*

In the late sixties concern was felt in the opposite sense: it then appeared that reserve creation through growth of holdings of national currencies would be insufficient to finance desired growth in world trade and members of the International Monetary Fund (IMF) adopted amendments to their Articles of Agreement (effective July 1969) enabling the Fund to allocate a new form of reserve asset called *Special Drawing Rights* (SDRs) to member states which are participants in the Special Drawing Account of the Fund.

The SDR was defined, like the pre-existing unit of account of the Fund, as equivalent to 0.888671 gram of fine gold but was not convertible into gold: its value depended upon

---

* with the cooperation of Brian Oliver.

the obligation of each participant in the account to accept SDRs for specified amounts and to provide its currency against them. It was designed to permit deliberate and internationally controlled expansion of world reserves to the requirements of feasible non-inflationary growth in world trade and production.

The small expansion coming from this source has since been totally overwhelmed by the uncontrolled accumulation of ever-increasing holdings of *national* currencies in official and unofficial institutions of other states. The growth of official reserves is set out in Table 1.

After the 1971 devaluation of the US dollar, which had previously been defined by the same gold content, the Fund adopted the SDR as the unit of account in all its operations; from July 1974 the value of the unit in transactions between the Fund and its members has been determined in terms of a weighted 'basket' of the sixteen currencies of countries whose 1968-72 exports constituted one per cent or more of world exports. In August 1975 agreement was reached that the official price of gold will be abolished and the countries in the Group of Ten have agreed to observe certain constraints to eliminate any attempt to peg the price of gold.

In principle it has been agreed that one sixth of the Fund's gold shall be sold for the benefit of developing countries and another sixth shall be restored to all members in proportion to their subscriptions, at the old and now obsolete official price (1).

1.3   *The Urgency of International Monetary Reconstruction*

World inflation and the forced modification of the Bretton Woods system make international agreement on fundamental reforms of the world monetary system more urgent than ever. The broad lines of such an agreement seemed to have rallied a broad consensus after more than ten years of the official debates initiated in October 1963.

Remaining obstacles to such an agreement, however, have increased as a result of the balance-of-payments disruptions and uncertain prospects triggered by the energy crisis. Governments are more reluctant than ever to tie their hands today by international commitments which they might feel unable, or unwilling, to honor tomorrow. This is perfectly understandable, but nevertheless regrettable, for two reasons:
(I) the first is that formidable balance-of-payments disruptions and world inflation *preceded*, and *contributed to*, the explosion of world prices; their seeds would still be with us tomorrow even if the oil problem could be solved;
(II) the second is that the international monetary reforms on which a broad agreement had previously emerged would provide a far more comprehensive, rational, and mutually attractive solution to the 'recycling' problem of OPEC surpluses than the 'Witteveen Facility', 'Kissinger-Simon safety net', and other palliatives now being negotiated.
After a comprehensive reform, all countries (and not the OPEC countries alone) would commit themselves to accumulate the bulk of their future surpluses in truly international reserve accounts with the IMF (broadly similar to SDRs), carrying adequate 'maintenance of value' guarantees, and available to finance mutually agreed policy objectives.

The January 1976 Jamaica agreement unfortunately confirms the practical burial — for the time being — of the comprehensive reforms previously envisaged and usefully

---

(1) Report to the Board of Governors of the International Monetary Fund by the Chairman of the Interim Committee on the International Monetary System September 1, 1975 (IMF Washington D.C.).

Table 1   *Sources and Beneficiaries of International Reserve Creation: 1970-74*
(in billions of SDR's = U.S. $ until 1971)

	World	Industrialized Countries			Third World Countries		
		U.S.	Other	Total	Total	OPEC	Other
I. *Bal. of Payments Surpluses or Deficits* (−)(= III-II)	= *Gold* 0.3	-66.2	22.5	-43.7	44.0	33.6	10.4
II. *Beneficiaries of Credit Reserve Creation:*	99.6	62.4	34.0	96.4	3.2	0.2	2.9
A. *Of Concerted Reserve Creation:*	7.3	1.2	2.8	4.2	3.2	0.2	2.9
1. SDR Allocations	9.3	2.3	4.7	7.0	2.3	0.4	2.0
2. Net IMF Lending	-1.4	-1.0	-1.2	-2.2	0.9	-0.1	1.0
3. Net BIS-EF Lending	-0.6	–	-0.6	-0.6	–	–	–
B. *Of Acceptance of Natl. Currencies as Intl. Reserves*	92.3	61.1	31.2	92.3	–	–	–
III. *Gross Reserves* (I + II):	99.9	-3.9	56.5	52.7	47.2	33.9	13.3
at the end of 1969	78.1	17.0	45.7	62.6	15.5	4.2	11.3
1970	92.4	14.5	60.0	74.5	18.0	5.0	13.0
1971	120.0	12.1	86.8	98.9	21.1	7.7	13.4
1972	145.6	12.1	104.7	116.8	28.8	10.0	18.8
1973	150.7	11.9	103.5	115.5	35.3	12.0	23.3
1974	178.0	13.1	102.2	115.3	62.7	38.1	24.6

Sources and Notes:
1. All these estimates are derived from the 'International Reserves' Tables of the January (for 1969) and May 1975 issues of *International Financial Statistics*, and regrettably exclude Communist countries for which no reliable estimates are published.
2. Net IMF lending (line IIA2) is the sum of IMF 'Gold deposits and investments' and 'Use of Fund Credit' *minus* the undistributed profits of the IMF, allotted here *pro rata* of quotas: 23% to the U.S., 49% to other industrialized countries, 5% to OPEC and 23% to other Third World countries.
3. Industrialized countries can be assumed to be the only beneficiaries of the Bank for International Settlements (BIS) and European Fund (EF) reserve credits (= excess of gold deposit liabilities over gold holdings) and of the accumulation of their national currencies as international reserves by foreign central banks.
4. The conservative 'guesstimate' of the U.S. share of reserve currency liabilities (2nd column of line IIB) includes only those reported as direct liabilities *plus* the liabilities of foreign branches of U.S. banks to official institutions reported in Table 19b of the *Federal Reserve Bulletin*. Liabilities to the BIS and the EF are not reported separately, but are included in the line IIB estimates.
5. Balance-of-payments surpluses or deficits (line I) are measured by the differences between the increases in countries' gross reserves (line III) and in their reserve liabilities (line II). Their net total for the world as a whole is equal, by definition, to the increase in world gold reserves, including those of the IMF, BIS, and EF.

recorded in *International Monetary Reform: Documents of the Committee of Twenty*. The draft amendments to the Articles of Agreement agreed in Jamaica hardly touch on the major issues previously identified as calling for fundamental reform and discussed below.

1.4 *Major Issues*

Three major issues had been identified as calling for fundamental reform. These issues were:
(I) The adjustment of world reserve creation to the non-inflationary requirements of potential growth in world trade and production;
(II) A prompter and more symmetrical system of balance-of-payments adjustment among member countries;
(III) A maximum reduction of disequilibrating capital movements and the neutralization of those which could not be effectively prevented.

1.4.1 *World Reserve Creation*

The existing uncontrolled method of world reserve creation had unquestionably become — and still is — a major *engine for world inflation*: world reserves, expressed in dollars, more than doubled from the end of 1969 to the end of 1972, *increasing over this short span of three years more than they had in all previous years and centuries since Adam and Eve.* They nearby doubled (increasing by 87%) even measured in SDRs. The resulting collapse, in August 1971, of the 'gold-exchange standard' — or rather of the 'gold-convertible dollar standard' prevailing since the end of the Second World War — and the generalization of 'floating rates' in March 1973 have not fundamentally changed the previous trend. World reserves have continued to increase at inflationary rates averaging approximately 11% a year, measured in SDRs and 18% a year, measured in dollars, over the two years 1973 and 1974 (2).

The use of national 'reserve currencies' as international reserves is the overwhelming source of this inflationary functioning of the international monetary system. The 'reserve currencies' component of world reserves nearly quadrupled from the end of 1969 to the end of 1974 and accounts for 92% of the total reserve increase over that period. (See line IIB of Table 1).

In contrast, physical gold reserves have remained practically unchanged (line I). Internationally concerted reserve creation (SDR allocations and IMF and Bank for International Settlements (BIS) credits) contributed only 7% of the total 1970-74 increase of world reserves (line IIA). International monetary negotiators had previously drawn the obvious conclusion from these facts: future reserve creation should centre on internationally controllable SDRs (or reserve accounts with the IMF), while gold and reserve currencies should be 'phased out' of the system.

1.4.2 *The Adjustment Process*

The same conclusion emerged inevitably from the debates concerning the second major objective of a well functioning international monetary system, *i.e.* the preservation or restoration of a healthy and sustainable pattern of balances-of-payments between individual countries. Such a pattern should *not* rule out temporary — even protected — disequilibria deemed more acceptable, both by surplus and deficit countries, than the consequences of their abrupt suppression. In the first years following the Second World War, for example, the redistribution of excess US reserves to war-torn, low-reserve countries was rightly welcomed by all concerned and accelerated the pace of

---

(2) For simplicity's sake, following estimates will be expressed in SDRs rather than in dollars.

postwar reconstruction. More generally, the transfer of reserves as well as other capital funds from high-reserve, relatively overcapitalized countries suffering from deflationary pressures to low-reserve, relatively undercapitalized developing countries suffering from inflationary pressures *should* obviously be welcome to both groups.

The same would be true in the event of speculative, reversible capital movements calling for collective off-setting action by the Fund rather than for exchange-rate readjustments susceptible of disturbing rather than restoring competitive cost and price relationships. What the international monetary system should definitely exclude is the excessive reserve financing of national deficits, exporting inflationary pressures to other countries, and of national surpluses, exporting deflationary pressures to other countries.

No individual country should be permitted to prevent or frustrate the readjustment of its disequilibria, whether surpluses or deficits:
(I) deficit countries, by forcing upon creditors their own currency or IOUs in settlement; or
(II) surplus countries, by accumulating the national currency of one or a few reserve-currency debtors in the expectation of being able to pass it on to other countries in settlement of future deficits.

We should, therefore, favour a strong presumptive rule of asset settlements such as is embodied in the proposed 'substitution facility' which provides both for the multilateral and symmetrical asset settlement — excluding 'reserve-currencies' liabilities — of future surpluses and deficits and for an acceptable system of consolidation of excessive balances of reserve currencies ('overhang') inherited from the past. This asset settlement rule should be a *presumption* to which exceptions could be made only by collective decisions that financing may be more appropriate than adjustment, for the reasons summarized in the first paragraph of this section.

Table 1 shows how defective the international monetary system has been in this respect over the last five years. Concerted international decisions (line IIA) accounted for only 7 per cent of the growth of reserves in 1970-74, and physical additions to the world monetary gold stock for less than half of one per cent. The acceptance of reserve currencies not only contributed 92 per cent of the inflationary explosion of world reserves, but in effect financed balance-of-payments disequilibria in a manner directly opposite to the criteria summarized above:
(I) The presumption of asset settlement was *totally reversed* for the reserve currency countries, *i.e.* primarily for the United States, whose cumulative deficits (measured by net reserve losses and SDR allocations) totalled more than SDR 66 billion over this period (nearly four times the US total reserve assets of the US at the end of 1969) and could be sustained only because 94 per cent of them were financed by increased liabilities (SDR 62 billion) rather than by asset losses (SDR 4 billion). Moreover, these increased liabilities served as a base for further uncontrolled expansion of dollar credits in the Eurocurrency markets.
(II) This huge reserve financing did not reflect any *collective* decision, but resulted primarily from the reluctance of individual surplus countries to let their currency appreciate vis-à-vis the dollar.
(III) Line II of the fourth and fifth columns of the Table shows that 96.4 billion (97 per cent) of this inflationary flood of reserve credits benefited 27 relatively affluent developed countries, and only 3.2 billion (3 per cent) the 99 poorer and least capitalized countries of the IMF.

These reserve loans and investments enabled the developed countries to finance overall balance-of-payments deficits of 43.7 billion (as measured by their losses of *net* reserves, shown on line I), but exceeded these deficits by 52.7 billion which they added to their *gross* reserves (line III), nearly doubling them over these five years, and contributing to their domestic monetary inflation.

Published estimates identify about half ($ 60.6 billion) of the $ 120.3 billion growth of foreign exchange reserves as liabilities of the United States, and $ 2.2 billion as liabilities of the United Kingdom, but unfortunately do not break down the residual $ 57.5 billion difference between recorded exchange assets and liabilities increases. The breakdown presented in the second and third columns of the Table is therefore highly conjectural. It merely adds to reported direct US liabilities to foreign official institutions the reported liabilities of foreign branches of US banks to the same institutions — less than half of the 'identified official Euro-dollar holdings' reported for the years 1969-1973 on p. 39 of the IMF *Annual Report* — and ascribes all the remaining residual to other developed countries (3). This may underestimate US liabilities and overestimate correspondingly the liabilities of these other countries. Yet, it shows the increase of US liabilities as two thirds of the total increase in reserve currency holdings (line IIB) and the total loans and investments received by the United States (line II) as having financed more than 94% (62.4 billion) of the cumulative US deficits over these five years (line I: 66.2 billion) (4).

Two striking observations emerge from this dismal record:
(I) The acceptance of national currencies as international reserves has been over these years the main source, by far, of frustration of the much vaunted process of balance-of-payments adjustment, as well as a major engine of world inflation. It enabled reserve-currency countries (primarily the United States) to run enormous and persistent deficits, and it enabled other countries (primarily Western Europe and Japan) to run equally huge and persistent surpluses, without forcing upon either group timely and appropriate changes in domestic policies, or exchange rates, or both.
(II) This lending and investment pattern ran directly contrary to the often repeated pious resolutions of the United Nations calling for an acceleration of capital exports from the richest and most capitalized countries to the poorest and least capitalized ones. The lending and investment mechanisms most fully controlled by national and international monetary authorities was used in exactly the reverse direction, bringing coal to Newcastle. It admittedly contributed to the ability of the recipient countries to expand their loans and investments in the Third World (5), but in amounts and directions determined unilaterally by them, on the basis of political as well as economic and humanitarian considerations.

A substantial portion of these credits, moreover, could also be diverted to other aims — such as military escalation and the takeover of enterprises through unrequited direct

---

(3) Reserve holdings of LDCs currencies may safely be assumed to have been insignificant up to now, but might conceivably include in the future some 'strong' OPEC currencies and, hopefully, the currencies of participants in existing and emerging regional arrangements. Small but growing, holdings of IBRD bonds are also grouped in the Table under the developed countries column.
(4) In the last two years of generalized floating rates, they even overfinanced the US deficits, adding 1 billion to the US gross reserves. Note also that the depreciation of the dollar in terms of SDRs entailed net foreign exchange losses of $ 5.3 billion for the other developed countries, and of $ 12.4 billion for the less developed countries (as measured by the difference in their *net* foreign exchange assets calculated in US dollars and in SDRs, at the end of 1974).
(5) And even to overfinance these countries' actual current account deficits, enabling them to quadruple their meager international reserves (see bottom lines of fifth column).

investments — which could hardly be regarded as serving the highest priority objectives of the international community or of the main reserve lenders.

1.4.3 *Disequilibrating Capital Movements*   The basic balance-of-payments maladjustments discussed earlier are primarily responsible for the dramatic increase of disequilibrating movements of speculative capital in recent years. While these would be difficult to measure exactly and to isolate from other capital flows, it is obvious that they must have contributed substantially to the dramatic increase of US private capital exports (including errors and omissions) from a yearly average of $ 5.5 billion in the 1960's to nearly $ 20 billion in 1971, yearly averages of $ 13.6 billion in the next two years and $ 25.4 billion in 1974.

Furthermore the measures taken by monetary authorities of surplus countries to ward off unwelcome inflows have encouraged very large deposits of foreign currencies in the hands of commercial banks in Europe and elsewhere. Supervisory authorities generally require banks which accept foreign currency deposits to employ the funds in the same currency or, if employed in another currency, to cover the exchange risk by forward contracts. Deposits in the Euro-currency market are difficult to measure because the market depends for liquidity on a network of inter-bank deposits, but gross assets and liabilities of reporting European banks in foreign currency are reported by BIS at $ 177 billion at the end of 1974. This total includes a relatively small but undisclosed proportion of official reserves, but it exceeds in magnitude the $ 160.8 billion reported by BIS as the total of official foreign exchange holdings of all countries. IMF reports official foreign exchange holdings of all members plus Switzerland at $ 153 billion at the same date.

The unofficial holdings can move from bank to bank and from currency to currency with bewildering rapidity when creditors or debtors find it necessary to protect themselves against — or to take advantage of — anticipated changes in exchange relationships. Informed speculators may well off-set temporary disequilibria and so smooth out price fluctuations; however, very few operators are now in a position to carry an 'open' position voluntarily from one day to another, still less from one month to another. Emphasis on the obligation to minimize exposure to exchange risks increases the volatility of rate movements, because the operator or trader who foresees a change is obliged to speed up his responses and sometimes so precipitates the expected movement with snowball effects.

The major action urgently needed to reduce the size of disequilibrating capital movements and make them manageable is to correct the *permissiveness* of an international monetary system financing blindly the basic maladjustments of the reserve-currency countries. Beyond this, international consultations should obviously aim at promoting:
(I) mutually agreed and enforced measures to encourage re-equilibrating capital movements welcome by the capital-losing as well as by the capital-receiving countries and to deter disequilibrating movements obnoxious to all alike;
(II) compensatory — or 'recycling' — action by the IMF itself, offsetting disturbing capital movements by a reshuffling of Fund's resources between the countries concerned.

1.5   **Concrete Conclusions and Recommendations**

The reconstruction of the international monetary order calls for an accelerated effort to negotiate as promptly as possible agreements on which a broad consensus had previously emerged from years of debates by the IMF, the Group of Ten, the Committee of Twenty, and others as well as by most independent observers.

1.5.1 *Reserve Creation*   International reserve deposits with the IMF — broadly similar, but more flexible and attractive than the present SDRs — should become the major settlement and reserve instrument for all countries (OPIC as well as OPEC), and an internationally defined unit of account — rather than gold or the US dollar — should be the common denominator (or 'numéraire') in which effective exchange rates are defined, measured, and changed when necessary by all member countries (6).

It is now clear that this unit of account will be the SDR, valued by reference to a basket of currencies, with discretion to the Board of the Fund to change the composition of the basket by a majority of 70% of the voting power.

Future lending and investment operations of the IMF should aim at adjusting the expansion of world reserves to the requirements of feasible, non-inflationary, growth in world trade and production (7). An annual 'fork' — maximum and minimum percentage — on the size of future reserve creation should probably be imposed by the Articles of Agreement as a *presumptive* rule, to which exceptions could be made only by special, weighted majority vote called for by recognized inflationary, or deflationary, trends in the world economy.

The lending power derived by the IMF from such a reform — in which reserve deposits in the IMF would be accepted in settlement and retained as reserves by all member countries — would be overwhelmingly of a long-term, rather than short-term character. It should be used exclusively for the financing of agreed objectives, carrying the highest priority for the international community. One of the major objectives of this sort repeatedly endorsed by UN resolutions would be the financing of development in the poorest and least capitalized countries of the Third World (8). Other eligible objectives would be the traditional operations of the IMF, including the offsetting of disequilibrating capital movements but also — when opinion becomes sufficiently enlightened to accept it — the financing of other high-priority objectives of the United Nations, the World Health Organization, etc.

The implementation of these reforms entails, as already agreed upon in principle, the 'phasing out' of gold and reserve currencies from the international settlements and reserve system (9).

(I) As far as *gold* is concerned, the consensus reached by the IMF Interim Committee in August 1975 and confirmed in Jamaica in January 1976 (10) provides a highly ingenious and acceptable compromise between very different, and legitimate, national and international concerns and objectives, and particularly:

(a) The confirmation of the existing 'demonetization' of gold, in the sense that gold will be assimilated to other commodities whose price is essentially determined by the market rather than stabilized through unlimited purchases or sales by some monetary

---

(6) See e.g.: Committee on Reform of the International Monetary System and Related Issues (Committee of Twenty), *International Monetary Reform, Documents of the Committee of Twenty* (IMF, Washington, D.C., 1974), June 1974 Report to Board of Governors, Section 24, p. 15, and also report to this Board of Governors of IMF by the Chairman of the Interim Committee on the International Monetary System, September 1st 1975. (IMF: Washington D.C.).

(7) Id. section 25, p. 15.

(8) Id., sections 29 and 30, pp. 17-18, and Annex 10, pp. 45-48. Also proposal adopted by Seventh Special Session of UN Assembly 16 September 1975 (A/AC 176 L.3 UN New York).

(9) Id., section 24, p. 15 and *passim.*

(10) See IMF Survey, January 19, 1976, pp. 18-19.

authority — national or international — against corresponding redemptions or issues of currency. The official gold price will be abolished.

(b) The possibility for national monetary authorities, as well as for the IMF, to mobilize previously accumulated gold holdings at a realistic price, both in their dealings with one another and with the market.

(c) Complex provisions through which a substantial portion of the accounting profits derived from the sale of IMF gold or its restitution to members at the present official price will benefit the less developed countries, and particularly those with 1973 per capita incomes not in excess of SDR 300.

(II) The 'phasing out' of *reserve currencies* from the international settlement and reserve system is even more crucial in view of their huge past and current inflationary impact and of the fact that they are the main source of frustration of the balance-of-payments discipline imposed upon, and accepted by, all other countries in deficit. International reserve deposits with the Fund should ultimately become the exclusive means of official settlement and reserve accumulation. For this to become generally possible, IMF reserve deposits must be 'no longer confined to official operations and settlements, but should be widely traded in and held by private markets' (11).

Deposits with the Fund should be more attractive to monetary authorities than any other form of reserve holdings. The 'basket' valuation of the Fund's accounting unit, and the 1974 decisions on remuneration and interest on Special Drawing Rights move in this direction. It would be necessary that the major authorities arrange to limit the growth of unofficial foreign exchange balances to a non-inflationary rate, and also agree to avoid further accumulation in official reserves of liquid claims expressed in other national currencies. In the transition period needed to develop a market in IMF reserve deposits, daily intervention in the exchange market will continue to require the use of more familiar national currency instruments but monetary authorities should avoid carrying excessive balances by turning over to the Fund for credit of the account of the depositing country and debit to that of the issuing country and national currency balances in excess of agreed criteria. The huge 'overhang' of reserve-currencies indebtedness inherited from the past could obviously not be debited overnight. It could be consolidated into a 'Substitution Account' as suggested on pp. 42-42, and 162-179 of the Report of the *Committee of Twenty*.

Unfortunately, this central and most crucial aspect of previous reform proposals is totally omitted from the draft amendment agreed in Jamaica and now submitted to all member countries for ratification.

1.5.2 *Re-adjustment Policies* Excessive and persistent disequilibria — surpluses as well as deficits — in a country's international transactions and settlements should trigger IMF consultations concerning which of the alternative readjustment policies should be least damaging and most acceptable to all concerned: changes in domestic monetary and fiscal policies, exchange-rate readjustments or floating, stimulation or deterrents to capital inflows or outflows through interest-rate adaptation or other measures, and/or further financing of such surpluses or deficits. Agreed measures should be implemented and enforced mutually by all countries concerned. Two cases, however, should be distinguished in this respect.

First of all, any country should receive the strong *'benefit of the doubt'* in such consultations regarding the measures which it is itself ready to adopt and implement to

---

(11) Id., p. 123. See also section 12, p. 12, Annex 3, pp. 32-33, and pp. 122-124, for more complex intervention systems not dependent on private SDR holdings.

correct its disequilibria. In the absence of agreement, the presumptive rule should be that it would be free to restrain or cease its interventions in the exchange market and let its exchange rate float, subject to the general guidelines adopted by the Fund. This should be particularly the case for relatively small countries whose surpluses or deficits are not of such a size as to exert a major impact upon the international community.

Secondly, however, other members and particularly the IMF executive Board, Council, or Managing Director should have the authority to *initiate consultations and proposals* with respect to surpluses or deficits whose size can have a major impact on others. Reserve increase or decreases exceeding an agreed percentage of world reserves and bringing a country's own reserves well above or below 'normal' levels (defined, as a first approximation, as a percentage of world reserves appropriate to its share in world trade and other identifiable balance-of-payments receipts and expenditures) should clearly trigger such an initiative and give the 'benefit of the doubt' to the other countries regarding the measures called for to remedy such a disequilibrium. In the absence of agreement, these countries should, at the very least, be relieved of any obligation to intervene in the exchange market at the cost of further reserve gains, or losses, interfering with their own legitimate anti-inflationary, or anti-deflationary policy objectives (12).

1.5.3   *Exchange Rates*   The most controversial issue least likely to be satisfactorily resolved on a worldwide basis in the near future is the degree of flexibility of exchange rates that should facilitate balance-of-payments adjustments without degenerating into incompatible, nationalistic actions and policies destructive of any international monetary and economic order.

Many countries – and particularly the developing countries – favour 'stable, but adjustable' par values and exchange rates, while the United States has veered strongly towards more 'flexibility' than is acceptable to them (13).
The wide fluctuations in the exchange rates of the dollar in recent years have prompted, inevitably and rationally, different reactions by other countries, depending primarily on the geographical pattern of their trade, financial and political relations. Some countries have continued to define and readjust their exchange rates in terms of the dollar and to be, in effect, members of a 'dollar area'. Some countries which found this link convenient while the dollar was depreciating in late 1974 and early 1975 were breaking the link as the dollar appreciated again strongly throughout the rest of the year. At the other extreme, the countries of the European Community are seeking to stabilize – and occasionally readjust – their exchange rates vis-à-vis one another rather than with the dollar, and aim at full economic and monetary union culminating eventually in an effective merger of their national currencies into a single European currency.

1.5.4   *Regional Integration*   This dichotomy imposes a painful choice upon other countries whose trading, financial and political relationships are less clearcut. This should accelerate the already existing trend towards regional integration in various parts of the world, such as in Central America, the Andean group of countries, the COMECON, the ESCAP, etc. These regional groups in turn, as well as individual countries, will tend to gravitate towards those with which they are more closely linked, and to seek formal or informal agreements with them. This should be encouraged as a way:
(I) to palliate the harmful results of the delays foreseeable in reaching worldwide agreements;

---

(12) See similar, additional, and different suggestions about adjustment in op. cit., sections 4-17, pp. 8-13, Annexes 1 and 2, pp. 24-30, and *passim.*
(13) Id., sections 11-13, pp. 11-12, Annex 4, pp. 33-37, and *passim.*

(II) to facilitate such agreements and relieve the IMF of responsibilities that can be more easily and efficiently implemented on a regional, less cumbersome and more decentralized scale;

(III) to exploit more fully the opportunities for closer integration — up to monetary, economic and political union — that will be possible, for a long time to come, only between countries whose close interdependence on one another can generate political support for, and acceptance of, the partial mergers of 'national sovereignty' indispensable for such beneficial integration of their policies and institutions.

1.5.5 *Summary of Conclusions* Let us note, in conclusion that the *substitution of reserve accounts with the Fund* for national reserve currencies as the major, or even exclusive, instrument for settlements and reserve accumulation *is the most crucial prerequisite for the fulfilment of all the essential objectives of international monetary reform:*

(I) The concerted adjustment of reserve creation to the requirements of potential, non-inflationary growth in world trade and production.

(II) The use of reserve creation for the financing of internationally agreed objectives, including particularly the financing of development of the Less Developed Countries (rather than for the indiscriminate underwriting of any official gold price or of the balance-of-payments deficits of one, or a few privileged reserve-currency countries).

(III) The reduction and offsetting of disequilibrating flows of speculative capital, a major source of which have been the overflows and overvaluation of reserve currencies.

(IV) The eventual return to stable but adjustable exchange rates, which will remain unacceptable to surplus countries as long as the world reserve system can be flooded by unpredictable overflows of national reserve currencies. This indeed was the major incentive to the suspension of stable but adjustable rates, as exchange-rate flexibility appeared to them as the only safeguard, available to them on a national decision-making basis, against inflationary purchases of reserve currencies paid for by inflationary domestic issues of high-powered money by their central banks.

To the extent that worldwide agreements, in this and other respects, remain thwarted by the rule of near-unanimity for amendments to the Articles of Agreement of the Fund, they should be implemented as widely as possible by concerted policy decisions and agreements among countries ready, and anxious, to reach such agreements with each other.

Other institutional reforms in the IMF machinery, proposed or already adopted, should accelerate consultation and agreement on the continuing evolution and functioning of an international monetary order, fair, acceptable, and beneficial to all member countries as well as to the international community as a whole.

Annex 2   Income Redistribution and the International Financing of Development
James Grant and Mahbub ul Haq

2.1   *Introduction*

In an increasingly interdependent world of rising expectations and of possibly slower overall growth of output, economic policy will need to give much more attention to issues of *distribution within and among nations*. The implicit social compacts shaped within and among societies during the past generation were based upon the expectation that a sharing of the benefits of high world growth rates between the rich and the poor would occur. This sharing has fallen much below expectations. The unprecedented trebling of gross global product in the years since World War II has taken place without adequate sharing either *between* the rich and the poor nations or *within* most countries. With a slowing of global growth rates, there will be increased need — and pressures — to devote greater attention to the distribution of the benefits of growth and to addressing mass poverty. Such pressures can be expected to grow within societies; more predictably, they will grow between societies. These trends can only accentuate the demands for the creation of a new international order.

As an essential element in the establishment of a new international order, it is important to develop a new framework for what the Seventh Special Session of the UN General Assembly labelled 'predictable, assured and continuous' *resource transfers from the rich to the poor* which is based on some internationally accepted needs of the poor rather than on the uncertain generosity of the rich. As was the case in the evolution of progressive national orders, provision of equality of opportunity to the poor nations must come to be regarded not as a matter of charity but as part of a new deal giving them a significant stake in an equitable social order. The success of the poor countries in pressing their claims on the rich countries on the grounds of equity and justice will depend both on their bargaining power and on the degree to which they can provide greater assurance than now exists for most countries that increased resource transfer will materially *benefit their poor majorities.*

2.2   *Characteristics of the Present Economic Order*

A brief summary of the characteristics of the present order is required for an understanding of the changes which are necessary for effective international support of development.

The starting point is to recognize that the spectacular achievements in science and technology in recent decades have made our century the first in the history of mankind in which fulfilment of the minimum requirements of a decent life for all represents more than mere conjecture. We are learning that poverty and disease no longer need to be the lot of the great majority of mankind. In recent decades we have witnessed rates of economic growth unmatched in any earlier period. Many Third World countries have grown much faster than the industrialized countries grew at similar stages of development. In the last decade alone, the countries of South Asia implemented a 'green revolution' in wheat production which demonstrated the remarkable achievements that are possible if science and technology are used intelligently to support economic development. Per capita income, on a global basis, has more than doubled since World War II, reaching more than $ 1,000 per head. The past generation has also seen unprecedented movement towards self-government and increased participation of people in the progress of society. Over 80 new nations have emerged and more than a billion people have been liberated from colonialism.

2.2.1   *The Emerging Crises*   Several sets of crises have begun to emerge, however, during the recent years in which the prospects for continuing material progress for all have increasingly been threatened by human folly. These centre around:
(I) growth without adequate sharing between countries;
(II) growth without adequate sharing within countries;
(III) overloads and breakdowns in international systems as a consequence of rapid growth; and
(IV) changing values as to goals and strategies for development.

A   *The Problem of Differences Between Countries*

One set of crises arises from the fact that there have been rapid increases in growth *without adequate sharing between* the powerful *industrial societies* and the more numerous *poor countries*. The enormous differential between the world's rich and poor is increasing rather than decreasing (cf. Chapter 6). There is a growing conviction in Third World countries that their increasing interdependence with the industrialized countries is on the basis of widespread inequality, while the interdependence of the industrialized countries with each other is on the basis of far greater equality.

Unfortunately, existing international economic systems tend to favour those economies which are already the well established 'haves' (1). The trade negotiations of the 1960's led to the halving of tariffs between industrialized countries but brought almost no reduction in the tariffs on the principal products sold by Third World countries. Moreover, during the last 10 years, a host of non-tariff barriers have been created, particularly those directed against the products of the Third World.

The poor countries, in their efforts to prosper, suffer from the additional disadvantage of having population growth rates which collectively are some three times higher than those of the industrialized countries. These rates, because of today's improved health and nutritional practices, are double, or even more, than those of the presently industrialized European countries at an historically comparable stage of development.

B   *The Problem of Differences within Countries*

The problems arising from *inadequate participation in − and sharing of − the benefits of progress* within rich countries today are primarily those of racial and cultural minorities; within most Third World countries, however, they characterize the lives of the poor majority of the people. In much of the Third World, the gap is widening dangerously between the minority for whom the system is working — factory workers, larger farmers, civil servants, businessmen, and politicians — and the poor majority left out of, or barely benefitted by, the system.

Western countries have been largely successful in their efforts over the past 50-100 years to obtain a *more equitable income distribution*. A more egalitarian income distribution has also been achieved in Eastern Europe at a lower level of per capita income. Inequalities have diminished substantially in the case of regional incomes, incomes per recipient, and incomes per consumer. It holds true for primary (pre-tax) as well as secondary (after-tax) and tertiary income (after complete redistribution). The *share of incomes from*

---

(1) This is amply demonstrated in Annex 1 which shows the extent to which the industrialized countries in general, and the US in particular have benefitted most from international reserves creation in recent years. Similarly, while the 'Kennedy Round' benefitted all nations, it was of particular advantage to the rich nations.

capital in Western European countries has been reduced from 40% around 1860 to 20% around 1960. Private income from capital is virtually absent in Eastern Europe. The average income of university graduates in the Netherlands was about 7 times the national average in 1900, and about 4 times in 1970, a period in which structural changes in the pattern of education occurred. This ratio is expected to fall to 2.5 times by 1990. Similar figures apply to the United States over a similar period. This reduction in Western countries is the result of two counteracting factors: technological development; and improved levels of education which afford greater opportunities to participate in economic and political processes, as through trade unions. Whereas technological development tends to increase the ratio, education and participation in the decision-making process tend to depress it.

So far, most countries historically have shown *increasing inequality* of income in the *earlier* and *decreasing* inequality in the *later phases* of this development. The experiences of the rich countries suggest that increased participation of the poor majority in the economic process, socialization, education, labour and capital mobility and progressive fiscal systems comprise means to reduce income inequalities. Some of these means can be (and indeed are being) applied at an earlier stage in the development of Third World countries than had been the case in the history of the presently industrialized countries. Most poor countries have not done so, however, and are suffering such acute pains from lack of effective address of the problem of their poor majorities that their longer term political viability is threatened. In addition, limits to international unskilled labour mobility, which are far more burdensome that existed when most Western countries were industrializing, increase the difficulties of development today.

The general strategies of most Third World countries in the past 25 years placed their bet – and therefore their incentives – on limiting consumption, investing heavily in the protected 'modern' capital intensive, already privileged sector of the economy as a means of raising savings and investment rates as rapidly as possible, and concentrating government expenditures on 'economic' as opposed to 'social' overhead projects such as education, health, housing, and sanitation. Insufficient attention was given to the composition of production, which has an important bearing on the participation of the poor majority in development and the distribution of income. The costs to the poorest 40 per cent of the population in many countries that followed this *'trickle-down' strategy* have now become clear. Not only have their relative incomes and standards of living decreased, sometimes markedly, but there is considerable evidence to suggest that the *absolute incomes of the bottom 10-20 per cent* may also have *fallen*.

Despite some successes to the contrary, income distribution continues to worsen in many Third World countries despite substantial GNP growth rates. Thus, in comparing income distribution between the top 20 per cent with the bottom 40 per cent, (2 : 1 in such countries as the US, UK, Japan, and Canada), evidence suggests high income disparity in such countries as Venezuela (8 : 1), Mexico (6 : 1), Jamaica (7 : 1), Brazil (6 : 1), Tunisia (5 : 1), and Ivory Coast (5 : 1) (2). In the early 1950's, the total income of the top fifth of the Mexican population was 10 times that of the lowest fifth; in 1969 it was 16 times as great.

Income maldistribution is a financial indicator of many acute social problems arising out of the inadequacies of present development strategies: extensive unemployment and gross underemployment; massive rural to urban migration which greatly outstrips urban

---

(2) See Annex A-10: 'The US and World Development: Agenda for Action 1975', J.W. Howe (ed.), The Overseas Development Council, Praeger, New York, 1975.

employment opportunities; educational and health systems which reach only a privileged handful; low agricultural productivity per acre, etc.

There is increasing evidence that a serious consequence of the present most common pattern of development, which leaves the poor majority to the limited benefits of 'trickle-down', is that it *encourages high birthrates* and perpetuates the 'population explosion' which now consumes so much of the benefits of economic growth. In contrast, in those relatively few countries and regions where the majority of the population has shared in the economic and social benefits of significant national progress to a far greater degree than in most poor countries – or in most Western countries during their comparable periods of development – birth rates have dropped sharply despite relatively low national per capita income and despite the relative newness of family planning programmes. Appropriate policies for making health, education, and jobs more broadly available to lower income groups contributes significantly towards the motivation for smaller families that is the prerequisite of a major reduction in birth rates.

C   *The Problem of Systems Overloads*

Another set of crises arises from the fact that the unprecedented rates of economic growth, and particularly the 5 to 6 per cent rates of increase in the global output of goods and services of the late 1960's and early 1970's, are outrunning the capacity of human institutions to respond and adapt and so constitute a systems overload. Like the short circuits in an overloaded electrical system, a rash of societal breakdowns are resulting from slowness in adapting our institutions fast enough to permit a continuation of the rapid increase in output of recent years.

Systems overloads have become the order of the day both within and among nations as the world moved from the $ 1 trillion economy of the late 1940's into the $ 3 trillion economy of the early 1970's. The world has begun to experience *ecological overloads*: pollution in the cities, eutrophication of lakes, and falling global fish catches. The unprecedented increases of the 1960's and early 1970's in population and affluence have so expanded demand that the demand-supply relationship for a growing list of commodities shifted to a *seller's market* from what for many years had been a buyer's market. Oil is a good illustration of the shift, and of how heretofore weak sellers among Third World countries have utilized their new power to settle longstanding economic and political grievances. These same forces for increased demand have led to actual multi-year shortages for a few critical commodities, notably food and fertilizers. *'Stagflation'* – double-digit inflation accompanied by stumbling economic output – is yet another symptom.

Events are making increasingly clear that the world can no longer confidently extrapolate a growth pattern for the next 25 years to a gross global product more than treble that of the present, that is similar to the trend line of the 1960's and the 1950's. This will raise serious political problems in an era of high population growth rates and raised expectations of perpetually increasing personal material well-being. It makes urgent the need to craft new systems more responsive to making the changes which are required in areas of tight supply if reasonably rapid rates of growth are to be maintained and the burdens of slowdowns in growth are to be allocated with some degree of equity. The dependence of each nation on jointly managed international systems is so great that the poor countries' lack of development frequently becomes a problem for the rich countries – just as the latter's waste, pollution and deepening recession often become their problems.

D   *Changing Life Styles and Self-Reliant Development*

A further characteristic of the present economic order is the growing *questioning of the meaning of development* in both the richest and the poorest countries; in the former as a consequence of being flooded with material goods and their consequences, in the latter because of growing awareness of the inappropriateness for them of much capitalist and communist experience.

Development has long meant to most people in the affluent countries the production of more and more goods — food, cars, homes, refrigerators, drugs and so on. Now that the necessities of life are being met for the great majority in the rich countries, many are learning that more goods do not necessarily mean more 'happiness', and, in fact, can mean just the opposite, as pollution, urban congestion, and other affluence-created problems multiply in number and increase in severity. Words such as technology, growth and urbanization, all of which evoke a positive reaction in many Third World countries, may now evoke a negative reaction among many in America and Europe. The counter-culture movements of several years ago, and the rash of such books as 'The Greening of America' (3) may have subsided, but the questions they raised are now permanently embedded in Western society. Abetted by energy and food shortages favouring the turning down of thermostats, smaller cars, and less grain-intensive meats as a means of meeting supply-demand imbalances through limiting supply, a *new value system* more appropriate to future needs may well emerge kicking and screaming in the decade ahead.

Parallel to this growing awareness of the inadequacies of a development theory targeted both capitalist and socialist societies on 'more, and still more' is the growing recognition that many of the presently poor societies of the world, particularly the poorest quarter of mankind, cannot hope to replicate the present North American and European levels of material affluence — and extensive waste — and need to develop *more self-reliant pattern* of development appropriate to their own circumstances (cf. Chapter 5). There is a growing belief that they need not only more cost effective systems which can deliver health, education, and agricultural services to the great mass of their populations rather than merely to a privileged minority as at present, but also new values as to what should constitute development and progress.

2.2.2   *The Main Characteristics of the Present 'Aid' Order*   It is only in this context that future relations between the rich and the poor nations can be reviewed and a new basis sought for international resource transfers. But before doing so, it is important to sketch some of the implicit assumptions of the present 'aid' order and what is wrong with them. The most important can be summarized as follows:

(I) The present resource transfers from the rich to the poor nations are *totally voluntary* dependent only on the fluctuating political will of the rich nations. The volume and term of most assistance are dictated by short-term decisions, with no longer-term perspective of assurances.

(II) As such, there is *no agreed basis* for resource transfers. 'Aid' is given for a variety of reasons, including cold war considerations, international leadership, political impact, special relationships with former colonies, domestic and international economic interest moral consideration — the relative weight of these factors changing greatly over time with each country. As an illustration, about 25 per cent of total resource transfers at present are still governed by 'special relationships' with a few former colonies (constituting only per cent of the total population of the Third World) rather than by the relative poverty growth needs of the poor countries.

(III) The only international deal which presently exists on resource transfers is enshrine in the acceptance by the rich nations of a target of 1 per cent of GNP, with *0.7 per cent* as official development assistance (ODA) on fairly concessional terms. However, the

---

(3) Charles A. Reich, 'The Greening of America', Random House, New York, 1970.

acceptance of this target by the rich nations was grudgingly slow (with many nations still not officially subscribing to this target or, as with the US, not having agreed to a date by which this target should be met). The actual performance has been most disappointing: official development assistance from 17 DAC countries has actually declined from 0.52 per cent in 1960 to 0.3 per cent in 1975.

(IV) So far, international resource transfers have been regarded primarily as the responsibility of the *Western* industrialized nations. Centrally planned economies have given little aid bilaterally and have not participated in any major multilateral channels of assistance. The newly-liquid OPEC countries are recent arrivals on the scene and have already started transferring significant amounts (an estimated 2 per cent of their combined GNP in disbursements in 1974 with the percentage expected to rise in 1975 and 1976 as a result of an estimated $ 11 billion — or 5 per cent of their GNP — in commitments in 1975) but are not yet systematically integrated into the overall framework of international resource transfers.

(V) Sufficient attention has not been paid in the past to the *terms* of international assistance or to the concept of *net transfer* of resources. As a result, the Third World has accumulated by now a total financial *debt* of about $ 150 billion, so that annual debt servicing is already taking away about one-half of the new assistance they receive.

(VI) While foreign assistance has played an important role in the development of some countries at certain times, the overall contribution of this kind of resource transfer to the level and character of economic development remains *shrouded in controversy*: there have been repeated accusations by the Third World that such assistance has at times been given in such a way as to undermine national resolve, conflict with national planning priorities, transfer irrelevant technologies, education systems, and development concepts, tie the recipient down to the source of assistance at a prohibitive cost, promote the interests of a privileged minority in the recipient country rather than the vast majority. The critics of aid in the industrialized countries allege that aid is largely wasted, that it goes to support repressive governments (or experiments in socialism), and that it discourages indigenous efforts to save and invest. These controversies are not an invariable guide to the truth in each case but they generally illustrate how unhappy the recipients are with the present pattern of assistance, how thankless the donors regard their current task to be and how urgent it is to make a new start.

2.3   *The Search for a New International Economic Order Framework*

The world has become so interdependent that, for the first time, it requires an economic order that takes into account the needs of the entire globe. It is now abundantly clear that a new world order must of necessity be based upon the recognition of the interdependence between both rich and poor nations and, therefore, on the reciprocity of advantages that this notion implies. This new global economic order requires first and foremost a response to the challenge to the industrialized nations of the North from the developing countries of the South embodied in their call for a New International Economic Order, with particular attention being given to the needs of the world's poorest billion. The prospects for the success of this new world economic order increases to the extent that it also responds to the needs of the industrialized countries in their efforts to cope with growing interdependence within this new framework. There is a clear need for seeking to respond to this challenge with such ingenuity that all principal parties realize that they will ultimately gain.

A *planetary 'development bargain'* which targets benefits to the Third World, and in particular to the poorest billion, should soon come to be viewed as beneficial to a large majority of governments in both the developed and developing countries. The reasons it is viewed as beneficial will vary greatly. The concerns will range from the purely humanitarian to the most calculatingly self-interested in both rich and poor nations. What may

bring these divergent governments and interest groups together is the shared recognition that a successful and jointly financed *attack on poverty* can ease the global problems of:
(I) population growth (by speeding the pace of the 'demographic transition' in Third World countries);
(II) food shortages (by increasing the labour-intensiveness of food production as part of rural development strategies);
(III) environmental damage (to the degree that it is related to sheer size of population);
(IV) growing unemployment in Third World countries;
(V) the political costs of an inadequate response to basic human needs.

Those governments unconvinced of the merits of this package might well be persuaded if the issue of rules of access to resources (for the industrialized countries) and to markets (for Third World countries), as well as cooperation on such joint needs as a greatly revised monetary order, were directly tied to the 'attack on poverty' compact.

2.3.1   *Income Redistribution* Justice and an effective world order require a substantial *narrowing*, preferably a halving, *of the relative income disparity* between the developed and the developing countries by the year 2000, with special attention being given to the poorest tenth of the world's people. If this goal is achieved, the problem of absolute poverty will be resolved in the process. These two goals — the narrowing of relative income disparities and the *abolition of absolute poverty* — can be achieved through three broad sets of measures:
(I) increased transfer of resources from the industrialized *to the poorer Third World* countries, with particular attention to the use of these resources to directly addressing the poverty problem;
(II) increased transfer of resources from the richer and advantaged minority within most Third World countries to the poor majority;
(III) revision of development strategies of most Third World as well as some industrialized countries to pay far more attention to ensuring *employment* and minimal levels of *education, health, nutrition, shelter and clothing*. This should pave the way for a more rational approach to family planning for their poor majorities. There is encouraging recent evidence from a number of Third World countries operating under a wide range of economic systems to suggest that the minimum essentials of human wellbeing can be met for the great majority of the population and birth rates reduced sharply while per capita income levels are still quite low when specific attention is given in development strategies to addressing the needs of the poor majority rather than the indiscriminate pursuit of GNP growth objectives.

The *intimate link between national and international economic orders must be emphasized*. Unless there are internal structural changes which permit external resource transfers to be channelled to assist in meeting basic human needs, the case for any expansion in external transfers will lose much of its legitimacy since such transfers may merely reinforce existing power structures. And unless there are internal structural changes in the rich countries to facilitate a rational and equitable redistribution of industries, domestic political forces in the rich countries will block the poor countries from having more adequate access to their markets for manufactured and processed goods.

2.3.2   *The Financing of Development*   A new framework for international resource transfers forms an essential part of the effort to establish a new international order. It will take time to negotiate such a framework and to put its various elements in place, but at least some of the principles on which this framework should be based can be spelt out.
(I) An element of *automation* must be built into the resource transfer system. To be realistic, the world community is still too early in its stage of evolution and recognition of its interdependence to accept the concept of international taxation of the rich nations for

the benefit of the poor nations. But the concept need not be accepted in its entirety: it can be introduced gradually over time through a variety of devices: (a) a larger share of international *liquidity* created by the IMF (either through SDR's or gold sales) can be made available for development either through international or regional financial institutions or directly to Third World countries; (b) certain *sources of international financing* can be developed – such as tax on non-renewable resources, tax on international pollutants, tax on the activities of transnational enterprises, rebates to country of origin of taxes collected on the earnings of trained immigrants from Third World countries, taxes on or royalties from commercial activities arising out of international commons – e.g. ocean beds, outer space, the Antarctic region; and various proposals for taxing international civil servants, consumer durables and armament spending; (c) if the rich industrialized nations are unwilling to tax themselves, *others can collect* and distribute these tax proceeds on the basis of what the rich nations consume – e.g. even a one-dollar per barrel 'development levy' by OPEC could create a development pool of over $ 10 billion a year. The devices are many: the more difficult aspect is to convince the rich nations that a more automatic system of international resource transfers will be in their own interest in the longer run as it will greatly reduce the present conflicts and endless controversies over the question of 'aid' between the rich and the poor nations.

(II) The focus of international assistance must *shift to the poorest countries* and, within them, to the *poorest segments* of the population. These are generally the countries below $ 200 per capita income, mostly in South Asia and Sahelian Africa, containing over one billion of the poorest people in the world. For higher income developing countries, what is important is their access to international capital market and expanding trade opportunities, not concessional assistance. At present, the poorest nations below $ 200 still receive only one-half of total concessional assistance. There is considerable scope for reallocating concessional assistance from middle income developing countries to the poorest nations and for compensating the former through larger trade concessions. If international assistance is so redirected, it is also essential that it be in the form of grants, without creating a reverse obligation of mounting debt service liability at a low level of poverty. As an intermediate objective, the target of at least 90 per cent of the international public assistance in the form of either grants or loans on IDA terms should be adopted.

(III) It would also be logical to link international assistance to *national programmes aimed at satisfying minimum human needs*, however tenuous the concept may be. This would give both a focus and direction to international assistance efforts and make it a limited period affair till some of the worst manifestations of poverty – malnutrition, illiteracy and squalid living conditions – are overcome both through the international efforts and the expanding ability of the national governments to launch a direct attack on poverty. These programmes, however, should not be based on the concept of a simple income transfer to the poor – which would create permanent dependence – but on increasing the productivity of the poor and integrating them into the economic system. It is difficult to estimate how much investment it may take to bring the majority of mankind to the level of minimum human needs: much conceptual and empirical work needs to be done. But a very rough estimate, based on various World Bank studies, shows that it may require a total investment of about $ 125 billion (in 1974 prices) over a 10 year period (e.g. food and nutrition $ 42 billion, education $ 25 billion, rural and urban water supply $ 28 billion, urban housing $ 16 billion, urban transport $ 8 billion, population and health programmes $ 6 billion). Of course, these estimates will vary considerably depending on the style of development pursued by various countries. However, the merits of articulating such a target for removal of poverty are that it can be easily understood by the public (and, hopefully, by the politicians) in the rich nations; it can be the basis of a shared effort between the national governments and the international community; it provides an allocative formula for concessional assistance; and it establishes a specific time period over which the task should be accomplished. Moreover, attention must be given to the composition of investment, particularly investment in human resource development. The satisfaction of the needs of the poor majority is, of course, not only a matter of investment. It is also a matter of social change, some aspects of which may not require substantial investment at all.

(IV) International assistance, on a more automatic and purely grant basis, should be accepted by the international community as a *transitional arrangement*, to be phased out as soon as some of the worst manifestations of poverty are removed. This is necessary both to protect the urge for self-reliance in the Third World and to underline that the essential element in the new international order is not so much the redistribution of past incomes and wealth as the distribution of future growth opportunities. *The stress must be on the equality of opportunity, not the equality of income.* Each developing country must shape its own pattern of development and its own life style and, for this to be accomplished, international assistance can only be regarded as a temporary supplement to domestic efforts in the poorest countries.

(V) *Who should provide* this assistance and how should the burdens be shared? Obviously, it should be done by the richest nations as measured by their per capita income. The problem for the next few years, however, is going to be that the rich industrialized nations — with an average per capita income of about $ 4,700 for DAC members — may experience balance-of-payments difficulties while most of the liquid OPEC countries (other than Saudi Arabia, Kuwait, Libya, Qatar and the UAE with an average per capita income of about $ 4,000) are hardly rich enough to provide large subsidy funds since their average per capita income is still less than $ 500. An obvious solution would be to combine the volume of lending from OPEC with the availability of subsidy funds from the industrialized countries and from the richest OPEC nations. But such a formula is likely to provide resources at intermediate terms, with about a 50 to 60 per cent grant element, rather than the pure grants recommended above. However, this *'second best' solution* may be the only course available for the next few years unless some of the automatic mechanisms suggested in (I) above come into play.

(VI) A major effort must also be made to provide a framework within which the richer *socialist countries* can play a much more substantial role than their present limited contribution.

(VII) If the framework of international resource transfers is to be restructured along the lines indicated above, it is a logical corollary that *multilateral channels* should be used increasingly for directing this assistance in preference to bilateral channels. This will be consistent with greater automaticity of transfers, allocations based on poverty and need rather than on special relationships, and a more orderly system of burden sharing.

(VIII) In order to develop a new framework of assistance, it is important to initiate fundamental change in at least three directions: (a) Arrangements must be made to provide a negotiating forum for an *orderly settlement of past debts*. It is time to revive the proposal of the Pearson Commission that a conference of principal creditors and debtors should be convened to discuss and agree on the principles for a major settlement to ease past burdens. For the poorest countries the most appropriate form of debt relief would be to consolidate their past debts and to refinance them on IDA terms. (b) Since the concessions, leases and contracts negotiated by the Third World countries with *transnational enterprises* in the past often reflect their unequal bargaining strength, and since there is an environment of constant agitation and uncertainty surrounding foreign private investment at present, a mechanism should be provided to permit an *orderly renegotiation of past contracts* within a specified period of time under some international supervision. The recent report of the Group of Eminent Persons to the UN Secretary General (4) provides a sensible framework within which a new code of conduct for the transnationals can be elaborated and adopted within the United Nations system and arrange-

---

(4) 'The Impact of Multinational Corporations on Development and on International Relations', UN, New York, 1974.

ments for international monitoring of agreements can be provided (cf. Annex 7). (c) It is also essential that the *structure of international institutions be revised* to enable them to work more effectively and to reflect new realities. Thus, the United Nations structure needs to be revised (the efforts now underway initiated by the report of the Expert Group of 25 may result in more effective and realistic arrangements) and the World Bank and other multilateral financial institutions need to provide for greater participation by new net donors (e.g. OPEC nations) and by recipient countries. A major effort must be made to integrate all resource transfers, including those from the socialist and OPEC nations, into an overall framework. Ultimately, there is a need for an equivalent of a *World Treasury* whose resources are derived from international taxation and ownership of international productive resources (such as ocean beds) and whose basic objective is equitable world development and eradication of world poverty.

To be realistic, it is not going to be easy to negotiate all the above principles simultaneously or to implement them immediately. The basic idea in spelling them out is to indicate the sense of direction that must be generated in negotiating a new framework for international resource transfers, rather than to offer a concrete blueprint which can only emerge out of hard, tough bargaining which seeks to balance various conflicting interests. An 'idealized' framework should include most of the elements mentioned above; a more practical framework will naturally have to settle for many compromises and 'second best' solutions, at least in the short run.

2.4   *Concrete Proposals: Implications for the World Bank*

Any new framework that is negotiated will have major *implications* for the future of the *World Bank*, at present the major international institution for channeling assistance to the Third World (5). The primacy of the role of the World Bank in the future will naturally depend on how well and how quickly it can adjust to changing realities. Before indicating the nature of the changes that the World Bank will have to face and accept, it would be useful to review very briefly the underlying philosophy of this institution since its inception in 1946.

The World Bank started out primarily as a US sponsored effort for the reconstruction of Europe and Japan, not as an international effort to channel assistance to the Third World. As late as 1964, about one third of its disbursements were still to the industrialized countries, now no longer included in its lending programme (the so-called 'past borrowers'). Over the last three decades, it has shown considerable dynamism in the light of changing situations. At first, it became an intermediary (through the instrument of IBRD lending) between the capital markets of the world and the more creditworthy countries of the Third World which could still not raise this capital on their own guarantee. As debt burdens increased in the poorest countries, it established a 'soft' window (IDA) in 1960 to provide long-term concessional resources to this group of countries. Its sectoral priorities also changed with the changing requirements of its recipients. While it provided mainly equipment and consultants for infrastructure projects in the earlier phase, it has promoted a direct attack on poverty in the last five years: for instance, about two-thirds of its total lending went to transport, power and communications in 1964-68 but a similar proportion is now devoted to rural development, industry, education, water supply, nutrition and population projects. It has increasingly phased out higher income Third World countries (above $ 1000) and focused its attention on the poorest countries (below $ 200), subject only to the limitations of the total availability of concessional resources: over 90 per cent of IDA resources are now directed to countries

---

(5) Much of what is said here also applies to the regional development banks.

below $ 200. Thus, the essential vitality of the World Bank has been reflected in its ability to adapt and improvise as the situation demanded.

The need to adapt will be much greater in the future. It is not possible to go over this ground in any great detail here but at least the general direction of change is already clear from the foregoing discussion and can be summarized quite briefly.

(I) In order to become a truly international institution and to shed its image of a Western club, the World Bank must aim at *universality of membership*, both among its potential contributors and among its recipients. Some of the original rules of the game, which make it difficult for new members to join the club, therefore have to be changed. For instance, if the IBRD capital base is expanded, the existing members have the first right to pre-empt the additional capital subscriptions so that new members can be inducted or relative quotas changed only with the tacit permission of the existing members. Similarly, the voting rights in IDA are based on cumulative contributions since 1960 so that if OPEC, for instance, is willing to contribute even 50 per cent to the next replenishment of IDA, it will obtain only about 10 per cent of the total voting rights which is not likely to encourage its participation. Again, a stumbling block in the way of the membership of the *socialist countries* in the World Bank has been the requirement that they must become members of the IMF beforehand, which they have been reluctant to do. The main point is that while it was inescapable that the World Bank should be conceived primarily as a Western club at the time of the Bretton Woods conference, it must now find ways of becoming truly international and actively negotiate the participation of OPEC and richer socialist countries in its affairs. In the emerging climate, universality of membership becomes one of the most important principles to pursue in its further evolution.

(II) It follows from the above that new formulas must be found for the restructuring of *voting rights* in the World Bank (including IDA). While voting rights have been revised over time, they still essentially represent the balance of economic, financial and political power which prevailed in the 1940's. For instance, the UK continues to have twice the voting power of Germany and nearly three times that of Japan; Belgium and the Netherlands together have more voting strength than OPEC combined; Iran has a lower voting power than India, and Pakistan nearly twice as much as Saudi Arabia, despite the fact that both India and Pakistan are by now aid recipients from Iran and Saudi Arabia. Overall, Third World countries (excluding OPEC) have only 31 per cent of the total voting power. It is important, therefore, to carry out a general and thorough-going review of the voting power structure, replacing the historical past with current realities so that OPEC can be persuaded to play a larger role, the Third World obtains an increased assurance that their voice will be heard more attentively on decisions which affect their development, and the established leaders continue to have an important, though necessarily reduced, role in the running of the institution. It is not necessary to start out with pre-conceived formulas: what is really needed is to set out with a clear recognition of the need for change and to provide appropriate negotiating forums where acceptable formulas can be hammered out.

(III) If international resource transfers tend to become more *automatic*, as argued earlier, the World Bank can emerge as the primary channel for these transfers, provided it can win the *confidence* of the international community as a whole. More automation in World Bank/IDA financial resources is needed in any case to free it increasingly from bilateral pressures and to enable it to play a truly multilateral role in the new economic order. Thus, efforts must be made to link at least a part of the future IDA replenishments with SDR creation, or gold sales, or some sources of international taxation, as mentioned earlier. For the IBRD, it would be logical that, instead of seeking the concerned government's permission before floating its bonds, it should have an automatic right to borrow in any capital market where the country has been enjoying an overall balance-of-payments surplus.

(IV) While the World Bank has shown considerable vitality in deepening its activities, it has not shown the same vitality in extending the *range of its services* (i.e. buffer stock financing, export credit financing, use of its guarantee powers, etc.). The latter aspects are likely to become even more crucial in the 1970's as trade expansion comes to be recognized as an increasingly important supplement to resource transfers.

(V) Though IBRD and IDA have served admirably as mechanisms for channeling assistance to the Third World, it is becoming increasingly necessary to evolve a new mechanism for obtaining and directing assistance at terms intermediate between IBRD and IDA. The recent introduction of a *'Third Window'* is, therefore, a pragmatic and inevitable response to changing circumstances. It is unfortunate that the scope of this facility has remained quite limited so far and it has been introduced only for a one year period. (VI) It is also

(VI) It is also timely that there should be a *general review of the Articles* of the World Bank which were conceived and drafted in the environment of the 1940's. This is necessary for a number of reasons. For instance, the original Articles expected, quite rightly at that time, that the bulk of the Bank assistance would be in projects and in foreign exchange, so that restrictions were built into the rules of the game against pro gramme lending and local cost financing. The Bank has improvised pragmatically in its actual operations to get around these restrictions as the need arose: still the long shadow of the Articles is always there and the needed flexibility is often missing. *Programme lending* and *local cost financing* still have to be justified, on a case-by-case basis, as deviations from a normal trend which is bound to influence the form and character of lending. One can find other instances of such restrictions in the Articles: e.g. procurement of goods and services restricted only to Bank members; extremely limited preference margin to developing countries for procurement within their own country; a strict financial rate of return criterion, etc. The Bank's practice has moved considerably, though not sufficiently, away from some of the restrictive aspects of the Articles. But it is time that the Articles themselves be reviewed, not only to bring them in conformity with actual practice, but to build into them enough flexibility to accommodate the needs of the 1970's and the fast changing role of the World Bank in the future.

Annex 3   Food Production and Distribution
Sukhamoy Chakravarty and Maurice Guernier

3.1   *Nature of the Problem*

Solution of the world food problem is of strategic significance in bringing about a new international order. However, opinions vary a great deal as to what constitutes the world food problem. On the one hand, there are those who believe that the entire problem owes its origin to the 'population explosion' in the Third World. On the other hand, there are analysts who view the problem exclusively in political terms, both in relation to domestic power structures in the developing world as well as in terms of unequal bargaining power between the developed and developing countries. While it should come as no surprise that a subject so sensitive as food should be the subject of much polemical discussion, no worthwhile solution can be offered unless the matter is studied with the greatest possible amount of objectivity. However, for an objective assessment, certain basic facts pertaining to the present situation need to be clearly recognized.

First of all, as of today, there is enough food in the world to feed everybody if the current production were equally distributed. The problem arises because this production is unequally distributed between different countries and within countries amongst different segments of the population. Table 1 illustrates the world nutritional situation with special reference to South Asia, which happens to figure very prominently in contemporary discussions on food. The table shows that in respect of every nutrient element, the situation is less favourable in South and S.E. Asia as compared with the developed world including Japan. The table also shows that in regard to intake of animal protein, the relevant figure for South Asia is less than one-tenth the corresponding figure for North America. This takes us to the second important feature of the present food situation.

This refers to the fact that while in developing countries most of the grain is consumed directly by human beings, the proportion consumed directly in developed countries is relatively small. Once again, on the basis of FAO balance sheets, in Canada out of a total consumption of nearly 2000 lbs. per person per year, grain directly consumed amounted to roughly 202 lbs. In India, out of a total consumption of 348 lbs. of grain per person, the directly consumed part amounted to 288 lbs. It is also interesting to note that while the range in direct grain consumption is quite narrow, the corresponding figure is much larger when total consumption is taken into account. Figures for US-Canada are five times as high as the corresponding Indian figure. A closely related figure is the starchy staple ratio in food consumption. In the US the current ratio is 20 per cent. The corresponding figure for India is nearly 74 per cent.

There would appear to be an emerging consensus that from the nutritional viewpoint, the intake of animal protein in the developed world is excessive. Furthermore, it is equally important to note that the pattern of consumption in the affluent countries and the way it is evolving imply that the *world's resources are being inefficiently used* from the viewpoint of providing the required calories to the world population after allowing for agroclimatic variations. This is so because meat producers are inefficient converters. It has been estimated that an animal must be fed between 3 and 8 kg. of grain to produce 1 kg. of meat. It would, therefore, follow that with the same amount of resources as are currently going into agriculture, world hunger could be met much better in the nutritional sense even though it would imply that affluent parts of the world will have to exercise a certain amount of restraint in regard to their food habits.

From the above data it would follow that to the extent that there is any truth behind

the 'demand' explosion hypothesis, it lies as much in the area of growing affluence resulting from post World War II boom in developed countries as in the increase in population
growth in many developing countries. This fact becomes apparent from the data given in

Table 1 *Nutritional Levels in Certain Selected Regions*

Nutritional Indicator	South Asia	S.E. Asia	Asian Centrally Planned Economies	Japan	North America	Oceania	W. Europe	E. Europe
Calories per day	2,037	2,161	2,069	2,537	3,261	3,283	3,051	3,181
Total protein (grams per day)	52.4	56.0	58.7	77.7	96.6	100.2	88.6	92.9
Animal protein (grams per day)	6.7	10.4	9.2	32.8	69.4	69.4	48.7	40.9
Total fat	28.4	28.2	31.5	52.8	153.1	144.8	123.8	88.0

Source: FAO: Agricultural Commodity Projections, 1970-80, Vol. 1, Table 6, p. 57. Column for Japan extracted from ECAFE
Bulletin, Vol. XXV, No. 1, June 1974.

Table 2, which shows that over the period 1950-70 the performance of the developing countries has not been an insignificant one if aggregate production alone were the criterion for assessment.

Thirdly, agricultural production in developed countries, some of which like the US, Canada and Australia are net exporters, use large quantities of industrial inputs such as chemical fertilizers, fuel oil, electricity and machinery to sustain their current levels of productivity. Developing countries, on the other hand, depend to a very large extent on the use of human labour power and power supplied by draft animals. In a recent study, energy requirements of US agriculture have been estimated at 2.9 million kilocalories for every acre planted to corn (1). It is also interesting to note that a large part of the energy consumed takes the form of nitrogenous fertilizers and gasolene. It is not, therefore, surprising that fertilizer response ratios are much lower in the US than in a country like India. Even in the US, the output-input ratios are steadily falling, suggesting that agricultural operations are being carried out in a regime of diminishing returns in terms of energy intake. In terms of kilo-calories, the ratio has declined from 3.70 in 1945 to 2.82 in 1970.

Developed country agriculture is, therefore, contrary to much popular thinking, more costly in terms of resource use especially in terms of the use of non-renewable resources as compared with agriculture in many developing countries such as India.

In addition to an appreciation of the structural factors mentioned above, it is also necessary to recognize that while the problem of food is one of the most serious problems facing mankind, the problem is one of devising and adapting institutional mechanisms to deal with increased production, on the one hand, and regulating demand, on the other. While regulating the rate of increase in population is of vital importance, especially in the long-run context, not much is gained in terms of understanding or in terms of identifying areas of action by evoking the spectre of Malthus or various doomsday scenarios.

It is much more productive to adopt a *planning* approach. In other words, the basic assumption should be the capability of human beings to 'invent' their future. For this purpose, one should begin with the assessment given by FAO and various other international agencies regarding the short term and medium term outlook regarding demand and supply based on an extrapolation of the trend that has been observed over the last twenty-five years. As these projections suggest that if the trend is allowed to continue, the gap between the developed and developing countries is going to widen much farther, accompanied in most cases by a growing stress on the balance-of-payments position of the oil-importing developing countries, corrective actions need to be initiated in a large number of areas covering differing time spans. While some of these policies can only be implemented by the countries themselves even if they were found to be otherwise fit for adoption, there are some important ones which cannot be initiated except on a regional or on an international basis.

3.2. *Short Term Outlook and Action*

Technically, the word short term is defined to include a time span during which the distribution of productive factors in different parts of the world can be expected to stay the same. The scope for short term action is, therefore, in principle, confined to variations in the *use of certain tradeable inputs such as fertilizers or fuel*, which can exert influence on the margin in increasing or decreasing regional surpluses/deficits in regard to

---

(1) See 'Food production and the Energy Crisis' by D. Pimental, L.E. Hurd, A.C. Bellotli, H.J. Foster, I.N. Oka, O.D. Sholes, R.J. Whitman in 'Science' vol. 182, pp. 443-449.

Table 2   *Rate of Growth of Food Production in Relation to Population, World and Main Regions, 1952-62 and 1962-72 (percentage per annum) **

	1952-62 Population	Total	Per capita	1962-72 Population	Total	Per capita
Developed market economies +	1.2	2.5	1.3	1.0	2.4	1.4
Western Europe	0.8	2.9	2.1	0.8	2.2	1.4
North America	1.8	1.9	0.1	1.2	2.4	1.2
Oceania	2.2	3.1	0.9	2.0	2.7	0.7
Eastern Europe and U.S.S.R.	1.5	4.5	3.0	1.0	3.5	2.5
Total developed countries	1.3	3.1	1.8	1.0	2.7	1.7
Developing market economies +	2.4	3.1	0.7	2.5	2.7	0.2
Africa	2.2	2.2	–	2.5	2.7	0.2
Far East	2.3	3.1	0.8	2.5	2.7	0.2
Latin America	2.8	3.2	0.4	2.9	3.1	0.2
Near East	2.6	3.4	0.8	2.8	3.0	0.2
Asian centrally planned economies	1.8	3.2	1.4	1.9	2.6	0.7
Total developing countries	2.4	3.1	0.7	2.4	2.7	0.3
World	2.0	3.1	1.1	1.9	2.7	0.8

* Trend rate of growth of food production, compound interest.
+ Including countries in other regions not specified.

Source: Assessment of World Food Situation, FAO, Rome, 1974.

food items. In determining the objectives for short term action, two factors should be kept in mind. First, world production actually declined in the year 1974, while population had gone up by another 70 million. Secondly, world reserve stocks in 1974 were considerably below what they were in 1961, a fact the significance of which is better appreciated when one takes into account the substantial growth of population that has taken place since then. In 1961, reserve stocks represented nearly 95 days' consumption whereas in 1974, they represented less than a month's consumption.

Following from these two basic factors characterizing the current situation, two main lines of action follow. In developing countries where food production has been stagnating or has declined because of high prices and/or restricted availability of essential inputs such as fuel and fertilizer, adequate *financial support* is necessary to compensate for their erosion in the capacity to import.

In addition, all oil-importing developing countries have had to cut back public investment in real terms as a result of global inflationary developments. Consequently, investment in critical areas such as irrigation has been kept below what would have been otherwise possible. International capital transfer for accelerated completion of selected ongoing major and medium irrigation projects in developing countries can be very helpful since water is often the *critical* factor.

The second line of action that would appear to be called for is to build up *reserve stocks* to a higher figure. In this context, several questions arise. What should be the size of the reserve stocks? How are they to be financed? How are they to be managed? While proposals to have internationally owned and internationally managed buffer stocks have been made by various individuals, including agencies such as UNCTAD, it is necessary to recognize that in many quarters there is a great deal of resistance to this idea. While the benefits of greater stability can be demonstrated for both net exporters as well as for net importers under faily plausible assumptions, there is no doubt that depending on the rules of the game adopted, some may gain somewhat more than others. In particular, if the carrying costs are to be borne exclusively by the net exporters, they would gain less than would be the case if the net importers were also made to contribute.

Since the *grain trade* is to large extent of a *residuary character*, and since an increase in food prices is in general likely to have considerable adverse impact on national welfare levels, risk averting behaviour on the part of net importers would suggest that they be willing to contribute to the funds needed for buffer stock management. Two difficulties arise. The first is the special problem of US surpluses which have generally encouraged the world to look to the US to do the reserve carrying function. Secondly, while the USSR has emerged as a big buyer on the world scene, it is still a fact that a substantial part of the imports is needed by countries which are extremely poor. If it is a fair presumption that the US will not be willing to continue the same role as it has played in the past, the obviously world food security demands that funds be made available for holding *international reserve stocks*. While contribution to such a fund should be made universal — even poor countries would be willing to own some share of buffer stocks so as to mitigate fluctuations, including possible emergency situations — it would be no doubt necessary to graduate the contribution on the basis of capacity to pay. Despite its many deficiencies, GNP per capita may serve as a proxy for this purpose. This will doubtless imply that some members of OPEC will figure amongst the donor sources.

If the shortsightedness that currently prevails in matters relating to international economic arrangements does not permit action leading to the setting up of a world food stock under international auspices, the least that needs to be done is to have nationally owned buffer stocks operated according to an internationally *agreed* set of rules. However, unless clear guidelines are given regarding floor and ceiling prices and there is agreement regarding when and how much to release, such a system may not provide much security in practice. An important prerequisite for setting up any system of international food security is regular exchange of information. At this time there are certain misgivings in this regard as it is felt by many developing countries that information may be misused, thereby aggravating speculation in grain trade. Such fears need to be allayed.

While buffer stocks of food grains need to be built up very urgently to mitigate the probable amplitude of fluctuations, sufficient care should be taken to ensure that the management of such a system does not jeopardize the policy of encouraging food production in developing countries. What is most important is that the *real price of food* i.e. food price divided by the index of wholesale prices, *stays reasonably stable*. This will certainly mean that prices will need to be brought down from the peaks to which they have recently soared. But equally clearly it is necessary to recognize that long term development in agriculture requires that prices should be attractive enough to currently marginal producers so that there is sufficient incentive to growth.

An indispensable adjunct to food management is the *management of fertilizer supplies*. Since fertilizer consumption is currently very low in all developing countries and several of these countries can increase food production significantly if larger quantities were made available at reasonable prices, it is very important to set up a world fertilizer pool with a view to insulating these countries against the uncertainties of the world fertilizer market. It would also be useful if the major fertilizer producing countries could be persuaded to *set aside a part of their fertilizer production* for deliveries at suitable prices involving a reasonable profit margin which would take care of the minimum requirements of developing countries defined among other factors with reference to population and a specified target of calorie intake per capita. Fertilizer sold over and above the minimum level can be left free to market forces. Special reference should also be made in this connection to the scheme adopted by the summit conference of OPEC in March 1975 whereby the member countries pledged themselves to producing and supplying fertilizers in quantities equal to two-third of total imports of Third World countries, to developing countries most seriously affected by the economic crisis. Such supplies would be ensured on a regular basis at cost price and be distributed under the aegis of FAO. In this and similar ways, a certain stabilizing influence can be imparted to the world food situation with little extra cost in the form of aid. Besides, maintenance of reasonable profitability in regard to fertilizer production may be expected to lead to an appropriate growth of capacity in the medium run, a point which will be discussed later.

As one of the major factors causing current pressure on the world grain market is the accelerated need for feed grains in developed countries resulting from improvements in their standard of living, a *meat excise* may serve the purpose of restraining demand to a certain extent. Besides, financial resources raised through such an excise may help in augmenting production in areas where growth is being inhibited because of shortage of financial resources. However, it is possible to maintain that a meat excise will not bring about the needed reduction in meat consumption, which is the basic objective of levying such an excise. In that event, the question of introducing meat rationing should be seriously considered. The loss of excise revenue can presumably be made good from other sources which are independent of meat consumption. The general thrust of short run action should be on removing those constraints to production which have been aggravated as a result of recent developments in the world economy. This implies that capacity to *import essential inputs* for agriculture should be augmented. In addition, efforts should be made to complete the implementation of ongoing *major irrigation and drainage projects* in different developing countries and regions. International financing for these projects, even on a partial funding basis, can serve as a powerful catalyst. If urgent action is taken along these lines, supply of food in the developing countries can increase somewhat above the past trend rate of 2.7 per cent although it must be considered very doubtful whether it can reach the Second Development Decade target of 4 per cent per annum for all developing countries taken together.

On the demand side, for developing countries there is little reason to assume that demand can be suppressed. Their reliance on the normal forces in international trade is not likely to lead to any improvement in per capita food consumption. Should an emergency arise like that which took place in 1972 when widespread drought conditions prevailed from the Sahelian Zone of Africa to Bangladesh, many of the most disadvantaged countries would be unable to avoid large scale human suffering. In the short run, therefore, it is necessary that these countries be provided with adequate *balance-of-payments support* both for taking up schemes for increasing production and, in certain situations, with concessional food sales. In some countries, such food aid may also be used as an instrument for stepping up real investment, especially when account is taken of large-scale prevalence or rural unemployment or underemployment.

3.3   *The Medium Term*

3.3.1   *Outlook and Requirements*   According to recent FAO projections, there is likely to be a gap of 76 million tons for the year 1985 in terms of foodgrains for the developing countries as a whole. For the Asian centrally planned economies, these projections imply a surplus of 9 million tons. Thus, the gap for the developing market economies is estimated at 85 million tons. Implicit in this calculation is the assumption that the demand will grow at the rate of 3.6 per cent per annum over the period up to 1985 and that production will grow at the rate of 2.6 per cent per annum, i.e., at approximately the rate that was experienced over the years 1962-72. It would appear that even if the average compound rate of growth of population over the years is assumed to be 2 per cent per annum which will imply some decline in population growth rates, this order of incremental food demand per capita would be consistent with an increase in per capita consumption in the order of 2.5 per cent, if the income elasticity of demand were put at 0.6 for the developing countries, a figure which is consistent with the known statistical estimates. On a very rough basis, this would be consistent with a growth rate of GNP of around 5 per cent per annum, allowing for some increase in the saving-income ratio for accelerating the growth rate. Any effort at redistributing consumption from the rich to the poor will increase the required rate of food demand to a higher figure. Furthermore, if the target rate of growth of GNP were put at a higher figure, say 6 per cent, the rate of increase in demand would naturally be higher. In India detailed studies showed that a rate of growth of at least 4 per cent per annum is necessary to raise the average level of consumption of the poorest three deciles to a *minimum nutritional standard*, on the assumption that population would grow by 2 per cent per annum and the aggregate rate of increase in gross national product was to be around 5.5 per cent per annum. Sensitivity studies carried out elsewhere would also suggest similar findings and for fairly obvious reasons.

It would appear, therefore, that even a modest target for improving the distribution of food consumption would require a rate of growth in food production higher than the trend rate of 2.6 per cent computed by the FAO. In fact, if the present rate is allowed to continue, it is beyond doubt that the distribution of world food consumption will register little or no improvement. Moreover, even a slight improvement in per capita consumption is contingent on an optimistic assumption concerning the reduction in population growth.

The assumption that with the continuation of the past growth rate in production the developing world can improve its per capita food *availability* to any significant extent, let alone the distribution to the poorest three deciles, would appear to be a great misconception when their capacity to import is taken into account. In addition, against the background of persistent shortages, the price at which such food is likely to be available will put it beyond the reach of the poor in the developing countries unless the sales were subsidized on a large scale. In turn such subsidies would pre-empt resources needed for development. The *inescapable conclusion is that the rate of growth of food production has to be increased*. On the basis of yield levels that currently prevail in the developing world and taking into account the fact that labour intensive, low energy demanding investment opportunities have opened up with respect to certain major cereals such as rice on irrigated lands or on land where water management is efficient, a rate of growth of 3.5 per cent per annum would not appear to be an unduly ambitious target for the medium term i.e. for the period 1985-1990. While detailed recommendations are made in the next section, it should be noted here that developing countries have grown over the last two decades at rates which are below 3.5 per cent but not way below. As Table 2 shows, over the decade 1952-62, they grew at the rate of 3.1 per cent per annum. While the growth rate over the period 1962-72 was somewhat lower, there is little evidence to suggest that agriculture in developing countries has moved into a regime of secular diminishing returns. In fact, a part of the reason lies in the fact that investment in agriculture has not taken place on the needed scale, because of the inability to mobilize domestic surpluses during a period when the flow of net aid was diminishing sharply (2). Another major contributory factor has been slow implementation of real agrarian reform measures in the developing countries. Since alternative options hardly exist, we cannot afford to accept either of these two factors as irreversible. It is precisely in our ability to change these trends that the crucial test would seem to lie.

Clearly an average rate of growth of 3.5 per cent of annum for the developing countries as a whole implies that some will grow faster and some at a lower rate. If the present trends in the world food economy continue, the slow growing ones will most probably import food from the developed market economies. *A more desirable course of development will imply a much greater degree of self-reliance on the part of the developing world as a whole in the area of food production.* This need not, however, completely preclude exchange between developed and developing countries, especially during the transitional period.

To sum up, along with the continuation of the existing trends for the developed market and centrally planned economies, an acceleration of the growth rate in the developing countries to 3.5 per cent per annum will provide for some improvement in the consumption levels in the developing countries while preventing major structural dislocation in developed country agriculture. Surpluses that may accrue to the developed countries during this period may prove useful in contributing towards world food security (3).

3.3.2　*Medium Term Action*　In the changed situation of the seventies and the early eighties, the achievement of the target rate of growth of 3.5 per cent for the developing countries will depend on several factors:
(I) In the ESCAP region this will require on an aggregate basis a substantial increase in yields per hectare. The contribution made by an increase in arable area is likely to be small excepting for a few countries such as Malaysia and the outlying islands of Indonesia. Potential for increase in arable area in Latin America would appear to be much larger, *prima facie*, although this is a matter of some dispute. In Africa, the experience of the sixties has been very disappointing. Reasons for this need to be carefully reviewed, although sparseness of population would be a major limiting factor. The nature of the techniques used, insufficiency of investment for land preparation and the nature of land tenure would also appear to be contributory factors. Country studies are called for with a view to identifying the constraints and for overcoming them in the least expensive way.
(II) Sown area can, of course, be increased by increasing the cropping intensity. In the ESCAP region, this possibility exists through the provision of irrigation and the introduction of rapidly maturing varieties.
(III) Land classified as fallow can be eliminated partly through irrigation and partly through changing the system of rotation. Furthermore, by encouraging transition from natural grazing to produced fodder, the area under cultivation can be increased. Forested land can also be economized by the introduction of farm forestry. These possibilities would appear to be particularly relevant for Africa and Latin America.

---

(2) It has been estimated by several eminent scientists that with world-wide control of pests and diseases, food supply can increase by at least 40% with little increase in farming costs.
(3) It should be noted that these assumptions taken together imply a growth rate for world agriculture somewhat lower than 3.5. per cent per annum.

(IV) Integrated production involving crops, livestock and poultry can reduce land needed for feeding the non-human population. The Asian Livestock Development Survey has indicated considerable possibilities in this direction.

(V) Assured water supply and management is an indispensable requirement for increasing yields in the greater part of the developing world.

(VI) Considerable scope for intensified use of chemical fertilizers exists in many countries. However, results are best obtained in combination with water, new varieties and pesticides.

(VII) Mechanization has very limited scope in ESCAP, but in Latin America, possibilities would appear to be greater.

In every region, *technology can prove useful in increasing yields provided the infrastructure of agricultural research and extension is adequate and the governments are sufficiently innovative in regard to rural institutions so that benefits can embrace the largest segment of the rural population.* Institutional adaptations such as land reforms and land consolidation are primarily needed in relation to the conjunctive use of ground water and surface water and for making suitable drainage arrangements. It is also necessary to minimize the extent of capital investment needed by promoting labour-intensive techniques. Basically, *a large part of the institutional problem boils down to devising measures for internalizing 'external economies', a problem whose importance cannot be over-emphasized in regard to a large class of agricultural investment.*

Experience of the so-called 'green-revolution' is sufficiently instructive to merit a special discussion. There is little doubt that the initial impulse behind the 'green revolution' has petered out because in the first instance it did not have as wide a research base as was desirable. Secondly, while it is basically scale neutral, the preconditions are assured water and credit which are generally very unevenly distributed regionally as well as between different segments of the rural population. As a result, benefits have accrued in a large measure to the more affluent class of farmers. On top of all this, the 'green revolution' has been heavily import biased with the result that vulnerability of agriculture to international economic fluctuations has increased. While an import bias is not in itself a bad thing, combined with a difficult and unstable foreign exchange situation, this has accentuated domestic instability. In addition, the use of locally available resources has been neglected (4).

Summing up, it is fair to conclude that while the 'green revolution', with its emphasis on yield increase through the seed-fertilizer route, was better adapted to the resource endowments of the countries in the ESCAP region, its effect on the Indian subcontinent, which includes Bangladesh, India, Pakistan and Sri Lanka, has been relatively modest. Apart from the need to development better varieties of rice which are drought and disease resistant — an area where some progress has been registered of late — it is absolutely essential to bring about reforms conferring a greater sense of security on tenant cultivators. It is also necessary to modify the skewed nature of land holdings which promote inappropriate mechanization practices. Such holdings tend to displace labour, including women, at a time when the rate of expansion of non-agricultural employment is likely to be slow. Adequate supply of credit to small and marginal farmers forms an essential component of any policy which aims at wider diffusion of technology.

---

(4) There is a voluminous literature on 'green revolution'. Attention is specially drawn to S. Ishikawa, 'Agricultural Development Strategies in Asia: Case Studies in the Philippines and Thailand'. Relevant literature on India is extensive. But as yet no definitive study has appeared. Whatever their merits, all studies bear out the points raised here.

As regards fertilizer and fuel supplies, possibilities of increased production cooperation amongst developing countries need to be explored very carefully. It is possible that a triangular relationship involving know-how from developed countries, availability of cheap feedstock in oil exporting developing countries and a guaranteed and rising market for fertilizers in developing countries can contribute substantially to a higher level of agricultural production accompanied by a growing volume of world trade.

Research, especially international research, can play a very important part in improving agricultural production. Our knowledge about tropical African agriculture is clearly deficient. Research efforts in the ESCAP region are currently proceeding at a more satisfactory rate. Nonetheless, the need for continuous improvement in varieties, especially in regard to pulses and oil seeds is very great. Given the protein deficiency of the developing countries, these items deserve a great deal more attention than they have so far received.

Considerable attention also needs to be given to technical factors involved in food production. The importance of these is often severely under-rated, The problem here is twofold: ensuring the effective transfer of appropriate technologies from the industrialized world and, more importantly, the development of completely new techniques and technologies specifically geared to the requirements of agricultural production processes in the countries of the Third World. These new technologies must fulfill three general requirements: they must be labour intensive; they must be ecologically sound; and they must be low or medium energy intensive. New technologies are particularly required with respect to irrigation and drainage, including the purification and desalinization of water which, at the present time, tends to be both too expensive and energy intensive. As noted earlier, water supply can be the limiting technical factor in raising agricultural production. The need to develop alternative methods of cultivation which are less soil destructive, a particularly important consideration in subtropical and tropical regions, must also be mentioned.

Long term funds on a concessional basis for agricultural investment with special attention to research are essential for most developing countries. (5) However, in this context, the potential complementarity relation between major food producing developing countries and some of the OPEC countries would need to be emphasized. This is particularly important not only for removing the payment imbalances of developing oil importing countries but also because one unit of fertilizer can go a much longer way in certain developing countries provided the development of rural infrastructural resources is not neglected. Since infrastructural activities are also highly labour intensive, regional cooperation along these lines can be conducive to generating expanded employment opportunities.

If the growth rate of 3.5 per cent mentioned earlier is to materialize, each one of the proposals mentioned above would need to be implemented with a vigour that has so far not been particularly conspicuous on the world scale. As yields on irrigated land are significantly higher than those in unirrigated areas, top priority would need to be given to irrigation and water management. Research on dry land farming needs to be intensified and human settlements patterns may need modification to suit agro-climatic conditions. In certain areas, tree production will need high priority. Above all, rural organizations must give scope for innovations while trying to mitigate existing inequalities. The question of cooperative village management requires serious attention from politicians and planners. Quite apart from the fact that such an arrangement will be more equitable, it

---

(5) Some possibilities in this respect are discussed in Annexes 2 and 6.

will also help in augmenting effective availability by reducing losses in storage and transportation. In addition, this is likely to have an indirect effect on production by promoting better health conditions all around.

The problem of ensuring an adequate supply of protein to the world population needs very careful attention. The meat route is clearly an expensive one for reasons which have been already mentioned. Two other routes that need to be fully explored are fish and allied products from the oceans and *grains involving a higher protein content*. In addition, soyabeans can provide some part of the protein needs in countries where they are not currently cultivated on any significant scale, such as the Indian subcontinent.

Unfortunately, world fish production having marked a steep ascent from 1950's to 1970's has been stagnating, a factor that needs to be rectified urgently. As regards protein fortification of grains, research has a long way to go. As far as soyabeans are concerned, no significant yield increase has been reported. Growth can, therefore, take place only by increasing acreage, which will require careful crop planning. Possibilities of processing oilseed cakes to make them edible for human consumption requires serious consideration.

An appropriate *price policy* is an important component of any reasonable plan for agriculture. Obviously, the farmer must be given a fair return on his investment, particularly in situations where he is expected to undertake risky investments such as trying out a new crop variety. In such situations, it will be necessary on the part of the government to *guarantee a support price* so that even if demand temporarily falls short of supply, the price does not slump so as to lead the farmer into a substantial loss. The interests of urban consumers can best be protected through a system of buffer stock operation. Since food prices determine money wages to a considerable extent in most developing countries, apart from whatever monetary-fiscal policy is pursued, the need for minimizing cost-push inflation arising from a sharp increase in food prices and the operation of the 'ratchet effect' that goes with it is a point that must be kept in mind by planners and policy makers. While the more affluent sections of the urban economy may require nothing more than reasonable stability in food prices, a price-based method of distributing food supplies may fail to do justice to the poorest three deciles of the population. For them *greater employment* must be accompanied by a method of controlled distribution of basic cereals up to a certain minimum level. The extent of the coverage will depend on the total amount of subsidies the government can afford. Since most governments operate under a severe budget constraint, the problem is a very difficult one in practice. However, there is no doubt that any aggregate rate of growth of food supplies will go a longer way in meeting the food requirements provided it is accompanied by a proper system of public distribution. For most countries, public distribution needs to be maintained on the basis of domestic production supplemented only on the margin by import of food on commercial terms. It may be useful to bear in mind, however, that in difficult years, concessional imports of food may need to be provided. Maintenance of an international buffer stock will help in stabilizing prices, thereby partially mitigating the possible need for highly concessional supplies in times of serious distress.

Finally, of special importance in the short term are attempts by Third World countries to reduce food wastage arising out of untreated plant diseases, pests, deficient storage and inadequate transportation arrangements. Rates of return on investments in these areas may in many cases be very considerable. Efforts to reduce post-harvest food losses should be organized with a view to reaching at least a 50 per cent reduction by 1985, as proposed and adopted by the UN Seventh Special Session.

In the long term, two major factors that need to be strongly emphasized are accelerated decline in population growth and changes in the consumption patterns of the wealthy countries.
In addition, the role of research cannot be over-emphasized especially in regard to non-conventional food resources as well as in economising on the use of non-renewable natural resources.

As regards the first line of action, so far as ESCAP is concerned, there are good reasons to believe that *population planning* will begin to have a more perceptible effect in these countries from around the middle eighties. This is because birth rates have begun to decline even in India, although to a small extent. In countries of East Asia, they have declined more substantially. As stressed throughout this report, the question of population growth cannot be treated in isolation. Success in this direction is dependent upon action, both national and international, in a range of interrelated fields.

The question of changing the consumption habits of the world's affluent minority is likely to prove a much more difficult matter. Attitude changes are very difficult to bring about in this respect. However, increased awareness of global problems may help in the long run. *Reduction in population growth* in the developed world, even though it is currently much lower than in the developing countries, should in view of per capita resource consumption, also be stressed (cf. Annex 8, viz. section 8.4).

For developing countries, as noted earlier, current deficiency in regard to protein is very much higher than in regard to calories. Even within protein, the contribution of animal protein is very much lower. Clearly, in a long term context, this situation must be rectified. Hence, the problem of how to meet the protein deficiency in the least expensive manner in ESCAP countries and in large parts of Africa would appear to deserve very urgent attention. In implementing a proper nutrition policy, the first step is to remove the calorie gap since this would appear to be the most urgent one. For children in developing countries, protein deficiency is, no doubt, very important as it can cause irreversible damages. But it would appear that without improving the calorie intake, the protein deficiency cannot be tackled satisfactorily, a fact which is of strategic importance in deciding on a appropriate nutrition policy.

Appropriate recycling of agricultural waste would appear to be useful in minimizing the need for chemical fertilizer, thereby preventing ecological degradation. There is a great deal of interest amongst scientists on the question of fixation of nitrogen for crop production. Currently a great deal of research work is going on which includes both biological and abiological processes. This includes enhancement of symbiotic nitrogen fixation of grain legumes, an area where fertilizer application has shown very little response. Similarly, if cost-effective methods of using solar energy are developed for agricultural operations such as solar pumps, they can help greatly in minimizing the need for fossil fuels (cf. Annex 8, viz. 8.5).

In the long-run, water is likely to prove a very critical limitation for sustaining a high level of agricultural production. This will require river basin wide planning as well as schemes for desalinization of sea water. Both require regional action, if not international cooperation. Also likely to prove of decisive importance in the future is the apparent trend toward fluctuating climatic conditions. The period between 1935-1955 may well come to be regarded as an optimum period in terms of growing conditions. The possibility of deteriorating climatic conditions underscores the need to create food buffer stocks organized on a regional basis.

On balance, it is, therefore, extremely hazardous to forecast the long term growth rate with any form of precision. All that can be said is that the target rate of growth of 3 per cent set in Chapter 6 of this report cannot be achieved through ad hoc improvisations. Only if sufficient foresight is deployed in regard to controlling population growth, in restraining the growth of demand by the wealthy and in directing technology into areas which promise to obviate potential bottlenecks, is it possible that a better balance will be reached between man and his environment than prevails currently.

No viable long run perspective can be forecast for the world economy, if we do not succeed in changing short term and medium term prospects. It would, therefore, appear necessary to undertake action on the lines recommended in the preceeding sections. In the short and medium term, fundamental problems arise largely from insufficiency of growth in the developing countries, chronic balance-of-payments difficulties, continuous increase in numbers and large scale adoption of technology and styles of living which are unsuited to their socio-economic environments. While corrective action needs to be initiated on all fronts, including institutional changes within the developing countries themselves, a more equitable international order can help substantially in the process of accomplishing the necessary structural changes from the long term viewpoint. Such a new order is of course incompatible with the international utilization of food as a means of exercising political pressure, in particular on developing countries.

Annex 4   Industrialization, Trade, and the International Division of Labour
Ibrahim Helmi Abdel Rahman and Helmut Hesse

4.1   *The Major Aims*

The new international economic order implies an optimal utilization of human and physical resources in the world as a whole, i.e. an optimal international division of labour. Since trade is inseparably linked with the division of labour, this optimum requires special rules governing international trade. Moreover, it requires a changing production pattern, especially in the field of manufacturing industry. The future evolution and emergence of trade policies and industrialization patterns which are required will, therefore, add a dynamic element to the concept of optimal international division of labour and will therefore indicate important variations from past experience. It should be noted that the expression 'international division of labour' refers to the geographical location of economic activities in the world, or to 'what is produced where'. This is frequently misunderstood to mean a static redistributive device which implies a shift of existing manufacturing infrastructure from one country to another. The expression 'international division of labour' is used here in a much more dynamic sense: the progressive shift in the pattern of production between regions and countries over time, so that all will benefit from changing comparative advantages and specializations.

Special technologies will need to be developed to suit the conditions prevailing in Third World countries (1), and also to help restructure industrial activities in the industrialized countries. Industrial policies and strategies at the national, regional and international levels will need to be formulated with the necessary procedures, information systems and instrumentalities of action to ensure implementation and harmonization at all levels. Moreover, it is obvious that the attainment of objectives in the fields of trade and industrialization entails a variety of changes and policies not only in the economic field but also in social and political structures.

4.2   *Analysis of Existing Situation in the Trading System*

The current trading system cannot be considered optimal for several reasons. First, the possibilities of a mutually advantageous division of labour between centrally planned-economy and market-economy countries are not adequately utilized, though the trade between these two country groups, hampered for a period of time by the 'cold war' and confronted with some difficulties arising from the different economic systems, has shown a rapid increase in the last years. It would appear that the state monopoly of foreign trade existing in the centrally planned-economy countries does not constitute an insurmountable obstacle to the development of their trade with the West. Nevertheless, further increase of flexibility in planning of foreign trade and in the management of foreign trade enterprises could contribute to the faster growth of this trade. It seems that in view of resource endowment – of the high degree of industrialization and of the abundance of qualified manpower in the centrally planned economy countries – there are ample possibilities for the developed and developing market economies of increasing trade with them. There is considerable scope for intra-industry cooperation, including mutual development of certain raw materials production, some types of joint ventures etc.

---

(1) Technological development and the question of appropriate technology are discussed in Annex 8 (Human Environment) and Annex 6 (Science and Technology). The role of transnational enterprises is discussed in Annex 7.

Secondly, the current pattern, practices, and institutions in the field of international trade between market-economy countries have evolved essentially from the requirements and according to the interests of the *major partners*. Reciprocity, one of the main elements of the General Agreement, is generally accepted as a fair principle in negotiations when all countries are economically and politically of equal strength; a bargain can only be struck between countries that either have something to offer or believe they have something to gain. Mutual bargaining, which has been typical of the trading system, on a reciprocal basis cannot ensure equity if the various partners are of *unequal strength*. The same applies to the most favoured nation principle, the other main element of GATT. It is an appropriate device for regulating trade relations among equals, but is certainly inappropriate for regulating trade between the industrialized countries and the Third World.

It is, therefore, quite understandable that the countries of the Third World have pleaded for an amendment of the MFN principle in that industrialized countries should be permitted to grant *preferential tariffs* to less developed countries whilst the latter should be able to grant preferential treatment to themselves. Though it is true that these claims have been duly considered in Part IV of GATT (effective 27 June 1966) and adopted within the General System of Preferences, it is no exaggeration to say that the tariff reductions in the whole post-war period have mainly favoured the industrialized countries. Since negotiations on the abolition of trade barriers in the past have been usually set in motion by the leading industrialized countries, it is not surprising that *tariffs on export goods of relevance* to Third World countries still remain comparatively high. In other words, because of the specific elements that have been chosen to regulate the trading system after the Second World War, the division of labour among industrialized countries (mainly an intra-industry division of labour) has developed far more quickly and more intensively than has the division of labour among industrialized and industrializing countries.

In addition, the concentration of tariff-reductions explains why the technique of bilateral bargaining has dominated the post-war period. *Multilateral* bargaining under global objectives is still *underdeveloped*. Thus, it is understandable that there have been only few cases in which international contracts were concluded not only on particular trade regulating measures but also, simultaneously, on the allocation of national resources to improve the *international* division of labour. Moreover, the exceptions have proved disappointing. The Long Term Agreement, for instance, actually took into consideration the cooperative and constructive action required to promote the development of world trade and also to meet the basic needs of developing countries for larger exports. These aims were meant to be effectuated by the removal of obstacles to trade and by furthering orderly adjustments in the industrialized countries. However, they have never been pursued. On the contrary, in the absence of any effective surveillance and obligatory arbitration, the agreement has been used as a charter for *restricting trade*, rather than as an obligation for the industrialized countries to encourage the reallocation of affected factors of production into new activities.

Because GATT failed to represent the interests and concerns of the Third World, the developing countries were induced to create a new organization, UNCTAD, which, in many respects, competes directly with GATT. The creation of UNCTAD marks the beginning of a gradual evolution towards institutional duality in the field of trade and development. This dispersion of activities constitutes a serious hindrance to the efforts to formulate a new order of foreign trade and division of labour at the international level.

The third reason why the current trading system is sub-optimal is that the international division of labour in the *agricultural sector* is weak. Most industrialized countries isolated their agricultural sectors from international competition. This can be largely explained by the fact that countries with a comparative disadvantage in agricultural products are often faced with a trade-off between the efficiency of world-wide resource allocation and national income distribution as well as national security. Given this situation, national policy aims have been given priority over the creation of a mechanism of international competition; virtually no serious efforts have been made to enable comparative costs to play a progressively more important part in international agricultural trade — efforts which would have contributed to an improvement in the international division of labour.

The fourth reason concerns the strong trend away from a single trading system based on the principle of non-discrimination towards greater regionalism in international economic relations and to the development of *inward-directed blocs* under the leadership of rich industrialized countries. Several groups of countries have exploited Article 24 of the General Agreement to negotiate preferential trade agreements. This trend towards regionalism in international trade enlarges the risk of political isolationism and commercial protectionism and even of trade wars. It determines the effectiveness of international organizations to the detriment of the Third World and the smaller industrialized countries. It generates pressures for certain developing countries to link to a particular bloc, thereby extending economic spheres of influence of already powerful countries. It should however be noted that the negative aspects of such groupings linking developed and developing countries can be mitigated by the generalization of the principle of non-reciprocity in their mutual relations.

All these pressures are obstacles to the improvement of a world-wide division of labour. However, as long as these pressures are felt, an appropriate degree of protection of the interests of the weaker countries is necessary. One of the effective ways of achieving this is economic integration within regional economic groupings and some degree of group-internal preferences without being forced to grant — according to the MFN-rule — these preferences to third countries. This is especially important for the developing countries, by developing economic integration these countries can — as several examples show — create broader markets for new products, realize economies of scale, avoid uneconomic use of scarce production factors by establishing so-called integration industries, and organize research in the field of technologies appropriate for their conditions. This also strengthens their position in the dialogue with the more developed partners. As positive as this situation in the present world may be judged, it has to be ensured that it does not result in a further step towards a world divided into strong and only inward-looking blocs of countries. Such would make it even more difficult to achieve a truly optimal international division of labour.

4.3 *Some Aspects of Industrialization Policies*

Although considerable differences exist between countries of the Third World with respect to their pattern and extent of industrialization, some general observations can be made. Compared with the industrialized countries, the developing countries have a small share of industrial production and industrial exports. The Third World accounts for only seven per cent of total manufacturing output, a ratio which has not increased appreciably over the last three decades. The corresponding ratios for the different manufacturing sectors vary from high values for food industries, textiles and leather, to low values for heavy mechanical and electrical equipment industries and for science based industries in general. Import substitution policies are generally followed which lead to local production protected by tariff walls and limited to captive local markets. The processing of local raw materials, including minerals, initiates a form of industrialization and increases exports, but rarely advances beyond a limited stage due to difficulties and trade barriers erected by the industrialized countries. Local assembly industries are started on the basis of imported components and intermediate products, but do not generally attain high productivity or competitiveness because of market limitations.

In the relatively advanced among the developing countries, and also in the large ones, it has been possible to establish a relatively strong and integrated industrial base, including heavy metallurgy, machine building and basic chemical industries, supported by the necessary research, design and marketing institutions. Traditional industries, as well as small and artisan industries, are generally privately owned, but modern and large enterprises are established with the strong participation and support of the public sector. Foreign participation in capital has not been as large as in the case of extractive industries, plantations and service industries, but is gradually increasing, bringing with it foreign technology and managerial experience. The distribution of net shares of profits depends to a large extent on conditions and specific circumstances.

The above remarks on import substitution policies require some qualification. In certain countries, and in certain phases of industrialization, such policies had to be maintained simply because opportunities for exporting manufactured goods and processed raw materials did not exist. In other cases, they were necessary, in spite of their clear short-comings, to help establish a broader industrial base or to safeguard against unfair dumping practices. Various phases and a certain degree of continuity of import substitution policies on a reducing scale should therefore be expected.

Apart from import substitution and the processing of local raw materials, with their limitations and difficulties, very few Third World countries have been able to develop and implement integrated policies of industrialization. Because of the shortage of capital and skills, labour intensive and small-scale industries have been advocated (2). The promotion of exports of manufactured goods has recently attracted attention, but can only be effective under very specific conditions. Regional integration and harmonization can help to the extent that it widens markets and avoids wasteful competition for capital; that the manufacturing industries correspond to regionally planned priorities and are effectively controlled by the countries entering into the integration process. The movement towards regional integration, however, has proved slow and beset with many difficulties.

In spite of all these difficulties, manufacturing industry still represents the most dynamic sector of growth in many Third World countries. The dynamism of industry is reflected in its generally higher rate of growth as compared to other sectors, in its requirement of building up new types of human skills and specialization, and in the important social implications of industrialization. Careful policies would have to be devised and implemented so as to avoid some of the more serious effects of wrong industrialization. In particular, coordination between agricultural and industrial developments is essential, especially in the coming years, in which demand for and prices of food are likely to represent higher demands on the resources of the developing countries. Provided that certain conditions are met, industrialization can be viewed as an essential prerequisite for building up the future economic structure of all Third World countries. Examples of success can already be found, and others can be expected to follow. This in itself provides some hope that a new international division of labour in industry can be established in the coming decades.

The present division of labour, as is well known, has its origin in a colonial period. Although it has since been modified marginally, it retains the general features of con-

---

(2) For a discussion of the advantages of labour intensive and small-scale industries see Annex 6.

centrating manufacturing industry and the development of technology almost exclusively in the industrialized countries. Generally, Third World countries have been left little more than raw material production and a minimum of local processing activities for the most basic needs. The increased imports of manufactured goods, which at a later stage justified policies of import substitution and the protection of infant industries, were related either to the production of raw materials, such as agriculture and mining, or were meant essentially to satisfy the needs of higher income and urban populations. It seems thus reasonable to assume that the industrialization which has taken place in most of the countries of the Third World has not been directed towards the satisfaction of the basic needs of low income groups and, therefore, can be justified less on social grounds than on economic grounds. The limited purchasing power of the poor, in the absence of deliberate policies of income distribution, has made it impossible to widen internal markets and to sustain integrated plans of industrialization. Exceptions to these observations can of course be easily found, but even in cases where serious efforts at income redistribution have been attempted, productivity of labour has not shown a corresponding increase, with the result that industrialization has met with other difficulties.

Industrial technology, as known at present, is almost exclusively created in the industrialized countries. The two main sources of financing and directing technology are military applications and large scale industrial profit motives. Given this situation, it is obvious that the technology developed will have little relevance to the pressing needs of the Third World. The difficulty in many cases, however, is that it is the only technology available. There is neither sufficient capacity nor resources to create technologies specifically geared to meeting the needs of the poor and disprivileged masses of the Third World. Worse still, the transfer of technology takes place on the basis of practices and conditions which are generally considered unfavourable to the recipient countries. And even if appropriate technology was to be developed, it would take considerable time and effort before it could make a major impact on trade and industrial production.

This situation should be remedied, otherwise appropriate and accelerated industrialization of the developing countries will not be possible (3). The problems posed for a new industrial technology suitable for the developing countries in the next 25 years must take into account the rapid growth required. It is most likely that a situation of technological and industrial duality will obtain. Because of population growth and the need to create jobs with low capital, a labour intensive technology will be required. For fast industrial growth, expansion of exports and provision of basic industrial inputs, a modern capital intensive industrial sector is required. The recent Chinese experience illustrates this situation, but need not be the only answer to this problem of duality. It is clear that accelerated industrialization should not entail mass unemployment or other disruptive factors in the social structure of the developing countries. These problems should be examined and long term objectives and policies to solve them established. It would not be sufficient to examine them on the basis of past experience alone.

4.4   *Aims of a New Industrialization Policy*

The establishment of an optimal international division of labour depends, in the long-term, upon the acceptance of the notion that the industrialization of the Third World does not run counter to the interests of the presently industrialized countries. It must also be realized that future industrialization patterns, as well as industrial technology, cannot be based upon the simple projection and continuation of past trends.

------

(3) The subject of technological development and conditions for the transfer of technology is discussed in Annex 6.

The countries of the Third World must endeavour, in formulating future industrialization policies, to set new priorities — priorities which must include the production of the basic commodities required to satisfy the needs of the poor majority rather than the production of more sophisticated goods to satisfy the predilections of the affluent minority. Food and energy must figure foremost among the priorities especially in those countries with food deficiencies. Certain industrial activities related to food and energy must, therefore, be given highest priority. These include fertilizers, insecticides, agricultural machinery and implements, processing, transport and storage facilities and agro-industries in general. Technology for producing basic textiles, building materials, pharmaceuticals and educational equipment should also be afforded high priority.

The future pattern of industrial production and consumption in the industrialized countries must also differ from that of the past. For one thing, limitations on the use of energy and raw materials will not permit simple extrapolation, while environmental constraints and changes in attitudes will, it must be hoped, lead to the more rational husbandry of world resources, including raw materials and energy for manufacturing industries.

In view of these considerations, the optimal division of labour must indicate the most efficient use of resources, including energy and human resources, according to certain patterns of inter-industry and intra-industry cooperation. It cannot be based simply on the division of industries into labour-intensive and capital-intensive and the assignment of one or the other to one group of countries. Such simple criteria are, in the light of industrialization experience, demonstrably insufficient. There is a need to consider industrialization as a social activity of human groups rather than the product of individual actions. The group approach would allow for a certain interlinking of different industrial projects to form complexes. It should also allow for the priority production of basic commodities, with the related stages and activities to make such production viable.

This picture of a future division of labour would have to take account not only of factors related to manufacturing activities but also of trade and technology factors. It should be noted that even under the ideal system of free trade, there will always be certain limitations imposed by stocks, markets and prices, and that new technologies can affect considerably the cooperative advantage of tradable goods from one time to another. This optimal division, therefore, will not be static, but subject to continuous and gradual adjustments to changing situations, including the availibility of capital, human skill formation and technological innovation. It must also of necessity be related to patterns of consumption and changing demand, which ultimately define the market for production and labour.

Attainment of the Lima industrialization target implies a rate of growth much higher than the 8 per cent recommended in the International Development Strategy for the Second United Nations Development Decade (4). It can only be realized, and then probably only partially, when a number of major changes and developments take place with respect to the transfer of capital and technology to the Third World, the training and expansion of skill and managerial capacity in the Third World, as well as to the restructuring of

---

(4) The Lima Declaration and Plan of Action as well as the declaration of the Executive Committee of the Third World Forum and the decisions of the Conference of the Non-Aligned Countries, as well as many other similar documents issued by intergovernmental and nongovernmental meetings during the last two years contain detailed proposals as regards recommended measures for industrialization of the developing countries within the framework of the New International Economic Order.

industrial activities in both groups of countries. In future it will be more essential than ever before to establish rational and careful programmes of international cooperation in order to avoid individual and erratic actions by countries or groups of countries which may lead to retaliation, economic and social disturbances and eventually military confrontation.

4.5   *Long Range Perspectives in the Trading System*

The establishment of a new international order implies the creation of a new trading system which will need to be created step by step. In the long term, this system should be characterized by at least three features.

Firstly, the importance of the principle of bilaterality as a negotiation technique should be substantially reduced: there should be only a few bilateral negotiations based on the interests of the partners leading to mutual concessions (which are then extended to all other countries). Instead, nearly all negotiations should be multilateral, carried out under global objectives, and aimed at international contracts. The principle of reciprocity should not govern these negotiations, though it should be accepted by all contracting parties that the agreements should effect an international division of labour being to the advantage of all.

Secondly, the agreements should not cover specific trade policy regulations only, e.g. tariffs or quantitative restrictions. They should also rule the behaviour of governments in influencing or regulating the allocation process in their countries. Codes of good conduct with internal responsibilities have to be negotiated which cover the interdependent areas of technological research, investment, production, and trade. They should ensure that the development strategies or growth policies of the partners are in harmony with one another and make possible an intra-industry division of labour between developing and developed countries. The contracts should include guaranties for access to supplies of raw materials and to markets.

Thirdly, the agreements should bind the partners. However, because the trade effects of agreements will be very difficult to foresee, it seems legitimate to demand that only those countries observing the rules established should profit by them. Therefore, in this connection, the unconditional most-favoured-nation clause should be substituted by the conditional MFN clause. In order to strengthen the binding character of the agreements, the principle of multilaterality should be introduced. It would not only stand for common responsibilities and joint decisions but also for international surveillance and the continuous presence of a concerned forum to which a country can address its complaints and seek mediation in respect to its grieviances with others. Even *obligatory arbitration* could be provided for, and it should be considered whether it would not be desirable to create a sanction mechanism by which countries having agreed on certain rules but acting against them should be made subject to discriminatory practices.

The preparation of agreements (including the organization of the information and consultation process) as well as multilateral surveillance and the control of the sanction mechanism, should be conferred upon a single *international trade organization*, thereby overcoming the problem of institutional duality existing at present. This organization should be established soon, either by merging UNCTAD and GATT or otherwise, and start to launch — pragmatically — the first agreements.

4.6   *Short and Medium Term Recommendations*

The Lima Conference adopted a Declaration and a Plan of Action on industrial development and cooperation which contained many detailed and specific recommendations, including the target of 25 per cent for the share of Third World countries in world industrial production by the year 2000 referred to above. The figure of 25 per cent is a target and not a projection. In the light of current and recent experience in world development, however, it could be viewed as being too ambitious, even unrealistic. Certainly its attainment will require concerted action in a range of inter-related fields. The Conference also recommended that a system of *consultations* be established in UNIDO and other appropriate international bodies between developed and developing countries. Such consultations may be held shortly for fertilizers and iron and steel.

The recommendations in the Lima Plan of Action are divided into actions at the national level of the developing countries, at the level of cooperation among developing countries, between developed and developing countries and, lastly, with respect to the group of least developed, land-locked and island developing countries. The Plan of Action concludes with a set of recommendations of an institutional character concerning the UN, including the proposal to set up an Industrial-Development Fund. The Seventh Special Session of the General Assembly of the United Nations held in September 1975, examined industrialization of the developing countries and passed a number of recommendations, generally endorsing the conclusions reached in the Lima Conference, especially with respect to the establishment of forums for industrial consultation between developed and developing countries. Some additional observations and recommendations, however, appear warranted. These are discussed under four main headings: information, the programming and management of resources; adjustment; and trade policies. Missing from this list are two subject areas which very much affect industrialization policies: the acquisition and transfer of technology; and the role of transnational corporations. These have been excluded for the simple reason that they are dealt with in Annexes 6 and 7 respectively.

It should be noted that the recommendations for action contained in this section do not generally call for the creation of new institutions, but rather the redirection and intensification of the actions of existing centres of decision-making and agencies of international cooperation. In recent years a project for the establishment of an *International Industrialization Institute* has been under study and has been recently recommended to the General Assembly of the United Nations by delegates of the United States.

4.6.1   *Information*   Several attempts have been made to increase the flow of information required for industrial development. This flow ranges from open studies and publications, through commercial and technical information on industrial equipment and commodities, to very specific forms of restricted information including patents, know-how and technological transfer. Owing to the accelerated pace of change and the disruption of markets and traditional procedures, more efforts will have to be made in all these areas, through a variety of means, including industrial fairs, export and investment promotion meetings, joint ventures and financing mechanisms, as well as intensive follow-up and analyses of current trends and recent technological developments. Not all of this information can be made public on a wide scale, and need not be. The exchange of information on a restricted scale must be furthered between interested parties in the developing and developed worlds. It is well known that the annual meetings of the World Bank and Regional Development Banks provide fruitful results for participants through consultation and exchange of information. Since 1969 UNIDO has organized annual consultation meetings between national, regional and international industrial banks and financing organizations. These meetings have grown in importance and serve a very useful purpose.

Prices and market situations of the main industrial commodities could form the subject of a useful information and consultation effort. Minerals and durable agricultural commodities have 'markets' with prices and agreed specifications. It is certainly time that fertilizers, basic chemicals, main metal products, and standard industrial equipment and products be organized in a similar manner; the creation of an organized supply-demand mechanism in fact constitutes a 'market' which, however imperfect, would comprise a positive first step in the right direction. Such products can be quoted for current delivery, as well as for future availability. This system of information and consultation could be later expanded to include more products, which would be capable of normalization so as to be suitable for offer and demand. It is unlikely that such a system would be useful for complex or specific equipment or for complete factories. For such cases, the present and only procedure of seeking quotations and comparing specifications should be improved.

Third World countries should be assisted in ascertaining — through data banks and reference organizations — the correct information on the products and the partners involved, including the competence and reputation of consultants and various advisory bodies. Data banks already store the results of large numbers of feasibility studies on industrial projects in different sectors.

If the Third World is to industrialize quickly and to give priorities to basic requirements and labour intensive technologies, a considerable amount of work will be required in the field of industrial project design and evaluation. The present procedures are too slow and in many cases depend upon the limited experience of a few (consultants). Some codes for consultation are badly needed.

Eventually, an *'investment' market* can be envisaged where the supply of and demand for finance, technology, management, and markets for specified industrial projects could be offered and negotiated. As noted earlier, Third World countries are in a particularly weak bargaining position with foreign suppliers or prospective investors, especially in the case of transnational corporations which have wide experience and integrated approaches. New systems of information and consultation should be developed to strengthen the position of Third World countries so as to enhance their capacity for industrial decision-making and effective implementation.

The 'investment promotion meetings' held over many years by UNIDO in different regions and for specific industrial branches are, in reality, aimed at creating such an 'investment market'. The idea has been the subject of a recommendation by the United Nations and was widely endorsed, though the experience of UNIDO could be considered as one of many possible forms. In effect, the role of the World Bank in promoting industrial investments through its project evaluation and the securing of capital from national, regional and private resources to supplement the limited share of the Bank itself, could be further enhanced so as to be more effective, not only project by project, but on the basis of a group of projects submitted by one country (as in the case of consultative groups and consortia) or in a specific branch, which is now the case with the high priority given by the Bank to certain industrial investments e.g. fertilizers.

The purpose of establishing 'an investment market' would be always to afford to the developing countries alternative proposals from a variety of sources, and to ensure that the projects are carefully prepared and evaluated. As in all 'good' markets, the benefits could be considerable to all parties.

It is the responsibility of the developing countries themselves to accept or refuse partnership in establishing industrial activities in their countries. They must ensure that such activities fall within the priorities established by the national plan of development, especially as regards direct and indirect forward and backward linkages which will be created by the new enterprise. Careful criteria must be established for the selection of such industries so as to ensure their fullest contribution to development and growth in the country and to their harmonization within the framework of social, economic, manpower and financial conditions. One would also hope that 'national plans' would in themselves be in harmony with wider regional and international 'plans' so as to ensure optimum contributions to a new international division of labour. For many years to come, national and regional policies will have to be dominant in this field of industrial cooperation. These objectives could be initially helped through the establishment of a comprehensive data bank covering industrial investment decisions and projects in progress combined with comprehensive and detailed projections of supply, demand and prices. Later, the information could be used for consultation and negotiation, whether in individual or collective cases, with the assistance of the appropriate machinery.

In this field of complex negotiations, new *rules of conduct* and *arbitration* will be required. Considerable progress has been made in the preparation of proposals in this field, especially with respect to the acquisition and transfer of technology. The whole area of conditions for and costs of technology transfer must be reexamined.

4.6.2   *The Programming and Management of Resources*   Sound industrialization policies will require new approaches to the programming and management of resources and development at the international level. The existing situation is characterized by the ad hoc formulation of policies and programmes in response to crisis situations: they are the result of crises rather than an attempt to anticipate them. This was the case with the environment, and more recently with food. In the light of the lack of foresight of the main oil importing countries, energy and oil policies seem destined to follow the same haphazard route.

It is now recognized that a more elaborate system of careful husbandry and management of raw materials and scarce resources is inevitable (cf. Annex 8). Certain opposition is encountered in those groups which benefit from the present chaotic situation, and from those who fear that 'too much' international regulation will inhibit competition or lead to adverse movements in prices and stocks. In any event, the complexities of the decision-making environment have resulted in an essentially unitary approach to policy and programme formulation, i.e. a concern with single commodities (for example oil) or with single problems (for example industrial pollution). Only recently have there been serious attempts to place policies in a wider perspective and to take account of and incorporate related issues i.e. a concern for comprehensive approaches.

The dangers of the unitary approach are particularly evident in the case of industrialization policy. Without more comprehensive approaches to decision-making, for example, a situation can be easily envisaged in which say 50 Third World countries, in the absence of knowledge concerning the total picture and the full range of options, are each sold the same capacity for producing the same products. Over-investment can be as damaging as under-investment. Fluctuations in demand occur in many industries and in many industrial countries; ship building, for example, is currently a case of oversupply, fertilizers a case of overdemand. The countries of the Third World, with their limited resources and experience, will not be able to withstand such fluctuations, nor would they readily accept advice unless it is supported by a system of verification of conduct and authenticity.

4.6.3   *Adjustments in the Industrialized Countries*   The industrialized countries, on their part, will have to introduce policies of *adjustment* and introduce gradually a set of rules for industrial location and environmental protection, and develop specialization in knowledge-based industries. Since attainment of the optimal international division of labour entails a large amount of intra-industry cooperation with the developing countries, the different processes and components required for the manufacture of a final product must be carefully examined in order to determine whether they can more advantageously be located or produced in countries or regions of the Third World. In reviewing relative advantage, the specific requirements of Third World countries must be identified.

New production processes must contribute not only to the attainment of international objectives, but also to the realization of national development objectives, especially those concerning the satisfaction of basic needs and the eradication of poverty. Viewed in this way, the adjustment measures adopted by the industrialized countries contribute not only to the attainment of the optimal division of labour, but also directly serve as an important instrument for raising the living standards of the world's poor and dis-privileged.

Of particular importance here are industrial development strategies at the national and regional levels. The patterns of industrialization in Third World countries differ considerably and some are as yet not well understood. Certainly, the simple assumption which formerly prevailed, that public authorities provide the infrastructure and private foreign investors do the rest, is no more accepted. The role of the public sector, either by itself or in conjuction with foreign and domestic private capital, especially with transnational corporations, will have to be carefully studied.

4.6.4   *Recommendations for Trade Policies*   Although we must ultimately strive for the creation of a new and integrated trading system, this will not be achieved overnight. It is important, however, that high priority be afforded to certain actions and measures which, not only of vital importance in themselves, could serve to catalyse the creation of and give shape to a new order. We believe that the immediate tasks of international trade policy reside in three main areas.

Firstly, it should enable an improvement in the division of labour between the industrialized countries and the countries of the Third World by a further reduction or even abolition of the tariffs imposed by the industrialized countries on the industrial products of the Third World. Likely to be of even greater importance is a reduction of non-tariff barriers (e.g. industrial standards) since these form a major hindrance to intra-industry trade.

Whenever trade barriers are abolished, particular sectors of industry in the industrialized countries will suffer as a result of increased import competition. To avoid unemployment and a return to protectionism (which would then be employment oriented), the industrialized countries, as part of their adjustment policy, should encourage the reallocation of affected factors of production into the new, more efficient activities, e.g. into the production of knowledge-intensive goods and services. Because this reallocation process will take time and be difficult, the industrialized countries can be expected to move for the inclusion of some escape clauses. Therefore, a temporary safeguard protection has to be provided for the industries affected. It should, however, be decreasing, in accordance with a definite timetable, and it should be strictly connected with adjustment measures.

An improvement in the division of labour between the industrializing and industrialized countries can also be effected by the developing countries themselves. In order to encourage the transfer of capital and know-how from industrialized countries, they should improve the investment climate. As long as foreign entrepreneurs fear the prospect of expropriation or believe they will be treated unfairly, they cannot be expected to encourage the transfer of capital, technology, and managerial assistance to the Third

World. Countries of the Third World must be prepared, therefore, to give proper guarantees to foreign investors. It goes without saying that such guarantees must be fair to both sides and not damage the legitimate interests of the country concerned. Guarantees of this kind could be arranged by common elaboration of international rules, the observance of which should be binding to all parties involved. It must be noted that direct investment is not the only form of cooperation between foreign enterprises and host countries. Recent years have witnessed an increasing tendency for developing countries to resort to other forms, such as consultant services, production, training and marketing contracts. Whilst these new forms of cooperation have tended to provide greater safeguards for the sovereignty of the host countries, their rapid extension needs to be regulated internationally to avoid the risk of unfair or disloyal practices.

Secondly, improvements in the agricultural sector would seem more difficult to achieve than in the industrial sector. This is due to the fact that governments stick steadfastly to those national goals linked to their agricultural policy, such as 'security' and 'equitable income distribution'. For this reason, international trade policies are unlikely to be successful if they fail to take account of the national agricultural policies of the countries concerned.

The first step in this direction should be to identify the agricultural products the particular countries are actually producing or could potentially produce with comparative advantage. Agricultural policies should then be organized so as to encourage the production of these and only these products and to induce a reallocation of resources respectively. At the same time, trade policy has to gradually bring about free access to the markets of all agricultural products in such a way that large employment problems do not arise. In addition, it should aim at multilaterally negotiated insurance – like contracts guaranteeing to every country a minimum supply of essential foodstuffs during political or economic crises, either from national and international bufferstocks or by performance guarantees of alternative exporting countries. Third World countries must be included in such a programme. In this case, the objectives should even be enlarged, especially by lowering price fluctuations and raising floor-prices for producers. This integrated commodity programme has to be seen as a step forward on the way to a new international economic order. It is an innovation in so far as it really takes account of global goals instead of only a few nations' goals.

Thirdly, efforts must be made to improve the division of labour between the centrally planned economy and market economy countries. Such efforts should not be restricted to the elimination of the remaining discriminatory measures by some Western countries. Effective steps towards achieving full multilateralism in trade relations should be undertaken. Bilateral agreements should be limited to a few obviously indispensable cases and governed by fair-trade-rules. Particularly important would be the broadening of the scope of industrial cooperation between the enterprises in the centrally planned economies and in the market economy countries. Common production of particular products and mutual exchange of their components and parts would contribute to the creation of permanent economic and technical links and a real division of labour.

The achievement of such a division of labour would require extensive exchange of information, consultation and cooperation on the inter-governmental level. The existing institutional framework, namely the United Nations Economic Commission for Europe, UNCTAD, UNIDO, and their secretariats, should broaden appropriately the scope of their activities.

The new situation emerging in world trade should be taken into account at the future revision of the GATT rules.

Energy, Ores and Minerals
Robert Gibrat* and Tetsuo Noguchi

5.1 *Structure of Annex: National Sovereignty and the Common Heritage*

5.1.1 *Structure of Annex*   In this annex problems of energy as well as non-energy mineral resources are discussed. They have been combined because they share certain common features. The combination implies, however, the need for an annex layout somewhat different from that of most other annexes. Three main issues are discussed: the most appropriate natural resources strategy for achieving a new international order (5.1); energy problems (5.2); and problems concerning non-energy minerals (5.3). Proposals and recommendations for action are listed in the respective sections.

5.1.2 *National Sovereignty over Mineral Resources*   The developing countries have emphasized the right to exercise national sovereignty over their energy and mineral resources. This intention is contained in a variety of statements made and subsequent resolutions adopted by the UN General Assembly as well as by UNCTAD and UNIDO (Lima, 1975). Points 80 and 82 of the 105-point Memorandum 'Oil, Raw Materials and Development' submitted by the Algerian Government in April 1974 to the Sixth Special Session, provide a clear statement of intent on this issue.
'The use of the rich raw materials of the developing countries gives rise to an income which is inherent in those materials. The developed countries have appropriated this income. The developing countries must recover it' (point 80).
'Over and above the recovery of income, the developing countries must use their basic materials to launch a process of economic development. They have not much time for this' (point 82).

The exercise of national territorial sovereignty over mineral resources is incompatible with acceptance of the principle of the 'common heritage of mankind' formulated by the UN General Assembly in 1970 (Resolution 2749XXV) with respect to the use of the seabed and outerspace; a principle which, in the context of complete human solidarity, is applicable to natural resources of all kinds. In this report it is argued that human solidarity must form one of the guiding principles for attaining an optimum international social and economic order. The strategies of the industrialized countries have not been based upon such solidarity and they have today a virtual monopoly over technological development and the production of capital goods. As long as the international order has not brought equity, the exercise of territorial sovereignty over natural resources is one of the few weapons available to countries of the Third World. Given the imbalances in the present international power structure, *it is a weapon which must be used in the struggle for a new international order*.

This is clearly recognized in the Algerian Memorandum. Point 16 states:
'In an unequal world . . . any struggle in which the poorest may engage on a national scale will achieve full efficacy only when it becomes part of a universal movement, of which it is both component and resultant, and to which it brings its own dynamism, while continuously drawing strength from it.'

The exercise of national sovereignty by developing countries over their natural resources is thus necessary and must be accepted as the basis for short and medium-range action. Once an equitable international order has been attained, the concept of territorial

---

* with the cooperation of François Callot.

sovereignty must give way to the concept of functional sovereignty (cf. Annex 10) and implementation of the 'common heritage of mankind' principle, i.e. the use of the earth's natural resources to the advantage of all world inhabitants. In this connection, it must be noted that short-term action is complicated by the fact that many developed countries (e.g. USA, USSR, Australia, Canada) are in fact major producers of raw materials and have acquired new economic vigour with the post-1973 rises in raw material prices.

5.1.3 *Growth, Environment and Energy Use in the Industrialized Countries* The dominant issues most related to our subject are:
(I) The growing debate in the developed countries on economic growth rates and the need for a new type of society differing from today's consumer society. The results of this debate will have a decisive effect on the exhaustion of energy and mineral resources, and of oil in the first place. All the stages of development of the Third World will depend on future rates of energy and mineral resource consumption. Point 28 of the Lima Declaration stresses that the developing countries' share of total world industrial production should be equivalent to at least 25 per cent by the year 2000. But the Third World may be thinking of industrial production and of consumer goods of the present Western type; the developed countries will probably have moved well away from this by then. Technologies will change. We must beware of the timelag; it may be very considerable.
(II) The debate on environmental problems, which the Third World sometimes seems to ignore (the word 'pollution' is mentioned only once in the 105-point Algerian Memorandum). Yet, to take only one example, oil, whether as a fuel for general purposes, producing sulphur, or as a motor fuel, producing oxides of nitrogen with carcinogenic effects, is the primary pollutant which needs to be controlled.
(III) Finally, the controversy over energy from nuclear fission raging in Western countries appears to be of little concern to the Third World. The West is gradually moving towards a *resigned acceptance* of this form of energy 'for a temporary and relatively short period in which the specific problems of nuclear fission, i.e. reactor safety, radioactivity, disposal of waste, remain within reasonable limits both quantitatively and qualitatively' (1). The short-term future will therefore be predominantly nuclear, but an inevitable consequence of such temporary acceptance will be to launch the developed countries into a fierce and almost desperate search for new sources of energy. And those expected to be available in the long term, primarily the sun and nuclear fusion, no longer require mineral raw materials.

It would be a serious mistake to underestimate the importance of these three points. In the Western world, those opposed to the current consumer society, who desire to protect the environment and are against energy from nuclear fission, have the same support from the population as a whole as was yesterday given in the Third World to the liberation movements and moves to recover lost income. In other words, public awareness of these problems in the developed countries, and the resulting implications for the property of individuals or of society, reflect the same fundamental aspirations as those expressed in the Third World's desire to recover its basic income in order to accelerate its development.

5.1.4 *No Conflict of Interests Regarding New Forms of Energy* The search for new sources of energy does not run counter to the medium and long-term interests of the Third World. We have a profound belief in the potential offered by solar energy, the realization of which will require an enormous research and development effort.

---

(1) Statement by Mr. Spaak, ex-Director of the European Community, at the European Nuclear Conference, 21-25 April, 1975.

Solar energy especially can contribute towards the rapid industrialization of the Third World; countries are generally favourably located for the use of this energy form, both by the quality of their sunlight and, above all, by the vast surfaces they have available for trapping it. The advent of the 'hydrogen civilization' (cf. section 5.2.6) also augurs well for increasing the productivity of the Third World.

5.2 *The Energy Problem*

5.2.1 *Short Term Tasks* In this section we will consider as short term those policies needed for securing energy supplies *up to the year 2000*. There is scope for doing so since:
(I) on the one hand, the success or failure of the two major technical adventures now available for developing energy supplies, namely breeder reactors and high temperature reactors, will not influence to a large extent the consumption of uranium; and
(II) on the other hand, unless a superhuman effort is made, no new sources of energy will be produced on an industrial scale before the end of the century.

We must be concerned today with developing those sources of energy already known to be technically feasible, such as *geothermal* and *tidal* energy. These sources were relegated to a second place by the low level of oil prices. Yet, in view of what is at stake, they can only be expected to exert a limited influence. The same applies to some other forms of energy derived from the *sea* (thermal, wave, etc.) and perhaps from the *winds*.

At the same time, countries with rich coal deposits, such as the United States, Poland, India and others, will develop coal distillation and other processes within the constraints imposed by the environment.

Further, the following discrepancies should be noted in developing alternative sources of energy for both rich and poor countries:
(I) the distribution of energy resources is rather *unevenly spread* over the planet;
(II) any large-scale conversion system will face the limits imposed by the carrying capacity of the *environment*;
(III) research and development on energy resources will in future be accelerated; the resistance of the general public to energy *conservation* programmes appears substantial.

The diversity of most of the alternative sources of energy (except nuclear energy) may imply substantial changes in technology and the development of a local potential, possibly not transferable to other countries.

Fossil fuels are not sufficient to supply mankind with the energy it requires to guarantee higher prosperity after the year 2000. Nuclear fusion as well as solar, geothermal and aeolian energy are considered the most promising alternative energy sources, diversified geographically according to natural conditions. Up to the year 2000, recourse to nuclear energy will unfortunately be inevitable. With the sole exception of tidal energy, all additional energy production is bound to affect climate, which remains a subject for urgent research. The problems of radioactive gaseous or liquid wastes do not seem to be serious. Accidents could conceivably happen; their probability, however, is comparable to the risks mankind has always had to live with.

5.2.2 *The Need for a World Energy Research Agency* A real danger, however, is the possibility of *nuclear proliferation*. More particularly, the greatest threat is posed by the possibility of *plutonium theft*. A recent research report on this subject concluded: 'some people (even single individuals) with elementary scientific training, in possession of 10 kg plutonium and a fair amount of conventional chemical explosives, will be capable of designing and constructing a rough fission bomb within a few weeks and can do so without any specialized knowledge and with equipment that can be purchased from any supplier of laboratories for teaching purposes' (2).

It is evident that, should nuclear installations proliferate in a given country beyond a certain limit, security will call for policing or other measures which are likely to prove more and more unacceptable. Hence it is necessary, without losing any further time, to set into motion a *gigantic effort* to stimulate as rapidly as possible the emergence of new sources of energy. Today, the scale of these efforts are ridiculously inadequate. The slowness with which the necessary means are made available has closed the options for the massive use of, for instance, solar or even fusion energy by the year 2000. The problem must be tackled *at the international level*; individual countries will always refuse to make available the necessary finance for long-term projects of this nature.

Hence our proposal to set up a *world agency, properly financed*, for instance by a tax on the kWhs of nuclear energy produced, in order to establish the necessary *link between the expansion* of the latter and *volume of research* into new energy sources, thereby contributing to the fundamental task of halting nuclear energy proliferation before it becomes insupportable.

Some information on new energy types is given in the subsequent sections (5.2.3-5.2.5).

5.2.3   *Nuclear Fusion*   The *fusion* process is fundamentally different from the fission process. The reactor under study is built on the principle of the fusion of two hydrogen isotopes: deuterium and tritium. Fusion implies a loss of mass and hence, in accordance with Einstein's law, a generation of energy. The required temperature is one or two hundred million degrees centigrade. Research is being directed into ways of ensuring that the mixture at that temperature does not come into contact with the reactor wall. This research, started about 20 years ago, uses the principle of magnetic constraint. The fields have proved highly unstable and only very recently, after many unsuccessful efforts, have some hopes emerged concerning the feasibility of a solution. With some optimism regarding the present programmes, scientists expect that industrial production could be started by the year 2000.

Two or three years ago, Teller, the father of the hydrogen bomb, revealed that a second possibility was being secretly studied in military laboratories, namely, that of a *micro explosion*. Gradually, the USA, the Soviet Union and France have been publishing their results. The conditions under which fusion takes place are the same as those of the thermonuclear bomb; the energy generated by the micro explosion, corresponding to the disappearance of one milligram of the deuterium-tritium mixture, is 80 kg TNT. Therefore, by exposing much smaller quantities to the process, one could hope to constrain a micro explosion in an adequate container and, by repeating it regularly, to generate energy practically continuously in the same manner as in an internal combustion engine. In the USA it is considered necessary to direct at the target an energy source of 20 to 30 g TNT in a nanosecond in order to set off a very small reaction that is sufficient for verifying the computations. Today, only one hundredth of this amount of energy can be produced in this time period. Progress on lasers is such, however, that it may prove possible to achieve the objective mentioned within two or three years. After this, a long series of prototypes and a programme of development will be required in order to make industrial production possible by the end of the century.

---

(2) M. Wilrich and T. Taylor: 'Nuclear Theft: Risks and Safeguards'. Report prepared for Ford Foundation, 1974.

Fusion is preferable to fission for various reasons. Firstly, on *ecological* grounds, because it does not produce radioactive waste and, in particular, no transuranic elements with a very long life. Secondly, the quantities of tritium stored in the reactor are very small (a maximum of 1 kg for 1000 MWE). However, the very potent neutrons arising from the reaction will activate, unless very great care is exercised, the structural materials at least as much as in fission reactors. But, in conclusion, it cannot be denied that there is a very clear advantage in fusion, particularly in comparison with plutonium breeder reactors. Hence the often raised question: 'Are breeder reactors indispensable between thermal reactors and fusion?' Would it not be possible, by stopping their further development, to save thousands of millions of dollars which will need to be committed before they reach the industrial production stage? The above clearly demonstrates that it is too early to give a reply to this question, despite its importance. Neither of the two paths towards fusion have as yet achieved the basic reaction needed. As noted already, the solution of the problems mentioned is barely within the possibilities of individual countries; this is why an *international agency* is viewed as indispensable.

5.2.4   *Solar Energy*   The solar radiation reaching the earth is estimated to be 5300 Q/year above the stratosphere, 3600 Q/year on the earth's surface and 690 Q/year on the total land area, as compared with consumption of man-produced energy in 1970 of 0.24 Q (3). Its potential capacity, therefore, is very large indeed. Its main advantage is its permanence and the absence of pollution. Disadvantages include its intermittent character, its unequal distribution over the globe and, so far, the high investment costs to 'catch' it. Further, large-scale utilization of solar radiation might affect the 'micro climate' in the area concerned.

Solar energy can be utilized in a variety of ways: in solar thermal processes, *photovoltaic* and *photogalvanic* processes. Solar thermal systems include solar thermal power generation, space heating or cooling and hot water supply by solar water heaters, solar distillation, solar refrigeration, ice making, solar furnaces for high temperature processing, solar cookers, multipurpose uses in agricultural technology such as in greenhouses, mulching, snow melting etc. Both photovoltaic and photogalvanic processes are suited for power and hydrogen production. Among the solar thermal systems, solar space heating, cooling and hot water supply, and solar thermal power generation are two of the most significant technologies in the research and development of solar energy science and engineering. Desalinization and agricultural solar applications should be considered very important from the viewpoint of food production.

The cost of solar energy might still be several times higher than that of fossil fuel in this decade. In the next decade, however, the respective costs can be expected to have narrowed considerably. In the earlier stage of research and development in solar energy technology, close international cooperation plays a significant role for standardization and measurement of isolation, testing methods for solar devices such as solar collectors and solar cells, while government incentives will be very effective for stimulating the development of systems for the heating and cooling of, for example, school buildings.

International cooperation will be important for the exchange of information and for the construction of large-scale test facilities. At the national level, the creation of incentives and the adoption of legislation concerning small-scale application must be recommended.

By the year 2000, up to 30 to 50 per cent of today's total energy requirement for space heating, cooling and hot water supply could be supplied by solar energy. Solar thermal

---

(3) 1 Q equals a billion (i.e. 10^{12}) kilowatthours.

and photovoltaic power generation will be coupled with other power generation systems, such as nuclear, SNG, hydrogen, aeolian and other energy sources. The rapidly expanding demand for water might also in future be met by the application of solar energy. For such applications it carries ecological and energy conservation advantages. Desalinization and solar refrigeration are potential additional applications in arid zones, and especially the tropical zones of developing countries. Research and development on industrial heat sources by the use of a solar concentrator and heat storage systems will possibly comprise the next steps.

5.2.5   *Geothermal Energy*   Most *geothermal energy* can be extracted from basins, formed by upheaval during the Cenozoic era, in the form of steam vapour, hot water or a mixture of the two. Though the net amount of geothermal energy (0.1 Q) is far less than that of solar energy, this energy available in the earth's crust might be accessible at temperatures up to 300°C at a depth of several kilometers.

The total output of geothermal power plants constructed as of 1973 was about 950 MW and that under construction was 720 MW for the world at large, mainly in Italy, New Zealand, USA and Japan. Geothermal energy has natural characteristics similar to that of solar energy and can be extracted without disruption. The technology of using geo-thermal energy for the production of boric acid has been developing at Larderello, Italy. Some 75 years of experience has shown that this energy source is competitive with fossil fuels. Transportation of geothermal energy is not, however, feasible and hence its application will remain restricted to specific locations only.

5.2.6   *The 'Hydrogen Civilization'*   There could be two energy distribution systems of about equal importance at the beginning of the twenty-first century: one of electricity, the other of hydrogen. Hydrogen would be cheap and available in large quantities since it would be derived from nuclear reactions (fission or fusion) or solar energy. It might be *gradually* introduced. Transport, storage, and distribution facilities available at present could handle 10 to 15 per cent hydrogen without having to undergo modification. Its transport in bulk would resemble the present-day transport of natural gas and should not give rise to major problems: in the Federal Republic of Germany a 300 km network already exists. A network of this kind would be five to ten times less costly than an electricity grid. Storage in underground reservoirs of several thousand million cu. metres could be achieved by using locations from which gas has been previously extracted and 'are now empty.

The advantages of hydrogen as a fuel are:
(I) the source of hydrogen depends on the availability of water which, as the most abundant molecular species on our planet, is at present generally cheap as well as easy to obtain;
(II) no disturbance is caused to ecological cycles since there will be no dissipation of carbon monoxide or sulphur dioxide and less nitrogen oxide than in the case of fossil fuels. The combustion product of hydrogen is water which can easily be assimilated by the natural environment;
(III) hydrogen fuel transportation through pipelines is much more economical than power transmission;
(IV) hydrogen fuel itself can form a component of an energy storage system since the use of surplus power may be utilized for hydrogen production by electrolysis and be coupled with an intermittent energy source such as solar energy;
(V) applications in wide varieties can be expected at temperatures ranging from 200° to 2200°C.

The decomposition of water could be achieved by the following processes:

(I) thermochemical processes with the combination of multistep reactions;
(II) thermal decomposition of water at high temperatures;
(III) electrolysis;
(IV) chemical radiation processes.

As noted earlier, production costs may be the prime determinant in the development of hydrogen as a major source of energy. Hydrogen fuel can be stored as a gas, liquid, or metal hydride; while pipelines for natural gas transportation may be used for those of a hydrogen system. The eventual costs of hydrogen transportation might in future fall between those of natural gas and electricity. In the development of hydrogen as an energy source, the active research and development on every step in production, transportation, storage and further safety and maintenance problems should be taken into consideration.

From an ecological viewpoint, the concept of a *total system* is recommended combining a hydrogen system with alternative sources of energy in the development of hydrogen fuel. The large-scale gasification of liquid hydrogen may even have a negative thermal pollution impact on the environment, although this and the problem of possible effects of a hydrogen system on the environment must be investigated further.

Hydrogen as an energy source carries a number of safety advantages. Although an inflammable substance, hydrogen has a high diffusion rate. This makes it easier to identify the location of a leak in the system. Since it diffuses more rapidly it is potentially less dangerous.

An evaluation of a hydrogen energy system and its economics should form another subject for an international cooperative effort.

5.2.7 *Climatic Changes*   One very important aspect of thermal energy production must finally be stressed. According to the second law of thermodynamics, thermal energy production requires two temperature levels, with the circulating fluid or gas being heated at one and cooled at the other; their function is symmetrical. The high level is obtained by use of the basic energy-producing material, and all the foregoing therefore applies. The low level consists of the atmosphere, which is indisputably a common resource of mankind. It seems certain that high energy concentrations acting on the atmosphere will result in modified micro-climates, although we do not as yet know the exact mechanism. It can be expected that world climate will itself be affected by the ever-increasing production of energy; but we do not know when, or how.

Meteorological phenomena are probably often unstable. Two examples may be quoted where, in one case, the natural equilibrium is stable, and, in the other, where it is unstable:
(I) heat is released under a clouded sky, evaporation is increased, hence also the volume of the clouds, hence also the albedo (reflection coefficient of solar radiation), thus the atmosphere is cooled and stability achieved;
(II) alternatively, heat is released on soil covered by snow: the snow cover decreases in volume, so does the albedo, the atmosphere is heated, hence there is additional fusion and there is instability.

It is generally argued that the heat produced by man is small in comparison to the heat exchanged between the land surface of the earth and the atmosphere. It must not be forgotten, however, that this additional amount of heat must first modify general circulation of the atmosphere before it can flow into interplanetary space and thus allow a new equilibrium to be established. This gives rise to a number of questions. What, for example, will this new type of circulation be? Will the change in temperature be proportional to the quantities of heat in question or will instability cause disproportionate modifications?

Until very recently only very general answers were formulated to these questions, and these were based chiefly on common sense; they fixed, generally speaking, the percentage of artificial heat production which might cause a noticeable modification of the climate at world-wide level at one per cent: this, at present economic growth rates, would give us fifty or perhaps one hundred years before the problem becomes serious. The National Center for Atmospheric Research, at Boulder City in the USA, has performed climate simulation on computers under conditions of enormous quantities of waste heat comparable with the well-known Weinberg scenario (15 kW per inhabitant and 20 billion inhabitants). The conclusion was that 'there is relatively small modification of the model earth atmosphere heat balance: the difference in numerous experiments with and without thermal energy input produced changes of the same order as the natural fluctuations of the model.' But a joint study begun in 1972 by the International Institute of Applied Systems Analysis (IIASA, Laxenburg, Austria), the UK Meteorological Office and the Research Centre Karlsruhe, using the UK numerical model, indicated that 'the amount of waste heat can have noticeable effect on both local and larger scales.'

True, these results are provisional and must be confirmed by much more complete studies which IIASA is at present undertaking. However, the results of analyses made to date suggest that the problem could indeed be a serious one and earlier apathy towards it may be unjustified. There is some evidence to suggest that possible climates are not a continuous sequence of states of equilibrium but rather separate climates obtained from the effect of heat fluctuations of varying nature and intensities. The equations of general atmospheric movements are of course not linear.

Indications of the probability of meteorological catastrophes, such as tornadoes, cloudbursts, windhoses, etc. can be obtained by comparing the incidence of forest fires (say in Australia or the United States) with corresponding thermal effects of the same order of magnitude. Forest fires will in all likelihood occur in the power concentrations sometimes envisaged (50GWe) and when the climate deteriorates in a zone round the power station. This zone may extend to 1,000 sq. km, depending on the prevailing topography. Given the power concentrations likely in the immediate future (5GWe), such fires would hardly appear possible. In any event, a great deal of progress will have to be made in meteorology before precise answers to all of these questions can be established.

It would therefore appear that the true limitation to economic growth may not lie in exhausting supplies of raw materials, nor in mankind being buried by pollution, but in the reaction of the atmosphere to thermal waste. For the first time, man has encountered an obstacle which he does not know how to circumvent or to conquer. Some hope may however reside in making use of deep ocean water. The mass of the oceans is two hundred and fifty times greater than that of the atmosphere, the specific heat of water four times that of air. The calorific capacity of the entire atmosphere equals that found in a depth of only 2.5 metres of the oceans' surface; it is only this depth that we are at present using.

Oceanography and meteorology are thus becoming vital disciplines in the study of economic growth. The proposed World Agency for Research on New Energy Sources should engage in the study of these and similar phenomena.

5.3 *Ores and Metals*

5.3.1 *The State of the Debate; Resources, Production and Consumption*   The fear of exhaustion of natural resources, together with the measures taken by the OPEC countries has started, at the international level, discussions on natural resources in general and non-renewable resources in particular.

For each mineral we must distinguish:
(I) The *known reserves* which are exploitable under current economic conditions. In the case of certain minerals (oil, lead, zinc, mercury), such reserves will not last more than twenty years at the present rate of consumption. For some others (coal, iron, etc.) there are sufficient supplies for more than a hundred years. These known reserves are reduced yearly by the amounts extracted, and increased by the amounts discovered by prospection. On average they remain stable in terms of time;
(II) *The planet's resources.* These are all the amounts which may be worked in the future and gradually revealed by prospecting. The quantity of metals and other useful elements contained in the first 1,000 metres of the earth's crust and in the seas represents, with the exception of oil, several million, or even several hundred million, times our annual consumption.

A general shortage of minerals in the near future does not thus appear a real danger. Future availability will largely depend upon:
(I) the rate of *exploitation*, which is closely related to the development of consumption in both the rich and the developing countries; and
(II) the rate of discovery and development of new deposits all over the world; and
(III) the development of *technology*, the *methods* of estimating reserves and the substitute materials available. Nonetheless, it would be dangerous to yield to an easy optimism concerning the permanent availability of substitution and innovation possibilities. The time needed to apply technologies developed industrially is long (from ten to twenty years) and changes in circumstances tend to accelerate. We are likely to witness a gradual rise in the cost of ores owing to the need to exploit poorer deposits in deeper mines; a doubling of the average technical operating costs is likely over the next few decades. This rise in costs should not unduly affect mankind's standard of living; the value of world mining production in 1973 represented only 3.5 per cent of the gross domestic product of the world as a whole (three-quarters of this for energy producing substances, i.e. oil, coal, gas).

Mining activity is of course very unevenly distributed throughout the world. A few figures, for 1973, serve to illustrate this:
(I) less than 10 per cent of the world's population lives in countries producing 50 per cent of world mining production and less than 25 per cent in countries producing 85 per cent;
(II) average per capita production world-wide is $ 42; for the inhabitants of the Third World (excluding China) the figure is $ 31 (5 per cent of the inhabitants of the Third World produce more than $ 140 per capita, while 55 per cent live in countries whose production is nil or negligible, totalling less than $ 2 a head); in the developed market-economy countries the figure is $ 78 per capita.

A rise in the price of ores, therefore, cannot, alone, provide a satisfactory means of transferring financial resources from rich to poor countries, *since it would profit only a minority of the inhabitants of the Third World.*

In 1973, the mining production of Third World countries was for the first time approximately equivalent in value to that of the developed market-economy countries, totalling $ 58 billion. In the case of energy-producing minerals, the Third World countries' share has increased continuously, rising from 17 to 40 per cent of the volume produced throughout the world between 1950 and 1973, while the share of the developed market-economy countries fell from 65 to 32 per cent. In the case of non-energy producing ores, the distribution of production has remained highly stable since 1950, with half the total production coming from the developed market-economy countries with the other half shared between Third World and planned-economy countries.

While the per capita mining production of the developed market-economy countries is 2.5 times that of the Third World, its consumption is about 16 times greater. The former are thus obliged to import about half their requirements (4) (energy-producing substances, metals and ores), primarily from the latter, while the latter consume only one quarter of their production, and the planned-economy countries are virtually self-sufficient (the USSR offsetting the deficit of Eastern Europe).

Recent analysis has shown the *strategic importance*, for the present industrial structure of the developed countries, of some mineral resources exported by the developing countries. Up till now, the relatively low prices of these resources have enhanced the growth of the developed countries. Producing countries are anxious to derive greater profit from their mining operations and, to accomplish this, are pursuing three main courses of action:
(I) processing ores produced locally in order to export products of higher value and to derive a greater share of the price paid by the final consumer;
(II) nationalizing foreign (especially transnational) enterprises so as to own and control their natural resources and to take advantage of the operator's profit (which is the larger the greater the quality of the deposits);
(III) increasing taxes (or, in the case of state corporations, increasing prices, which comes to the same thing). Such policies have been adopted in recent years primarily by the OPEC countries in the case of oil, and Morocco in the case of phosphates.

A systematic increase in prices, and thus in the tax revenue of the producing states, has not so far been possible for other ores, since such an increase would have encouraged substitution, and above all the exploitation of high production cost deposits in countries willing to accept a lower revenue per ton produced (in the industrialized countries for instance).

A feature of the price of certain minerals is a high degree of market *instability*, which is reflected in large price *fluctuations*. This is particularly noticeable in the case of metals such as silver, copper, lead, tungsten, etc., and is caused by a periodic failure of adjustment between supply and demand in the absence of any regulating mechanism. This causes the revenue of the producing countries to fluctuate, and these fluctuations are exaggerated by the fact that, in the short term, the volume of minerals sold generally varies simultaneously with, and in the same direction as, prices.

The prices of other metals are much more stable, either because they are fixed by a dominant producer, or group of producers (aluminium, nickel), or, as in the case of tin, covered by a market regulating agreement. The tin agreement, the only one in the ore sector, has been regularly renewed since 1950. An International Tin Council, on which the producing and consuming countries are equally represented, fixes a scale of prices which is periodically reviewed (5), manages a buffer stock in order to keep the market price within the fixed scale, and, in the event of over-production, fixes quarterly export quotas for the producing countries to keep the price at the required level.

---

(4) The USA and Canada are only 25 per cent, Western Europe 75 per cent, and Japan 94 per cent dependent on imports.
(5) In constant-value dollars, the price of tin rose by an average of 2.6 per cent a year on the London market between 1950 and 1974, as against 1.6.per cent for all ores (metalliferous and otherwise).

In some cases (copper, tin) the ores are usually *processed locally* into metals. In others, the ores are exported after being subjected, in some cases, to a simple concentration process; this applies in particular to iron ore, both from the developing countries and from Western countries (Sweden, France, Canada, Australia). Other ores (lead, zinc, aluminium etc.), and crude oil, are in an intermediate position.
The subject of local processing of minerals is clearly related to problems of industrialization and the international division of labour which are dealt with in Annex 4.

Some *apprehension* is currently felt by the users of minerals in the industrialized importing countries (primarily Western Europe and Japan; the United States are much less dependent on imports and seem determined to reduce such dependence even further). It derives from their observation of two facts: that the mining industry requires very large capital expenditure, both for exploration and development, and that many Third World countries do not possess sufficient capital either on their own account or through the United Nations agencies, and are suspicious of transnational enterprises; such companies are in any case often very reluctant to invest in these countries. This leads to the fear (so far experienced only in specialist circles) of *a delay in prospecting for and developing new deposits*, which in a few years would result in an imbalance between supply and demand and further disruption of the world economy, with a tendency for the industrialized countried to opt for self-sufficiency to the detriment of the Third World. We shall bear this in mind when formulating our proposals.

5.3.2 *Elements of a Solution to the Problem*   The variety and complexity of the problems are such that, as UNCTAD has already suggested, questions of exploitation and use of mineral resources, from the production to the consumption stage, must be approached carefully in conjunction with a number of other products. The experience of the Lomé Agreement might be taken into consideration, along with some of its particular aspects. At present two closely-linked factors are receiving special attention: the use of the growing revenue from these resources as an element in attaining a fairer distribution of income on an international scale, and the reliability of the consumer countries' access to sources of supply.

In order to arrive at a solution, the following principles should be afforded special consideration:
(I) Producer countries should receive for their products a *fair share* of the prices paid by consumers. Market organization and price formation have to be studied in order to decide whether producers may receive a higher price through *local processing*, by the elimination of *market imperfections* and *excessive trade margins*, by better credit facilities and distribution systems.
(II) Price stabilization or indexation should not be used as a *pretext to refuse* price rises.
(III) Consumer countries must be *assured of long-term supplies* without fear of deliberate interruption or delay in the provision of production capacity. Countries possessing mineral resources must be urged to take the necessary steps to explore and exploit them at the proper time in order to meet the demands of the world economy. If the use of foreign capital and/or techniques is needed for this purpose, then the possessors of such capital and techniques and their host countries should seek an equitable formula to ensure that the necessary mining operations are carried out in due time.
(IV) *Producer associations* must be approved as legitimate negotiating bodies to counteract the strong pressure exerted by the economic power of the buyers.
(V) A World Agency for Natural Resources is needed to supervise the execution of commodity agreements.

5.3.3 *A World Agency for Mineral Raw Materials*   We recommend the creation of a World Agency for Mineral Raw Materials. It could operate under the aegis of the UN Natural

Resources and Transport Centre or be formed by expanding the powers and competence of UNCTAD. The proposed agency would be responsible for:

(I) coordinating and continuing the activities of agencies specialized on individual products and arranging for agreements on products not yet covered;

(II) compiling and circulating *information* on known *reserves*, reserves likely to be exploitable in the future, ten-year trends in operating costs and trends in demand. This information will be useful to public and private concerns for their prospecting and exploration programmes;

(III) compiling and circulating *information* on *commercial transactions*;

(IV) managing agreements on the *stabilization of export revenues*;

(V) *consulting*, when requested, on the fairness of agreements to be concluded between governments and mining companies and on the viability of processing projects;

(VI) *arbitrating*, when requested, in any disputes on the execution of agreements;

(VII) periodically putting forward comments and suggestions to countries on their conduct of their mining policy, as the OECD now does to its members on their economic policy and its International Energy Agency does on energy policy, *with individual countries retaining full sovereignty and entire freedom to reject such suggestions*.

5.3.4 *Long Term Proposals* Our long-term proposals are based on the following facts:

(I) mineral resources are distributed unevenly over the earth;

(II) their exploitation advantages a small number of countries which have been favourably endowed by nature;

(III) the industrial development of the presently less developed countries will increase their consumption of mineral resources and more and more countries will need these resources.

In view of the above, it is important that conditions be created which make it possible to treat mineral resources as *a common heritage of mankind* (cf. section 5.1.2) and to gradually shift from the exercise of national territorial sovereignty over mineral resources to the exercise of functional sovereignty. The concept of common heritage should imply:

(I) a *real world market* for all mineral resources;

(II) a *world tax system* to replace the national taxes on mineral resources.

The revenue collected should then be redistributed among the developing countries — possibly through an agency such as IDA — according to certain criteria (taking account of, for instance, the size of population, income per capita, income redistribution projects, etc.) and which would not necessarily exclude the producing countries themselves. This tax could be introduced as one of a moderate rate and gradually be raised to something in the order of 70 per cent of profits on fossil fuels and 50 per cent of the value of production of ores (including uranium ore) (6).

Such a tax would, as the present taxes on oil products, *be paid in fact by the consumers* and would have three advantages as compared with higher prices:

(I)' it would *help all developing countries*, whilst a price increase only improves the situation of producer countries (which include some of the most developed countries);

(II) it would *not disequilibrate the market*, since it would not raise the price received by producers and hence not raise production beyond demand;

(III) it would not affect the relative competitive situation of one mineral in comparison to the others;

---

(6) A tax on profits seems to be preferable in the case of fossil fuels to encourage the exploitation of high-cost deposits (undersea oil, poor coal seams); it seems to be less necessery in the case of ores, where a tax on selling prices seems preferable as being easier to apply.

(IV) such a tax, at the rates proposed, would probably induce consumers to restrict their consumption of mineral raw materials (economizing on their use, recycling and substitution by non-mineral materials, etc.). Perhaps a slight slowing down of the sales of mineral resources by the developing countries would result, but the revenue of the tax which they would share would enable them to create other industries, or to embark on further exploration of their resources.

5.3.5   *Recycling and Heat Losses*   An immense effort needs to be made at the world level and countries should be strongly invited to intitate action especially with respect to the following:
(I) the suppression of unnecessary consumption of primary resources and the avoidance of waste;
(II) the expansion of recycling activities;
(III) the recuperation of part of heat losses, particularly in thermal power plants.

Points (I) and (II) concern not only primary resources but also agricultural (paper for instance) and animal wastes. The tax suggested in the preceding section would, if levied at a reasonably high rate, induce consumers to economize, to recycle and to provide substitutes, and therefore tends entirely in the right direction. In initiating and supporting action on the above, we should be conscious of the fact that all problems mentioned are *very difficult*, especially those relating to the recuperation of heat losses.

5.4   *A Final Note*

We are convinced that growth is not something which can be bought with money or the transfer of which can be compelled by political means. It is easier, for example, to buy a nuclear power station than to provide the countless services for its operation and above all for its maintenance which require the backing of the people as a whole. In his speech in April 1974 to the General Assembly of the United Nations, President Boumedienne advocated a genuine industrial revolution for the developing countries: 'Each country which really wishes to look after its future must take over responsibility for its own development, that is to say it must first of all mobilize all its own human and material resources.' This is the practice adopted in the past by Japan, which learnt to import growth while abiding by the rules of the game applying in the industrial countries. And it is what China, with its approach of 'relying on its own strength', is doing today.

Since the rules of the game will have to be changed to create a new international order, a popularly-based desire for *solidarity with the developing countries* must be established in the developed countries (whether or not they have a planned economy), in order to ensure that growth is 'exported'. The structure of the institutions of the new international order are basically of little importance, provided they offer a meeting place from which new ideas can be made *to reach to the heart of the people*. The time has come to try this in the energy and mineral resources sector.

Scientific Research and Technological Development
Alexander King and Aklilu Lemma

6.1 *Introduction*

Technology, arising directly or indirectly from scientific research followed by technological development, has been a motor force in creating the kind of world in which we live today. Indeed, from man's earliest beginnings technology has been his main agent in the struggle upwards from subsistence towards a decent, healthy and long life. From the shaping of the first flint tools, the discovery of the wheel, the lever, the plough and the use of fire, man has assiduously, and by empirical means, shaped a technology to serve his material needs. Technology is then no new phenomenon; what is different today is that the discovery of natural laws through scientific research has given a new dimension to technology, of such massive impact that it not only offers infinite promise for the relief of poverty and the provision of healthy conditions of life, but also, as a consequence of its force, brutality and lack of systematic control by human wisdom, threatens patterns of life, the ecology of the globe and even the survival of the race.

In this annex we shall focus on the role of science and technology in development from two points of view. We will first deal with the fundamental problems of advanced science-based technology as it now exists in the more industrialized countries and consider new approaches to ways of making it more available for the general use and benefit of mankind as a whole. Considering the fact that most of the advanced science-based technologies are beyond the reach of and foreign to many of the less developed countries who might benefit, we shall also consider more traditional, empirical, technologies used by the great majority of the world's populations, still living at subsistence levels, which, with the assistance of modern science, are capable of considerable improvements and which can help in alleviating the human condition and improving the quality of life of the majority.

Science-based technology has led to the emergence of highly developed and rich societies in several parts of the world, but has, as yet, had little major impact on the great masses of humanity. It has tended to increase the disparities between the rich and the poor of the world, both between and within nations. In the context of the New International Economic Order, the continuation of technological development and the research on which it is based, will only make sense if it can be harnessed to the process of development, both economic and social, and thus evolved to the benefit of mankind as a whole.

The distribution of a capacity for scientific research and technological development across the spectrum of national conditions is very disparate and does not conform well to the needs of each. Certainly some countries, such as India, have a sophisticated capability the oil-producers have, of recent years or months, begun to build such a capacity and even in the least developed countries there is a small elite of people with scientific understanding and training. On the whole, however, the world's now massive scientific and technological capacity is concentrated in the few highly industrialized countries which are responsible for well over 90% (possibly as much as 95%) of the total research and development effort. There is thus a need to create a New Scientific and Technological Order within the new international order, based upon the establishment and the strengthening of local scientific and technological capacity in developing countries, if research and development are to become a motor force of economic development in the global sense and not merely a means for the already rich amongst nations to become still richer. Such a New Scientific and Technological order represents, moreover, the only politically feasible alternative to the present situation in which science and technology from the rich countries have dominated the poor nations after their political decolonialization.

Nowhere then is the disparity between the industrialized and the Third World countries more marked than in the field of scientific research and technological development. It has long been recognized that scientific research, in making possible the development of modern industry, has contributed greatly to the pattern and growth of the economy. It is only recently, however, that economists have given more systematic attention to *the role of technology in economic growth*. It is now evident that both education and research are major factors in the growth process, mainly by enhancing the quality of the two main inputs of capital and labour. Education and training at all levels, from that of top management to unskilled labour, are determinative of the performance of the work force, while technology likewise is essential in upgrading the utilization of capital, in suggesting new and improved products, increasing the power per capita of labour, producing new chemical intermediates and structural materials and, above all, in making possible vastly quicker and more effective processes and work methods. This does not mean to say that research and better education will always and automatically yield higher economic growth. This depends on the quality and relevance of the education and the choice of appropriate research and development, as well as on how effectively these are assimilated and articulated with the process of innovation and growth. Hence these factors have to be regarded as an integral part of national development programmes and priorities.

If, then, the experience of the industrialized countries is that science and technology have been major instruments of economic development, it would seem an easy assumption that this would be true also for countries at an earlier stage of economic development. Indeed, we might have expected that their progress would have been more rapid than has in fact been the case, since the technologies and skills already exist, evolved slowly and at considerable expense by the industrialized countries during the two centuries since the industrial revolution. Certainly great advances have been made by the direct transfer of skills and techniques; communications form a world-wide network, certain devastating diseases such as malaria, smallpox and tuberculosis are under control, agriculture in some parts of the Third World has been greatly assisted by the use of fertilizers and the introduction of high yielding varieties by genetic selection based on research. Nevertheless, on the whole, and especially in the industrial sector, advance has been much slower than desirable if the economic gap between the rich and the poor nations is to be bridged in a reasonable time. Furthermore, there is evidence to suggest that in many places such benefits as have accrued from the transfer of modern technology to the Third World countries have been reaped mainly by a small privileged minority and that the masses of those living near the subsistence level have been largely untouched. Thus, the relative failure of the technology transfer process is due both to the intrinsic ineffectiveness of the process itself as part of the existing economic systems and partly to social and political factors in the recipient countries.

The reasons for these inadequacies in the process of technology transfer are deep and complex. They reside, in part, in the *inherent complexity of the process of technological innovation* itself and, in part, in the ownership structures of modern technology produced by large transnational and national enterprises situated in the industrialized countries. One of the first difficulties is the availability of capital. In Third World countries with very little in the way of surplus resources – the classical 'savings' of the economists – capital is exceedingly scarce and subject to greater competition than in the industrialized countries since it is in urgent demand for the building up of every sector. Furthermore, the technology of the already industrialized countries has been deliberately evolved to increase the productivity of manpower and hence is both capital and energy intensive. In so many Third World countries, on the other hand, unemployment and under-employment are widespread and so a dominance of capital-intensive industry is not necessarily to be welcomed. Consequently, much of the technology 'on the shelf' is not, a priori, appropriate to the economic and social needs of the Third World. The choice of technologies with new work positions costing, say, $ 5000 each as compared with others at $ 250 per capita may, in reality, be a choice between half a million jobs with high economic yield or ten million jobs with a lower per capita outcome. Moreover, a large segment of modern technology owned by the transnationals is often available only as part of a package, which includes foreign capital investment. In the spirit of contemporary nationalism, some Third World countries are reluctant to see the entry of technology associated with foreign capital, feeling that this further strengthens their dependence on the rich world and makes it more difficult to develop an indigenous technological capacity.

A further difficulty in the way of successful transfer of technology to the Third World is the local *lack of* availability of sufficient *skills* — managerial, engineering or manual — which must be provided through an appropriate, highly developed and sustained educational system. In many countries; the general basis of education is insufficiently evolved, both quantitatively and qualitatively, and its building up, including the funding of the necessary resources, the training of teachers etc. is a very long process. In addition, there is often a lack of both middle and higher technical training and of facilities for management education.

Still another difficulty is the *absence* in many countries of *an infrastructure of science* and technology and of a deliberate science policy. Without such an infrastructure, science and engineering have difficulty in sustaining the necessary vitality; facilities even for routine testing of materials and the control of manufacturing performance and quality are rudimentary, auxiliary services, for example of chemical analysis or engineering design, are difficult to provide and the general national awareness of the promise of new scientific and technological possibilities throughout the world, which might benefit the country concerned, is generally insufficient. The matter is further complicated by the apparent satisfaction of local elites with the consumption oriented technologies imported in the form of goods and services produced locally by subsidiaries of transnational enterprises. Lack of technological innovation in the Third World is due not only to the absence of conditions propitious to such a process, but also because there is limited demand for the products which might result from it.

These difficulties should not be taken to mean that the adoption by Third World countries of advanced technologies is inadvisable or unnecessary. A certain proportion of advanced modern processes, despite their high cost and low employment generation, may contribute greatly to the economy and provide resources for employment in other sectors. Furthermore, they are important in raising technical and managerial competence of the country in general, with a considerable spill-over effect on the technical levels of other industries. It is suggested, however, that each technology should be carefully chosen, within the overall plan of economic development, carefully prepared for well in advance and that its consequences, including those of a social nature, be reviewed before the decision to adopt them is taken. This becomes possible only when a country has built up its own scientific and technological capacity — institutions, manpower and an appropriate environment. Furthermore, the adoption of advanced technologies should be compensated by careful efforts to improve existing and basic technical methods in manufacture, agriculture and handicrafts, which could have immediate and widespread benefits.

The question arises as to whether the Third World could achieve major industrial and economic breakthroughs exclusively on the basis of technologies evolved elsewhere. The example of Japan is attractive, but not generally cogent. Its emulation would necessitate the building up of educational, research and development capacities on a considerable scale in a carefully phased plan made many years ahead of achievement. Reliance on foreign technology alone may be useful at the early stages of industrialization, but unless it is accompanied by the building up of an indigenous technical structure, including the necessary research and development capacity, it is unlikely to be efficient and will perpetuate in the nations which adopt such a policy a reliance on the purchase of the ideas and processes which have surfaced several decades earlier in the industrialized countries, that is, a continuing technological backwardness. Furthermore, there will be a continuing acquisition from abroad of modern consumption-oriented technologies, pandering to the tastes of small, local elites and thus helping to perpetuate internal social and economic inequities. We are convinced, therefore, that the building up of national capacities for research and development is essential, both for the effective selection and quick assimilation of imported technologies and for the inculcation of an innovative potential for the future.

This brings us back to the question of *research and development disparities*. The great mass of new scientific and technical discovery is made in the industrialized countries and it would appear that the existing scientific capacity of the Third World countries is quite submarginal to their needs, including that of enabling them to exploit effectively the existing world store of technological knowledge, by modifying it for adaption to the use of raw materials and manpower possibilities as well as to the features of both domestic and possible export markets. The disparities are indeed greater than the overall statistics suggest, since it seems that the less developed a country is, the greater the proportion of its small scientific effort is devoted to fundamental research in contrast to applied research and technological development, an understandable situation since such countries generally lack the industrial infrastructure to provide sophisticated skills, equipment and other facilities to carry promising basic research possibilities through the applied research and technological development stages to productive use. It must be remembered too that, on the average, the technological development stage costs about ten times that of the research on which it is based and requires engineering in addition to scientific skills. The United States and the Soviet Union each possess about 18 engineers per thousand of the population, the European countries rather more than half of this while in most of the countries of Asia and Africa, the number ranges from about 1.5 per thousand down to practically nothing. The reduction of these disparities would be an essential initial objective of the scientific and technological element of the new international order.

6.3 *Technology, Appropriate and Otherwise*

The main objectives which have justified the large research and development expenditures in the decades following the Second World War have been defence, national prestige (such as space research) and economic growth. Relatively trivial efforts have been made in other directions, such as improvements in the social and service sectors including health. It was only towards the end of the 'sixties that world expenditure on research on military matters ceased to form the most important single element.

Until recently it was assumed, somewhat naively, that increase in the research and development of a country would automatically result in an increase in economic performance. Studies of the so-called 'technological gap' between the European countries and the United States, however, have indicated that there is no direct correlation between the research effort of these countries and either their economic or trade performance. It appears that at this level of development, the diffusion of new technology across frontiers through commercial arrangements (sale and exchange of patents, know-how etc.) is sufficiently rapid to compensate for deficiencies in domestic research effort. This applies only, however, to countries already possessing a sophisticated technological capacity, industrial infrastructure and skilled labour and management. It cannot be assumed, therefore, that more research inevitably means higher growth; so much depends on the relevance of the research undertaken and on the existence of conditions propitious for its assimilation in the economic process.

Attention now focuses, therefore, on the totality of the process of *technological innovation* in which research and development, whether domestic or imported, is only an initial, although essential, input and whose effective use depends on numerous other factors, such as the availability of risk capital, entrepreneurship, levels of education and training at all points from top management to unskilled labour, fiscal policy, management/labour relations, national psychology and cultural patterns to say nothing about marketing ability. This holds equally for Third World as for industrialized countries.

In the industrialized countries there is much concern and resentment with regard to the negative side-effects of technology. Foremost amongst these is pollution which, in the extreme, could give rise to irreversible and disastrous changes in the oceans, the terrestial environment and the climate of the world. There are, however, many others which together suggest a deterioration in the general quality of life. Furthermore, there are the resource implications of indiscriminate technological growth. Much of the new technology and the products which flow from it are developed to meet an artificially stimulated demand for novel and luxury goods which do not always contribute to human well-being and add to the clutter of material possessions, requiring still greater quantities of raw material and energy in their manufacture. In a world of limited resources and in which the disparities between the material possessions of the 'haves' and the 'have-nots' are so great, it is questionable how far this process of stimulated consumption and waste can continue. On the other hand, it is an organic element of the total economic system of the market economy countries and to modify it would be economically and socially difficult.

The continuation of economic growth by the industrialized countries necessitates further development of technology. Should this continue as at present to mushroom without control, pollution and all the other difficulties are likely to go on increasing to the extent of producing social and other disturbances. There is thus considerable concern that future technology should be evolved so as to be *socially acceptable*. This would necessitate a much more careful selection and management of technology in the future and there is increasing need to develop effective means of technology assessment.

This brings us to the concept of *appropriate technology*. If technology is a major agent of economic development, how can it be evolved appropriately to meet real human needs? This question, essentially ideological and political, is basic to the concept of a new international order — but appropriateness can only be agreed and achieved on the basis of an accepted value system for global human development.

Appropriate technology is thus a necessary concept for both industrialized and Third World countries and not merely a euphemism, as many feel it to be, for persuading the Third World to adopt inferior technical and hence economic performance levels. The term appropriate technology should be taken to mean the devising and utilization of processes and work organization most suited to particular circumstances, both economic and social, of a particular country or sector. For the industrialized countries, present technologies are far from fully appropriate to present and forseeable needs; in the future they will need to be made more appropriate in that they will have to take into account social concerns, pollution control and conservation of materials and energy, in addition to the desirability of a longer life for their products — a transformation which will necessitate changes in both public and industrial behaviour.

In such countries, research and development has been aimed at the creation of processes to achieve high levels of labour productivity and large scale production to provide for large markets and thus take advantage of economy of scale. Towards this end they have been appropriate; where they have deviated has been in their failure to take account of social and environmental factors. There is no reason to suppose that an equal effort of research and development directed to the creation of highly efficient, but more *labour* intensive, technologies would not have been equally effective and have provided a much higher degree of work satisfaction. Many Third World countries have a permanent need to provide employment and, with the present demographic structures, this need will increase in the future. It would seem, therefore, that much of their technological effort, aided by research, should be directed to this objective. Such technologies should not have any status inferiority as compared with the often inappropriate capital-intensive technologies in such environments. There need not be any dogmatic distinction between the status and desirability of different types of technology and both can coexist. Indeed, many different mixes of 'modern', labour intensive and primative technologies will be necessary and appropriate in different national circumstances. For the Third World countries much 'free' technology is available, for example to achieve important substitution with regard to many traditional and bulky goods now obtained from abroad and, in other cases, much social and economic benefit would flow from the devising of small scale, labour intensive methods, capable of being decentralized, thus relieving urban pressure and bringing wealth to rural areas.

Indeed, special attention is required with regard to the more *traditional technologies*, developed over long periods of time by empirical means, throughout the Third World. In almost all developing countries there exists the so-called 'modern' sector of the society which comprises the comparably very few elites, side by side with the 'traditional' sector which includes the great majority of the population, particularly those living under subsistence level in rural communities. Most of the needs of the 'modern' society of developing countries are more or less similar to those of people in developed countries. The needs of such societies are largely met by imported technologies with little, if any, adaption. The rest of the population, mostly rural, has been hardly touched by this process of technological modernization, and remains more or less in the same state of poverty and backwardness that has been its lot for generations. Thus the 'gap' between the 'modern' and 'traditional' sectors of societies within the same developing country is real, and similar to the 'gap' between the developed and developing countries. Furthermore, it is widening, with the apparent result that those who already have something are getting more while those who have nothing remain the same.

In elaborating policies for science and technology in many Third World countries, there is a paramount need to devote considerable effort to improving the empirical technology of the traditional sector, generally neglected and often despised. So far this has been attempted mainly by replacing the age-old traditional methods and tools by imported technology, with uncertain success and often with social resistance and inefficient operation, since these innovations are not always seen immediately as conforming to local needs and cultural habits. Very much could be done through the application of well understood and often simple scientific principles to the improvement of the traditional tools and methods, with the possibility of great improvement in efficiency and increase of product and the minimum of cultural disturbance.

To sum up, the technological needs of Third World countries, although exceedingly diverse, demand, as essential, the creation of a technological capacity, including manpower, skills, facilities and the right environment with the following functions:
(I) to screen, select and absorb, within the framework of national economic and social objectives, science-based technologies developed elsewhere, and to modify them to take

account of local materials, work methods, manpower availability and human skills;

(II) to introduce a wide range of established technologies, usually freely available, for the manufacture of basic products or consumer goods now imported;

(III) to create research and development effort which might, in part, be undertaken with advantage by cooperation between countries with similar needs, to evolve efficient, but labour-intensive processes;

(IV) to provide a service at both national and local level to improve the empirical methods and instruments of the traditional sector, by the systematic application of scientific principles and to encourage production based on these.

6.4   *The Reduction of Technological Disparities*

The prerequisite to any radical attempt to reduce the economic disparities both within and between countries is the existence of a *political will* to do so on the part of both the industrialized and Third World nations. The history of the aid process hitherto shows that this has not always been the case. With deepening understanding of the nature of the disparities and recent recognition on the part of the industrialized countries of the reality of interdependence within a finite world and the consequences of ignoring it, however, the concept of the new international order no longer sounds hopelessly idealistic. Economic disparities are intimately linked with technological disparities and it is improbable that the economic 'gap' can be bridged without a new approach to the diffusion and assimilation of technology.

The system of science is very different from that of technology. By long tradition, research results in basic science are *published freely and internationally*, thus research contributions from the developing as well as from the scientifically advanced countries are additions to the world's repertory of knowledge, and not the exclusive property of or even of specific interest to the country of origin. Indeed, they are likely to be exploited by the most strongly industrialized countries with their superior facilities for scanning the new knowledge, for applied research, technological development and production. The process of the expansion of scientific knowledge consists of the addition of new elements of discovery, wherever they may arise, to the existing mosaic: scientific research is thus essentially a global process, but its fruits are plucked by those with the instruments to do so.

Despite the absence of direct economic gain from a nation's fundamental research, it is essential for each country to cultivate it to a degree; it imparts a sense of contemporary flavour to the educational process, contributes to the level of scientific and technological awareness and is an excellent training means for applied research workers. Without this scientific culture and awareness, even if it be concentrated in the minds of a relatively few individuals, it is well nigh impossible for a country to select from the vast number of discoveries in the world of potential applicability and from the range of technological options, those which are particularly relevant to its development. In such a situation, the country is at the mercy of outside interests which may endeavour to sell it processes, to the advantage of the originators rather than of the importers.

Technological knowledge, in contrast, and especially the newer and more advanced varieties, are very rarely a free commodity, but rather take the form of *industrial property*, owned by individuals, corporations or states. It is a valuable commodity which is bought and sold on the national and international markets and hence carefully guarded. Thus most advanced processes and the know-how to use them are not automatically available to Third World countries and so the transfer of technology can be a costly business which, in common with other commercial transactions, requires great care in the choice of expensive items before purchase. However, it must be remembered that the life of a patent is relatively short and there therefore exists a vast accumulation of useful technological knowledge which is freely available, at least from a legal point of view. Even here, however, the successful application of available processes depends on experience and know-how accumulated over the years by those who have operated them and may have to be purchased at considerable cost.

It must be admitted, however, that the availability of technologies which can be freely or cheaply required, is not sufficiently visible. There is need then for information banks and exchange mechanisms as suggested at the Seventh Special Session of the UN General Assembly to bring such information to the attention of interested countries and to share applied research findings. This could well become a function of UNCTAD and UNIDO.

There are two main requirements for the effective transfer of technology from industrialized to Third World countries:
(I) easy access to and equitable conditions for such transfers;
(II) the building up of appropriate capacities in each country to permit the selection and assimilation of imported technologies and skills, both technical and managerial, necessary for their efficient exploitation.

Major problems exist with regard to both of these needs. For the efficient *transfer of technology*, new attitudes and approaches are required on the part of both donor and recipient countries. As already explained, the governments of the industrial market economy countries are not in a position to direct their industries to part with their technological property which in many cases has involved the firms concerned in very high research and development costs and possession of which determines their competitive status in both domestic and foreign markets. This being said, it is necessary to introduce greater rationality and equity into the international framework of technology transfer, eventually through a multinational, legally-binding instrument for facilitating transfer, eliminating restrictions and strengthening the technological capacities of all countries. For this and other reasons a review of the patent and industrial property system should be undertaken within the framework of attempts to establish a new world order. This should ensure that the interests of the importers of technology are safeguarded and should reflect the generally accepted principle of preferential and non-reciprocal treatment in favour of the developing countries.

In the meantime, there are considerable possibilities for great improvements in the *terms of transfer*, by new means, as yet largely unexplored. For example one could envisage negotiations between the various market economy industrialized countries with a view to establishing agreed, preferential terms for the sale of various categories of patents and know-how to Third World countries, the difference between such terms and those between the industrialized countries being borne by the governments. In this way, the competitivity of the firms involved would not be disturbed on world markets. A further approach would be to establish in the donor countries policies which would enable them, as part of their aid policy, to subsidize the sale of technological property to the Third World on an ad hoc basis. Special arrangements would have to be made between the industrialized countries with regard to such transactions where transnational corporations are concerned; these have, of course, been one of the main channels for technology transfer in the past, although both the reality and effectiveness of such transfer in favour of Third World countries have been repeatedly questioned.

Within the receiving countries, the prime necessity is to establish deliberate policies for technological development. Such policies must be related organically with their long term economic and social objectives, the acquisition of a detailed knowledge of the process of technological innovation including fiscal, manpower planning and market survey aspects.

It is exceedingly important that there should be a capacity to select the optimum processes for particular purposes; it is all too easy for a country lacking the depth of knowledge of the range of world scientific and technical trends to select inappropriate processes or products to manufacture, and hence to innovate for obsolescence.

Here the second of the main requirements for technology transfer is encountered, namely, the building up of an *indigenous* capacity for research and development. Without the knowledge of the real growing points of science, which can hardly be gained without such a capacity, a country is unlikely to reach a threshold of technological awareness which will enable it to select the technology, negotiate its purchase and ensure the effective assimilation of that technology which its economic and social objectives demand. The indigenous research capacity is also necessary for long term purposes, as a training facility for the acquisition of modern technical skills and for the generation of new innovative possibilities. Unless such a capacity, which need not be very large but must be of high quality, is evolved, the Third World countries will be in danger of indefinitely running several decades behind the technologically active countries. The example of Japan is often advocated for Third World countries to emulate. It should be recognized, however, that Japan's industrial success — based, it is true, on imported technology — was prepared years in advance through the building up and modernization of the educational system to provide the necessary skills when required and a research effort was gradually mounted to sustain the national technological effort at a high level of quality. This research capacity has now itself become an originator of new products and processes.

The successful use of foreign technology, then, is much more than a matter of access to foreign patents and know-how, or even the availability of capital to exploit them. It necessitates the adoption of deliberate policies of technological innovation as part of a long term economic strategy. Such policies would be concerned, inter alia, with the following:

(I) the acquisition of a detailed understanding of the innovation process and of the factors which encourage or inhibit it;

(II) the careful selection of technological processes to be purchased from abroad, so as to achieve a balanced economic effort with minimum attention to prestige innovation or the acquisition of methods which do not accord with national cultural conditions;

(III) the adoption of fiscal and tariff policies aimed at facilitating the introduction of new processes and techniques, protecting new manufactures during the early, critical stages, but not to the extent of rendering the products non-competitive or of condoning inefficiency or low standards of quality;

(IV) the stimulation of research and development by locally owned industrial enterprises through temporary tax concessions;

(V) the encouragement of innovation and quality performance through government purchase in accordance with specifications of quality, measures of standardization and quality control and by providing contracts for research and development in appropriate cases;

(VI) achieving a balance between the conflicting needs to possess a proportion of high capital-intensive industry with high economic yield and that for the generation of employment;

(VII) instituting forward manpower planning, especially for scientific, technical and manpower skills, and the redesigning of programmes of education and training to ensure that such skills are available when required;

(VIII) the provision of information networks for the use of industrial enterprises, government planners and researchers to transmit selected and relevant knowledge of a practical nature from all parts of the world, in relation to technological opportunities, economic, marketing and social data;

(IX) the creation of industrial advisory services, corresponding to the extension services of agriculture, to assist industrial firms to achieve the best general practice of the sectors concerned and assist in the introduction of improved techniques;

(X) the adoption of policies of resource management and encouragement of research concerning new uses for indigenous materials;

(XI) the encouragement of both basic and applied research in the universities and independent research institutes of relevance to long term national needs and the stimulation through their teaching programmes of interest in national development and its technological needs;

(XII) the integration of technology transfer considerations with national planning and science policies and the establishment of regulations for technology transfer contracts;

(XIII) supplement the national efforts of Third World countries by cooperative action between them, in particular through the establishment of sub-regional and inter-regional centres for both the development and transfer of technology in general or specifically in critical sectors of particular interest to groups of countries.

(XIV) on the international level, the establishment of a code of good practice on technology transfer.

Such comprehensive policies could not be implemented fully in a short time in many Third World countries and both support and guidance from other countries and the international organizations would be necessary. Such efforts should be viewed as essential to attempt to shape a new international order.

6.5   *The Need for Relevant Policies for Science and Technology*

With the increase of government expenditure on research and development, both directly and through contract with industries and the universities in the industrialized countries, it has been found necessary to establish *national science and technology policies* both for the management and creativity of their scientific efforts and in order to achieve its fullest use in the solution of the pressing problems of the different sectors. A comprehensive science and technology policy, covering the whole range of activity from fundamental research to technological development, will be seen as complementary to the industrial and innovation policies described above and related to them through the planning mechanism. Science and technology, therefore, should not be regarded as autonomous areas of policy, but be evolved in articulation with economic, social, health, educational and other policies. Consequently, the formulation of science and technology policy should be approached through systems analysis that considers relationships between the science and technology system, the production and education system and politics.

Science policy is generally conceived as a deliberate and coherent basis for national decisions influencing the investment in scientific activities, institutional structures, creativity and utilization of scientific research; it is thus not only concerned with the orientation and management of the national research and development effort, but also with the problems of ensuring that new thinking and scientific discoveries permeate all sectors of national activity. This stress on application implicitly includes technology within the term scientific policy. No country has, as yet, succeeded in implementing such a comprehensive approach; many are, however, striving in this direction.

The need to ensure that the science effort is vigorously directed towards the real needs of a country is equally important in the Third World as in the industrialized countries and many of them have created councils or other instruments for this purpose. These, however, do not always interact sufficiently or realistically with the national economic and social plans. In the present technological world, 'science is too important to be left entirely to the scientists'. National Science Councils should include in their membership a representative range of scientists and engineers, to be sure, but also economists, industrialists and those concerned with overall national policy. Otherwise it is all too easy for such bodies to become vested interest groups, pleading for resources for their own enthusiasms and only incidentally and marginally contributing to the attainment of broad national objectives. It is easy to slide into a situation in which the small scientific community of a poor country, most of the members of which have been trained in advanced centres of research abroad, see themselves as expatriates from the world scientific community, working exclusively on the basis of intellectual interest, but in unfavourable conditions outside the mainstream of national development.

6.6 *'Brain Drain'*

'Brain drain', the problem of skilled human resources flowing out of economies where they can make the greatest contribution to human welfare into economies already well-supplied with trained, capable, scientific and administrative personnel, is a loss of a vital human capital resource. It is a loss without compensation.

It has been estimated, for instance, that, between 1949 and 1961 43,000 scientists and engineers, 'many' of whom came from the less developed countries, emigrated to the United States. In 1964-65, some 11,000 interns and residents in US hospitals (out of a total of 41,000) were graduates of foreign medical schools and more than 8,000 of these came from developing nations. The drain from Asian nations, particularly Taiwan and Korea, is most serious. Over 90 per cent of Asian students who arrive for training in the United States never return home. It is estimated that the United States would have to build and operate 12 new medical schools to produce the manpower derived through immigration (approximately 1,200 per year). The annual dollar value of this 'foreign aid' to the United States approximately equals the total cost of all its medical aid, private and public, to foreign nations.

The situation is not without its ironies. France takes pride in her aid to former colonies, yet the new state of Togo has sent more physicians and professors to France than France has sent to Togo. Great Britain, alarmed by the exodus of its talent to the United States, relies increasingly on foreign doctors, mainly Indians and Pakistanis, to man its National Health Service. According to official statistics, 44 per cent of its junior medical staff is foreign. There are more specialists of all kinds from other commonwealth countries working in Britain than there are British specialists working elsewhere in the Common-wealth. There are more American-trained Iranian doctors in New York alone than in the whole of Iran.

As mentioned repeatedly, human capital is indispensable to a country's economic development. This is even more true of certain key skills, the loss of which may trigger cumulative 'external' effects on other sectors of society. Moreover, to the extent that top-grade professional manpower is expensive to produce, and to the extent that it usually embodies substantial public investment, its loss through migration represents a 'gift' from one country to another — typically from a poor country which cannot afford it to a rich country which does not need it. Such uncontrolled migration of brain power today favours the most advanced and affluent nations.

It suggests that some interference, analogous to the protection of infant industries against premature international competition, is necessary to assure less advanced countries and particularly underdeveloped countries against the loss of the specialized manpower they vitally need if they are to realize their growth aspirations.

Migration is an index of an extraordinary 'pull' from abroad or 'push' from at home. It is an overt manifestation of some structural maladjustment — some deviation from equilibrium — in the country of emigration or immigration, or both.

In the final analysis, the brain drain is an index of the structural maladjustment in both the 'sending' and 'receiving' countries. In the case of the latter, it indicates an inelastic supply of certain talents and skills, based in part on the monopolistic entry restrictions which are allowed to operate in the professional sector of the economy. It may also indicate an inadequate amount, wrong type, or faulty administration of foreign aid and technical assistance to other countries. In the case of the 'sending' countries, the brain drain may be the index of retarded development or underdevelopment. In all cases, the brain drain is simply the symptom of the disease rather than the disease itself; effective policy, therefore, must be directed to the roots of the problem rather than its surface manifestations. This requires, above all, an unsentimental, dispassionate, hard-headed approach.

With respect to the developing nations, the 'brain drain' is both cause and effect of all the economic, social, and political factors which we group together under the term 'underdevelopment'. It points to the sad fact that economic development is not just a matter of producing needed skills, but of producing the opportunities to use them. It explains the strange paradox that needed manpower will emigrate from a country even though that country has crying need for human capital. Like it or not, the basic problem is the lack of opportunity and absorptive capacity, in the sense of effective economic demand, which characterizes most developing countries.

It is imperative that the new international order recognizes the paramount importance of the 'brain drain' problem, especially as it affects the skilled manpower in the general field of science and technology, and envisages the development of a global policy to control it at both the receiving and sending ends, with the twin objectives of optimum and fair resource allocation, and particularly, in the interest of the economic growth of the less developed countries of the world.

In order to combat effectively the *'brain drain'* phenomenon, several important *measures* must be considered. These include: revision of salary structures; increased professional opportunities; better local receptivity to change; restructured investment in education and rationalized manpower policies; promotion of economic integration and resistance to political 'balkanization'; elimination of discrimination and bigotry. Clearly, the developing countries, in full recognition of this problem, should refrain from pursuing policies which might encourage the exodus of their trained personnel.

6.7 *Science at the International Level*

Science and technology are inherently international in nature and in practice. New knowledge is a mosaic of painstaking, individual advances made in all parts of the world. Equally, the problems which science will have to tackle are fast becoming internationalized. We are witnessing the emergence of a wide range of interacting, global problems, such as the 'population explosion' with its food, health and employment consequences, exploitation of the oceans, deterioration of the geo-environment etc., some of which arise as unwanted by-products of earlier scientific successes, unwisely applied. The need is pressing, therefore, for the development of a global approach to science itself, both for the attack on impending difficulties, for the prevention of further unwanted side effects which could threaten the world and humanity as a whole and for the attainment of universal well-being. But research is an extremely costly business and, as it becomes ever more sophisticated, will become ever more so. It can be argued that many of our present problems involving important research and development components are beyond the means of all but the largest and richest of countries and even they will be strained to the limit to provide the necessary resources. Such a situation suggests that there is a need to move towards the construction of global science policy and action in which there are two immediate desiderata:

(I) common formulation of objectives for the application of science and technology to the solution of common problems, agreement on priorities and programming of the main lines of research for mankind as a whole; and

(II) sharing the costs of research and development by dividing the tasks between the nations and, in the case of certain large projects, operating international cooperative schemes.

In the period since the end of the second world war, many attempts have been made, especially in Europe, to build up cooperative, cost-sharing ventures in research in particularly expensive fields on an international basis. It must be admitted that these have been by no means uniformly successful. However, much valuable experience has accumulated concerning the organization of such schemes and the new need for common effort and sharing of resources has become so great that the time is ripe for a new impulse to be given to international research and the shaping of a global policy for science within the framework of the New International Economic Order.

The United Nations, through its Specialized Agencies and Programmes, has been responsible for much activity in this field. On the whole, however, its performance has been disappointing for many reasons, including the dispersal of responsibility and activity over many agencies with consequent duplication, sub-marginal effort, lack of cohesion and often of realism. In the present attempts to restructure the machinery of the United Nations, special attention should be given to its role in science and technology which are essentially horizontal activities, permeating almost all of the activities of the United Nations system. We therefore make two proposals for immediate consideration.

6.8   *Proposals for Immediate Consideration*

6.8.1   *Science in the United Nations*   Because of the widespread impact of the advancement of science across the whole spectrum of human and political activity, there is need — if science is to be used effectively in the common interest of mankind — for an effective *Council for Science and Technology* in the top structure of the United Nations Organization to enable discussion to take place between the nations on broad policy considerations and strategic requirements. The Council would be composed of national representatives, with a limited membership representative of the various regions of the world, sufficiently small for effective discussion, with different nations having a seat by rotation.

Likewise, the Secretary General should be given means of direct access to advanced scientific thinking within the socio-economic perspective which we have advocated in this paper. For this purpose, an *Advisory Group of independent scientists*, economists etc, should be constituted, reporting directly to the Secretary General, but available also to advise the Council for Science and Technology. The Advisory Group would replace the present Advisory Committee for the Application of Science and Technology for Development (ACAST) and, because of the wide impact of science in all the fields of interest of the United Nations, would, like the Council, have a scope greater than ACAST, i.e. beyond that of ECOSOC.

These two bodies would be responsible for selection of the major points of emphasis to be given, within the programmes of science and technology of the United Nations system as a whole, as well as strategic and policy aspects of securing the effective application of the results of research and of supervising UN scientific advisory functions. In this work, due attention would be given to the conflicts and reinforcements likely to result from meeting the agreed objectives, sector by sector. Questions of the social acceptability and assessment of the consequences of new technological developments would also be discussed.

Under the aegis of the Council for Science and Technology, a planning and programming activity is envisaged in which the secretariat of the Council and the representatives of the Specialised Agencies and Programmes would, with the assistance of independent experts as necessary, together formulate the broad lines of a science and technology programme for the UN system as a whole, taking account of the priorities laid down by the Council. Their consequent task would be to allot responsibility for carrying out the elements of the programme by the most appropriate of the UN bodies in each case, making use, not only of the in-house capacities of the latter, but of the relevant outside bodies where necessary, whether national or international. Particular attention would be given to such elements of the programme as concerned two or more of the organisms within the UN system.

6.8.2   *A World Technological Development Authority*   The above recommendation concerns essentially the research and development programme of the UN system. While this would, as it evolves, become increasingly influential in determining the broad lines of a global science policy, the main operational concomitants of such a policy would, as now, remain outside the UN framework as such. There is, however, an increasing number of technological development topics which are increasingly global in their significance or too costly for individual nations or corporations. In future it will be difficult to tackle such problems on an effective scale other than through the cost-sharing mechanism of international cooperation. Examples here include the development of non-traditional energy sources and the devising of techniques for the exploitation of the resources of the deep sea bed. It is proposed, therefore, that consideration be given to the establishment in due time of a *Technological Development Authority*, backed up by an *International Bank for Technological Development*. The former would *not* be an operational body with its own laboratories and pilot plant facilities, but a planning, programming and training organization which would carry out feasibility studies, devise detailed programmes of research and development, arrange for their implementation in cooperation with the Bank, by contract with the most appropriate experimental institutions for each specific project or sub-project — research institutes, state enterprises, industrial firms —, supervise the progress of the work in each case and act as custodian of such industrial property as might accrue, on behalf of the participating countries. The advantages to Third World countries would be their participation in the planning and decision stages, their joint ownership of the property and the long term benefits of training of their nationals in practical research and development activities and of intimate familiarity with the new techniques and know-how which would be evolved. It should be noted that the proposed Technological Development Authority need not be a completely new agency, but rather formed by expanding the powers and competence of a body already active in the field of scientific research and technological development.

It should be recognized that these two suggestions do not involve creation of new international bodies; they are rather functional in nature. The first is essentially a proposal for restructuring and would not lead to institutional proliferation; the latter might be an additional function within a broader international investment bank.

These two suggestions might serve as topics for discussion at the proposed conference on Science and Technology, planned by the United Nations for 1978 or 1979. They could serve as important elements in shaping the new international order.

Annex 7 **Transnational Enterprises**
Idriss Jazairy, Pieter Kuin and Juan Somavia

7.1 *Introduction: History and Present Situation*

7.1.1 *Structure of this Annex*   This annex consists of three main parts. In the first part, a sketch is given of the recent history and present situation of transnational enterprises. In section 7.2, an attempt is made to formulate a long-term view on the position of trans-national enterprises with respect to a new international order. This requires that some attention be given to national orders and desirable developments within them. The final section, 7.3, is devoted to the formulation of proposals and recommendations on trans-national enterprises relevant in the short and medium range.

7.1.2 *Recent History and Main Characteristics of Transnational Enterprises*   The rapid growth of transnational enterprises has been one of the major developments which has shaped the existing international order.

The importance they have acquired is illustrated by the fact that the value added by each of the ten largest transnational enterprises is more than $ 3 billion — a figure in excess of the GNP of 80 of the world's nations. In 1971, the total value added by transnational enterprises reached $ 500 billion, thus accounting for 20 per cent of total world GNP (excluding the socialist nations). Without changes in present trends, transnational enter-prises could control 41 per cent of world production (excluding the socialist nations) by 1988. (1)

Further, it is estimated that transnational enterprises are at present responsible for an expanding part of international trade. The largest 300 US enterprises and their 5,200 foreign subsidiaries alone account for 28 per cent of world exports, including 47 per cent of exports of primary products and 20 per cent of manufactured products.

From a monetary viewpoint, transnational enterprises own vast international liquidities which are linked to their business operations. The liquidities of US enterprises alone account for $ 200 billion which is more than twice the amount of the total reserves held by all central banks and international monetary institutions. Speculative operations on only 1 per cent of these liquidities could thus provoke severe stress on a particular national currency; even without speculation, normal 'leads and lags' could have similar consequences.

For these reasons, and in the absence of clear institutional frameworks to orient and control their activities, transnational enterprises, in pursuing their normal business activities, have considerable power in forging the structure of national and international development; their decisions also influence society in a number of non-business aspects. Events have demonstrated that they can become politically disturbing factors.

The 'old' international order, as it has evolved, favoured the development of the production structure of centre countries over that of peripheral countries. A system was progressively set up, the objectives and principles of which stimulated the growth and transnational expansion of national enterprises of centre countries. To that end, the goals became flexible. They were liberal when necessary (reduction of barriers to trade, liberalization of payment and financial systems, stimulus to the free flow of foreign investment) or restrictive when necessary (rigid patent system protecting the property of technological development, acceptance of liner conferences as 'organizers' of international maritime services). These objectives were legitimized through the existence of international agreements (GATT, IMF) or, in the absence of agreements, when the free play of power forces was required.

It is for these reasons that transnational enterprises cannot be analysed or fully understood if they are separated from the historical sequences from which they emerge or from the geographical location of their principal head offices. As a social science phenomenon they are one of the principal expressions of the transnational expansion of contemporary capitalism. The large majority originate in a few countries where capitalist rationale — through different formal ways — constitutes the guiding criteria for economic decision-making.

At the micro-economic level, the overall expansion of the activities of transnational enterprises, and in particular their expansion in less developed countries, can be ascribed to a number of reasons, including:
(I) the desire to maintain a high rate of growth;
(II) the objective of profit maximization by taking advantage of international wage differentials and of possibilities of guaranteed access to other low-cost factors of production and through expansion of sales in protected markets;
(III) the use of all available financial resources outside the transnational enterprises' home country; and
(IV) the improvement of international transport and communications.

By the very act of investing in a foreign country transnational enterprises create conditions for international disputes. This had led to cases of subversive political interventions, acute confrontation over the exercise of the right to nationalize, use of businessmen as cover for intelligence activities, political and economic retaliations by home governments, situations where affiliates of transnational enterprises have been exposed to unilateral measures by host governments, conflicts of jurisdiction, and a number of politically related problems. In particular, the growing recognition, based on proven and admitted disclosures, that corrupt practices have become a standard norm for the conduct of business of more than 30 United States corporations, has given new impetus to the allegation that the power of such enterprises tends to give them the feeling, and sometimes the conviction, that their actions are above the rule of the law. Worse still, the fact that such corrupt practices have become known after investigations at the highest political levels, forcing corporations to admit them, sheds a mantle of distrust over all other transnational enterprises, whether or not they indulge in such practices. These particular events are a renewed expression of the need to create a framework of social accountability for these enterprises.

Uncertainties concerning the performance and real interests of transnational enterprises are compounded by the fact that a surprisingly large number of them are legally engaged in the production or exportation of armaments. According to information made public in the United States by the Bureau of Munition Control of the Department of State, 1,033 US companies are licensed to export or produce arms. Among them are 152 of Fortune Magazine's list of top 500 corporations and, among the 152, are 32 of the largest 50. Many US companies, long identified in the public image with appliances, cameras and toys, are also producing arms, munitions and implements of war!

It is a fact that many transnational enterprises operate in countries where respect for fundamental human rights is systematically disregarded. It is also a fact that a number of societies have not fully embodied in their statutory laws or practices the whole range of intellectual, political, social or cultural rights and freedoms recognized by the Universal Declaration of Human Rights. From these two realities stems a fundamental question. Is it morally justified to initiate or maintain operations in a country where it is palpably evident that the social and political order is maintained on the basis of systematic disregard for basic human values; and consequently to reap profits that originate — partly at least — in varying forms of human exploitation? To what extent do such regimes persist precisely because they are backed and sustained by foreign investment? Such issues cannot for long be ignored. Except for a few cases, transnational enterprises have in the past not given due consideration to such issues when making decisions on whether to initiate, maintain, expand, reduce or close operations in a given country.

An analysis of the possible role that transnational enterprises can play in establishing a new international order must not be cast in either moral or ideological terms, although both may play a role in evaluating their usefulness. The objective fact is that both home and host countries are increasingly uneasy with transnational enterprises. To find solutions it is thus necessary to concentrate on the areas where problems exist. Essentially, it is a question of defining the practical conditions under which the nature of the relationship between transnational enterprises and host and home countries can be adapted to the requirements of a new international order.

7.1.3   *Transnational Enterprises' Decision-making Process*   Transnational enterprises excel in two fields: they have accumulated vast technological and marketing knowledge and they have developed a highly effective process of transnational decision-making. The use of these capacities put purely at the service of their private rationale oriented towards growth and profit sometimes clashes with larger human, social and economic dimensions of development emerging throughout the developed and developing world. Transnational enterprises are not only a north-south issue but a global one.

Although subject to the national legislation of the countries where they operate, there is no real framework of accountability for the actions of transnational enterprises as global enterprises. The sum of the often divergent and contradictory national regulations does not add up to an effective framework to control their activities. By not being globally accountable to anyone, the question of the exercise of power without due responsibility emerges as a major issue. All of the so called 'constituencies' to which the enterprises feel responsible (shareholders, consumers, suppliers, host country, home country) have only a partial view of the total activities they engage in and consequently cannot exercise the social function of overseeing and controlling the exercise of their power.

Furthermore, in view of their international mobility, which enables them to shift their operations from one country to another or to expand them in one and level them off in another, transnational enterprises have the possibility of exercising pressure on governments of host countries or even of playing host and/or would be host countries one against the other. In a number of cases, transnational enterprises have used diplomatic channels to serve their interests, especially when based in a powerful country. Bribes have also been known to have been paid for the same purpose by transnational enterprises to influential officials in host countries, although the initiative may or may not have come from representatives of transnational enterprises.

7.1.4   *Product Mix*   It is in the nature of private enterprise to tend to maximize profits. This is why the product mix of transnational enterprises, although meeting a demand of the market, does not necessarily coincide with that which would meet basic human needs. In their pursuit of continuous growth, they must have an increasing number of responsive buyers and must, therefore, try to expand effective demand: hence the importance of advertizing in their market strategies. There may be in some cases, therefore, a bias of transnational enterprises towards the production of non-essential goods. This bias may find support in the policies of the host countries themselves where such policies are not primarily concerned with the well-being of the masses of their population and where they are influenced by the aspirations of a local 'elite' to a Western life-style. In order to reconcile the profit motivations of transnational enterprises with the objective of satisfying basic human needs, less developed countries should introduce, where necessary, the required internal reforms and take appropriate action, individually or collectively, in order that transnational enterprises be made to adapt their policies accordingly.

7.1.5 *Technology and Prices of Capital, Labour and Know-how*   In view of the absence of locally available technology, less developed countries are to a large extent dependent on imported technology, mostly controlled by transnational enterprises. Responding primarily to the strategy of these enterprises, such technology, when transferred, acts as a support for the transfer of the economic pattern of production of the transnational enterprises' home country. Such a pattern may not be best adapted to the requisites of the host country at its particular stage of development. Moreover, transfers of technology by transnational enterprises often take place between the parent company and its foreign affiliates as a purely internal process, and without in any way increasing the technological autonomy of the host country. In any event, technologies used by most transnational enterprises have been developed in their home countries and are geared to the capital labour endowment of the developed world.

In a general way, this implies that these technologies are not adapted to the evolving factor endowment of the host country and that, more often than not, they are more capital intensive than the host country can permit itself if it is to seriously attempt to create employment opportunities for the population of working age. It must also be admitted that the authorities in many host countries insist on ultra-modern technology. One should not underestimate, however, the flexibility and pragmatism of the international business community which enables it to adapt profitably to labour intensive processes and to take advantage of specific labour conditions prevailing in developing countries.

In some cases the technologies chosen by transnational enterprises have, given the international market structure, tended to result in minimizing the value-added of their production in less developed countries. This has been further aggravated by the excessively high prices at which some technological know-how is supplied, by the so-called 'tie-in clauses'; the protection built into the tariff structure of industrialized countries with respect to processed goods and by tariff provisions in the transnational enterprises' home countries which relate to the preferential treatment accorded only to re-imports of materials which may only have been superficially processed in less developed countries (such as, for example, items 806.30 or 807.00 of the US tariff schedule).

The raising of local capital to participate in direct investments by transnational enterprises may constitute a way of simply replacing the financial effort incumbent on the transnational enterprises to the host country. It also occurs that the negotiating power of the local partner, whether or not requested by the government, does not enable it to effectively take part in the decision-making process. There may be disadvantages to the community in financial terms as well as in terms of autonomy if a structure of dependent relationships thus become firmly established with strong local roots. This can be obviated only when the government of the host country, as the local partner, yields greater countervailing power than private local capital.

7.1.6 *Product Prices and Taxes*   Another group of problems surrounding transnational enterprises concerns prices of products bought or sold, including prices of inputs (raw materials), prices of semi-finished products, such as those delivered to the headquarters or establishments of transnational enterprises in countries other than the host country and prices of goods sold to consumers and other customers (outputs). On the input side, the size of a transnational enterprise may imply its power to buy at low prices; on the output side it may imply its power to sell at high prices — both being examples of an oligopolistic market. Little is known about the extent of the advantages thus obtained overall, though evidence of such advantages exists in the cases of specific countries. Complete knowledge can only be derived from greater transparency in, and larger disclosure of, the accountancy of transnational enterprises.

Prices used in the transfer of goods to other establishments of a given transnational enterprise can be affected fairly easily by the enterprise and shifts in these prices imply shifts of profits shown in each of the countries involved. An important determinant of the transfer prices actually applied is the profit taxes to be paid in the various countries concerned. Thus, should a developing country consider levying relatively high taxes on profits, the transnational enterprises will, in order to reduce recorded profits, tend to apply low transfer prices for goods exported from that country and high transfer prices for employment, components and technology imported from its parent company. If, however, a developing country applies low taxes or acts as a tax haven, the opposite tendency will prevail.

In both cases this logically implies a loss of potential income for the host country. Some checks may be possible if the transfer product has a market price but an important number of raw materials, for instance bauxite, and some semi-finished and manufactured products do not have a perfect market and may even be controlled by the transnational enterprises themselves. The problem is further complicated by the tax treaties existing between countries and the taxation principles adhered to by the transnational enterprises' home country. If the home country applies the exemption system, profit taxes are collected by the developing country concerned. It is different when the credit system is adhered to, as is the case in the USA. In a number of cases, excessive profits have clearly been made by transnational enterprises. Their remittance might have been prevented by effective foreign exchange control, although this would be by no means easy to achieve.

From the above it is clear that the lack of cooperation among governments in tax matters provides opportunities which have been used by transnational enterprises to maximize profits after tax. Because of their size and relations, transnational enterprises can use to their advantage the existing differences in tax policies among countries; they are even assisted by tax policies to minimize total tax beyond that required to establish an optimal division of labour among countries.

The Euro-currency market, basically controlled by transnational enterprises, is a new structural characteristic in the international economic system and is used as a borrowing 'haven' to stimulate the international growth of foreign investment. The financial assets over which transnational enterprises have control or can influence, are of such magnitude that a 'private international liquidity' has in fact emerged. It is characterized by high mobility and is administered according to the specific needs of transnational enterprises. This is compounded by the universal appearance of certain selling techniques designed to pressure the consumer into buying. At the same time, it serves as a source for financing operations when other sources are insufficient. Faced with this situation, national governments have, in various ways, provided the liquidity to ensure the workings of this form of expansion, generating high increases in money supply and consequent inflationary tendencies (cf. Annex 1). Finally, it has become apparent that the oligopolistic structure has increased rather than decreased and that a 'correlation' has appeared between higher concentration in industrial sectors and the tendency towards higher relative price increases.

7.1.7 *Concluding Remarks and Illustrations*   Let us try to summarize our description of the present situation while adding some illustrative material. Transnational enterprises introduce into developing countries the phenomenon of a dual economy (1), which has been found to be one of the important causes of inequality in income distribution (2). Some believe that this dualism is an inevitable characteristic of a certain phase of development; they refer as evidence of this to the Soviet model of development. We are not convinced, however, of its unavoidable character and consider that such dualism should be fought from the early stages of development.

Governments of developing countries have often been anxious to implement policies of modernization — Myrdal's definition of development — with potential partners from industrialized countries, including transnational enterprises. In the negotiation process between the developing country and a transnational enterprise, the bargaining power of the latter is strong because of its know-how, its market position and relations. In choosing their product mix, prices and technology, transnational enterprises are able to use, and possibly abuse, their power, especially if backed by diplomatic power in the case where the transnational enterprises' home country is a large country. In determining the role of a transnational enterprise in a developing country, the existence of a national development plan which sets out the general framework of the goals to be pursued is essential. Compliance of transnational enterprises' action with this plan should be ensured by host countries through appropriate means.

The governments of developing countries can easily become the victims of the paucity of information on technologies and on the activities of transnational enterprises, although recently more information has started to be disclosed in the form needed to conduct negotiations in a more appropriate way. Transnational enterprises are not accountable to the world community because of the lack of integration among governments which badly lags behind in the transnational decision-making process (this applies to governments of both developed and developing countries) and because of the inadequacy of the data provided.

There are considerable differences in the attitudes of transnational enterprises, reflecting such factors as the size and power of their country of origin, their policies on research and development, the location of their affiliates, the degree of centralization in their decision-making process, the extent to which political pressure is resorted to (in some cases transnational enterprises, especially those based in powerful countries have abused their power by interfering in political matters) and, in general, their capacities to adapt to local circumstances. Thus, while some have succeeded, to varying degrees, in producing and distributing products to satisfy basic needs and within the reach of the poor masses, others have not.

Some developing countries, such as those of the Andean Group, have to some extent been able to strengthen their bargaining power through cooperation. Before their integration, 317 of the 409 agreements of the countries concerning transnational enterprises prohibited exports of the latters' products to other countries; after their decision to integrate a considerable number of improvements could be obtained in renegotiations, summarized in UNCTAD document DT 107 (1971).

---

(1) For a description of this see J.H. Boeke, 'Objective and Personal Elements in Colonial Welfare Policy', in W.F. Wertheim c.s., eds., 'Indonesian Economics: The Concept of Dualism in Theory and Policy', 1961.
(2) See I. Adelman and C. Taft Morris, in W.F. Wertheim c.s., op.cit.

7.2 A Long Term View on the Place of Transnational Enterprises in a New International Order.

For the formulation of consistent short- and medium-term policies aimed at shaping a new international order, a broad long-term view of this as well as national orders is required. By national orders we refer not only to national aspirations but also to the type of society required to best serve the interests of the population at large.

Many of the objectives of self-reliant development described in Part II of this report collide with the present rationale of transnational enterprises. Self-reliance is a style of development based on a recognition of cultural diversity and, as such, it is an instrument against the homogenization of cultures. Transnational enterprises' rationale, on the contrary, is based on the proposition that most products can be profitably marketed in almost all of the countries where they operate, taking due account of their development levels. Selling the same, or substantially similar, products everywhere is a foundation of their strength. To the extent that they can homogenize the markets of the world, they attain their own maximum efficiency.

If their markets were to be disaggregated and made increasingly responsive to local cultural and taste determinants, their 'raison d'être' may be jeopardized. Their interest lies not in maximum response to local requirements, but in incorporating local capacity into global consumption models where they are the predominant producers. Their 'efficiency', in terms of their own objectives, lies in the fact that their subsidiaries or representatives are producing basically the same or related products, not different products. Should local investments adopt production policies geared to the satisfaction of local needs, the economies of scale on which their global cost structures are based would be adversely affected.

The new society we consider desirable would be characterized by cultural diversity; its structure would be chosen so as to guarantee each nation's security and no doctrinaire a priori elements would be imposed. Self-reliant and participatory development should be furthered without impairing the country's productive capacity. In fact, a synthesis of equity and productivity will have to be aimed at. This also implies that excessive bureaucracy be avoided. We see new forms of cooperation between private initiative and the community, as represented by governments, at various levels and publicly owned enterprises. Among the main social aims are a more equitable distribution of incomes and jobs, both within and between countries. In particular, the basic needs of a country's population must be met as efficiently as possible.

New forms of cooperation between private initiative and public authorities will have to be characterized by a certain balance of power, so as to serve society's aims as well as possible. Efficiency should be understood in the social sense, that is, comparing social benefits with social sacrifices and striving for a maximum of benefits over sacrifices. There is a certain optimal size of production units which varies widely among branches of activity. Enterprises that are too large – that is those surpassing optimal size – cannot be considered to be in the interests of society; they are rather an example of hobbyistic empire building. American anti-trust legislation is based upon an awareness of this danger. In many cases, corporations built up as 'federations' of their departments have understood this and thus spread the decision-making process within their own structure. This may also be applied to branches of industry. Moreover, although in certain circles it is believed that monopolies are characteristic of the present phase of development in Western countries, the share of profits in national income has not increased, but rather markedly decreased. This seems to show that some countervailing power has been at work, possibly in the form of trade unions, governments, and consumer groups. This countervailing power should lead to a situation where transnational enterprises are made accountable to the world community.

New forms of transnational enterprises' activities may be developed when complementary production factors can be made available originating in different countries. Such factors could include the supply of financing, employment or consulting activities from developed, and natural resources and labour from developing countries, provided they can conclude agreements as equal partners. Thus, there is a multiplicity of new forms of cooperation which can be envisaged as parts of the new international order. In particular, the present structure of transnational enterprises should not be considered an immutable phenomenon. The possibility of genuine internationalization of some transnational enterprises or transnational operations should be further investigated. They could be owned, controlled and managed by an international development authority. The pharmaceutical industry could be used as an initial test case for analysis because of its international social implications. Proposals regarding the seabed are another one in point (cf. Annex 10).

7.3 *Concrete Proposals for the Short and Medium Term*

7.3.1 *Governments of Host Countries* We will group our proposals under five main headings, indicating the various actors involved. We start with those immediately involved — the governments of host countries — which, in our context, are especially the developing countries.

The aim of attaining maximum welfare for present and future generations and the means to be used for that purpose must be specified in a development plan. Compliance by transnational enterprises with this plan could be obtained through individual and collective measures taken by the developing countries, such as:
(I) at the national level: public approval of investment projects, establishing the 'public utility' nature of certain enterprises, the presence of public representative on boards, adequate orientation of the credit system, public ownership of certain industries which constitute the 'commanding heights' of the economy; and
(II) at the international level: the realization of all possible forms of collective self-reliance between developing countries.

Participation of local capital in transnational enterprises should be made dependent, possibly on the basis of a sliding scale, on the contribution to be expected in the implementation of the national plan and, in particular, with respect to the satisfaction of the people's basic needs. Better planning than has so far been used in developing countries requires, however, a further elaboration of macro-economic and social concepts and of methods of rational choice of projects. It is up to national governments, in their negotiations with transnational enterprises, to choose between alternative ways of cooperation. Governments not wanting transnational enterprise owned production facilities in their country or region might study alternative forms of using the potential of transnational enterprises, such as joint ventures, minority participation, production sharing contracts, management contracts or other contractual devices, and seek prospective partners for such contracts, possibly with the help of UN agencies, such as the World Bank and UNIDO.

The exercise of national sovereignty is one of the rights of nations which in the present phase of development of developing countries improves their power position. It implies the possibility of nationalization of enterprises — national or transnational — which have not lived up to the standards expected. Thus, state-owned enterprises, if closely supervised from the viewpoint of consumer interests, could be used for the attainment of a proper balance in cases where direct government supervision and control of private enterprise is not effective. In particular, they can be thought of as a weapon against the possible monopolistic or oligopolistic practices of transnational enterprises, both national and foreign, producing essential goods or services. Nationalization giving rise to compensation effectively based on the objective evaluation of the net inflow of capital, technology and know-how provided by the transnational enterprises should not, of course, affect negatively the future flow of foreign capital.

Cooperation between governments of nations in one region or sub-region is an important means of improving their bargaining position vis-à-vis transnational enterprises. In this connection, the establishment of joint codes concerning foreign investment at the sub-regional or regional level has proved its capacity to increase the bargaining power of the host countries. Such codes should address themselves to such questions as ownership and control, financial flows and balance-of-payments, research and development, commercialization of technology, employment and labour, consumer protection, competition and market structure, transfer pricing, taxation, accounting standards and disclosure. Specifically, the following policy alternatives could be explored: limits to direct and indirect profit remittances, orientation of research and development towards technologies best fitted to the factor endowment of the developing countries, resort to transnational enterprises in the context of production contracts rather than through direct investment, elimination of discriminatory treatment in favour of transnational enterprises, restrictions on access to local financial sources, strict control of intra-company transactions and minimum disclosure standards. Other forms of joint actions by developing countries include the setting up, where appropriate, of joint inter-governmental holding bodies where direct investment by transnational enterprises is maintained.

7.3.2   *Governments of Home Countries*   Governments of developed countries, in which the seats of transnational enterprises are almost always located, should cooperate with other governments with a view to preventing any political intervention of transnational enterprises in developing countries and all unfair or restrictive practices. Governments of home and of host countries should also cooperate in order to improve the tax structure regarding transnational enterprises so as to limit and eliminate the distortion of the international division of labour among countries. The immediate objective might be to allow taxes to be collected on profits where these are in fact made (territoriality or exemption principle), rather than on the basis of the residence country principle (3).

Another objective — certainly longer-term — might be to conclude an agreement against tax havens. Governments of developed countries might also subvention the prices at which technological know-how is offered by transnational enterprises to developing countries, providing the technology is appropriate. This endeavour may be combined with the creation of a pool of technological knowledge (cf. Annex 6). Developed countries could also restrict the immigration of workers from developing countries, providing adequate additional capital and technological flow to such countries is supplied in order to create employment for the workers concerned in their own country, while, at the same time, avoiding that transnational enterprises use the latter as 'dirt-havens' to fight pollution at home.

---

(3) For a Dutch view, see J.H. Christiaanse, 'De fiscale positie van de multi-nationals', in 'Opstellen aangeboden aan Prof. Mr. J.J. Hofstra', Kluwer Deventer, 1975, p. 17. (English: 'The Fiscal Position of Multinationals'). A Swedish study on a related subject is in preparation.

7.3.3   *The International Community*   First priority must be given to the recommendation of
the 'Group of Eminent Persons' to the Secretary General of the United Nations to collect
more useful information on the activities of transnational enterprises. Steps towards
uniform accounting systems to be applied by all corporations, national and transnational
enterprises, may be helpful in improving the quality of information (4). A further
measure could consist of the creation and financing of an international body of voluntary
technical advisers in order to help strengthen the bargaining power of the governments
of prospective host countries.

In certain fields, transnational enterprises may in future be replaced by publicly owned,
truly multinational enterprises or authorities, for instance in the fields of international
rail and air transportation and the management of oceans.

The international community should formulate minimum standards of behaviour of
transnational enterprises within the context of a code of conduct with legally enforceable
elements. This code could include such subjects as obligations to refrain from intervening
in the host countries' political affairs and to avoid restrictive business practices, the
respect of the development priorities of the host countries, and the implementation of a
fair labour policy. It could also include criteria on the optimal size of enterprises based
on sound socio-economic principles. An adequate framework should be devised in order
to enable all interested parties, at the national and at the international level, to contribute
to the elaboration of such a code and subsequently to its implementation.

Furthermore, an international register could be held concerning the country by country
performance of transnational enterprises, to be made readily available to all concerned.
This could be done in the context of the UN Information and Research Centre on Transnational Enterprises with the support of regional institutions such as the planned
Information and Research Centre of the non-aligned countries.

7.3.4   *Transnational Enterprises*   Transnational enterprises should, as noted earlier, comply
with the aims of the host countries' development plans. They should be aware in
particular of the overwhelming importance of maximizing employment and value-added
in the developing countries. They should, again as noted earlier, refrain from all forms
of political interference in the affairs of host countries and avoid restrictive business
practices. They should cooperate in the study of the alternative tasks they could
undertake to carry out, such as shifting towards advisory, management and training
contracts with governments of developing countries.

7.3.5   *Trade Unions*   Trade unions should further increase their endeavours to reinforce their
countervailing power at the international level. They will have to work out rules and
procedures to reconcile within themselves the often conflicting interests of national
trade unions, keeping in mind the differences in the acuteness of the needs of workers in
different areas and countries, and differences in levels of productivity between countries.

---

(4) See A.J.H. Enthoven, 'Accountancy and Economic Development Policy',
Amsterdam-London-New York, 1973.

8.1   *Introduction: Stockholm and After*

The UN Conference on Human Environment held in Stockholm in June 1972 proclaimed environment — the global habitat of man — a matter of continuous concern for the nations of the world and set up in the form of the United Nations Environment Programme (UNEP) embryonic machinery to deal with this newly recognized dimension both of development and international affairs. In the long series of UN conferences, Stockholm stands thus high for its success in identifying a new global problematique and in reaching North-South consensus on ways of approaching it. Confrontation was avoided. The Third World countries understood that, far from being an exclusive problem of the industrialized world, environmental degradation and overtaxing of nature formed very much a part of their predicament. On the other hand, the industrialized countries abandoned their initial narrow technocratic view of environment and ended by admitting that patterns of resource use and maldistribution were an important aspect of the problematique. Both sides really grasped that they were living on *only one earth* and that the existence of international commons — oceans, sea-bed, weather and climate — as well as the finiteness of spaceship earth, were binding them into a pattern of real interdependence.

Failure to take this into account, given the unprecedented scale of human interference with nature and ecological balances, might prove disastrous to all. Egoistic policies of resource appropriation by the rich minority, the dumping of waste into seas progressively transformed into cesspools and the release of ever increasing quantities of heat, must give way to the more balanced management of world resources and environment. Balanced management must aim simultaneously at waging an immediate battle against poverty and at safeguarding the interests of future generations through the legacy of an habitable planet. Both are predominantly political and not technical issues; both belong to attempts to shape a new international order.

In view of this, the largely verbal consensus reached in Stockholm about principles, positive as it may be, should not distract us from the tasks ahead. Translating general principles into action is bound to be exceedingly difficult because of the resistance of powerful vested interests that favour the present pattern of resource use and management. This resistance is already evident in the rather low-key performance of UNEP and its modest financial capacity, and in the indifference — if not hostility — of most industrialized countries towards a programme-oriented document like the Cocoyoc Declaration (1). It is also manifest in the failure of the Law of Sea Conference (cf. Annex 10), where it proved impossible to create a regime of sea-bed exploitation capable of harnessing the resources of international commons for the war against poverty and thus to provide UNEP and UNDP (United Nations Development Programme) with an independent Source of financing.

Radical action is urgently needed. If the present trends in deterioration of human

---

(1) This declaration, issued in October 1974, as a result of a meeting of experts jointly sponsored by UNEP and UNCTAD, emphasized a need-oriented and environmentally sound approach to development planning. Its basic principles were further elaborated in *'What Now'*, the report of the 1975 Dag Hammarskjöld Project on Development and International Cooperation.

environment are allowed to continue over the next quarter of a century, we may reach in some areas a situation of no return; irreversible damage to the prospects for genuine development and effective removal of poverty from our planet, if not for the survival of mankind.

Emphasizing the problematique of human environment is a way of forcing politicians, decision-makers, international and national instutions to face the challenge of long term sustained socio-economic development.

8.2 *Problem Setting*

Man is unique among the animal species in adapting himself to a remarkably broad range of ecological niches, in transforming the natural environment up to a point where it may become almost entirely man-made and in living thus in two closely connected and inter-penetrating environments: the natural and the cultural. He is part of nature and dependent upon it for his survival and material enjoyment — air to breathe, water to drink, food to eat, plants and minerals transformed with harnessed energy into countless goods.

But civilization confers on man the power to act on nature on an ever increasing scale. For good and evil. He invents new uses for the inanimate elements present in the bio-sphere, as well as its flora and fauna (turning them into resources); he covers the surface of his planet with fields, pastures and gardens, towns and roads (using space as a resource); he enhances the surroundings in which he lives (improving his natural and artificial and dangerously reducing the genetic pool of animals and plants; he destroys soils through abusive usage, causing erosion, inundations, and unwelcome and unexpected changes in climate; he menaces biological life in oceans, lakes and rivers by polluting their waters; he poisons the atmosphere with noxious fumes; and he concentrates industrial and commercial activities in overcrowded areas up to a point where external diseconomies of congestion, accumulated pollution and alienation of modern industrial and urban life more than nullify the gains in the quality of life obtained through the increase in material standards of well-being.

The widely prevalent inequalities in income and wealth distribution both between and within countries give the poor of the Third World the worst of the two worlds. On the one hand, poverty condemns them to lives of squalor in the backyards of towns and cities; they lack drinkable water and elementary sanitary protection; they are deprived of access to schools and are often severely undernourished. On the other hand, they are the victims of the pollution caused by affluence and for which they are by no means responsible. People in the poor quarters of big cities do not travel by car and more often than not they do not have jobs in factories. But they are the most seriously affected by the motor-car and by industrial pollution because of their appalling housing conditions and location.

As for the rural poor, they are often the agents of ecological disruption. They cultivate the slopes that should be left under tree-cover or allow their sheep and goats to overgraze pastures. In this they have no other choice so long as the fertile valley belongs to the big landowner. Theirs is an economy of despair and not of farsighted husbandry of resources. And it is bound to be so until they have access to a plot of land capable of ensuring decent living to a peasant family on a sustainable basis. Ecological disruption by the poor is the consequence of inequality in wealth and land distribution. Inequality that breeds at the one end of the social spectrum overuse of soils and erosion and, at the other, subutilization of latifundia (e.g. in the form of extensive cattle breeding) and wasteful patterns of resource use for the conspicuous consumption of moneyed elites. In such a case, by no means far removed from reality, an ecologically sound management of resources cannot by achieved without land reform. Natural and social processes thus appear closely interwoven.

The combined effects of industrialization, population growth and urbanization achieved in the twentieth century, and more particularly since the end of the Second World War, lifted the Gross World Product to a level undreamt of by the generation of our grand-fathers. At the same time, however, they magnified the income differentials between rich and poor, both between rich and poor countries and within poor countries (with the notable exception of China, N. Korea, N. Vietnam and Cuba). They also brought us nearer to the brink of irreversible ecological disasters and the depletion of some essential resources. They have given rise to a number of important questions. Can we, for example, afford to continue undisturbed along this path, piling up wealth, maldistribution and ecological hazards? Should we instead stop growth, both material and demographic, and move towards a steady state? How much time is left for such a transition?

These questions were raised in a dramatic (and probably overdramatized) way by the 'Limits to Growth' report and several other more or less apocalyptic writings. All of them stem from the trivial and indisputable observation that exponential growth in a finite environment cannot last forever, either because of overcrowding or on account of the depletion of non-renewable resources and/or of the disruption of ecological cycles that account for the reproduction of renewable resources. A third scenario of the collapse might be the extinction of the human species due to the deterioration of the quality of the environment up to a point where air would become unbreathable; in this case, man-kind would disappear in the midst of plenty instead of being progressively brought to starvation (and mutual extermination in the struggle for scarce food).

The question, however, is not whether outer limits, the transgression of which would be fatal, do exist at all. Unless one indulges in wild and totally unwarranted technological optimism, their existence can be taken as granted. Instead, we should try to ascertain how close we have moved to them and, still more important, what can be done to push them further away. It is important in this connection to realize that the concept of outer limits is not an absolute but a relative one in at least two ways. Because of the tremen-dous differences in the intensity of resource exploitation and space use, outer limits are likely to make themselves felt at local levels long before the cumulative global effects are felt for spaceship earth as a whole. Moreover, the pattern of resource use will be decisive in pulling them closer to us or pushing them further away for a given volume of economic activity. Consider, for example, the dissipation of heat (thermal pollution); its amount is determined by the second law of thermodynamics and depends on the quantity of energy used. It makes all the difference, however, whether we decide to utilize solar energy – a source which flows to earth and is reflected – or whether we release additional quantities of stored heat from fossil and nuclear sources.

In the former case, the global thermal balance of the earth will not be affected; in the latter case it would. By the same token, we shold foster substitution of depletable resources by renewable resources, assuming their ecologically sound management, so as to ensure their regular reproduction. The same argument applies to the recycling and imaginative use of waste as raw material. For a given demand, the taxing of nature can thus be drastically reduced and the risk of transgressing the outer limits consequently diminished.

Viewed in this perspective, rates of economic growth are less important than rates of exploitation of nature, supposing that is that we know how to measure them. Situations can be imagined where a low or even a negative rate of growth is accompanied by rapid depletion of the stock of non-renewable resources (capital of nature) and considerable environmental degradation. And conversely, a fairly high rate of economic growth may prove ecologically sound and sparing of potentially scarce resources by resorting to the flow of renewable ones. This is easier said than done; it has the merit, however, of showing that there may be a way out of the (false) dilemma: growth versus environment.

The more so if, instead of pursuing present patterns of growth inequality, we look at the possibility of changing the uses of growth by giving priority to the satisfaction of the fundamental needs of the whole population, starting with the eradication of poverty. To the extent that this would entail the curbing of conspicuous material consumption and of artificially stimulated needs (be it by advertising, be it by the so-called demonstration effect), the most glaring instances of wasteful use of resources and environmental disruption would be attacked. In this way, more time can be bought for the transition. Growth in equality would make it less difficult for people to accept the principle of self-restraint in the satisfaction of material needs — the ideological cornerstone of the future 'steady state'. It would equally create the necessary social conditions for self-control of family size and the consequent reduction of population pressure; birth-control campaigns are likely to remain largely ineffective (unless enforced by coercion, which is clearly unacceptable) up to the time that peasants are freed from material insecurity, that infant mortality rates go down, and that the use of unpaid child labour is no longer necessary to make ends meet.

Viewed in this light, there is clearly little to be gained from speculation about impending catastrophes and the likely dates of their occurence. As for the depletion of resources, playing with compound rates of interest is suggestive only and may result in the exaggeration of dangers of impending scarcities. Possibly the only lesson which can be derived from such arithmetical entertainment is that it is unwise to extrapolate trends for the next century or so on the basis of patterns of growth observed over the past 25 years. Instead, we require more exact knowledge of the growing energy intake of mining and processing of poorer or deeply seated grades of ores, and of the dwindling ratio of net to gross energy output since this may well become the critical issue.

We have enough time (counted in decades if not centuries) to plan and implement an orderly transition without resorting to the economic euthanasia of a zero-rate of material growth that would perhaps ensure a better quality of environment to those on the top of the social pyramid but at the price of postponing indefinitely the satisfaction of the most pressing needs of those at its bottom. Of course, lip service to redistribution would be of little use. Our past record shows that we have been unable to redistribute even in periods of very rapid increases of income. A fortiori we shall fail when the rate of growth is reduced.

Exaggerating the closeness of impending dangers may prove self-defeating in both ways. On the other hand, it may lead us to despair and predatory practices ('après nous le déluge'). On the other hand, and, on the grounds that there is no time to loose, it may lead us to desperate actions; valuable options and carefully phased strategies (starting with the accelerated social and economic uplift of the rural poor of the Third World) may be overlooked. The removal of the Sword of Damocles above our heads should not be misunderstood as an invitation to forget about the environment and the ultimate finiteness of spaceship earth. To review the possibilities of harmonizing social and economic development with ecologically sound resource and environment management makes considerable sense; it stands on its own merits even without the threats of imminent disaster.

In the light of the previous argument, environment appears as an additional and important dimension of development, rather than as a subject per se, a sector, or an anternative to development. It affects development in two ways: as a challenging resource potential that ought to be used for the benefit of mankind in an ecologically sound manner; and as a direct component of the quality of life through the physical and aesthetic values of its natural, man-transformed or man-made components. From another viewpoint, environmental awareness means in reality, as already mentioned, the intro- duction of the long term, of the diachronic solidarity with future generations. Sparing resources, avoiding predatory practices and protecting environment is tantamount to ensuring that our grandchildren (and their grandchildren, etc.) will be given a fair opportunity to develop. To the extent to which the protection of environment may entail costs, these should be looked at as an investment in the future, offset as always by a sacrifice in current consumption and in most cases justified on economic grounds by the reduced cost of preventive actions as compared to the costs of remedial ones.

In this report it is argued that development should be self-reliant and endogenous — i.e. based on an autonomous decision-making and future designing capacity — need oriented and environmentally sound. In order to make operational the later conditions we require:

(I)   a set of expanded social rationality criteria for resource management and use, based on development ethics;
(II) an institutional machinery for global resource management; and
(III) a specific strategy to harmonize social and ecological objectives.
Let us look briefly at each of these requirements.

The two main principles of development ethics have already been referred to: solidarity with the poor of our age and solidarity with future generations. All people must be guaranteed the right to have their fundamental needs satisfied not only with respect to food, shelter, health protection, and access to education but also regarding enhancement goods and opportunities for creative work in order to fulfill their personalities; the problem is not one of providing feedlots for passive creatures but to foster human activity. The prevailing maldistribution of resources must be accordingly corrected. The universal right to a decent minimum entails a ceiling on personal material consumption.

Furthermore, to ensure that the interests of generations that will succeed us are really taken care of, it is necessary to broaden considerably the time-horizon within which resource-use decisions are taken and, in some cases, to learn to value the future more than the present. This is clearly in contradiction with prevailing practices with their heavy discount of the future. The consequence of this argument is that resource allo- cation cannot be left entirely to uncorrected market mechanisms and to the one-tracked, profit-oriented rationality of the enterprise. An appropriate institutional machinery is called for to enforce the criteria of expanded social rationality. The same holds true with respect to space-use: preservation of options for the future and harmonization of various uses for the same space will not be achieved without public intervention.

Finally, while it is conceivable to expect from enterprises steps designed to curb pollution that affects their functioning as a negative externality, global ecological equilibria will never be achieved through the sum total of these partial steps even by enforcing regu- lations inspired by the rather principle 'the polluter should pay' (2).

An authority must therefore be entrusted with global resource and environmental management. Its responsibility would consist of monitoring the changes in the stock of the capital of nature and in the working of basic ecological cycles that sustain the flow of renewable resources (such as the cycle of water, the renewal of soils, weather and climate) in reviewing the interfaces between the different groups of resources that are treated by sectoral agencies (seas, inland waters, soils, forests, energy, mines) and also the interactions between different ecosystems (high mountains, river basins, coastal plains, seas). The authority should establish management rules based on a systems approach and promote in this way the elimination of wasteful uses of resources such as water (3). In the long run, global management of inland resources will prove decisive in preventing the pollution of the seas.

The positive effects of global resource management would, however, be lost to a great extent should the present strategies of wasteful growth through inequality be pursued. The need is, therefore, to explore alternative development styles — the latter word emphasizes the margin of subjective societal choice — socially oriented, more egalitarian intra- and internationally, and environmentally sound. This calls simultaneously for the reassessment of lifestyles and consumption patterns, the search for appropriate technologies and the skilfull location of human activities.

8.4   *Lifestyles and Consumption Patterns*

Although it has become a commonplace to stress the need for a change in lifestyles, we know precious little about how to make this concept operational. Is it possible to move to alternative patterns of lifestyles without changing our towns, villages and transportation systems? Is is a problem of software, hardware, or both? How far can we move by modifying the patterns of time-use (aménagement du temps) — individual and collective — day, week, year and life-wise? At what level of labour productivity does it make sense to reduce working hours in favour of disposable time instead of further increasing material wealth and marketed services? How much marketed consumption is enough, and what could be the share of household or collective non-professional activities performed as an hobby? How do patterns of time-use interact with patterns of space-use and of habitat?

All these questions are additions to the classical problems of apportionment of consumption between collective and individual, material and non-material, delivered through the market or as a social service. While analysing the many options open to society in

----

(2) The polluter should pay for what: the compensation for damage done, the cost of antipollution which may become the right to continue to pollute, the shift to low-waste technologies? On the other hand, who is going to bear the cost; the polluter by squeezing his profit margin, the State by receiving less taxes, or the consumer by paying a higher unit cost for the product? The reply to the latter question depends of course on the configuration of the market, the price elasticity of demand etc. The theoretical case constructed on the unlikely assumption of a perfectly competitive market for a good with a high price elasticity of demand is likely to prove an exception rather than the rule.
(3) Water management offers the most striking example of wastefulness, due to poor design of urban water supply and irrigation systems, lack of recycling facilities in industries, etc. The impending shortage of water can be successfully met by better management, except in particularly arid areas. Even there some hopes may be attached to desalinization of water with solar energy and, as far as agriculture is concerned, to more skilfull use of arid zone plants as well as resorting to techniques based on closed water circuits.

response to these questions, it is possible to introduce resource and environmental considerations as relevant criteria: we may, for instance, decide to choose a low-energy profile for our consumption patterns and give in this respect preference to housing, urban transportation and time-use systems that are low energy-consuming.

8.5 *Appropriate Technologies*

The next step will consist of looking for appropriate technologies (cf. Annex 6). The appropriateness of a technology cannot be evaluated in absolute terms. It always requires contextual analysis and a clear specification of pertinent criteria — be they social, economic, political or ecological — to be applied in a given historical situation. We may, however, suggest some broad guidelines for use in the search for environmentally prudent technologies, which are defined here in a less restrictive way than so-called 'soft technologies' (4).

First of all, such technologies should be low-waste. The rule of the game for the enterprise in an unrestricted market economy is to internalize profits and to externalize social costs and, therefore, to dump pollution onto society. Under the pressure of anti-pollution regulations, the enterprise may eventually fit at the end of the production-pollution chain as an anti-pollution link. This is better than nothing. From a social viewpoint, however, it remains a very poor solution. Anti-pollution adds to GNP in the same way as armaments. But its contribution to the satisfaction of positive societal needs is nil. It is, therefore, crucially important to seek new ways of internalizing the environmental dimension at the technological level. This calls for the design of low-waste technological systems that resort, wherever possible, to recycling and to complementary production processes in which the waste of one level is used as a raw material in the next. In matter of fact, the single most important consequence for economics of the new awareness of environment may well be the rediscovery of the ecological cycle as a paradigm for production systems, techno-industrial complexes and the articulation of human settlements with industry, agriculture and aquaculture.

Another approach is to lengthen the life-cycle of equipments and durable goods with the consequent possibility of reducing the consumption of energy and materials incorporated in these products (and not subject to recycling or, otherwise, requiring substantial amounts of energy for recycling). In many cases it would be both possible and desirable to counter the present trend towards accelerated obsolescence of products both by introducing changes in their technological design and by better organizing their maintenance. The choice of the rate of obsolescence should form the subject of deliberate social policy. This would make it possible to evaluate the trade-offs between conservation or recycling of materials, between more durability and a lower rate of introduction of technological progress, etc. (5).

---

(4) We are all for 'soft technologies' characterized by low environmental impacts, moderate use of depletable resources, high labour intensity, absence of economies of scale, and conviviality. Except for the fact that the universe of such technologies meeting reasonable productivity criteria is for the moment very limited indeed.

(5) A special case is offered by the building industry. Are we interested in building today schools that will remain for centuries, making difficult future changes in the educational process? The so-called 'flexible architecture' seems to offer a compromise between the use of durable materials and the possibility of easy adaptation of the interior of the building. Let us also note that in some very specific cases ephemerization of goods is to be preferred (e.g. the one-shot syringe or the paper handkerchief).

Finally, we should stress the already mentioned substitution of renewable resources by non-renewable ones. In the field of energy, this calls for a grossly increased research effort on solar techniques, the only ones capable of offering a lasting and entirely safe solution to the energy problem. It is far superior to nuclear energy since it involves neither a Faustian bargain nor complications with the earth's thermal balance. After a quarter century of unprecedented research, nuclear plants supply only a tiny fraction of our energy needs; the costs of the plants go up (largely because of security requirements) and recent studies indicate that the ratio of net to gross energy produced is likely to be lower than initially expected. Under these circumstances, the least one would expect is the benefit of the doubt and that those scientists who take an optimistic view of solar energy be strongly supported. This for no other reason than as a strategy of insurance for the future. Instead, futile cost-benefit calculations are evolved which suggest the advantages of the nuclear option; these must not be allowed to influence a choice that may prove decisive for the fate of mankind.

We are not arguing for a complete stop to the construction of nuclear plants. Such would be impossible at this stage. But what still lies in our power is to work for a strategy of transition from an oil to a solar age in which nuclear energy would play a restricted and transitory role, while conventional sources of energy are fully exploited in an environmentally sound way. In a sense, we might say back to the solar age, since our life on the planet has always been conditioned by the bio-conversion of solar energy. Quite apart from solar power plants and of the less spectacular but immediately feasible applications of solar energy in housing, agriculture and post-harvest technologies, bio-conversion appears, after the spectacular rise in oil prices, as a very convenient supplier of raw materials for industries. Recent studies have emphasized the scope for the production under economically competitive conditions of bio-energy in the form of methane, methanol, ethylic alcohol from forest products, energy plantations (e.g. sugar-cane or cassava), agricultural and urban waste as well as aquatic plants. A further slight increase in the relative price of oil might open the market for a vast spectrum of chemical products such as, for example, plastics processed from vegetal raw materials and waste. It is expected that their range and competitiveness will rapidly increase with the progress of biological and enzymatic engineering. Building materials offer another promising area where materials based on bio-conversion could stage a spectacular return. Finally, let us mention the production of protein either by direct extraction from non-edible leaves or by growing micro-organisms on cellulose and waste substratum. When used as animal feed, these proteins would make it possible to release for human food production the areas now used for fodder crops.

Thus, bio-conversion of solar energy could become once more the cornerstone of many industries. Interesting as this may be for all countries, irrespective of their climate and industrial advancement, this new turn in technology should be particularly welcome in tropical regions that enjoy a comparative advantage as far as natural conditions for photosynthesis are concerned. A unique opportunity seems to be unfolding for them to industrialize on an entirely new technological basis, well adapted to their climatic conditions and environmentally sound, provided it is supported by rational management of renewable resources, systematic replanting of forests, etc. Otherwise, such industrialization might lead to a major ecological disaster (6).

---

(6) A rationally managed forest is a renewable resource. An unmanaged forest is but a mine of trees.

8.6 *Patterns of Space Use*

The same economic and human activities are bound to have widely diverging environmental effects according to their location. The inconvenience of overcrowding and also of very low densities are only too well known and ecologists have put forward the concept of the carrying-capacity of an ecosystem. Under certain circumstances, badly chosen locations can magnify environmental problems in an often explosive way, as cumulative and synergistic effects may appear and thresholds of tolerance be transgressed. And conversely, a wise locational policy can play a major role in harmonizing socio-economic development with environmental concern by avoiding further congestion of heavily industrialized and urbanized areas, but also the progressive desertification of rural areas not well endowed with fertile agricultural land.

The spectrum of locational policies is very large indeed. It ranges from the choice of the topographic site for a factory, passing through the design of a balanced network of human settlements up to the international division of labour and redeployment of industries on a world-wide scale. Considerations of space, resource availability and environmental concern, add strong new arguments in favour of rapid industrialization of Third World countries.

8.7 *Ecodevelopment*

The concept of ecodevelopment, actively sponsored by UNEP, is an application of the framework outlined above. It stresses the need to look for concrete development strategies capable of making a good and ecologically sound use of the specific resources of a given ecosystem in order to satisfy the basic needs of the local population. Ecodevelopment insists on the variety of ecological and cultural situations and, therefore, on the diversity of proposed solutions as well as on the importance of citizen participation in the identification of needs and resources, the research of appropriate techniques, the design and implementation of development schemes and structural changes when needed. It is not a mere set of ecotechniques, although redefinition of technological options is likely to play a major role.

Ecodevelopment was first thought of as a guideline for defining microregional or regional development strategies in predominantly rural tropical areas. Hence its interest in evaluating, through ethnobotanical and botanical surveys, the potential of local forest, field and water plants, domesticating local animal species, designing and testing mixed crops, fish and cattle breeding systems well adapted to the forest, ecological farms producing their energy from waste, wind, small waterfalls, etc. and emphasizing to the maximum all the complementarities. Of course, there is always room left for the introduction of 'exotic species', but preference is given in such a case to plants and animals from similar ecosystems.

Applied to housing — both rural and urban — the ecodevelopment approach stresses the need for ecologically sound designs for both human settlements and for individual dwellings. Software in this area is decisive and, furthermore, it should be possible to supplement it with some low-cost, soft technologies for water cooling and heating, climatization, etc. Local building materials are of course to be used and trees and plants must play an important functional as well as an aesthetic role. Energy could be obtained either from a small waterfall or through a combination of non-conventional techniques, preferably linked in a system, so as to ensure reasonable reliability of supply. The argument in favour of development of industries based on bio-conversion of solar energy may be interpreted as the addition of an 'industrial floor' to ecodevelopment strategies and in this way extending enormously their applicability, both in Third World and industrialized countries.

We have referred to harmonization strategies at the national and local level. Let us now turn to the international aspects of such strategies.

First of all, it must be recognized that the pressure on world resources and environment comes at present mainly from the industrialized countries. There is much talk about the 'population explosion' but millions of non-consumers weigh little on the balance of resources and ecological equilibria, at any rate far less than the minority of rich. The non-consumers are, however, highly vulnerable to ecological hazards which can strike far away from the source of pollution. This situation must be recognized and the responsibilities clearly assumed; responsibilities concerning both the cost of global environmental management and the much more complex issue of finding ways and means of reducing the present maldistribution of resources — the main subject of this report.

A more specific problem is to set up adequate machinery for the likely redeployment of industries in an environmentally sound manner. Third World countries should by no means become 'pollution havens'. Neither should they give up the possibility of rapidly increasing their relative share in world output of basic industrial goods. The way out is to design and enforce strict environmental policies for new industrial projects seeking a location in the Third World. This is, in the last instance, a matter for national governments. To the extent, however, to which careful screening of each project will be required so as to ascertain its environmental impact under precise siting conditions, UNIDO should set up a special unit to assist governments in this task.

Finally, let us return to the regime of the 'international commons' extending this term not only to oceans and the sea-bed but also to air, outer space, climate and weather. We have here two different problems. On the one hand, an International Control Agency must be set up to monitor, prevent or denounce, whatever the case, abusive usage of international commons e.g. for dumping of noxious waste or modifying climate with possible adverse effects on other countries, etc. On the other, and as already mentioned, the sea-bed and other resources constituting the 'common heritage of mankind' should be used for the benefit of the poorest section of mankind and as an autonomous source of finance for UNEP and UNDP activities. To accomplish this, an ocean-toll could be imposed on vessels and on aircraft by analogy with tolls paid by trucks on highways. Given the considerable volume of sea-traffic, even a very modest unit-fee per ton of merchandise transported across the oceans to ports situated in the industrialized countries would give the United Nations a substantial source of additional development financing.

8.9   *Medium Term Proposals*

Certain research priorities have been emphasized in this annex. Those relevant in the medium term can be summarized as follows:
(I) We require a better understanding of the working of outer limits and, in this connection, of the interactions between natural and social processes. 'Nature accounting' must be developed to enable us to follow the changes in the stock of nature capital. It must be then brought in line with social indicators of quality of life and economic accounting of costs of development strategies. Ways must be equally found to quantify the wastefulness of present patterns of resource use. A major re-assessment of technological effort is called for in order to foster new uses of solar energy and renewable resources, with special emphasis on technologies for decentralized use of nonconventional sources of energy. We must learn to design techno-industrial structures as true systems and to explore the interfaces between lifestyles, urban design and production systems.

Ecodevelopment requires mass mobilization of participatory research on specific solutions to local problems. The range of subjects explored in an ecodevelopment perspective should cover all basic needs in the realm of food, habitat, health and sanitation, as well as education. As ecodevelopment also calls for bold institutional and organizational innovations, life-size experiments should be promoted with active support from UNEP, UNDP and international funding organizations without forgetting, however, that the primary responsibility for endogenous development is by definition vested with concerned populations and their political bodies.

(II) National agencies should be created with responsibilities for global resource management. They should be entrusted with the supervision and coordination of the activities of sectoral and regional bodies.

(III) The viability of the proposal to change development styles depends upon our ability to outline transitional strategies. Such strategies should give special attention to alternative uses of existing productive capacities, redeployment of industrial activities, substitution of non-renewable by renewable resources, and the creation of new job opportunities in resource management and social services activities. Work on these should start as soon as possible.

(IV) Life-size ecodevelopment experiments should be promoted in different ecosystems and cultural settings and the experience thus gained compared, analysed and disseminated.

(V) At the international level, it is necessary to define the regime of the 'international commons' and to set up an agency to exploit their resources in the interest of the poorest section of the world's population. The introduction of ocean-tolls and air-tolls should be considered. Another agency should be established to control the use of 'international commons'. UNIDO could be entrusted with setting up a technical assistance unit specialized in the evaluation of environmental impacts of new industrial projects.

8.10   *Long Term Proposals*

Global management of resources and environment will have to be increasingly tackled at a transnational and even world level, as well as at the national level. The issues involved are very complex and politically sensitive. We do not have as yet effective machinery for dealing with conflicts arising out of the management of rivers, lakes and sea basins belonging to several countries nor for the transnational effects of pollution.
Attention must be given to this matter by the United Nations and, above all, by UNEP.

Useful as it may be, an institution for conflict resolution cannot replace positive machinery for dealing with global resource and environmental management and in this way, it is to be hoped, preventing the emergence of conflicts. A supranational agency does not seem feasible even in the long-run given the sensibility of governments to the question of sovereign control over resources. Efforts must, therefore, be directed towards some form of continuous formulation and voluntary coordination of national resource, environmental and locational policies. Ultimately, such a procedure will involve a considerable degree of harmonization between economic plans that will have internalized environment as one dimension of development. This is a major and very difficult challenge to the new international order, even as a long term objective. It is to be hoped that the Mediterranean Project initiated under UNEP sponsorship will provide some relevant inputs and lessons. At any rate, thinking on possible institutional designs should start without further delay and UNEP should give it high priority. Proposals made in Annex 10 on ocean management for the establishment of functional confederations of international organizations and the creation of integrative machinery would appear particularly relevant in this respect.

Arms Reduction
Inga Thorsson

9.1 *Introduction*

It is a fact of life that nations at present interpret their security problems as requiring the kind of measures which make the prospect of a disarmed world very distant indeed. And it is an interpretation which seems destined to persist into at least the forseeable future. Despite this 'fact of life' — and of death — the quantitative and qualitative level at which armaments are kept and from which the armament race continues unabated, is such that it demands the urgent attention of everyone who is concerned about the future course of mankind: a course towards a meaningful and constructive existence in search for human fulfilment or towards a display of an increasingly meaningless destructive capability, threatening the very survival of the human race.

The superpowers have, between them, built up a nuclear arsenal equivalent to more than a million Hiroshima bombs (1). The US alone has a stockpile of nuclear weapons corresponding (in 1974) to 615,385 Hiroshima bombs. Based on estimates of casualties of that cataclysmic event in August 1945, this represents a potential 'overkill' capacity 12 times the present world population. Besides, the burdens imposed by military expenditures on the economies of societies and human beings everywhere have now grown into such proportions that they constitute serious obstacles to anything worthy of the term 'human progress'.

9.2 *Analysis of the State of Armament*

At constant (1970) prices and exchange rates, *world military expenditures* in 1974 stood at $ 210 billion. This represents an increase in annual spending, in constant prices, of 68 per cent in the 20 year period between 1954 and 1974. The sum total is approximately divided, as an analysis of the military budgets of the 12 countries responsible for three-quarters of world military expenditures will show, into the following categories: 30 per cent is used to pay for uniformed personnel; another 30 per cent to buy weapons and equipment; a third 30 per cent is spent on construction, operation and maintenance of weapons and equipment. The remaining 10 per cent is used to finance research and development in the field of armaments.

Current prices expenditures in 1973 were $ 244 billion. This means that in every hour of that year the nations of this earth — rich and poor — spent $ 30 million on their armed forces and on armaments (2). The increase seems to continue unabated, as current expenditures in 1975 are estimated to be *close to $ 300 billion*.

These enormous sums must of necessity be compared with total world financial transfers from rich to poor countries specifically aimed at the betterment of human conditions. Official development assistance in 1973 amounted to $ 10 billion which means that it stood at 4 per cent compared with every dollar spent on armaments. Military expenditures should also be compared with sums spent on international cooperation for peace and development through the United Nations system. At approximately $ 1.5 billion (excluding the World Bank Group), these are 163 times less than armament costs.

_____

(1) Stockholm International Peace Research Institute (SIPRI) Yearbook, 1975.
(2) Ruth Leger Sivard: 'Let them Eat Bullets', Bulletin of the Atomic Scientists, April 1975.

It is a self-evidence fact that the military alliances in general and the super-powers in particular are the great military spenders. In 1974, NATO- and Warsaw pact countries were responsible for *80 per cent of total world expenditures*; the US, the USSR, the UK and France accounted for 67 per cent; the US and the USSR together for 60 per cent. A development worthy of attention, however, is that in the 20 year period between 1965 and 1974, the share of Third World countries in world military spending *increased from 6 per cent to 17 per cent* — without any corresponding increase in these countries' share of total world financial resources.

Behind this trend lies a rapidly growing *export of arms* from rich to poor countries, a part of a process whereby the rich get increasingly richer and the poor increasingly poor in terms of their capacity to satisfy basic human needs. In 1974, the value of arms exported to Third World countries was 40 per cent higher than in the preceding year.

Non-nuclear arms export generally amounted in 1974 to *$ 18 billion*. Of this the US appeared to be responsible for about two-thirds or $ 12 billion. It has been pointed out, however, that even more important than the figures themselves is the fact that, in contrast to the situation prevailing earlier, the arms trade now encompasses the most technologically advanced weapons, 'hot off the design tables' (3). According to the Stockholm International Peace Research Institute (SIPRI) Yearbook 1975, weapons are often sold to other countries even before they enter the arsenals of the producing countries. Flows of sophisticated weapons are rapidly moving into the politically unstable parts of the Third World, as Table 1 clearly shows.

Table 1   *Regional Distribution of Major Weapons' Exports to the Third World in 1974*

Region	Per cent of total arms exports of			
	US	USSR	France	UK
Middle East	67.5	74.8	19.5	50.1
Far East (excl. Vietnam)	9.4	3.6	–	6.7
South Asia	0.4	9.3	8.1	8.3
Africa	4.6	7.2	45.2	7.3
Latin America	6.8	4.5	10.6	27.5

Source: 'Disarmament or Destruction', SIPRI 1975.

A second important trend is the establishment of national defence industries in several Third World Countries, particularly those which, for a variety of reasons, fear a disruption in their regular arms imports. While in 1960 there was virtually no production of arms in the developing world, the SIPRI register of licensed production of major weapons listed 18 Third World countries with such production. The majority of these, 14 countries, are referred to by SIPRI as possessing their own design as well as production capacity.

The *resource implications* of world military expenditures are enormous and should be reviewed, however briefly.

According to the most common estimates, about 50 million persons are employed,

---

(3) Anne Hessing Cahn: 'Have Arms, Will Sell', Bulletin of the Atomic Scientists, April 1975.

directly or indirectly, for military purposes — as members of regular armed forces and paramilitary forces as well as employees in defence ministries and industries (4). Particular attention should be given to the fact that close to *half a million scientists and engineers* — almost *half* the world's scientific and technical manpower — devote their talents and skills to military research and development, at a cost of between $ 20 and $ 25 billion annually. These sums represent 40 per cent of all, public and private, R&D expenditures. To state it differently: the civilian part of the world economy embracing economic and social development — 94 per cent of world GNP — utilizes only 60 per cent of the world's scientific and technical talents to satisfy peaceful human needs, while the military sector — accounting for 6 per cent of world GNP — commands 40 per cent of these talents to improve existing arms and to develop new ones. This is the result of the increasingly high sophistication of weapons, as is shown by the fact that countries with developed military industries employ a far greater proportion of the labour force and, even more so, of scientists and engineers for research, development and production of military equipment than the military expenditures percentage of the GNP (5).

Military expenditures represent, to varying degrees, the use of a wide range of *raw materials* for military purposes. Some of these natural resources will almost certainly become scarce in the long term. Their continued military application already prevents them from being used for badly needed civilian economic purposes. A UN report published in 1972 reviewed the consumption of selected raw materials for military purposes in the United States in 1970. The estimates of percentage total use of each commodity are shown in Table 2.

Table 2   *Consumption of Selected Raw Materials for Military Purposes in the United States in 1970*

Raw material	Estimate percentage used for military purposes	Raw material	Estimate percentage used for military purposes
Bauxite	14.0	Tin	8.8
Copper	13.7	Chromium	7.6
Lead	11.3	Iron	7.5
Zinc	11.0	Manganese	7.5
Nickel	9.7	Petroleum	4.8
Molybdenum	9.3		

Source: 'Disarmament and Development', Report of the Group of Experts, United Nations, 1972.

The other 1972 UN report, already referred to, states as self-evident that the present level of arms imports and arms production in the Third World constitutes an impediment to the pursuit of alternative opportunities for economic growth and development. Since 1972, as indicated above, military expenditure — and as a direct consequence the military use of scarce resources — has grown sharply, thereby increasing the diversion of these resources from civilian use.

Up to now reference has been made to armaments and armament costs generally. Special

---

(4) See for example 'Economic and Social Consequences of the Arms Race and of Military Expenditure', United Nations, 1972.
(5) Idem.

attention must, however, for obvious reasons, be given to the existence of a huge and growing *nuclear* arsenal. Since the dawn of the nuclear age in the summer of 1945, mankind has been under a constant, serious and growing threat of nuclear extinction. The states possessing nuclear weapons have found neither the will nor the capacity to dismantle their nuclear arsenals and forswear the use of a nuclear capability for military purposes. They have not even found themselves able to reach agreement on a comprehensive ban on all nuclear weapon testing.

The unbelievably destructive power accumulated, with an *'overkill' capacity* many times the present world population, exists in a great variety of forms, which are under continuous improvement through sophisticated and costly R&D. The nuclear arsenal is composed of so-called strategic and so-called tactical weapons. It is the strategic capability which has received the most attention and which forms the main subject of on-going bilateral super-power talks on the limitation of nuclear arms. Tactical nuclear weapons have received much less attention, a situation which, in view of their incredibly destructive capability, needs urgently to be rectified. In continental Europe alone, the US and the USSR have deployed 10,500 (7,000 + 3,500) tactical nuclear weapons. Should they ever be put to use, they would result in the obliteration of the European continent and the end of the European civilization as we know it: military strategists are virtually unanimous that it would be impossible to prevent nuclear escalation should nuclear weapons of any kind be used. The same threat of course exists in all other parts of the world where nuclear weapon states have deployed their 'overkill' resources.

9.3 *Prospects for Arms Reduction*

What has been said about the armaments race and its implications in terms of the use of scarce human and material resources for negative and destructive purposes has a direct bearing on the possibilities of this generation of mankind to *rectify past and ongoing errors*, to steer away from the inhuman use of our common resources, a state of affairs determined by power domination and resulting in severe inequities, injustices, human suffering and the ever present threat of devastation.

Always implicit in the present situation of great power domination through military force is the threat of a new world war with its only too obvious end result.

The present state of affairs in the field of armaments is incompatible with the quest for a new international order and every effort will need to be made to change the present and likely course of events. In the first instance, more substantive results must be seen to emerge from arms limitation negotiations.

The results attained from multi- and bilateral *disarmament negotiations* are very far from impressive. Multilateral negotiations have been going on in their present form since 1962, first through what was called the Eighteen Nations Conference on Disarmament (ENDC) convened by the US and the USSR under the auspices of the United Nations, later transformed into the Conference of the Committee on Disarmament (CCD) with a membership of 31 states (although France has never participated, making it 30). In various forms, including bilateral talks and summit meetings, the super-powers have meanwhile kept their disarmament conversation going. This conversation has taken place without the participation of other states. These have been able to do little more than await possible results — results which, of course, have global implications.

A list of the major multilateral and bilateral achievements during years of tedious disarmament negotiations since the early 1960's would read as follows:

A   *Multilateral agreements*

1   Antarctic Treaty, prohibiting any measure of a military nature in the Antarctic, 1961.
2   Treaty banning nuclear-weapon tests in the atmosphere, in outer space and under water (Partial Test Ban Treaty), 1963.
3   Treaty on principles governing the activities of states in the exploration and use of outer space, including the moon and other celestial bodies (Outer Space Treaty), 1967.
4   Treaty for the prohibition of nuclear weapons in Latin America (Treaty of Tlatelolco), signed in 1967.
5   Treaty on the non-proliferation of nuclear weapons (Non-Proliferation Treaty - NPT), 1970.
6   Treaty on the prohibition of the emplacement of nuclear weapons and other weapons of mass destruction on the seabed and the ocean floor and in the subsoil thereof (Seabed Treaty), 1972.
7   Convention on the prohibition of the development, production and stockpiling of bacteriological (biological) and toxic weapons and on their destruction (BW Convention), 1975.

B   *Bilateral agreements between the US and the USSR*

1   Agreement on measures to reduce the risk of outbreak of nuclear war between the US and the USSR (Nuclear Accidents Agreement), 1971.
2   Treaty on the limitation of anti-ballistic missile systems (SALT ABM Treaty), 1972.
3   Interim agreement on certain measures with respect to the limitation of strategic offensive arms (SALT Interim Agreement), 1972.
4   Agreement on the prevention of nuclear war, 1973.
5   Protocol to the Treaty on the limitation of anti-ballistic missile systems (SALT ABM Treaty), signed 1974.
6   Treaty on the limitation of underground nuclear weapon tests (Threshold Test Ban Treaty), signed 1974.

The rather unanimous view within the disarmament community would seem to be that this list is far from impressive. Efforts must continue, in a spirit of realistic appraisal but not disillusionment.

As part of such a realistic appraisal, an answer should be sought to the question of whether — in spite of repeated references to the spirit of détente — a degree of polarization still exists between the two super-powers which constitutes a serious obstacle to progress in their bilateral negotiations, in terms of real and genuine disarmament. This question would seem to be even more important since such a situation would also have a decisive influence on multilateral disarmament efforts. However, a case could be made for the view that other circumstances are wholly or partly responsible for the slowness in bilateral talks. One such circumstance is the fact that the two super-powers are motivated towards continuing the armaments race by their considerable mutual distrust. Another is the observation that there seems to exist a mutuality of professional interests among the military establishments in both super-powers, resulting in — possibly tacit — mutual agreement to eliminate, through agreements or treaties, only such weapons or activities which seem of little or no significance to these military establishments. Examples to be quoted can be taken from the list above: The Seabed Treaty and the Bacteriological Warfare Convention. One conclusion which could be drawn is that while this mutuality of interest results in a reinforcement of each others position, the arms controllers and disarmers on their side are weak, divided and ineffective, thus finding themselves in an exposed and poor bargaining position.

The question of a possible agreement on the *reduction of military expenditures*, as a step towards disarmament, is from time to time placed on the agenda of the international arms control debate. The Soviet Union suggested in 1973 that an item be placed on the agenda of the XXVIII session of the UN General Assembly entitled 'Reduction of the military budgets of States permanent members of the Security Council by 10 per cent and utilization of part of the funds thus saved to provide assistance to developing countries" The Assembly subsequently requested the Secretary General, assisted by a group of experts, to prepare a report reviewing this possibility; it was to cover not only members of the Security Council but also other states with a major economic and military potential. This report was submitted to the XXIX Assembly session in 1974, which invited governments to communicate to the Secretary-General, their views and suggestions on its content before 30th June 1975. Encouragingly enough, the Coordinating Bureau of Non-Aligned Countries meeting in Havana, Cuba, in March 1975 had this to say on the subject: 'Within the context of the economic crisis, efforts to reduce the enormous armaments expenditures and use the resources thus saved mainly to aid the developing countries, has acquired a renewed importance'. This statement was followed up at the meeting of Foreign Ministers of the Non-Aligned Countries in Lima, August 1975, when, in their final statement, they emphasized the urgent need to convert the resources used on armaments into resources for economic and social development. They suggested that if the proposed World Disarmament Conference should not prove possible, a special session of the UN General Assembly should be convened in order to deal with the disarmament problem.

As noted earlier, the way in which national security interests are interpreted obviously dictate the size of military budgets. At present, interests are understood in such a way that their safeguarding requires the commitment of vast human and material resources. International armaments debates have however resulted in fairly widespread agreements on the supposition that national security interests can in fact be realistically safeguarded by *considerably lower levels of armaments* than are at present the case. A fact enforcing this argument, and already referred to, is the conclusion being reached by increasing numbers of states, including the great powers, that the rapid growth of costs stemming from the rapid advances in military technology constitutes a grave strain on their economies. This suggests that a reduction in armaments spending need in no way jeopardize national security. The savings involved would not only benefit the economies of nations involved but could also serve to give new dimensions to development cooperation efforts.

Economists specializing in the analysis of military budgets seem agreed in seeing certain advantages in reductions of military expenditures as a means of approaching disarmament. Limiting the monetary resources available for military purposes has, in their view, an element of flexibility and practicality which might be attractive to governments, allowing them, within limits, a certain freedom of action. To counteract, on the other hand, any negative effects on other states of this very freedom of action, it seems to these economists of decisive importance to combine agreements on reductions of military expenditures with measures aimed at limiting weapon systems. Particularly important here are weapons of mass destruction and offensive systems, such as nuclear weapons and biological and chemical weapons.

None should be surprised that *nuclear disarmament* has been on the agenda and has been given the highest priority in disarmament efforts made since the early 1960's. The achievements so far, in terms of certain limited agreements, are, as stated above, completely unsatisfactory in that they imply no reduction whatsoever in the horrifying stockpile of nuclear armoury.

The future fate of the whole non-proliferation regime, as embodied in the Non-Proliferation Treaty, may well be placed in serious jeopardy if the nuclear-weapon states do not show the will and capacity for disarmament that was so strongly requested at the Conference on the Review of this Treaty, held in May 1975. In the Final Declaration adopted by the Conference it was expressed as follows:

'The Conference appeals to the nuclear-weapon States parties to the negotiation on the limitation of strategic arms to endeavour to conclude at the earliest possible date the new agreement that was outlined by their leaders in November 1974.

The Conference looks forward to the commencement of follow-on negotiations on further limitations of, and significant reductions in, their nuclear weapons systems as soon as possible following the conclusion of such an agreement.'

This is all the more important in view of the fact that the world community possibly faces a considerable increase in nuclear explosion capability as a result of the ongoing expansion of nuclear energy programmes in a great many countries, a development which could place the nuclear Non-Proliferation ideology in serious jeopardy. In the view of a number of experts, around 35 states could, within the space of ten years, develop the capacity to explode a nuclear device — for peaceful or non-peaceful purposes — as a side effect of their nuclear energy programmes. This of course has all kinds of consequences for mankind's struggle for meaningful survival. It should be noted that the five expert participants attending a Harvard/M.I.T. Arms Control Seminar in autumn 1975 agreed that a nuclear war seemed likely before the end of the century.

Increased worldwide attention must also be drawn to the fact that the expansion of nuclear explosion capability will result in the establishment of rapidly growing stockpiles of plutonium, with the equally growing need for shipment of this material. This will increase, to a dangerous extent, the possibilities open to irresponsible groups and individuals for obtaining amounts of plutonium which could be used for purposes of sabotage or blackmail. The technical know-how required to manufacture a crude nuclear device is becoming increasingly easy to obtain. Most of the other materials required can be found in a school chemistry laboratory.

As a result of the Review Conference, it is hoped that, by its request for a Second Review Conference in 1980 and for the inclusion in the General Assembly agenda in 1976 and 1978 of a review of the implementation of the conclusions of the first Review Conference, the non-nuclear world community will be able to keep alive that element of dynamic momentum in efforts that is urgently requested *to make non-proliferation and nuclear disarmament successful.*

The horrors of a possible nuclear war notwithstanding, one should also be aware of the *developments in conventional warfare* in recent years, leading up to the deployment of increasingly indiscriminate and unnecessarily cruel weapons. These have been tested on the battlefield, on civilian populations and on the human environment in recent wars. They are rightly called 'terror weapons' and their use should be officially condemned and banned.

9.4   *Some Reasons for the Present Stalemate in Disarmament Negotiations*

While it would, as a matter of course, be difficult to make an exhaustive list of the reasons for the present highly unsatisfactory state of disarmament negotiations — current political crises in different parts of the world would for example hardly lend themselves to correct estimates of their impact on armament levels — some factors of more principal importance could be listed:

(I) Technical development in the armaments field, particularly by the two super-powers, seems to have a life of its own and to follow its own laws as if directed by 'anonymous forces'. This gives rise to new military doctrines and strategies, resulting all too often in new obstacles to real and genuine disarmament.

(II) The military establishment — or to expand the concept to what is sometimes called the military-industrial complex — seems to exercise a considerable pressure on political authorities, and forms an obstacle to concessions which might lead the way toward disarmament.

(III) Excessive secrecy concerning present levels as well as type of armament expenditure, quality and capacity of various types of arms seems to create an atmosphere of mutual fear and distrust, leading to probably unnecessary countermeasures and a spiralling arms race.

(IV) New weapons and/or new weapon systems seem to be introduced as "bargaining chips" into disarmament talks; if these momentarily fail to achieve results, these weapons and/or weapon systems are further developed and, in some cases, ultimately deployed, leading to new and higher levels of the arms race.

(V) The concept of national security still seems — in year 31 of the nuclear era — to be equated with military security, a concept which gradually assumes less credibility with every phase of continuing horizontal and vertical nuclear proliferation.

(VI) Military strength and capability, and in particular the possession of a nuclear capacity, still seem to confer prestige and esteem on nations — several examples could be quoted.

These factors — of a material and a nonmaterial character — will have to be carefully examined and assessed as part of continued disarmament efforts.

9.5 *Ultimate Aims of Disarmament*

The ultimate aims of disarmament efforts must be:

(I) to remove the threat of future devastating wars, even — in the worst of cases — the extinction of human civilization as we know it; and

(II) to re-allocate resources presently used for military purposes to peaceful, constructive and developmental purposes, in a spirit of international solidarity.

The fact that the 1970's have been proclaimed the *Disarmament Decade* as well as the Second UN Development Decade provides the necessary link between these two purposes. The real facts behind this link were examined by the Expert Group referred to earlier, convened by the UN Secretary-General in 1971 and chaired by Alva Myrdal. Its report is of the utmost relevance to the ongoing review and appraisal of the objectives of the Second Development Decade as well as efforts to establish a New International Economic Order.

On the basis of first calculations, the group reported that a 20 per cent general reduction in military expenditures could contribute not only to the satisfaction of urgent economic needs of both developed and developing countries, but also to the reduction of the economic disparities between the two groups if development assistance was raised globally in the same proportion or slightly more. The group found, moreover, that most of the resources released by disarmament, total or partial, would be readily transferable to other uses — for example manpower, food, clothing, transport, fuel and products of the metal and engineering industries. According to an analysis made of the United States economy, the number of industries likely to suffer the negative impacts of transferring some of the resources now absorbed by military expenditures to other purposes would be smaller when replacement was specifically aimed at increasing the level of assistance to the Third World rather than when replacement was geared to increasing domestic personal consumption.

The importance attached by the group to the *transfer of skilled human resources from military to peaceful purposes* is further underlined in, for example, the answer given by the Swedish Government to the UN Secretary-General in June 1975 on the expert group report on reductions of military budgets referred to earlier. A crucial point of armament activities in the present technological age, increasingly specialized and isolated from the needs of civilian society, is the allocation of resources for R&D. Whatever reductions could be made in this field would constitute a long-term restraint on military procurement. Efforts should thus be concentrated, for the dual purposes stated above, on minimizing the commitment of resources for military R&D, thereby effectively hampering further technological advance in these fields. Such efforts would, of course, in the spirit of the Myrdal expert group report, have to be pursued in a clear understanding of their disarmament effects. There would certainly appear to be an important role which could be played by the international scientific community in this respect. It must be encouraged to issue a strong and urgent appeal aimed at enlisting the support of all scientists in the world in efforts to devote skills and capacities to peaceful and constructive, as opposed to military and destructive, purposes.

An early request by those motivated by the need for disarmament and appalled by the profits of private companies in the arms industry, has been for *nationalization of this industry* or some of its parts. This has taken place in several countries. It could be doubted, however, whether such a measure, by taking the profit motive out of arms production, would contribute significantly to a slowing down of the arms race and, particularly, the arms trade. It could be argued that governments in most countries already have a considerable, in several cases decisive, influence on arms export; such countries would seem to include some of the most prominent arms dealers. This would lead to two conclusions: that even governments are motivated by profit motives in concluding deals in the arms field i.e. improvements in balance of payments; and that in addition to such considerations, political-military alliances and/or political-military interests direct to a considerable extent the world flow of arms. Nationalization of arms industries would not significantly change this dismal situation.

Results so far of disarmament efforts have, as has been stated repeatedly, been generally frustrating and far from impressive. The case for uniting the support of the overwhelming majority of human beings behind disarmament efforts is very strong. Hopefully, informed and united public opinion can prove of decisive importance in giving new impetus and shape to disarmament negotiations. Many disarmament experts seem to be increasingly of the opinion that the partial disarmament measures aimed at so far only seem to have assisted in pushing the arms competition into new and more virulent directions and that the only way out may be through a comprehensive approach (6). If, as seems to be their view, it has been futile to engage military technicians in arguments over technical details, perhaps more success could be achieved by bringing the argument back to matters of principle, to questions of economics, of ethics, or morality and, quite simply, *survival* (7).

Matters of principle are indeed involved in the question of disarmament. Since mankind's future is inextricably linked with the need for drastic change in world management, disarmament must be included as an *integral*, and important *part of the global issue of survival*, that is, of the new international order.

---

(6) Bernard T. Feld: 'The Charade of Piecemeal Arms Limitation'. Bulletin of the Atomic Scientists, January 1975.
(7) Idem.

A widening of the definition of national security to encompass also progress in the social, economic and cultural fields seems to be one way to break the deadlock of disarmament. As pointed out by Miriam Camps (8), even in such a traditional realm of high politics as security, we are beginning to be aware of new interdependencies and of new tasks requiring international action. No political leader, however, has so far initiated a debate on the relationship, if any, between security and military resources in a nuclear age now 30 years old. Mr. Camps quotes Leonard Beaton in his posthumous book *The Reform of Power* (9), where he develops the thesis that there should be no competition between international and national security interests and advocates a step-by-step approach to the building up of an international system taking "cognisance" of the existence and purposes of all kinds of military force, and eventually leading to a capacity of management and control.

Meanwhile a number of *concrete requests* must be made to the world's political leaders. In the first instance, ongoing multilateral and bilateral arms limitation negotiations must be requested to yield more decisive results that has hitherto been the case. Serious efforts must be made to involve all the great powers, permanent members of the UN Security Council, in multilateral disarmament negotiations. The efforts under way within the United Nations to examine the possibilities of a reduction in the military budgets of states with a major economic and military potential must be pursued with urgency. Efforts to establish a negotiated time table for consecutive reductions in military budgets of these states, and the simultaneous and effective transfer of resources thus released to constructive civilian use, including development purposes, are recommended. Likewise, countries of the Third World are recommended to seriously consider reversing the trend reflected in figures given earlier in their military budgets. Special attention must continue to be given to efforts to halt the horizontal and vertical proliferation of nuclear arms and nuclear explosion capability, as well as to a very considerable strengthening and extension of safeguards of all kinds of nuclear facilities and material in use, transport and storage, in order to prevent thefts and diversion from civilian purposes. Very few countries have so far pledged their support of and contribution to a standing UN Peace Force. Every effort should be made to promote progress in establishing such a force as a means for peace-keeping.

The increased emphasis that seems to be attached to bilateral disarmament talks between the superpowers, as compared to multilateral negotiations, seems particularly ill-boding. Thereby, nations and peoples around the world, whose future fate is dependent on the outcome of these talks, have been deprived of any possibility to influence whatever results may emerge from them. There seems to be an urgent need of finding ways and means to strengthen the efficiency of the *multilateral disarmament efforts.* Therefore, the decision by the XXX Session of the UN General Assembly to establish an *ad hoc* Committee to review the role of the UN in the field of disarmament, with the aim of submitting to the Assembly's XXXI Session recommendations and proposals for strengthening this role is to be welcomed. The purpose of the Committee seems to be very much in line with the views and suggestions of Miriam Camps and Leonard Beaton, as quoted above. In this context, there would appear to be a need to establish, within the framework of the United Nations, a *World Disarmament Agency* vested with the responsibility of supervising the gradual implementation of disarmament through agreements aimed at an authentic overall reduction in military budgets, especially those devoted to nuclear armaments.

---

(8) Miriam Camps: 'The Management of Interdepence, a Preliminary View'. Council on Foreign Relations, 1974.
(9) Leonard Beaton: 'The Reform of Power'. Chalto and Windus, London, 1972.

Ocean Management
Elisabeth Mann Borgese and Arvid Pardo

10.1 *General Significance of the Oceans*

The traditional legal order in the oceans is being rapidly eroded by technological and political developments and must be replaced by a new legal order if escalating tensions, depletion of living resources and serious deterioration are to be avoided. There are many factors which make such a change imperative. Amongst the background factors are the population explosion which is creating a demand for increasing quantities of food and water as well as the worldwide intensification of industrialization which will consume enormous and increasing quantities of water, raw materials and energy and is already a major cause of environmental degradation. In broadest terms, the current transformation of the international order in the oceans must be considered in the context of a twofold revolution that is shaking the entire order during the second half of this century. Its components: the change in the structure of international relations owing to the entry of the *new nations* into world affairs and the *technological revolution* which transcends the traditional nation-State and transforms traditional concepts of sovereignty and property.

Up to the present, man has intensively used little more than half the area of emerged land. There is scant hope that this portion of the globe — over the balance of this century — can provide all the water, food and raw materials required. There is a strong incentive, therefore, to utilize with increasing intensity those areas of our planet previously considered either worthless or inaccessible to sustained economic activity. *Ocean space* is by far the largest and most valuable region of our planet which still awaits full utilization. Technology is providing the tools to penetrate, use and exploit ocean space in all its dimensions.

Ocean space covers more than two-thirds of our planet. It comprises the surface of the seas, the water column, the seabed and its subsoil. The seabed has all the features of emerged land: mountains, plains and valleys, a varied flora and fauna, and mineral resources.

Ocean space is of vital importance for the following reasons:
(I) It contains more than 95 per cent of the world's water, probably more hydrocarbons and certainly vastly greater quantities of a wide range of hard minerals than are found on land; it also contains vast living resources which can make a far greater contribution to world food supplies than at present. Some of these resources, such as krill and marine plants, are still virtually unexploited;
(II) It is an immense potential source of energy which awaits exploitation;
(III) It is not merely the last and greatest resource reserve of our planet; it also offers space for a variety of activities which are at present land-based, and it is an essential medium for the expansion of knowledge of the planet, for international trade, and for the maintenance of national security, as perceived today;
(IV) It is of fundamental importance to climates, indeed to life on earth, and is the ultimate sink of the enormous, growing and increasingly toxic wastes produced by our expanding industrial society.

Since the manner in which ocean space will be used and exploited affects the perceived national interests of every nation in the world, it is vitally important in the creation of any new international order.

10.2 *The Traditional Law of the Sea and Current Trends*

10.2.1   *Sovereignty and Freedom in Ocean Space*   For the past three centuries the law of the sea has been governed by the twin principles of sovereignty and freedom. Sovereignty of the coastal State, limited only by the doctrine of innocent passage, was recognized over a narrow belt of sea adjacent to the coast called the territorial sea. Beyond territorial waters were the high seas where freedom, in theory, reigned, subject only to a reasonable regard for the interests of other States in the exercise of the same freedom.

The principle of sovereignty was, and is, based on the nature of the international community composed of sovereign States and on the security and economic needs of coastal States *in the technological conditions of three centuries ago.*

The principle of freedom of the seas was explicitly based on the assumption that the living resources of the seas were inexhaustible and that the oceans were sufficiently vast to accommodate all navigational uses without need for regulation. Implicitly, it was assumed that man could not seriously impair the quality of the marine environment and that the oceans were so vast and their uses so limited that serious conflicts of use were impossible.

It is obvious that the assumptions on which the principle of freedom of the seas is based are, at best, obsolescent. Visible contamination of some areas of the sea has aroused concern and requires the adoption of measures of control of *marine pollution* which cannot be effective under a regime of Freedom of the seas. We now know that the living resources of the sea are not inexhaustible and that they can be depleted; effective measures of *conservation and management* are now required, but they cannot be implemented under the concept of the Freedom of the seas. Intensified exploitation of *hydrocarbons*, and soon of *hard minerals*, and many of the new uses of ocean space – from offshore ports to offshore petroleum storage tanks – require the exercise of recognized authority to protect investments, control marine pollution, reconcile competing uses in ever wider areas of the seas, and facilitate the equitable participation of the less developed nations. The emergence, furthermore, of increasingly sophisticated technologies, which potentially could change the natural state of the marine environment over vast areas, raises fundamental political questions that cannot be solved under the old Freedom of the seas principle.

The gradual extension and diversification of man's activities in the marine environment involves an expansion of the interests of coastal States and has been accompanied by a progressive extension of coastal State jurisdiction. Thus the 1958 Geneva Conventions on the Law of the Sea, apart from codifying major areas of customary law, recognized expanding coastal State interests by giving international recognition to the concept of *straight baselines*, to the concept of the *contiguous zone*, and to the concept of the *legal continental shelf*, in which the coastal State exercises sovereign rights for the purpose of resource exploration and exploitation. The special interests of the coastal State in the maintenance of the productivity of the living resources of the sea in areas of the high seas adjacent to the territorial sea were also recognized. However, neither the rights and duties of States within these areas nor their limits (apart from the limits of the contiguous zone) were clearly defined. Furthermore, the revolution in our uses of ocean space, caused by technological advance, was not anticipated. Most important, the obsolescent principle of the Freedom of the seas was maintained.

The revolution of our uses of ocean space is proceeding at such a pace and involves so many activities that there is no reasonable prospect that the slow process of negotiation of specific treaties and technical agreements can sufficiently alleviate, within the foreseeable future, the adverse effects of the *abuse of the high seas* and of their resources which are the inevitable consequence of technological advance, diversifying use and intensifying exploitation in a world of competitive nation-States.

Thus, due both to the need for resources and the need to avoid adverse consequences of other nations' activities in the general vicinity of their coasts, coastal States are under increasing pressure to take *unilateral* and, occasionally, *regional*, action to subject ever wider areas of ocean space to their authority — a process which is facilitated by the ambiguities and deficiencies of the 1958 Geneva Conventions. There is often a further motive for the extension of coastal State maritime jurisdiction, and that is the strong desire to equalize opportunities of ocean uses, since the ability to use ocean space freely and exploit its resources is an important factor in the disparity between technologically-advanced maritime countries and other countries. Since equalization of opportunities cannot be achieved under the present law of the sea, the alternative for weaker maritime States is to subject progressively wider areas of the oceans to their own jurisdiction, thus attempting to restrict the area in which technologically advanced maritime countries can freely exploit ocean resources. If present trends continue unchecked, there is a serious possibility that the greater part of ocean space could be covered by sometimes conflicting national claims.

A division of ocean space between coastal States on the basis of sovereignty, however, is a solution as dangerous and as obsolete as the maintenance of the freedom of the seas. National authority can deal effectively with the uses of the ocean connected with the extraction of mineral resources. *Fragmentation of ocean space* between more than one hundred different sovereignties, however, would be virtually certain to obstruct significantly vital transnational uses of the marine environment such as overflight, navigation, and scientific research. The latter, of course, is an essential prerequisite to rational resource management and development. Management of several important commercial fisheries would be very difficult if ocean space were divided between coastal States on the basis of sovereignty, and effective control of marine pollution would be almost impossible. Most importantly, a division of the oceans — assuming the practicability of peaceful delimitation of the respective areas of coastal State jurisdiction — would measurably *aggravate world tensions*. About twenty nations, the majority already rich, would appropriate some two-thirds of ocean space, thus exacerbating the gross inequality between States and potentially inflicting grave economic damage of geographically disadvantaged countries.

In conclusion, *neither sovereignty nor freedom* are suitable as a basis for a viable and reasonable equitable legal regime for ocean space under contemporary conditions. A new, international legal order must be created, based on a new principle which constrains both sovereignty and freedom in the common interest.

This should be the task of the present Conference on the Law of the Sea which was convened by the United Nations General Assembly to consider all matters relating to the Law of the Sea in the multiple interrelationships (UNGA Res. 3067, XXVIII). Four sessions have so far taken place (New York, 1973; Caracas, 1974; Geneva, 1975; and New York, 1976).

10.2.2   *The Informal Single Negotiating Text*   The Geneva session of the Law of the Sea Conference ended with the publication of an *Informal Single Negotiating Text*, presented in three parts, to which a fourth was added later in 1975. This Text served as a basis for discussion during the fourth session which took place in New York from March 15 to May 7, 1976. In New York important changes were introduced in the Text, ranging from technical and editorial improvements to significant, and not, in all cases, positive transformations of basic concepts. In spite of significant progress in the negotiations towards a consensus in some areas, the Revised Informal Single Negotiating Text, in four Parts, released at the end of the New York session, still has the status of an 'informal' document, drafted under the sole responsibility of the Chairmen of the main working Committees and of the President of the Conference.

Part I of the Single Negotiating Text deals with the conduct of States on the seabed and ocean floor and the subsoil thereof beyond the limits of national jurisdiction, based on the principle that this part of the oceans is a 'common heritage of mankind' and as such should be reserved for peaceful purposes and should be used, and its resources exploited, for the benefit of mankind as a whole. The waters above the international seabed area retain the traditional status of High Seas. In order to implement the principle of common heritage, it is proposed to establish an international agency, called the International Seabed Authority, 'through which States Parties to the Convention shall administer the area'. While the Authority, in principle, is the recognized competence with regard to all activities in the international seabed area, its proposed structure is geared essentially to the exploration and exploitation of mineral resources, particularly the manganese nodules of the abyss. The principal organs of the Authority are: an Assembly, a Council, a Tribunal, an Enterprise, and a Secretariat.

The Assembly, according to the Revised Text, is 'the supreme organ of the Authority', and as such it shall have 'the power to prescribe the general policies to be pursued by the Authority on any questions or matters within the competence of the Authority by adopting resolutions and making recommendations', while the Council of 36 members, elected by the Assembly, partly 'in accordance with the principle of equitable geographical representation' and partly 'with a view to representation of special interests', is conceived as the executive organ of the Authority, with the power 'to prescribe specific policies to be pursued by the Authority on any questions or matters within the competence of the Authority and in a manner consistent with the general policies prescribed by the Assembly'. The Council is assisted by an Economic Planning Commission, a Technical Commission, and a Rules and Regulations Commission. The Tribunal is given final and binding jurisdiction over any dispute concerning the interpretation or application of this Part of the Convention, any dispute 'concerning the conclusion of any contract, its interpretation or application or other activity in the Area', over questions on the legality of measures taken by any organ of the Council or the Assembly, or any violation of the responsibilities of the Secretary-General or his staff. The Tribunal must also render advisory opinions on the request of any organ of the Authority. The dispute settlement system of the Authority is completed by an alternative provision for adjudication by 'special chambers' consisting of three arbiters appointed by the Parties to the dispute.

A number of Articles of Part I of the Single Negotiating Text contain interesting innovations in the current practice of international organization, but it is the proposed creation of an Enterprise which shall, 'subject to the general policy directives and control of the Council, conduct activities in the Area directly', that poses the greatest challenge — not yet adequately met by the text — and potentially distinguishes the proposed Authority from all present and past international organizations. The activities to be undertaken by the Authority through the Enterprise are defined as 'all activities of exploration for, and exploitation of, the resources of the Area'. But, as the Chairman of the First Committee explained in his introductory note to the Revised Text, 'this does not mean that other activities would not be governed by this part of the Convention'. This is the first time that a global public international organization is charged with the responsibility of resource-management, and this is a breakthrough, even though the importance of manganese nodule mining beyond national jurisdiction is likely to be comparatively small, and the Enterprise, which will have to be financed by States, voluntary contributions, and loans, will have to compete with private transnational companies and with States, on the seabed both under national and international jurisdiction. Part I of the Single Negotiating Text has been completed by three Annexes. The first sets forth the basic conditions of Prospecting, Exploration and Exploitation; the second contains the Statute of the Enterprise; the third, the Statute of the Seabed Dispute Settlement System. A 'special Appendix', finally, contains provisions for financial arrangements. Two alternatives, 'Approach A' and 'Approach B' are presented: one more, the other less stringent in its controls and regulations.

Part II of the Single Negotiating Text develops existing trends in the present law of the sea with regard to such complex and important questions as the limits of marine areas under national sovereignty or jurisdiction, the rights and duties of States therein, and the regime of the High Seas. In general it may be said that the Negotiating Text extends coastal State control in ocean space over wide areas of formerly High Seas. At the same time, the limits of coastal State jurisdiction are not precisely defined and no clear criteria are proposed for the delimitation of national jurisdictional areas between States lying adjacent or opposite each other.

The marine area covered by the regime of the High Seas is restricted as a consequence of the proposed extensions of coastal State jurisdiction. The High Seas regime is also limited to the surface and water column of areas beyond national jurisdiction, while the seabed is governed by the totally different principle of the common heritage of mankind. While some constructive changes are proposed to the present regime of the High Seas, this regime cannot be easily reconciled with the new regime suggested for the seabed beyond national jurisdiction.

Part III of the Negotiating Text deals with *environmental protection, scientific research* and the *transfer of technology*. In the field of environmental protection, it established a general obligation of States to protect and preserve the marine environment, to take all necessary measures to ensure that marine pollution does not spread outside their national jurisdiction and to cooperate in the formulation of international rules, standards, and procedures in this connection. This section of the document also contains articles providing in general terms for monitoring of the marine environment and technical assistance for the prevention of marine pollution. Finally there are articles on the establishment and enforcement of vessel-source pollution standards by coastal and flag States.

In the section on *scientific research*, general articles affirm the right of all States to conduct scientific research in ocean space and the general duty to promote international cooperation in this area; at the same time, the right of coastal States to control scientific research in marine areas under national jurisdiction (such as the continental shelf and the exclusively economic zone) is affirmed, and the conditions with which such research should comply are prescribed.

Part III of the Negotiating Text is completed by a section urging international cooperation in the *development and transfer of marine technology*. Finally, responsibility and liability of States for environmental damage and for the conduct of scientific research are affirmed in general terms.

Part III proposes no specific machinery to implement the principles and provisions of the Negotiating Text with regard to the environment, scientific research and the transfer of technology. Throughout the text, however, there are general references to 'competent international global or regional organizations', and the Revised Text concludes with an Article providing that 'the competent international organizations referred to in this Part of the Convention shall take all appropriate measures to ensure, either directly or in close cooperation amongst themselves, the effective discharge of the functions and responsibilities assigned to them under the provisions of this Chapter of the Convention'.

Part IV, which was redrafted after a week of intense debate during the New York session, and now has the same status as the other parts of the Single Negotiating Text, establishes a dispute settlement system in the oceans apart from the seabed beyond national jurisdiction, for which a special system is established in Part I of the Single Negotiating Text. It is not clear whether the two dispute settlement systems interlink.

The system proposed in Part IV is comprehensive and flexible and combines general and special or functional procedures in a new way.

Contracting Parties which are parties to a dispute are first referred to Article 33 of the Charter of the United Nations or to any obligation they may have accepted under a general, regional or special agreement to settle disputes by arbitration or judicial settlement or to any special dispute settlement procedures provided in other parts of the proposed Convention. If these procedures are either not applicable or fail to settle the dispute, the Single Negotiating Text proposes the following specific dispute settlement procedures: (I) conciliation by a specially established Conciliation Commission, the findings of which are not binding on the Parties to the dispute; (II) arbitration by a specially established Arbitral Tribunal, the award of which is final and without appeal; and (III) judicial settlement by a Law of the Sea Tribunal, the members of which are elected by the Contracting Parties on the basis of equitable geographic distribution and of the representation of the principal legal systems of the world. While the judgement of the Tribunal is final and without appeal, it has binding force only between the Parties to the dispute and does not constitute a precedent. In addition, there is also access to the International Court of Justice, in cases where its jurisdiction applies.

The system envisaged covers in principle any dispute between Parties to the future Convention relating to its interpretation or application. There are, however, important exceptions. In the Geneva version these were so significant that they might have incapacitated the whole system. In the revised version they have been more carefully circumscribed. 'Nothing contained in the present Convention shall empower any Contracting Party to submit to the dispute settlement procedure provided for . . . any dispute in relation to the exercise of sovereign rights, exclusive rights or exclusive jurisdiction, 'except when it is claimed that a coastal State has violated its obligations under the present Convention by interfering with the freedom of navigation or overflight, the freedom to lay submarine cables or pipelines or by failing to give due regard to any substantive right specifically established by the present Convention in favour of other States; or when it is claimed that any other State when exercising the aforementioned freedoms has violated its obligations under the Convention, or the laws and regulations enacted by a coastal State in conformity with the present Convention; or when it is claimed that a coastal State has violated its obligations under the present Convention by failing to apply international standards or criteria established by the present Convention . . . which relate to the preservation of the marine environment . . .' When ratifying the Convention, furthermore, a Contracting Party may declare that it does not accept some or all of the procedures for the settlement of disputes specified in the Convention with respect to one or more of the following categories of disputes: (I) disputes concerning sea boundary delimitations between adjacent or opposite States, or those involving historic bays or titles, provided, however, 'that States making such a declaration shall indicate therein a regional, or other third party procedure, *entailing a binding decision*, which it accepts for the settlement of these disputes'; (II) disputes concerning military activities; and (III) disputes in respect of which the Security Council of the United Nations is exercising the functions assigned to it under the Charter.

Special dispute settlement procedures are envisaged for questions relating to fisheries, pollution, navigation, and scientific research. In these cases, at the request of any of the parties, disputes may by submitted to a special committee of five members selected from a list of experts established respectively by COFI/FAO, UNEP, IMCO, and IOC/UNESCO. The decisions of the special committee are binding on the parties to the dispute, but are not necessarily 'conclusive'. These provisions add significantly to the functions exercised by the Agencies concerned.

The Informal Single Negotiating Text, in its four Parts, is a document without precedent in the history of international law and organization. While Parts I and IV are, at least potentially, 'systems transforming', however, Part II is entirely 'systems preserving' and Part III is systems transforming in its principles but systems preserving in its applications. In the present context, therefore, it is to be feared that the systems-transforming functions may be made largely ineffective by the systems-preserving limitations, and by the numerous ambiguities and contradictions still in the text. All of this may indeed lead to an increase rather than a decrease of inequalities between States, to a multiplication rather than a reduction of conflicts, and to considerable uncertainties with regard to the law. Many States have failed to see the relevance of the law of the sea for the building of a new international economic order. As a consequence, the Law of the Sea Conference does not take into adequate account either the emerging new uses of the seas and their harmonization, or fairness and equity between States. Instead, a consensus seems to have developed, at least amongst coastal States, that an acceptable new law of the sea can be achieved merely by shifting the balance of the existing law from freedom over the greater part of the oceans to national sovereignty over the greater part of the ocean space. This is merely a change within the existing legal framework and is counterproductive from the point of view of constructing a new international legal order.

In spite of this, however, the Revised Informal Single Negotiating Text may contain the seed of a new order in the seas.

10.3   *A Comprehensive Approach to Ocean Affairs*

10.3.1   *Purposes and Principles*   Ocean space is a new world which is gradually opening to full utilization and intensive exploitation by man. All States are vitally interested in the legal regime which will govern man's activities in ocean space.

The increasingly serious problems arising in the oceans are insoluble on the basis of the present law of the sea. Nor can they be solved merely through accommodation of the interests of more influential States in the context of a massive appropriation of ocean space and its resources. This would sow the seeds of lasting tensions by increasing inequalities between States since scarcely more than a score of States with long coastlines fronting on the open oceans would acquire some two-thirds of that vast portion of ocean space which the Single Negotiating Text proposes to place under national jurisdiction; landlocked States would acquire nothing and the remainder very little. As has already been mentioned, fragmentation of ocean space between more than one hundred sovereignties, large and small, would not be conducive to rational management of most living resources, to effective pollution control or to the unhampered exercise of transnational uses of the sea, such as scientific research or navigation. The Law of the Sea Conference, therefore, must aim not merely at an accommodation of national interests but at their accommodation within a legal framework conducive to the achievement of more general, highly desirable goals: reduction of world tensions, reduction of inequality; reasonable protection of the marine environment; control of emerging dangerous technologies; promotion of international cooperation; management and conservation of living resources with the full participation of developing nations, etc. This requires the creation of a new international order in ocean space which (I) safeguards the common interests of all peoples in ocean space as a whole; (II) flexibly accommodates multiplying inclusive and exclusive uses of ocean space; (III) provides expanding opportunities to all countries, especially the developing ones, in the use of ocean space beyond national jurisdiction; and (IV) makes possible, through effective management, development of the resources of ocean space beyond national jurisdiction for the benefit of all countries, especially the poorer ones, and equitable sharing in the benefits derived therefrom.

To achieve these ends, international agreement is required on:

(I) The concept of *ocean space* comprising the surface of the sea, the water column, the seabed and its subsoil. This is essential because activities in the marine environment increasingly involve the seas in all their dimensions.

(II) The concept of the *common heritage of mankind*, which must supersede the traditional freedoms of the sea. This concept has five basic implications. First, the common heritage of mankind cannot be appropriated. It can be *used but not owned* (functional concept of ownership). Second, the use of the common heritage requires a *system of management* in which all users must share. Third, it implies an *active sharing of benefits*, including not only financial benefits but the benefits derived from shared management and the transfer of technologies. These latter two implications, shared management and benefit sharing, change the structural relationship between rich and poor nations and the traditional concepts of development aid. Fourth, the concept of the common heritage implies *reservation for peaceful purposes* (disarmament implications); and fifth, it implies *reservation for future generations* (environmental implications).

(III) The concept of *functional sovereignty* as distinguished from the traditional concept of territorial sovereignty exercised by States. Functional sovereignty means *jurisdiction over determined uses* as distinguished from sovereignty over geographic space. This transformation of the concept of sovereignty is in line with the transformation of the concept of ownership. Functional sovereignty permits secure accommodation of inclusive and exclusive uses of the sea or, in other words, the interweaving of national and international jurisdiction within the same territorial space. Conceptually, it opens the possibility of applying the concept of the common heritage of mankind within marine areas under national jurisdiction and management.

(IV) The concept of *regional development* within the framework of global organization. A number of activities, including most aspects of fisheries management and pollution control, the management of mineral exploitation and the harmonization of uses, can usually be dealt with successfully on a regional basis, while other activities, such as navigation or scientific research, are more directly of global concern. No oceanic region is a 'closed system'. While global organization, to be effective, must be articulated in an infrastructure of regional organizations, regional organization to be effective must be developed in the context of global organization.

(V) The clear and precise definition of the *limits of national jurisdiction for all purposes*. If agreement cannot be obtained on this point, coastal State jurisdiction will inevitably continue to expand.

(VI) The creation, not merely of a seabed agency, but of a *balanced international system for ocean space*, with comprehensive powers of administration and resource management beyond national jurisdiction. Only thus can there be some assurance that the present jurisdictional vacuum in the seas will be filled, that the provisions of the future Convention will be complied with by the States, that all States will benefit in some measure from the future international order and that serious attempts will be made to control environmental and other abuses beyond the limits of national jurisdiction.

10.3.2   *Medium and Long Term Proposals*   In ocean space we have to create, for the first time, international institutions charged with the responsibilities for *resource management* and its economic and ecological implications; with the *control and management of science and technology*; with the *harmonization and integration of uses*, including questions arising from the *impingement of military uses* on an environment, resources, technologies, and management systems reserved for peaceful uses only; and with the *interaction of national and international management systems*. In the oceans we are challenged concretely, for the first time, not only with the need for but also with the opportunity of, initiating an *international redistribution of income*. For on the one hand, the international management and development of resources that are the common heritage of mankind generate an income that can be used for international development purposes; on the other hand, and far more significantly, not only resource exploitation beyond national jurisdiction but also other major ocean space uses could be made to generate income for the international community, particularly poorer countries. It would be possible, for instance, to evolve a system by which States would make contributions, based on their use of the ocean and its resources, to international ocean institutions. A prerequisite for such a system would be that information and statistics on ocean uses and their economic value should be greatly improved to establish a rational basis for a schedule of fees; furthermore it would be necessary to take into account factors such as population, gross national product, economic dependence on sea uses, etc., of the different countries involved.

In the oceans, finally, one might make a concrete beginning towards controlling the international activities of *transnational enterprises* involved in ocean space activities: on the seabed, in international shipping and sea-borne trade, and in fishing, seafood processing and marketing. The international ocean institutions, forming part of a regionally and functionally decentralized network, would provide the proper framework to implement in their area of competence the 'Report of Eminent Persons' on transnational enterprises, published by the UN Secretariat in 1974.

Thus a concrete beginning could be made in the oceans to build the *New International Economic Order*.

The present elements of the UN System dealing with ocean space have only a sectoral competence and no independent capability. A new international order in the oceans will require considerable changes in the nature and functions of existing United Nations Agencies whose activities are centered on the marine environment. These changes must be initiated by the Agencies themselves, but the Law of the Sea Conference and the General Assembly of the United Nations can stimulate action. It would also be up to the Conference to create an *integrative machinery* which must ensure stability and fairness for all States and which must provide for a credible system of dispute management with regard to the controversies which may be expected to arise from the progressive development of ocean space. Part IV of the Single Negotiating Text is, in this sense, already a part of this 'integrative machinery'.

A practical model for an effective integrative machinery could be constructed on the basis of existing United Nations Agencies or segments thereof, the activities of which are centred on the marine environment (hereafter called *basic organizations*). These are: the Inter-Governmental Maritime Consultative Organization (IMCO), for navigation; the Committee on Fisheries (COFI) which presently is part of FAO, for living resources; the Inter-Governmental Oceanographic Commission (IOC), presently part of UNESCO, for scientific research – in addition to the International Seabed Authority (ISA) proposed by the Conference on the Law of the Sea, for nonliving resources. If the United Nations Environmental Programme (UNEP), which deals with environmental problems in the broadest sense in the oceans, on land, and in the atmosphere, were to establish a sub-organ dealing exclusively with the protection and conservation of the marine environment, this organ should be included amongst the 'basic organizations'. This would be in line with the Revised Informal Single Negotiating Text. In the long run, such a development could be useful. In the meantime, to meet the management and regional requirements mentioned, the other four agencies must be structured or, respectively, restructured as follows:

(I) The Seabed Authority, as prototype embodying international resource management functions, could provide a model for the restructuring of the other 'basic organizations', although there are obvious differences in the problems arising from the international management of mineral resources, living resources and services like navigation or scientific research;

(II) IOC and COFI should be detached from UNESCO and FAO respectively and made autonomous Agencies to enable them to assume their new managerial, judiciary and other functions, which would be difficult within the organizational and budgetary constraints within their mother organizations;

(III) It will be necessary for each of the 'basic organizations' to make appropriate provision for cooperation with other agencies and organizations active (though not exclusively) in marine affairs both within and outside the United Nations system, such as WMO, WHO, IAEA, ILO, the International Hydrographic Bureau, etc., and for proper interaction between international, national, and regional management systems.

To meet the structural requirements of coordination and integration of policies and activities, we propose an *integrative machinery* with the following functions:
(I) To provide a forum for the discussion of major problems relating to ocean space in their multiple interrelationships;
(II) To deal with ocean space questions beyond national jurisdiction not falling within the specific competence of any of the basic organizations;
(III) To integrate the policies of the basic organizations;
(IV) To establish guidelines for multiple ocean space use, taking into account the need for cooperation between national and international management systems;
(V) To ensure cooperation with technologically less advanced countries in the development of national ocean space;
(VI) To ensure equitable sharing of the benefits derived from the exploitation of resources of ocean space;
(VII) To promote the progressive development of the law of the sea;
(VIII) To assume those functions with regard to dispute settlement which are of a preeminently political nature.

The integrative machinery must have a broad base at the level of policy-making: i.e. it must be based on an assembly system composed of elements derived from, or delegated by, the Assemblies of the 'basic organizations'. This is essential because more than traditional cooperation at the inter-secretariat level between the 'basic organizations' is required. What is proposed, on the other hand, is not a new international organization of the traditional type, but a *functional confederation of international organizations*, with functions which are novel in international law. This would seem the proper organizational response to the requirements arising from the new concepts of *functional sovereignty* and *functional ownership* (common heritage of mankind).

A functional confederation of international organizations has a number of advantages. In the first place, the 'integrative machinery' would require less international bureaucracy than the traditional type of international organization, since staff and delegates from existing 'basic organizations' would be used. Furthermore, it combines *integration at the policy level* with a maximum of *decentralization at the operational level*; each of the 'basic organizations' would be largely autonomous in its activities, and the integrative machinery would be no more than just that: an integrative machinery.

Integration of policies at the assembly level has additional advantages over coordination at the secretariat level as currently practiced in the UN system. In the present situation, States can discuss policies only sectorially (fisheries in the Assembly of COFI; science in the Assembly of IOC; navigation in the Assembly of IMCO; minerals in the Assembly of ISA). There is no forum for States to discuss policy on interaction of uses. An Intersecretariat body is too restricted to make policy decisions. The Assembly system here proposed will give to States this opportunity.

At the same time, the structure proposed provides a *balanced system of functional interests*. For each 'basic organization' would be represented in the Assembly system by the same number of delegations. Thus, while each State would have one vote in the Assemblies of each of the 'basic organizations' as heretofore, each 'basic organization', in turn, would have the same number of votes in the Assembly system of the integrative machinery. The new structure thus would interweave State representation and regional and transnational functional interests in a new way.

Finally, this kind of functional confederation of international mechanisms, autonomous yet united in purpose and action, could not only be a *model* for international organization in other sectors; it could become *part* of an even wider structure: it could be expanded into and flexibly connected with functional confederations in other fields. Twenty-five or fifty years from now, one might indeed imagine international resource management systems for energy and food, for outer space and satellites, for weather control and modification, and all these systems could be linked and coordinated.

We have strayed into the future — a future, however, that has already begun. This study shows how the present work of the Conference on the Law of the Sea can be fitted in its totality into the proposed model. The model restores a focus and a goal to the efforts of the Conference which seemed entirely lost but has begun to re-emerge in the Single Negotiating Text. We must move on from here.

The proposed model, providing an *institutional framework for the new international economic order*, as applicable to a sector of the world economy that is of enormous and increasing importance, would benefit most immediately the small, disadvantaged, and poor nations who have the strongest interest in comprehensive, strong international organization. It will be resisted by large, technologically developed nations in an advantageous geographic position which believe they still can benefit from the freedom of the sea and from the proposed vast extension of their maritime sovereignty. Of great importance will be the cooperation of those United Nations Specialized Agencies which we propose to develop into 'basic organizations'.

10.3.3   *Proposals for Immediate Action*   The New York session made, at least, a beginning in the direction here indicated. The Delegation of Portugal circulated a paper listing the numerous references, throughout the Revised Informal Single Negotiating Text, to 'appropriate' or 'competent' regional or global institutions which would have to implement various functions connected with the management of living resources, scientific research, environmental protection, the transfer of technology, and navigation. Based on this document, the representative of Portugal introduced, in the closing meeting, a proposal that, before the next Session of the Conference, a second document be prepared, this time by the Secretariat of the United Nations: an 'annotated directory' of UN agencies and institutions, describing briefly their structure and functions, their responsibilities and competences. The proposal was accepted by consensus. A comparison between the two documents, the Portuguese and the Secretariat's, will then show up the direction and the extent of the needed restructuring. This could be beyond the scope of the Third United Nations Conference on the Law of the Sea, but it could well be initiated by it. At the same time, it would be up to this Conference to make provision for some kind of 'continuing mechanism' with specific functions and responsibilities.

Also on this point, the New York session made at least a beginning. Three delegations — Sri Lanka, Surinam, and Portugal — and one non-governmental organization — the International Ocean Institute — pointed to the desirability of establishing a 'continuing mechanism' of a political nature, to interpret the Convention and continue the development of the law of the sea in the broader context of building a new international order in its institutional and economic aspects. All four speakers agreed that the most appropriate form for such a mechanism would be a periodic meeting of contracting parties — the same, probably, that would have to be called anyway to elect the Judges of the Law of the Sea Tribunal, if the final text of the Convention maintains this provision of the Single Negotiating Text.

This periodic meeting of contracting parties should be supported by a small Secretariat, and its work might be complemented by a Commission or Committee of Experts or Eminent Persons, to advise on appropriate measures to accelerate and coordinate the process of restructuring of COFI, IOC, and IMCO in order to enable these agencies to become effective organizations in the new ocean system.

It is a simple and practical proposition, not involving a high cost (the modest financing needed could easily be drawn from the five organizations which, from now on, will be basically involved in ocean affairs: ISA, IMCO, COFI, IOC, and probably UNEP, or a part thereof , and it is to be hoped that the next Session of UNCLoS will act on it.

There are, besides, a number of measures that could be taken, or initiated, in the imminent future, quite independently from the Law of the Sea Conference. These could bring some incremental improvements and enhance the participation of developing nations in ocean management.

Regional cooperation and organization could be strengthened in several areas such as the Mediterranean, the Caribbean, the Indian Ocean, etc., and could deal not only with environmental protection, as does the recently concluded Barcelona Convention for the Mediterranean, but also with fishing and the management of living resources, scientific research, the transfer of technology and the furnishing of science-based services. This would indeed be in accordance with the provisions on regional cooperation of Part II of the Single Negotiating Text, but it could be initiated independently, through regional economic commissions and fisheries commissions and through ad hoc agreements among States bordering enclosed or semi-enclosed seas. Regional institutes for marine sciences and technology could be established by any group of nations, especially in less developed regions, through regional banks or the UNDP. Their coordination through global organizations such as IOC should be assured. The participation of developing landlocked States and small island States in the marine economy could be strengthened through bilateral or multilateral agreements, in the wider context of UNCTAD recommendations. Appropriate steps could also be taken to increase the participation by developing nations in world shipping tonnage and sea-borne trade, and the UNCTAD Code of Conduct for Liner Conferences should be enforced. Finally, steps could be taken by the appropriate international fora not merely to declare certain marine areas Zones of Peace but also to seek international agreement on effective arms control measures within such areas.

Thus a new international order in ocean space may progressively become a reality commencing perhaps in the 1980's, consolidating the first phase of what already manifestly is a revolution in international relations. If the Law of the Sea Conference were allowed to close before proposals for effectively dealing with this marine revolution were adopted, a unique opportunity would be lost, as Secretary-General Waldheim made it clear in his inaugural address to the New York session of the Conference. 'We will have lost a unique opportunity, and one that may not occur again, if the uses made of the sea are not subjected to orderly development for the benefit of all, and if the Law of the Sea does not succeed in contributing to a more equitable global economic system.' For, he concluded, 'it is not only the law of the sea that is at stake. The whole structure of international cooperation will be affected, for good or for ill, by the success or failure of this Conference.'

List of Abbreviations

ASEAN	Association of South East Asian Countries
CMEA	Council of Mutual Economic Assistance
COFI	Commission on Fisheries (of FAO)
DAC	Development Assistance Committee (of OECD)
ECOSOC	Economic and Social Council of the U.N. `
EEC	European Economic Community
ESCAP	Economic and Social Commission for Asia and the Pacific
FAO	Food and Agricultural Organization
GATT	General Agreement on Tariffs and Trade
GNP	Gross National Product
IBRD	International Bank for Reconstruction and Development (World Bank)
ICC	International Chamber of Commerce
IDA	International Development Association (World Bank group)
IDS	International Development Strategy
IFAD	International Fund for Agricultural Development
IFC	International Finance Corporation
ILO	International Labour Organization
IMCO	Inter-Governmental Maritime Consultative Organization
IMF	International Monetary Fund
INTELSAT	International Tele Communication Satellite
IOC	Intergovernmental Oceanographic Commission (of UNESCO)
ISA	International Seabed Authority
MFN	Most Favoured Nation
ODA	Official Development Assistance
OECD	Organization for Economic Cooperation and Development
OPEC	Organization of Petroleum Exporting Countries
OPIC	Organization of Petroleum Importing Countries
SDRs	Special Drawing Rights
SIPRI	Stockholm International Peace Research Institute
TNEs	Transnational enterprises
UNCTAD	United Nations Conference on Trade and Development
UNDP	United Nations Development Programme
UNEP	United Nations Environment Programme
UNESCO	United Nations Educational, Scientific and Cultural Organization
UNIDO	United Nations Industrial Development Organization
WFP	World Food Programme (of FAO)
WHO	World Health Organization
WMO	World Meteorological Organization

Silviu Brucan

As a Marxist, I do not agree with every concept and formulation of RIO. However, this qualification does not extend to the validity of a Report designed to become a *common platform* for the struggle of billions of people with so different a culture and lifestyle, ideas and beliefs. Disagreements here and there are inevitable in a text whose authors belong to various schools of thought, nations and institutions. Under such requirements and circumstances, I consider RIO as a fair compromise between the views and interests of the main world social forces that must unite to succeed in this lengthy, hard and painful overhaul of the old unjust order.

Sukhamoy Chakravarty

In Part I, I would have preferred a little more emphasis on history. In Part II, I have reservations about Chapter 5 in terms of emphasis, illustration and analysis. As an example, while the concept of 'public power' is correctly stressed, it is delinked from the question of ownership of non-human productive assets. Realignment of property rights is often basic for an effective exercise of public power. I agree that this requires generalization of the concept of property as a 'zero-one' variable. Further, we need comprehensive planning. Emphasis on wasteful consumption is inescapable within the current market system. In part III, on food, inadequacy of intra- and international distribution needs more stress. As regards TNEs, their role in the long run is not clear to me. On technological change, the question of 'focusing mechanisms' needs to be highlighted. Subject to these observations, the Report brings out the relevant issues in reshaping the international order forcefully.

Robert Gibrat

A report of this kind (21 specialists of different nationalities and tempera-
ments, innumerable individual studies, joint discussions for several hundreds of hours) cannot claim to receive the agreement of everyone on all
its details. As far as I am concerned I only disagree on points of minor
importance, which I will not examine here, and I totally agree with the
Report as a whole even if sometimes it reflects a little too much the political positions of the Netherlands or Sweden.

However, I want to underline the necessity of a profound agreement of
the great masses. The Report is too optimistic. The present policies of
self-reliance of the Third World, even if one can see them in a perspective
of a *trial of strength*, weaken its popular image each day a little more.

James P. Grant

I have valued participation in the RIO project because greater equality of
opportunity among and within nations is a necessity if millions are not to
continue dying unnecessarily each year and if the pace of world growth
and development is to be resumed under circumstances more appropriate
for the last quarter of this century. This report has important ideas to contribute to needed discussions in the United States. Unfortunately the final
drafting of RIO in which I did not participate resulted in a text particularly in Parts I and II so asymmetrical in its treatment of the responsibilities
of developing as well as developed countries in advancing equality and so
apparently faulty in some of its discussion and facts that I fear too few
concerned Americans will find convincing those many parts of its analysis
which are eminently sound or properly provocative or will consider with
sufficient seriousness the important recommendations in Part III.

Maurice Guernier

I give of course my total agreement to the RIO Report which constitutes the most important progress realized in the field of planetary balanced development. In my mind, however, I think that it gives too much emphasis to — what we call in French — 'l'économisme' and too little emphasis, if at all, to humanism. Development implies a constant destruction of sociological and psychological structures. The real problem of development is cleverly to balance positive and real improvements with severe destructions.

In this respect, for example, I think that a rate of growth of 5 per cent per capita during 42 years in Asia and in Africa — as mentioned in Chapter 6 is not only unrealistic but overall undesirable from a humanistic point of view.

It is the responsibility of every nation to make its own choice between economic progress and socio-psycho structures destructions, and to define its own fundamental objectives for real development, which is the development of man as a totality and of the totality of men.

Mahbub ul Haq

Over two hundred years ago, Rousseau declared that 'man is born free but everywhere he is found in chains'. Few years later, the French revolution set the new mood for the movements of political liberation all over the world.

Today, in a major part of the world, the real battle is for the economic liberation of man. For, in an economic sense, all men are not created equal and most condemned to poverty at their very birth. A new economic order cannot emerge unless the principle of equality of opportunity is firmly established within and among nations.

This may be a simple statement but, in its inplications, it is a revolutionary manifesto, requiring fundamental changes in political, economic and social power structures all over the world.

If I have to pick one major recommendation in this Report to which I attach the greatest importance, it is the elimination of the worst forms of poverty over the course of the next decade through a grand compact between developed nations and the poorest developing countries. Among the instruments of implementation at the international level, I attach the highest priority to the introduction of international taxation and establishment of an international central bank.

Helmut Hesse

Although I am fully convinced that the present world economy is in disorder, due to the problems described in this Report, and though I agree with the argument that global cooperation, as elaborated, is needed to overcome these problems, I cannot agree with some of the value judgements, arguments and proposals made. Especially, I cannot agree with those value judgements which come near to egalitarianism. I cannot blame the Western industrialized countries for the severe inequalities in the world in the way suggested in this Report. Nor can I agree with a far-reaching substitution of market forces by a global planning and management system. Finally, I do not believe that an indexation of prices and self-sufficiency in food production, instead of taking advantage of comparative cost differences, etc., could be parts of a really optimal world economic order.

Idriss Jazairy

I will confine my remarks to 'Transnational Enterprises' (TNEs). Although agreeing with the proposals, I must stress that the underlying analysis — tending to underestimate the negative impacts of TNEs on suppliers, consumers, small shareholders, labour and, generally, on home and host countries — reflects the spirit of compromise prevailing among the authors.

Whilst adverse effects on democracy and equity of the concentration of power with a few ubiquitous enterprises escaping all parliamentary and public control has lead to claims for more transparent and ethical behaviour, the ICC 'Guidelines' issued in response have not prevented some TNEs from interfering in political affairs, indulging in corruption, currency speculation, illegal transfers or other unfair practices, as recent events have shown. Such will also be the fate of the recent 'please do this' OECD code which even The Economist refers to, on 26 June 1976, as 'unnecessarily weak'.

The report, therefore, rightly suggests a code of conduct for TNEs, legally enforceable by the international community, as the way of ensuring social accountability and not only profit maximization to guide future action of TNEs. Their past record cannot enable impartial observers to consider them as allies of the public at large, in developed or developing countries.

Alexander King

I am in general agreement with the final text and subscribe fully to its suggestions. Of course there are many matters of detail which I would have expressed otherwise or have given a somewhat different emphasis.

However, we have somewhat understressed the consequences of the doubling of the global population in some thirty years; and secondly, the needs for reform within the developing countries. Seeing the development activities in developing countries, one increasingly realizes how much effort is in support of small Western influenced elites, with little amelioration of the lot of the poor masses. Egoism, chauvenism and love of power are certainly not the monopoly of the rich countries and their leaders. Unless people in *all* countries can sublimate these human characteristics and include in their views the possibilities for their children and grandchildren, the outlook for the New Order is bleak; it can only succeed if there is political and individual will to make it do so.

Finally, we have said little about the great need for institutional innovation in *all* countries. Our institutions were constructed for simpler times and are not capable of facing the problem of scale, complexity, change and uncertainty which mark our contemporary world.

Pieter Kuin

I will confine my co-responsibility to my special field, transnational enterprises (TNEs). I agree with most concrete proposals; they should help to create clarity and reassurance. However, I do not share the negative feelings from which these proposals partly arise. Too often incidental faults are generalized as typical characteristics. The preponderantly beneficial effects of TNEs are mostly underestimated. It is their business to provide useful goods and services, and I have seen physical toil reduced, popular diets improved, yields per acre increased, distant areas opened up, education facilitated, and social activities rendered possible as a result of TNE production. Usefulness to the people and to governments is the main explanation of the rapid growth of TNEs and their real *raison d'être*.

Seen globally, TNEs excel in effective international resource allocation, matching rising needs with growing possibilities. They have probably done more than governments so far to build a true world economy. Many of them have shown great responsibility both in the conduct of affairs and by initiating or endorsing guidelines for good conduct (ICC 1972, OECD 1976). They should be looked upon as allies, not enemies, in the struggle against poverty.

Elisabeth Mann Borgese

The team spirit developed under Mr. Tinbergen's leadership has been remarkable. Most of the concepts and ideas dear and important to me have been incorporated in the text; and I know my colleagues on the team have made the same experience.

If I should still try to indicate a shade of difference between my own views and those incorporated in the text, I would turn to Chapter 5, its assessment of faults and weaknesses of the rich countries, and its recommendations and priorities. The evils of the 'consumer society', to my mind are more symptom than cause of the disarray within some affluent nations. A voluntary change in consumption patterns or 'life style', promoted, in the first place, through education, therefore, does not appear to me as a convincing priority. This notion still reflects the basically a-political and, therefore, evasive approach exemplified by the 'Greening of America'.

The cause underlying consumerism, arms race, the misuse of technology *and* neo-colonialism is, in internal as in international politics, the 'power structure': the industrial-military-scientific complex, the 'corporate society'. The cause is structural and deeply political. To break its nefarious influence, is, to my mind, the first priority. All the rest will follow.

Arvid Pardo

The report is in general very good, but I would like to stress some points concerning Part III.

General perspective for proposals: The proposals assume cooperation on the part of all significant countries, including *socialist* countries, and they also assume that all significant countries can and will closely coordinate economic and social objectives, policies and priorities.

International Monetary Order: I am a supporter of the gold standard (currencies convertible to gold at internationally agreed rates). I am frankly sceptical about the long-term value of SDRs.

Food production: It would be useful to mention the potential role of cooperatives. A surprising omission is any reference to the need to provide adequate incentives to farmers in order to increase production.

Energy, ores and minerals: Not merely 'uninterrupted supply' is needed but 'adequate and uninterrupted supply at prices remunerative to efficient producers and fair to consumers.'

Human environment: Among many other things, there is no mention whatsoever of the need to develop international law with respect to international responsibility and liability for damage caused to the environment.

Arms reduction: It could be mentioned that the arms race is intruding into new environments (outer space and the ocean deeps) with consequences that are unpredictable.

This Report — an important effort at compromise — inevitably reflects limitations in conceptual coherence. I believe more emphasis should have been given to:

(a) The establishment of a NIO is essentially a political operation. Technical proposals and measures are a function of political objectives; only in that context 'functional sovereignty' can be discussed.

(b) The latent contradiction between the implications of a quantitative reduction of differentials and the aspirations for 'another development'; these lines of thought appear juxtaposed rather than integrated.

(c) The 'Poverty Compact' focuses on poor countries rather than poor people, poverty and exploitation in Third World countries having relatively higher per capita incomes are undeniable.

(d) Changes in the United Nations system will be superficial unless the control of industrialized countries over its secretariats is clearly modified.

(e) People will not understand the need for changes in all countries unless the existing transnational information structure is radically modified.

(f) That one code of conduct can deal with all problems of all TNEs in all countries, is a dangerous political mistification for Third World countries. Joint action by Third World countries and a sectorial approach are central to this issue. Only changes in the presently mimetic development strategies can really change the relationship with TNEs.

Víctor L. Urquidi

This report is a major contribution to a clear understanding of the international and global issues of our time, with a view to reaching over the next two generations a number of basic objectives for mankind. It is essential that sufficient awareness of our problems be created within a short space of time in order that actions, at the national and international levels, may be pursued intensively. The performance of governments, individually or through international organizations, is disappointing and does not measure up to the magnitude and complexity of global problems. Current debates between national and international bureaucracies are largely sterile. There is need for more general involvement of people through appropriate groupings. It is my hope that this report reaches wide circulation and gives rise to widespread debate. We must all strive for a better world society in which inequality is drastically reduced.